ISLAMIC ECONOMICS

THEMES IN ISLAMIC STUDIES

A (new) Brill Series including short histories and concise surveys of appealing themes in the field of Islamic and Arabic Studies The various titles give an accessible overview of a specific aspect or topic. Scholars and graduate students find in this series easy reference tools to current subjects in Islamic history and culture. Several titles are edited compilations of articles from the Encyclopaedia of Islam (second edition).

VOLUME 3

ISLAMIC ECONOMICS

A SHORT HISTORY

BY

AHMED A.F. EL-ASHKER

AND

RODNEY WILSON

TUTA SUB AEGIDE PALLAS · 1683 ·

BRILL

LEIDEN · BOSTON
2006

This book is printed on acid-free paper.

Library of Congress Cataloging-in-Publication Data

El-Ashker, Ahmed Abdel-Fattah, 1943-
Islamic economics : a short history / by Ahmed El-Ashker and Rodney Wilson.
p. cm. — (Themes in Islamic studies)
Includes bibliographical references and index.
ISBN-13: 978-90-04-15134-5
ISBN-10: 90-04-15134-6 (hardback : alk. paper)
1. Economics—Religious aspects—Islam. 2. Islam—Economic aspects. I. Wilson, Rodney II. Title. III. Series.

BP173.75.E42 2006
330.088'297—dc22

2006049043

ISSN 1389-823X
ISBN-13: 978-90-04-15134-5
ISBN-10: 90-04-15134-6

PRINTED IN THE NETHERLANDS

To the memory of our fathers.

CONTENTS

PREFACE

Comparing the often sorry reality of the present day Islamic World with the Islamic World of yesterday with its many achievements, when Muslim governments were powerful and setbacks less disasterous, provides us, with the benefit of hindsight, rich empirical evidence and lessons to derive conclusions from. Historical evidence should be treated with caution however, as history has inherent distortions when it comes to extracting evidence, as the prevailing conditions of the past may differ from those dominant in the present. History contains useful lessons to be learned, however, providing that this be received with an examining mind and an inquisitive attitude. In Islamic economics, historical examination can tell us that the Islamic system per se has the capability of providing an operational norm and the workable model, as long as the surrounding environment was helpful. As the present is an unbroken chain with the past, it is, in a similar historical fashion, a continual link with the future. And Islamic economics, in a historical sense, is no exception.

This study intends to link the past with the present, in preparation for the future. The remit covers the development of Muslim economic thought from the emergence of Islam, long before economics became a separate discipline. Concern with economic issues predates the development of the analytical tools associated with contemporary economics, and these concerns were evident in the writings of the early Muslim jurists. The introductory chapter examines the economic and financial environment in ancient Arabia from which Islam emerged. The second chapter is concerned with the Islamic economic concepts and ideas in the Qur'ān and Sunnah up to the time of the death of the Prophet. This is a particularly important chapter as Islamic economists, both the jurists in the early centuries of Islam and the contemporary writers, inevitably base their treatise on the subject on the two primary sources of the religion: the Qur'ān and Sunnah. Islamic economic thought during the Rightly-Guided Caliphate, and the development of Islamic society and economy during that period, which are much quoted in the writing of modern Muslim economists, is the subject of the third chapter. The fourth chapter deals with societal changes during the dynastic caliphates, the Umayyads and the Abbasids, and the administrative and economic reforms in the early powerful periods of these two dynasties. The golden age of the intellectual development of Islam and the appearance of the first specialized books on Islamic economics is the focus of chapter five, while the sixth chapter deals with the crucial stage of Islamic history associated with the political decline of the caliphate. Despite this setback there was significant intellectual development during this period. This was to influence the subsequent economic revival, the subject of the seventh chapter that considers the increasing power of the Islamic state during the periods of the Ottomans, the Safawids and the Mongols. In this chapter socio-economic and political changes are highlighted with a view to looking into the effect of these changes on the intellectual development in general and the development of Islamic economic thought in particular. Chapter eight covers the Islamic reform movements up to the present stage of the Islamic revivalism. The emphasis in this chapter is on the effect of revivalist movements on the development of Islamic economic thought and applications that have become more obvious in the twentieth century, notably the emergence of Islamic banking. Finally, chapter nine concerns the present, focusing on the development of Islamic economics and the partial Islamisation of economic and financial systems. Some observations are made on the prospects for Islamic economics in the light of its history, a future that is in many respects full of promise.

ACKNOWLEDGEMENT

We are very grateful to many people and institutions for the valuable help we have received, without which the completion of this book would have been more difficult than it has already been. Of those, we wish to highlight the following in particular.

We have received valuable help from the Institute of Middle Eastern and Islamic Studies, Durham University, United Kingdom during the various stages of completing this work. To the Institute and the University we are very grateful.

At Prince of Songkla University, Thailand, we are grateful to the President of the university, Associate Professor Dr Boonsom Siribumrungsukha. We are particularly thankful for his support and encouragement in his continuous effort to make the university a national and international centre of excellence in research and teaching. To Dean of Faculty of Management Sciences, Director of College of Islamic Studies and Head of Department of Islamic Studies at the same college, we owe special thanks for their enthusiasm and encouragement and for providing the logistical support and study leave needed for the completion of this work.

The assistance from library staff proved invaluable. To the library staff at the University of Paisley, Scotland, the former place of work of one of the authors, Durham University and the Prince of Songkla University, at both Pattani and Hat Yai campuses, Thailand, we extend a big thank you.

Our list of acknowledgement would not be complete without giving special thanks to Arthur Probsthain, Oriental bookseller and publisher, London, for their valuable help and assistance in coping with our requests and in advising us on source material.

TRANSLITERATION OF ARABIC LETTERS

Vowels

ā	اَ , اِ
ū	و
ī	ي
ʻ	ئ
ʻ	ء (end of word)

Consonants

a	أ ,ء	ŝ	ص
b	ب	dh	ض
p	پ	Ť, ț	ط
t	ت ,ة	ž	ظ
th	ث	a	ع
g	ج	gh	غ
j	چ	f, ph	ف
ĥ	ح	q	ق
kh	خ	k	ك
d	د	l	ل
ż	ذ	m	م
r	ر	n	ن
z	ز	h	ه
s	س	t	ة
sh	ش	w	و
		y	ى

CHAPTER ONE

PRE-ISLAMIC ARABIA POETRY, TRIBAL RIVALRY AND HEROISM (800 B.C.–610 A.C.)

Introduction

Despite the difficulty that surrounds the study of Arabia before the rise of Islam, the study, incomplete as it may be, is important to any researcher in the field of Islamic civilization. Unlike other ancient civilizations, which were established on riverbanks with the help of a permanent source of water, Islamic civilisation emerged from arid land. Arabia, the cradle of Islam, did not have sufficient national resources that would serve as a prerequisite for establishing a civilisation. It was Islam that had played a decisive role in changing the position of Arabia in early history. It transformed its inhabitants, the Arabs, into one nation, by unifying them under one religion and preparing them for a wide series of world conquests. The religious factor here is quite distinct. A brief description of Arabia before the coming of Islam is, therefore, important for three main reasons: (a) to examine, as far as is possible, the level of civilization that had developed, (b) to investigate how much of this civilization was in existence at the time of the rise of Islam and how much influence it may be claimed to have had on Islamic thought and (c) to assess the effect of the socio-economic conditions of pre-Islamic society on the early concerns of Islamic economic thought.

Biblical Connections

The term Arabia claims an etymological origin from ancient history. From Biblical sources, the word suggests a Semitic origin, derived from the Hebraic root word "aravi" that means "to be arid" (Aid to Bible Understanding, 1971). The Biblical reference manifests this meaning when it speaks of Arabia as the arid land or "the desert plain", Isaiah 21:13. Also, the word could be a different version of the word "Arabah" that carries a similar Hebraic meaning: the desert plain. (Deuteronomy 3:7, Joshua 3:16; 11:16 and Jeremiah 52:7). However, while the Biblical reference is applied to the area from the Sea of Galilee down to the Red Sea the definition of Arabia, or Arabah, as being the arid land or the desert plain could also be widened to include all the arid land down to the north of Yemen. There is no evidence to suggest that the nature of land in the heart of the peninsula, with its aridity and lack of water sources, was any less arid than that of the Biblical reference.

The origin of the Arabs has also a Biblical reference. Some tribes were Semitic, descending from Shem, or Sem (hence Semitic) the son of Noah, through Joktan; others were Hemitic, descending from Haman the son of Noah, through Cush. (Genesis 10:6, 7, 26–30). Some of the descendants of Prophet Abraham (Islamic version Ibrāhīm) through his son Ishmael (Islamic version Ismāīl) also inhabited Arabia and "took up tabernaciling from Havilah near Shur, which is in front of Egypt, as far as Assyria". (Genesis 25:1–4, 12–18). Essau's offspring, dwelling in the mountainous region of Seir, also came under the general classification of Arabians. (Genesis 36:1–43, Aid to Bible Understanding, 1971). However, the general term used for Arabs in the Bible is the Ishmaelites. This is because after the coming of Islam, Jewish tradition regarded the Arabs as fellow-descendants of Prophet Abraham, and because of the birth of Isaac, the older son Ishmael was superseded as a natural heir whose descendants would inherit the promised land (Peter Mansfield, 1982).

Early Muslims, or Arabs, maintain that they are descendants of Ismāīl, the son of Prophet Ibrāhīm, who is regarded as the father of monotheism. According to the Islamic version, the Prophet Ibrāhīm, brought his Egyptian second wife Hagar and his son from her, Ismāīl, to the valley of Makkah and abandoned them in the middle of the desert without much to sustain them. Then Prophet Ibrāhīm prayed to God, the True One God, "Lord, I have settled some of my offspring in a barren valley near (what will be) Your Sacred House. Lord, so that they may observe true worship put in the hearts of people kind towards them, and provide them of your bounty, so that they may give You thanks" (Qur'ān 14:27). According to Genesis God assured Prophet Ibrāhīm that no harm would fall on them, "Let it not be grievance in your sight because of your child and because of your bondwoman. Of her son will I make a nation because he is your offspring" (Genesis 21:13). According to both Biblical and

Qur'ānic versions, with some variations, the story continues to say that God had provided them with water and bounties and the child kept growing and became an archer, dwelling in the wilderness of Par'an, in the valley of Makkah.

The rest of the story has a particular significance for the Islamic movement and played an important role in the economy of Pre-Islamic Arabia. In Islamic traditions, the source of water provided by God was a spring under the feet of Ismāīl, which Hagar tried with her hands to stop from going into the sand saying "zumm, zumm" meaning stop and accumulate. The spring, which was to become sacred, was called Zumm Zumm, a name that is still used until the present day. When Prophet Ibrāhīm eventually returned to see them, he found Bedouins dwelling around the spring and with the help of Ismāīl he built the Ka'aba as a temple to the True One God. The Ka'aba and the Spring have constituted the focal base for the sacred shrine of Makkah, to which pilgrims paid homage before and after the rise of Islam. Pilgrimage has played a significant role in the life of the Arabian Peninsula since then.

The Land and the People

In a broad geographical sense, Arabia could be divided into three distinctive parts, north, central and south. It is the whole of the Arabian Peninsula which starts from the south of Palestine in the north, stretches to the Persian Gulf and Gulf of Oman in the east and the Red Sea in the west, and stops at the Indian Ocean in the south. It is a vast land, as large as one fourth of Europe and one third of the United States. The classification of the Peninsula into three distinctive parts is dictated by the nature of land and the level of civilizations that had developed in Ancient Arabia. The North and the South enjoyed fertile lands, which allowed the development of a viable economy and helped establish significant civilizations (Della Vida, 1944). But the Central part, the land from which Islam emerged and the home of the Arab stock that had lead the Islamic conquests for centuries, was, apart from sporadic oases, entirely arid. There is no evidence to suggest that there was a civilization in this central part comparable to that of the North or the South.

But had Central Arabia always been arid? This is a question that has been asked by historians in their attempt to establish a "theory" for the origin of the Semites. The existence of "wādies", which are dried-up river beds, has provided assumptions for a theory that suggests that pre-historic Arabia was fertile and was able to accommodate settled inhabitants before it suffered from progressive desiccation, before the beginning of history (ibid.). Dried-up river beds, "wādies", played an important role in the development of trade in Central Arabia. They served as trade routes between the South and the North, and proved to be the most convenient routes in a most hostile land.

As the nature of land of pre-historic Central Arabia is unresolved, so is the origin of the early inhabitants of the land. Whether they were purely Semitic or a mixture of Semitic and non-Semitic is a question that has attracted the attention of anthropologists. The connection between the Hemitic and the Semitic languages lends support to the hypotheses that the inhabitants might have come from Africa. On the other hand, the cognatic similarity between the Hamito-Semitic, Indo-European and Ural-Altaic languages seem to suggest that the early inhabitants came from the north (ibid.). Biblical sources state that some of the inhabitants were descendants of Shem and others from Ham, the sons of Noah (see above) who dwelled in the North and North West of Arabia. Some of these tribes could have moved down to the South along the Red Sea. This provides theological support to the assumption that the Arabian inhabitants came from the North. Furthermore, taking into account the version of the Islamic traditions concerning the story of Prophet Ibrāhīm who brought his second wife and his son from her, Ismāīl, to the valley of Makkah, it could be suggested further that some Arab tribes were Ismāīlītes. Other tribes, those Bedouins who came to the water spring provided by God to Ismāīl and his mother in the Islamic traditions, must have come from somewhere. However, anthropologists and theologians do not always fully agree.

Social Organization and Settlement Patterns

The nature of society of the inhabitants of Arabia could be divided into two, though unequal, types, nomadic and sedentary. Apart from Southern Arabia, where some civilizations were developed as we will see shortly, sedentary settlements were concentrated mainly in the sporadic oases of Arabia and in the main caravan towns on the trade routes between the prosperous South and the fertile North. The first type of sedentary settlements were agricultural, such as Yathrib and Najran, while the others were of strategic importance to trade, such as Makkah, Petra and Palmyra. Makkah, where Islam emerged, had a further strategic importance enhanced by the religious factor where it was, and still is, the final destination of pilgrims. This gave Makkah a special position among Arabian towns, a position that gave her the name "Omm al-Qra", mother of the villages. Despite the existence of these settlements in Arabia, the predominant style of life was nomadic. The line of differentiation between nomads and sedentaries is very fine, however. There were stages of semi-Nomadism and of Quasi-urbanism where some ex-Bedouin townsfolk still betrayed their nomadic origin, while other Bedouins were towns-people in the making (Hitti, 1963). It is even argued that the sedentary populations were originally Bedouins who were able, during their search for better living conditions, to take possession of the many oases within the peninsula and sometimes to penetrate the neighbouring regions conquering oases already inhabited (Shahid, 1970).

The Bedouin existence was, therefore, the main feature of society among the inhabitants of Arabia, which shaped their thinking and determined their way of life. Several features characterised the life, personality and the economic behaviour of the Bedouin: endurance, individualism, clanism, hospitality, fortitude and enthusiasm for conflict.

ENDURANCE. Endurance is the most obvious example of the effect of environment on man. As an arid land, Arabia did not have much to offer, and in order to survive in such a hostile environment the Bedouin had to learn to adapt to the difficult conditions of the land both mentally and physically. Mentally they had to learn to be patient, "*sabour*", since he could do nothing to change the basic set-up of their inhospitable land. The Bedouin learnt that mental endurance "*sabre*" is the first ingredient for survival. Physical *sabre*, the Bedouin had to learn how to endure the hardship of the desert life. Their food was meagre, mainly dates and a mixture of flour and milk or water, and their clothing was as scanty as their food.

Endurance was a supreme virtue to the Bedouin, a virtue that has been sung proudly in Arabic poetry as one of the tribe's traits and the traits of its individuals and has also been emphasised repeatedly in the Qur'ān as a distinct Muslim characteristic. This high degree of endurance played, among other factors, an important role in building up a strong army during the expansion of the Islamic state. Because of the high standard of endurance, the armies consisted of strong units who were able to survive on less food than that of other armies. With lighter provisions than those of the Byzantine and Persian troops, the Islamic army must have been able to move faster and to travel further. (A remarkable example could be taken from the history of the early expansion of the Islamic state when the Islamic army crossed the desert from southern Iraq to the south of Syria to engage with the Byzantine troops in a quite unexpected move). The scarcity of economic resources and the need to preserve them is stressed in the Islamic approach to consumer behaviour. The concept of moderation is emphasised in Islamic economic theory where the no-niggard-no-extravagant pattern of consumption is ordained in the Qur'ān (Qur'ān: 7:31, 17:29), as will be discussed in due course.

INDIVIDUALISM. This was another distinct trait of the Bedouin character. Individualism was twofold: loyalty to the "self" and loyalty to the clan. Beyond these two levels, with a descending priority, the interest of others was not the individual's concern. This characteristic was also a reflection of the effect of the environment. The desert was vast and open, which gave the Bedouin the sense of freedom and liberty. If it became difficult to live in a land where there was a repressive political regime they would move somewhere else. Also, individualism was enhanced by, or was a product of, the hardship of desert life. The law of survival in such a hostile environment would force a descending priority: self, then others. The Bedouin, as Hitti says, has never been able to raise himself to become a social being of the international type, much less to develop ideals of devotion to the common good beyond that which pertained to the tribe (Hitti, 1963).

That sense of individualism seems to have penetrated deeply in the Bedouin character to the extent that even after the coming of Islam, with its social caring teachings, a Bedouin is reported to have pleaded, "O Lord, have mercy upon me and upon Muĥammad but upon no one else besides!" (Abū-Dawood, 1280, quoted in Hitti, 1963). Regardless of whether such society was qualified for the description of being "capitalist", the society bore one of the early signs of the spirit of capitalism, individualism.

Islam acknowledges individualism and concedes the drive for it, and for that, it, among other things, assigns a considerable weight to private ownership. But no harm should be fallen upon others in pursuit of individualistic interests, and this is a fundamental prerequisite for accepting individualism in Islam. And on the educational side, Islam teaches and preaches the virtue of self denial, alms giving and societal caring.

Clanism. Strange as it might seem, clanism was a twin image of individualism in Arabia. The Bedouin, or the Arabian, had loyalty to his clansmen in a patriotic fashion. He would defend members of the clan, as he would be protected by them, and would engage with them in any war that might be launched by the clan on the neighbouring ones. The sense of individuality to self and clan seemed to have developed the feeling of loyalty to the clan and to have shaped the form of political structure in the Bedouin society. The clan as a social unit had its own titular head, a *sheikh*, who was chosen by the members of the clan by virtue of his seniority in age, experience, wisdom and other personal qualifications and who represented the clan in relation to other clans, but did not have the absolute authority in all matters regarding the clan (Ĥassan, 1959). In serious judicial matters and in questions of inter-clan conflict he would have to consult with a council consisting of the heads of the families in the clan. The sense of individuality, on the other hand, emphasised by the high regard for personal freedom, made the Bedouin treat the *sheikh* on an equal footing. The *sheikh* was not a king, and apart from the peripheral areas of the Persian and Byzantine empires the leaders of which were given the title kings by these empires, but in South Arabia such titles were never used by Arabians in reference to their tribal heads (ibid.).

The two twin forces, individualism and clanism, seem to have helped establish the basis of democracy in the tribal society. This democracy was not far away from that of modern times. The sense of individuality and the feeling of loyalty to the clan also shaped the economic structure of pre-Islamic Arabians. With the force of individuality, private property was emphasised, but through the bonds of clanism matters of common economic concern were observed. Representing the clan as a whole in a community that lived on common economic resources, the head of the clan would have to draw the line between what was regarded as private interest and that which could be considered as of common concern. The role of the individual and that of the state in running the economy, to use modern terms, was therefore outlined.

That system of democracy in pre-Islamic Arabia survived the coming of Islam, though it was modified so that it would conform to Islamic norms (ibid.). Islam does not deny the sense of individuality, though it does not overemphasize it. Nor does Islam discard the feeling of clanism, although it does not support group conflicts. Islam redirects the natural feeling of belonging, and probably the need for that feeling, and replaces the concept of the clan by the concept of Islamic community, *ummah*. Between these two pivots, the individual and the community, and with no supremacy of either, Islamic political philosophy and economic theory is established.

Hospitality. Hospitality was a dominant feature of life in pre-Islamic Arabia. It was a principle that was deeply rooted in the desert life, and a virtue that was sung by early poets, the journalists of the time, alongside bravery, fortitude, enthusiasm and endurance (Al-Ṭabarī, 1991). No matter how much of an enemy a person was, if he descended on someone as a guest he should be treated with the utmost hospitality. A breach of hospitality would bring dishonour to the individual and probably to the clan. Such deeply rooted principles of hospitality might seem contradictory to the kind of life the Arabian lived, with its lack of economic resources. But the principle could be indeed a product of such life. The mutual feeling of helplessness in such a hostile environment developed a need for the establishment of hospitality as a highly regarded duty.

The principle of hospitality, nevertheless, signals an important observation: the needs of a helpless individual were taken into account. In addition, as the assertion of the pride and the honour of the individual and that of his clan was a main motivation for hospitality, besides mutual interests, it can be said, in purely economic terms, that the consumer utility function of the Arabian could be twofold: the satisfaction of goods consumption and moral satisfaction. In Islamic economic theory the utility of the Muslim consumer is threefold: the satisfaction of goods consumption, moral satisfaction and the satisfaction from a divine reward during life and thereafter (as will be discussed later).

Invasion for economic gains. Driven by the lack of economic resources, the tribes that did not have enough to feed their members had to launch a military invasion on those who had more than they needed. The purpose of the invasion was entirely economic. No blood should be shed except in cases of extreme necessity (Hitti, 1963). Although such invasions do not seem acceptable, to say the least, from the perspective of modern society, they should be looked at in the context of the mentality of those days. It was an action of force conducted by those who had not against those who had, which aimed to reallocate economic resources in the community. In the absence of a state that would assume such a reallocative role by various economic and legitimate devices, individuals "took the law into their hands". The fighting mode that was prevailing in the desert society at that time seems to have reinforced these actions even further. Ethical values that emanate from divinely inspired religions, or the lack of it in Arabia at that time, did not seem to have played a significant role in preventing these economically-motivated military actions. Christian tribes, too, such as Banū-Taghlib, practiced it without any reservations (ibid.).

After the coming of Islam these practices were tamed: its purpose was changed by emphasising the religious drive, rigid rules were established to avoid any destruction or unnecessary bloodshed and it was re-directed towards foreign conquests. The right of the poor to the wealth of the rich is, however, a well established principle in the Islamic tradition, "in their wealth there is a *right* (italics ours) to the beggar and needy", (Qur'ān 51:19), though such a right is exercised by the state, not individuals, through economic devices such as religious taxes (as will be discussed in due course).

Fortitude and enthusiasm for conflict. Nothing could be a source of pride to the individual and the clan as courage and fortitude. This was a predominant feature of the personality of the inhabitants of Arabia. Like lack-of hospitality; cowardice was the worst trait with which an individual, or a clan, could be described. Courage was a particular source of pride, even if it meant the loss of life. We hear a classical poet stating with pride that he was from a tribe that lost many of its knights as a result of their being the first to come forward on hearing a call for a duel (Nicholson, 1993). This might not be much of praise to the fighting skill of the duel fighters of his tribe, but at least it showed that they were far from being hesitant in confronting danger or military combat. In another example, in glorifying the tribe's military and status hegemony, we hear another poet boosting with pride that they, him and his clan, are tyrant oppressors, never been oppressed and when they and their herd go to the spring, they drink first, clear and pure water leaving the others to come after them to drink of what they left, mud and muck (ibid.). The sense of justice would seemingly take a lower priority to courage and oppression, if the former was mistaken for weaknesses and leniency. Islam, needless to say, came with the most threatening terms to those who acted unjustly: God's wrath and retribution.

Fortitude continued to be a source of pride to the Arabian Muslim after the coming of Islam. It was tamed and later well organised, however. Courage at combat ought not to be directed to fellow Muslims or for causes not meant to be for the sake of God. Cowardice is not the trait of Muslims, no matter how the danger might be, and those who do not respond to the call of military jihād are condemned as hypocrites who will dwell in Hell Fire (Qur'ān 9:90, 97–101, 120). As for those who die in battle, for the sake of God, they are not dead in Heaven; as martyrs, they live in paradise among prophets and blessed ones (Qur'ān 2:154, 3:169–171).

Arabian Civilizations

Now we turn our attention to the study of the civilization that existed in the peninsula at the time of the rise of Islam. This will be divided into three main parts: South Arabia, North Arabia and Central Arabia

South Arabia

In South Arabia, between the Indian Ocean and the Red Sea, there was a highly developed civilization, the origin of which is, however, not known for certain. Mesopotamian civilization has been suggested as a source, though evidence suggests that the bulk of the civilization was not of Mesopotamian origin and points toward an independent development of monarchic government in South Arabia and Mesopotamia (Della Vida, 1944). The dispute over the origin of such a civilization, though important to historians, is not the main concern of this book, however. Equally unimportant to our study is the unresolved question of how old the South Arabian civilization was, which could be said to have started as early as the fifteenth century B.C.

or earlier (ibid.). It is sufficient to focus on the socio-economic elements of the civilisation with a brief description of its political dimension.

Different from the environment elsewhere in Arabia, the south had fertile land caused by rainfall. South Arabians were skilled enough to build dams to help irrigate the land. The dam of Ma'rib was perhaps the most famous, the older part of which was built around the mid seventh century B.C., and was constructed in the city of Ma'rib, the capital of Saba' (ibid.). This allowed water to be divided into many streams running into a wide plain. As the skill developed, the Ma'ribeans constructed a dam at the narrow point between the two mountains east of the city with gates that allowed controlled distribution of water (Haykal, 1976). In contrast to wandering Bedouins in the north, the people in the south had a sedentary existence.

Four main Kingdoms were established in South Arabia: Saba', Ma'in, Qatabān and Ĥadramawt.

Saba'

Saba', biblical Sheba, was the most dominant of the four kingdoms. Besides the fertile land, the strategic position on the India trade route and the nearness to the Red Sea contributed to making Saba' the most important kingdom in the south. The Sabaean period extended from about 750 B.C., or 1500 B.C. according to some, to 115 B.C. (Della Vida, 1944). The kingdom started as a theocracy first, where the king had priestly authority, but in about 610 B.C. it became secularised with a change in the royal title that did not bear a priestly character and with a new capital, Ma'rib. Gradually, the kingdom of Saba' overshone, and absorbed, the other kingdoms in the south. The Qur'ān refers to an encounter between the Queen of Saba' (Queen of Sheba) and King Solomon. King Solomon learned from his intelligence sources that the Sabaeans with their rich and powerful queen were worshiping the sun, not God. He wrote to the queen inviting her and her people to believe in God and to give up worshiping the sun. The Qur'ānic reference indicates a few interesting points related to Saba': (a) the deity of the kingdom at that time was the sun, (b) Saba' kingdom was very rich and powerful, (c) the kingdom had a very powerful army, (d) the Queen had a wise council, and (e) the Queen was not an autocratic monarch as she is reported to have sought the opinion of her council, "I am not to take an action (on this matter) unless you are part of it".

After some intriguing events, attractively mentioned in the verses, the Qur'ān tells us that she eventually joined King Solomon in worshiping his one true God (Qur'ān 27:20–44).

Ma'in

The second kingdom in South Arabia was Ma'in (biblical Ma'on, Me'un and Me'in), meaning spring-water. The Minean period lasted from about 700 B.C. to 70 B.C. (ibid.). The kingdom was famous of its produce of frankincense and other aromatic products, which were of importance for temple worship. For the Egyptians in particular, they were also used for mummification. Like the Sabaean, the kingdom began as a theocracy and ended up secularised. The Minaean kingdom also occupied an important place on the trade route.

Qatabān and Ĥadramawt

The other remaining kingdoms were Qatabān and Ĥadramawt. The former lasted from about 400 B.C. to 50 B.C. while the latter lasted from about 450 B.C. to the end of the first century A.C. (ibid.). These two kingdoms though were overshadowed by the Sabaeans and the Minaeans, who played an important role in organising the spice trade

Starting from 115 B.C. the four kingdoms were under a new influence, that of the tribe of Ĥimyar which emerged from south west Arabia. The first Ĥimyarite kingdom lasted until about 300 A.C. The Ĥimyarites who inherited the Sabeo-Minaean trade had the same culture and language as that of the Sabaeans. The socio-economic structure of the Sabaeo-Ĥimyarite community consisted of a mixture of the tribal system, caste stratification and feudal aristocracy and monarchy (Hitti, 1963). At about 300 A.C., which marked the beginning of the second Ĥimyarite kingdom, the Ĥimyarites annexed Ĥadramawt and Qatabān and continued ruling South Arabia, with a short interruption by an Abyssinian occupation from 340 A.C. to 378 A.C., until the beginning of the sixth century A.C (ibid.). The period, however, was one of winds of change religiously and politically.

A Change of Faith and Fate

Religious factors had played a decisive role in determining the destiny of South Arabia, or al-Yemen as it was known by then, from the mid fourth to the beginning of the sixth century A.C. The religion in the area was initially of a planetary astral system in which the prevailing moon-god was referred to by various references according to the different tribes, such as, love, lover, father, health giving God and paternal uncle. The first sign of religious changes began with the first official Christian missionary sent by the Emperor Constantius in 356 A.C. which is said to have carried political implications instigated by the rivalry between the Roman and Persian empires to control such a strategic area (Hitti, 1963). The missionaries, and other less official ones, succeeded in promoting Christianity in the area and in building up churches in different locations. Judaism also spread in the area and the last of the Ĥimyarite kings, Dhu-Nuwas, became a Jew. Rivalry between the followers of the two religions began. In October 523 A.C. Dhu-Nuwas, the Jewish king, massacred the 20,000 Christians of Najran by throwing them in a trench which was then set on fire (Al-Ťabarī). The Qur'ān refers to this massacre by saying, "By the heaven with its constellations! By the Promised Day! By the Witness and that which is witnessed! Cursed be the diggers of the trench, who lighted the consuming fire and sat around it to watch the faithful being burnt to death! Nor did they torture them for any reason save that they believed in God, the Mighty, the Praised One; the Sovereign of the heavens and the earth, the Witness of all things", (Qur'ān 85:1–9). This dramatic event led to a major political change in the area. As the protector of Christianity the Roman Emperor, Justin I, asked the Negus of Abyssinia, the nearest Christian force to the area, to intervene. The Abyssinian army crossed the Red Sea, conquered the kingdom and occupied the land from 525 to 575 A.C. (Hitti, 1963). Furthermore, to circumscribe the religious influence of the Ka'aba in the north as opposed to his newly built church in the south, the Abyssinian commander, Abraha, led a military expedition to Makkah to destroy the Ka'ba. The expedition did not succeed and the army was destroyed by smallpox. This is said to have happened in 570 or 571 A.C., the year when the Prophet of Islam was born.

The year 575 A.C. witnessed a new political power in South Arabia, the Persians. As the struggle continued between the Christian Arabians on the one hand and the Jewish and Pagan Arabians on the other, and since the former were backed by the Abyssinians representing Christian Byzantine, the latter sought help from a rival empire—the Persian. The Persians must have found it the right opportunity to eliminate the control of the Byzantines, through the Abyssinians, over South Arabia. Six ships of the Persian army sailed from the Persian Gulf towards al-Yemen, two of which sank on the way and the other four reached al-Yemen in 575 A.C. and defeated the Abyssinian garrison (Al-Ťabarī). Instead of only coming to help, the conqueror, as usually happens, occupied the land and soon al-Yemen was converted into a Persian province, and one master was changed for another. In 628 A.C., al-Yemen fell into the hands of Muslims and the fifth, and last Persian ruler converted to Islam.

The political strength of the South Arabian kingdoms was based on economic strength. As was mentioned earlier, the fertility of the land coupled with the strategic location on the trade routes helped South Arabia to develop its economic strength. Agriculture flourished and various agricultural products were grown: corn, vegetables, fruit, and vines and, most important for trade, spices, myrrh and frankincense. Besides exporting their own products, of which spices, myrrh and frankincense were highly demanded, the area lay on a very important trade route to India. Saba᾽ was a transit place for many products coming from different areas: pearls from the Persian Gulf, silk from China, swords and fabrics from India, and gold, ivory and ostrich feathers from Ethiopia. The Sabaeans, as Hitti says, were the Phoenicians of the Southern sea (Hitti, 1963). They commanded a strong commercial fleet, which connected the two sides of the Indian Ocean with South Arabia. Also, due to the navigating difficulty of the Red Sea, overland trade routes were developed between al-Yemen and Syria along the western coast of the Peninsula with several caravan cities, such as Makkah, Petra, and Palmyra. Another trade route was developed between Ĥadramawt and Ma'rib, where it joined the south-to-north route.

The economic development of South Arabia suffered a setback by the end of the third century A.C. Three major factors could be said to have contributed to the setback: the increased external maritime competition, internal schism and the breaking of the dam of Ma'rib. External maritime competition appeared first through the intervention of the Ptolemies, though the Romans followed suit. The Ptolemies developed such a strong navy that they transferred the northern part of the Red Sea into a Ptolemic lake. By reopening the canal between the Nile and the Red Sea by Ptolemy II, a canal which was dug originally during the rule of Sesostris 1700 years earlier, part of the overland trade which was controlled by the South Arabians was transferred to the Red Sea. The final blow came when the Ptolemies mastered the navigating problems of monsoons in the south of the Red Sea by the end of second century B.C. and entered the Indian Ocean, establishing a direct trade route between India and Egypt (Della Vida, 1944). That was the start of an economic decline in South Arabia. Internal schism instigated by religious differences between the newly converted Christians, Jews and pagan Arabians marked a stage of political disturbances, which the feudalistic socio-economic system did not help to alleviate. Political disturbances, as usual, led to adverse economic consequences. The breaking of the dam of Ma'rib, possibly during the rule of the Abyssinians, was an economic disaster. The reasons for the breaking of the dam are not known for certain but it could be attributed to inefficient maintenance work. However, the breaking led, with other factors, to a dramatic economic decline in the area (Haykal, 1976).

North Arabia

On the northern end of the peninsula lay several kingdoms: the Nabataeans, the Palmyrenes, the Ghassānīds, the Lakhmīds and the Kindaites.

The Nabataeans

The Nabataeans were the first significant Arabian state in the north. Although the exact origin of the Nabataeans is not known for certain, historians agree that they were emigrant nomads who came to the area from Transjordan and the northern part of Central Arabia, possibly in the early sixth century B.C., and occupied the land of the Edomites between the Dead Sea and the Gulf of Aqabah. The third, or perhaps the fourth, century B.C. was the starting point of their uprising; they occupied important cities such as Petra, Bostra and Gerash, the major caravan cities on the South-to-North trade route, and stretched their territory to Damascus at the time of Christ. The year 105 A.C. witnessed their end however, when the Emperor Trajan annexed the area and declared it a Roman province, a "Provincia Arabia", (Hitti, 1963).

The Nabataeans developed a high level of civilization with the help of two major economic factors: agriculture and trade. Although they were originally nomads, the Nabataeans developed an agricultural life and built several important cities. Also, being on the northern part of the south-to-north trade route at Petra, they partially controlled the route, breaking the South Arabian monopoly over it and increasing their prosperity on the account of that of South Arabia. The Nabataeans had two languages: spoken Arabic and written Aramaic, borrowed from their Syrian neighbours. In this sense they were bilingual. Their religion was a mixture of Arabian and Aramaic features. Briefly, the Nabataeans arose to a level of civilization that may stand comparison with any other of the states in the Near East in ancient times (Della Vida, 1944).

The Palmyrenes

The Palmyrenes were Arabians, as their personal names and the names of their kings revealed an Arabian origin (Hitti, 1963). Some of the inhabitants seemed to have come from al-Yemen before the destruction of the Dam of Ma'rib (Al-Ṭabarī). Palmyra (Arabic Tadmur and Semitic Tadmor), developed from being an oasis in the middle of the Syrian Desert to becoming a rival and a successor to Petra of the Nabataeans. It is not known exactly when the Arabs came to Palmyra, but by 9 B.C. the city seemed to have gained its importance as a trade centre between the Roman and the Persian empires (Della Vida, 1944). The location of Palmyra on the West-to-East trade route, coming from India through the Persian Gulf to the Euphrates then crossing the desert to the Syrian coast, gave the city a strategic importance particularly after the fall of the Nabataeans. Palmyra reached its zenith between 130 and 270 A.C. when, under the protectorate of the Roman Empire, it enjoyed a high level of prosperity with a wide range of international trade stretching east as far as China. In 270 A.C. the Palmyrenes succeeded in extending their military influence to as far as Alexandria, in Egypt, and to defy the Roman Empire pushing the Empire's garrison as far back as Ankara in Asia Minor (Hitti, 1963). In 272 A.C. the Palmyrene Queen was defeated and the Romans entered Palmyra bringing its destruction.

The ruins and inscriptions of the Palmyrenes reveal a developed civilization. Although the Palmyrenes were of an Arian stock, their civilization was a blend of Greek, Syrian and Parthian elements (Hitti, 1963). They spoke a dialect of Western Aramaic and their religion was influenced by Aramaic and Mesopotamian concepts and traditions.

The Ghassānīds

The Ghassānīds are said to have originated from a tribe that emigrated from South Arabia at the end of the third century after the destruction of the dam of Ma'rib and established itself to the south east of Damascus on the South-to-North trade route (Hitti, 1963). Some are said to have emigrated to the area shortly before the destruction of the dam (Al-Ṭabarī). Like other tribes in the area, which emanated from an Arabian origin, the Ghassānīds who were Christianised had two languages; Aramaic and Arabic. By the end of the fifth century they came under the influence of the Byzantines. The Ghassānīds were allies, and perhaps clients, of the Byzantines and served as a buffer between the Byzantine Empire and the nomads' sporadic attacks on the Empire's borders and at the time of the Islamic conquests the Ghassānīds fought alongside the Byzantines in the battle of Yarmūk in 636 A.C. (Hitti, 1963). Later, the Ghassānīd king embraced Islam (but renounced it afterwards and fled to Constantinople when the second Caliph wanted to reduce him to a Bedouin status in a dispute that erupted between them). The Ghassānīds period is marked with important achievements in architecture, houses of basalt, palaces, triumphal arches, theatres and churches. Poetry, as the art of word at the time, was encouraged by the Ghassānīd kings, whose generosity in paying poets was renowned.

The Lakhmīds

The Lakhmīds, in some aspects, were the mirror image of the Ghassānīds in the east. They originated from Yemenite tribes, called Tanukh, who emigrated to North Arabia around the beginning of the third century A.C. and settled in the west of Euphrates (ibid.). With the establishment of the Lakhmīd dynasty in al-Hira, the Lakhmīds became allies, or perhaps clients, to the Persian Empire and, similar to the Ghassānīds, served as a buffer area between the Persians and the prevalent attacks of the Bedouins on the Empires frontiers. The Lakhmīds who spoke Arabic, but used Syriac in writing, were mostly pagans, with a Christian minority (ibid.). The influence of Christianity increased, however, during the reign of the last king, al-Nu'man III (580–602 A.C.), when the king, whose mother was Christian, became Christian. The Lakhmīds civilization did not reach the level of its counterpart in Petra and Ghassānland. However, they also encouraged poetry and rewarded poets generously.

The Kindites

Once again, the Kindites were of South Arabian origin. The influence of South Arabians on the Northern Arabian kingdoms was more obvious in that kingdom than in others, as the first Kindite king was appointed by the South Arabian king to rule over some tribes in Central Arabia, whom the latter had conquered in 480 A.C. The Kindite kingdom lasted from 480 to 529 A.C. At its zenith the Kindite kingdom extended to the Euphrates, and after the death of the Persian Emperor the Kindite king stretched his influence to the capital of the Lakhmīds (Hitti, 1963). The end of the Kindites came at the hand of the Lakhmīd king in 529 A.C. when the latter defeated them and put their king to death along with many others from the royal family. The rest of the Kindite prominent members went back to Ĥadramawt, from where they originally came. After embracing Islam the Kindites showed a great zeal in the Islamic conquests in Syria and Iraq and some of them were rewarded by being appointed provincial governors. Also, some of the Kindites became great Islamic thinkers such as Ya'qup ibn-Ishaq al-Kinidi who earned the title "the philosopher of the Arabs" (Shahid, 1970).

Though short lived, Kindah provides an interesting case of Arab uprising. Different from the other Northern Arabian kingdoms, which were to some extent client-kingdoms influenced by the power of the two great Empires in the north, Kindah was neither a Persian nor a Byzantine client-kingdom. It was the first attempt by the inner Arabs to unite their tribes under one leader. In this sense, Kindah could be regarded as a precedent for the Islamic state that emerged from Central Arabia.

The study of the above civilizations in North Arabia, as Hitti says, is significant not only in itself but as an illustration of the cultural heights which the Arabians of the desert were capable of attaining when the proper opportunities present themselves (Hitti, 1963). A common factor among the above civilizations was that they were founded by Arab stock: the language was Arabic and personal names and the names of the kings were also Arabic. This ability was reflected in the development of Islamic civilisation and Islamic thought.

Central Arabia

Nomadism was the main feature of life in pre-Islamic Central Arabia. This was dictated by the nature of land which, apart from sporadic oases, was arid. The inhabitants, who had a Semitic origin, lived a primitive life, residing in tents and moving with their flocks in pursuit of pastoral locations. As mentioned earlier, the inhabitant of the desert, the Bedouin, developed a high level of endurance, individualism, hospitality and fortitude, which might be regarded as a product of the hardships of the desert life. Furthermore, the Bedouin strongly adhered to their history, language, religion and traditions, and any "liberated" ideas of changing his inherited set of beliefs and customs would be strongly resisted. This, despite the negative approach to change, helped preserve one of the main assets of the Arab heritage, the language.

Sedentary life existed in pre-Islamic Arabia in oases and caravan centres, though Bedouins' characteristics were the main nature of the society (Shahid, 1970). Most important of these sedentary settlements and most mentioned in early Islamic history were Makkah and Yathrib. Makkah was the city where the Prophet of Islam was born, in 570 or 71 A.C., and proclaimed his message, and Yathrib was the city to which he emigrated, in 620 A.C., which was called al-Medīnah after the emigration, meaning the city.

Makkah, like Palmyra, grew around a spring-water in the middle of the desert. Two major factors played a significant role in the economic development of Makkah, its strategic location on the South-to-North trade route and its reputation as a sacred shrine. With its fresh water supply and geographical location on the trade route from South Arabia to Syria, Makkah occupied a strategic position on the route and partially took over the trade from the South Arabians. Makkah grew wealthy and Makkahn merchants became rich and powerful (Ĥassan, 1959). The sacred features of the caravan city emerged from the belief that Makkah was the place where Prophet Ibrāhīm left his second wife and son in the middle of the desert with little to sustain them, and the spring was the water sent to them by the divine power. Makkah became the centre of pilgrimage, which was a source of income to the city. The caravan and pilgrimage city developed an advanced social and political system with some aristocratic features in those families which were leading the trade and organising the pilgrimage seasons. The tribal features were still, however, predominant in the Makkahn society (ibid.).

Yathrib, al-Medīnah, was another sedentary city approximately 200 miles to the north of Makkah. Despite the similarity of the tribal set up of the society in both cities, they differed in their economic activities. While trade was the main economic activity in Makkah, agriculture was the chief activity in Yathrib (Shahid, 1970). As an oasis, it also owed its existence to a water spring. The city gained its reputation after the rise of Islam, the Prophet emigrated to it with the support and invitation of its inhabitants. It was the base from which Islam spread in the peninsula, and it remained the capital of the Islamic state until the reign of the Umayyads.

Unlike their neighbours in the north and south, pre-Islamic Central Arabians did not develop a civilization of their own. Their only, though very important, contribution to the Arab heritage was that they preserved the language. Speech was the only artistic nature they possessed and transferred through generations until the Arabs of today, "the beauty of man lies in the eloquence of his tongue", goes the Arabic general saying. Or as Hitti puts it, "No people in the world, perhaps, manifest such enthusiastic admiration for literary expression and are so moved by the word, spoken or written, as the Arabs. Hardly any language seems capable of exercising over the minds of its users such irresistible influence as Arabic does, (Hitti, 1963). This helps explain why the Qur'ān is regarded by Muslims as having a miraculous literary character "i'jaz", which with its style and composition challenged the Arabs in their most artistic skill: speech. Makkah served as a centre of cultural "civilization" in this sense. Cultural fairs were held outside Makkah, in a place called Sūk Ukaz, where poets would come from all parts of Arabia contesting their poetic ability sometimes with long odes (Haykal, 1976). Among the famous odes were the seven golden odes, *mu'allaqat*, meaning suspended, which were written and suspended on the door of Ka'aba. Poets, who were also engaged in various avenues of life as traders or warriors, represented the political voice of the tribe as the journalists of the day.

The religion of Central Arabians was of a mixed nature. Astral deities existed where sedentary populations worshipped the sun and nomads worshipped the moon. Natural objects, such as palm trees, wells, stones and caves were also sacred. In Makkah, the sacred shrine, idols also existed with several idols erected on the top of the Ka'aba representing gods for different tribes (Sirat-Ibn-Hishām). The concept of one God was not discarded either, but these idols were regarded as intermediaries between worshippers and God. Islam calls this period the age of ignorance and confusion, "jahiliyah". Judaism, perhaps coming from South Arabia, also had a certain influence in Central Arabia mainly in Yathrib (al-Medīnah) and Khyber. Christianity also existed among some tribes such as the Banū-Taghlib, though it was not influential. In many respects, however, Central Arabia was ripe for the spiritual rejuvenation, which was to come with the rise of Islam.

Trade and Finance in Makkah

Apart from the nomads in Central Arabia, trade prospered in the South, the North and in Makkah, the cradle of Islam. The Makkahn traders traveled south and north, in two journeys one in the summer and another in the winter as the Qur'ān is telling us in citing the bounties bestowed by God on the Makkahn Qurayshites (Qur'ān 106:1–4) who had settled in the city and accumulated great wealth and power. Financially the development of trade had created three distinctive financial situations: the demand for, and supply of, finance, the appearance of money changers and the necessity of insurance. The need for, and provision of, finance was necessitated by the expansion of the trade. The mode of finance took three different forms depending upon the level of risk the financier, or the investor, if a modern term is to be borrowed, was willing to bear. For those willing to accept risk for a greater return, partnership was a suitable form. For those not willing to accept the risk, loans were the alternative.

In a partnership, a group of people may agree to enter into a financial arrangement to finance a trade trip, to the North or the South, whereby some of those involved may be sleeping partners while the others were managing partners. Restrictions may be placed on to the authority of the managing partner(s) and to reduce risk the type of goods traded and the terms of transactions should be clearly defined (El-Ashker, 1987). The duration of the partnership could be limited to the period of the trip, at the end of which the partnership was to be dissolved, or extended, to cover a renewed period with either the same partners or new ones. The managing partners would join the caravan as independent participants, with their goods and funds, enjoying the protection of, and facilities provided by, the caravan organizers who were mainly the Qurayshites. A fee would probably have to be paid to the caravan organizers for the facilities provided in general and the military protection in particular. Part of the fee would probably go towards the protection money the caravan organizers would have to pay to the powerful tribes along the trade route for a safe passage through their land. In the absence of hard evidence to the contrary, it is conceivable to "hypothesise" that these were the sort of arrangements that prevailed given the particularly harsh reality of the surrounding environment.

The profit of the partnership was to be shared according to predetermined proportions, but the loss was to be borne by the fund supplier with the non-financier managing partner having to work without material compensation (ibid.). The Prophet is said to have taken part in these caravans acting for a wealthy lady, Khadigah, who later became his wife. The partnership, or Mudharabah as it was known then, was approved of after the coming of Islam and continued to serve as a legitimate mode of business finance under Islamic law until the present day. If all partners provided finance, including the managing partners, the Mudharabah was to be called Mushārakah; a slight differentiation to indicate that the funds were provided by all, which would have some important implications for the distribution of profits or allocations of losses. The Mushārakah may employ a working manager for a predetermined pay. Mushārakah also survived the coming of Islam and continued to serve as an acceptable Islamic mode of business and finance until the present day. Islamic banks, which were established in the late twentieth century, use Mudharabah and Mushārakah in their financing.

In a busy trade centre, like that of Makkah, money changers must have existed and exercised a significant role in what was at the time an international trade. They were the traveling merchants who had centres in Makkah and who were more able than others to compare the value of currencies, realize the change of value when it occurred, and acknowledge the differences resulting from possible tampering with the quality and quantity of the metal in the currency (Wilson, 1983). Pilgrimage would have necessitated the need for their services further. In addition, as they became wealthy merchants they were able to provide finance when it was required. Finance was needed for two purposes: business and personal.

Lending for business and personal purposes was provided at a rate calculated on the basis of the amount borrowed and the period of the loan to maturity. If the borrower was not able to pay in time, a deferment of payment may be granted by the lender but with an additional charge. The loan capital would therefore be subject to an additional payment based on the amount borrowed and the total period covered, including the additional deferred payment period (El-Ashker, 1987). The deferral may carry a financial penalty, which can be referred to as an increase. To increase means in Arabic 'yarbu', the noun of which is 'Ribā', which corresponds to the noun increase in English. The total amount paid by the borrower would be the principle, the capital, which is in Arabic 'r'as al-Māl' and the increase. The Qur'ān is emphatic in prohibiting the increase, Ribā, and warns those who charge Ribā of war from God stating that they "shall rise up before God like men whom Satan has demented by his torch", and to reply to any claim that might be made that the increase in money from lending is like trade, God has a similar warning because, "they claim that Ribā is like trading, but God has permitted trading and has forbidden Ribā", (Qur'ān 2:275). And to the counterargument that Ribā, the increase, may be allowed providing it is not excessive, the Qur'ānic verse is unequivocally clear, "if you repent you have the right to only your capital, *ru'aūs amwalikum*, (the plural of capital)", (Qur'ān 2:275). In other words there is no differentiation between interest and usury, all interest is usury. Therefore, while partnership, with its various forms was permitted and survived the coming of Islam, lending at interest was categorically forbidden.

Insurance became known to the Arab traders through the need to minimise the risk encountered in the trade (Rahman, 1979). The caravans would pass through dangerous territories and likely hostile lands and the possibility of loss of assets as well as lives through hazardous conditions or intended hostile action of plunder by others could not be ruled out. A form of loss financing risk management through collective, or mutual, insurance existed whereby the losers were compensated either wholly or partially from a collective fund organised prior the trade. A story is told that when Prophet Muĥammad was engaged in one of the trade journeys before the coming of Islam, a trade caravan was lost in the desert which lead to the members of the contributory insurance fund paying compensation to cover the loss of merchandise, horses and camels to the survivors as well as to the heirs of those who did not survive (ibid.).

The insurance fund would remain in operation for the caravan period beyond which it would be either terminated or renewed for another trade journey. If renewed it would take the form of an open-ended fund where new members may be permitted to join and existing members may be at liberty to leave. New members permitted to join would be subject to satisfying conditions regarding the degree of the additional risk they are bringing to the fund, depending upon how risky the new members are thought to be in terms of their personal character and tribal connection, the level of compensation expected to be paid out of the fund in line with the amount of capital involved and the amount of contribution, or risk premium, made by the new comers. Satisfying these preliminary conditions would be necessary in a mutual insurance, as all insurance was at that time. Although the process may not be as sophisticated as insurance is today, pre-Islamic Arabian insurance must have required a high degree of organization and clear rights and obligations that were very advanced for their day.

The Bedouin in Islam

It can be said, therefore, that in Central Arabia, where Islam first emerged, there was no civilisation to serve as a prerequisite for what later became the Islamic Empire. It was Islam as a religion that consolidated the mutually hostile tribes, tamed the Arabian character and pushed the inhabitants of Arabia forward towards world conquests. But not all of what existed in pre-Islamic Arabia was condemned and discarded. While Islam was unequivocally decisive on matters related to Man and God, the new religion was more tolerant, selective, and sometimes agreeable, in matters related to the character of the individual as a person. "The Bedouin is the raw material of Islam", is a saying that is attributed to the second Caliph Umar (Hitti, 1963). Some of the personal traits that were sung in the Arabic classical poetry were equally honoured, if not demanded in the Qur'ān and the Prophet's Sunnah. Patience and endurance, hospitality, and fortitude are particularly praised in the Qur'ānic verses and the Prophet's sayings. Several verses refer to the endurance as being the character of the real believers in God and His message. In Islam, endurance has been widened, however, to include endurance in facing the hardships in life, endurance in the consistence of the devout worshiping God, endurance in resisting forbidden temptations and not going astray, and endurance in military jihād.

Hospitality is equally emphasized, repeatedly, in the Qur'ān and Sunnah. This is widened to include, conceivably, hospitality to the poor and the needy and in spending in the cause of God. Going even further, the Qur'ān is explaining to the Prophet that, even "If one of the unbelievers sought your refuge (hospitality and protection), grant it to him and let him hear the words of God and, then, (if he is still not believing) accompany him to a place of safety (and let him go)," (Qur'ān 9:6). No example can serve better than this verse in demonstrating how sacred the value of hospitality is in Islam, how tolerant Islam is, and how important it is in Islam to extend protection to those individuals who are desperately in need for protection even if they are not Muslims.

Fortitude in Islam, needless to say, is a duty on the Muslim when a call for a military jihād is made. Those who die on the duty of jihād are promised a continuous life after death, dwelling in Heaven with angels and apostles, and those who remain alive are given due reward in life and hereafter, "do not consider those who were killed in the cause of Allah dead, they are alive and are given bounty in Heaven", (Qur'ān 2:154, 3:169–171).

Individualism has never been annulled in Islam, nor has the sense of belonging, clanism, been repealed. The reassurance of private ownership in Islam and the special regard given to protecting it is a demonstrable proof of the recognition of individualism. But it is not the absolute individualism that aims to fulfill the individual's whims and desire with no particular regards to the surrounding community. Rather, it is a well organized form of individualism that while it acknowledges the free will of the individuals to enjoy the bounties God has bestowed on them, it conditions such freedom with the stipulation that "no-harm" should incur to the surrounding community. Similarly, pre-Islamic clanism was tamed, though the concept of the individual being part of the whole was not dismissed. The clan became the Islamic community, ummah, the whole to which all Muslims belong.

Hard work, a main feature of the life in the inhospitable Arabia, is sanctified in Islam so much so that it is regarded as a kind of worship. Plus, work ought to be deemed as a continuous process with no excuse for interruption. "Whoever had a small plant which he was about to plant and heard the call of the Day of Judgment let him plant it first before the Day comes," the Prophet is reported to have said (Śaĥīĥ Muslim).

Some Pre-Islamic forms of trading were accepted and some of the financial arrangements in pre-Islamic Arabia survived the coming of

Islam. Commenda contracts, *mudharabah*, which were used in pre-Islamic trade were accepted and declared legitimate under Islam. The pre-Islamic forms of commercial insurance were also allowed to continue and survive the coming of Islam.

But lending at interest, for economic purposes or otherwise, was condemned; Muslims were to recover only their loan principle, capital, "you have the right to only your capital, '*ru'aūs amwalikum*'" (Qur'ān 2:275).

But the pre-Islamic Bedouin is also condemned and is often charged with hypocrisy in the Qur'ān, "the Bedouins said: 'We believe' (in Islam), say: 'You believe not, but you ought to say, 'we have surrendered' (to Islam) for faith has not yet entered your hearts'", (Qur'ān 49:14). This was particularly the case when it came to the fulfillment of the call for Holy War, *jihād*; they were described as being reluctant to take part in military jihād but were in a hurry to claim a share in the spoils of war (Qur'ān 9:90, 97–101, 120).

The condemnation of the forms of life in pre-Islamic Arabia that has led to rightly declaring them un-Islamic appears also in the Sunnah, in which the Prophet is reported to have warned his followers against having a behavioural attitude to each other as that of *al-Jahiliyyah*, the pre-Islamic Arabia's Age of Ignorance and Confusion. However, the Qur'ānic and Prophet's reference to the age of *jahiliyyah* should be inferred as related to those beliefs, actions and patterns of behaviour that were not per se accepted in Islam. These can be divided into three main categories as follows:

First, although the pagans believed in God as the creator and sustainer of the universe, "If you ask them (the unbelievers) who has created heavens and earth they will say Allah (God)", "if you ask them who has created heavens and earth and subjected the sun and the moon, they will say Allah", and "if you ask them who sends down water from the sky and gives life to the earth after being dead, they will say Allah", (Qur'ān 31:25, 29:61, 63, respectively), they also believed in God's associates, as intermediaries between man and God. These were forms of deities mostly of their own making to reconcile between them and God. Gradually they perceived these man-made gods equal to God and began to worship them as His associates. This was not accepted. The educational approach and the resort to the power of reasoning can be seen clearly in the Qur'ān in guiding the human mind to the truth before God's retribution is promised to the stubborn mind. We read the Qur'ānic verses educating, "Say (if you ask them), 'who has provided for you from the sky and earth, who has the all hearing and all seeing, who brings out the living from the dead and the dead from the living, and who controls the affairs of the universe?', they will say 'Allah (God)', say, 'Will you not then be righteous in worshiping Him (alone)?", (Qur'ān 10:31). To show the helplessness of God's associates, the Qur'ān continues to preach and reproach, "Say, 'is there of your associates (who you claimed to be God's equals) who could have made the Creation, or can remove it and remake it new?' Say, 'God has made the Creation and can remake it new', why then you are leading yourselves astray?" (Qur'ān 10:34), and "Is there of your associates (of what you have made as God's equals) who can guide to the Truth? Say, 'God guides to the Truth'; then is He who guides to the Truth is worth following or he who does not guide to the truth have you lost your senses!" (Qur'ān 10:35). Believing in God's associates would, therefore, attract the wrath of God and His retribution, as there is No God but one and He has no equals, "Say: he is God, One, the Everlasting Refuge, who has not begotten, and has not been begotten, and equal Him is not anyone" (Qur'ān 112:1–4), is the message, clearly put and unequivocally ratified. Moreover, all purpose of life is to be for the sake of God, as God teaches His Prophet, "Say verily my prayer, my sacrifice, my living and my dying are all for (the sake of) God, the Lord of all worlds, (who) He has no equal. Of this I have been commanded and I am the first of Muslims" (Qur'ān 6:162–163).

Second, the pre-Islamic Arabian could not perceive the notion of life after death, so he dismissed the belief in resurrection with the Day of Judgment that comes with it, "And they say, 'even if we were decayed bones and decomposed corpse, are we (how could it be possible) to be resurrected creation-new'" (Qur'ān 17:49). The Qur'ān is emphatic in confirming resurrection, Judgment and life in the hereafter with associated reward and punishment. In reply to their argument the Qur'ān continues, "Say, 'be stones or steal, or any of the formation you may arrogantly think of', they will say, 'who will bring us back the way we were', say, 'He who has created you (from nothing) in the first instance' they will turn their defiant heads to you and argue, '(and) when is that?', say 'it may be neigh (nearer than you think),'" (Qur'ān 17:50–51). Indeed, the Qur'ānic verses tell us about apostles of the past who wondered how God would resurrect the dead, though the verses advise that their motivation was not emanating from a disbelief in God's ability as much as it was from a wonder of how it could be done in their attempt to understand God's wisdom.

Third, social justice did not seem to be an embedded trait of the pre-Islamic Arabian as the concept did not appear to be fitting in with the harsh reality of the life prevailing then. The pre-Islamic Arabians, it seems, had associated social justice with weakness and feebleness, something they would not like to be linked with; so they dismissed it. This does not necessarily imply that charity was absent; indeed a charitable attitude could be inferred from their history and poetry; supporting the needy and protecting the weak was also sung in their poetry as an additional source of pride to the powerful clan. But charity, when extended to the poor, the needy and the weak, was meant to demonstrate a position of power, wealth and privilege. In Islam this is not the case. With the concept of social justice well embedded in the roots of religion, Islam came with a clear message, "in their wealth there is a *right* (italics ours) to the beggar and needy", (Qur'ān 51:19), and "So give to the kindred his *right* (italics ours) and to the poor and the wayfarer" (Qur'ān, 30:38). Furthermore, while equal respectability of individuals was not known to be the case in pre-Islamic Arabia except among the privileged few, Islam, though acknowledged the differences among individuals as a result of the differences in their ability, wealth and earning capacity, it has ordained equal respectability among individuals, as persons; they are as equal as the "comb's teeth". In that sense Islam, as will be discussed in the next chapter, does not call for an equal distribution of wealth but it advocates instead an equitable distribution.

In brief, Islam, on socio-economic matters, did not come to pre-Islamic Arabia to destroy a nation, as in A'd and Thamud, drown a king as with Pharaoh and his army or flood the world except for those in Noah's arc, in order to rebuild. Islam came, instead, to teach, mend, guide and direct, and to make a nation of no nation and a system of no system. Perhaps God was more merciful with the Arabian pagans because they still believed in Him as the creator of the universe and as their sustainer and as they served His sacred shrine in Makkah and the pilgrims with pride and devotion. He spared them the torture He gave other nations perhaps because that was a favourable response to the prayers of His messenger Prophet Muĥammad when he said, "O Lord, if you torture them they are Your slaves, and if you have mercy on them they are Your slaves". Prophet Muĥammad's prayer was, as Muslims believe, analogous to that of Jesus Christ's before him, O Lord, "if You torture them, they are Your slaves, and if You forgive them, You are the Only All-Mighty and All-Wise", (Qur'ān, 5:118), but in contrast to that of Noah's, "O Lord leave not one on earth of those who disbelieve in You", (Qur'ān 71:26). The disbelief of the pagan Arabians was, after all, a disbelief emanating from ignorance, Jahiliyyah. Ignorance needed enlightenment, education and redirection, and these were what Islam offered. And this is part of the strength of the religion.

CHAPTER TWO

THE BIRTH OF THE ISLAMIC STATE ECONOMIC THOUGHT IN THE QUR'ĀN AND SUNNAH (610 A.C.–632 A.C.)

Introduction

In 610 A.C. Central Arabia was on the verge of a dramatic change that would transform not only its history but also the history of many other nations for centuries to come. At that date, Makkah heard for the first time the Prophet Muĥammad (571–632) proclaiming a new religion to which he was the Messenger.

The new religion is called Islam, meaning the full submission to one supreme God and the entire surrender to His divine power. God in Islam is one true God, the God of Prophet Ibrāhīm, and the faithful should believe in this "one God, in His angels, in His Books, in His Apostles, in the Day of Judgment and in the Divine decree of good and evil", (Ŝaĥīĥ Muslim). The Arabic word for one supreme God is Allah, a name which should not be thought of as a different God from Prophet Ibrāhīm's God; He is the same God. The only difference is that the word Allah is an un-translated Arabic word for the word God. It should not be conceived as an exclusively Islamic God that is different from the monotheistic God in Judaism or Christianity. It explains why Judaism and Christianity are acknowledged in Islam as divinely inspired religions. Antecedent Apostles and Prophets are highly regarded. What distinguishes Islam from Judaism and Christianity, however, is that, among other things, it does not discriminate between religion and politics. Hence it is both a religion and a political institution. Moreover, Islam emphatically confirms that, "Say: He is God, One, the Everlasting Refuge, who has not begotten, and has not been begotten, and equal Him is not anyone" (Qur'ān 112:1–4).

Like the previous two monotheistic religions, Judaism and Christianity, Islam was resisted. The Bedouins of Arabia were strongly attached to their past religion and traditions, as mentioned in the previous chapter. They could not accept any ideas that would challenge their inherited beliefs and customs, at least not without great resistance. Moreover, the political input of the new religion adds a further reason for resistance; it introduced radical changes not only in religion, but also politically, socially and economically. It, therefore, threatened the power base of the assumed authority at that time, hence it was met with great resistance from the elite of the society, particularly in Makkah itself.

Islam found support in the sedentary Medenite society. Two main factors could be said to have encouraged the Medineses to lend support to Islam; the rivalry between the Arab pagans and the Jews in Medina and the continuous conflict between two major clans in the city itself. Firstly, the Jews reproached the pagan Medineses for their paganist deity, taking pride in their own divine religion and the expected Messiah. The Arab Medineses found in Islam the counterpart religion to that of the Jews and hoped that the new Prophet, who spoke the word of God, could be the often mentioned and expected Messiah. Secondly, the rival clans hoped that the new Prophet would play a reconciliatory role in unifying them.

After ten years of limited success in Makkah, the Prophet emigrated to al-Medīnah, in 620 A.C., having advised his followers to emigrate before him. From his base in al-Medīnah, the Prophet directed his missions to the rest of Arabia. After several battles with the Makkahns, he finally achieved victory over them and took over Makkah in 630 A.C. In 631 A.C. a treaty was concluded between the Prophet, and the Christians and the Jews of Tabūk, on the borders of Ghassānland, and without any military engagement they accepted to be taken under the protection of Islam for the payment of a poll tax called *jizyah* (Ibn Hisham). (The poll tax on non-Muslims replaces Zakāh tax which is imposed on Muslims only). Furthermore, during 630–631 A.C. delegates were sent to other parts of Arabia and to Egypt, to convert people to Islam. Tribes from Central Arabia, Oman, Ĥadramawt, al-Yemen, Hamadan and Kindah joined in. Arabia, as Hitti says, which had hitherto never bowed to the will of one man, seemed then inclined to be dominated by the Prophet Muĥammad and be incorporated into his new scheme, (Hitti, 1963). Arabia at last was united. This is known in history as the birth of the Islamic-Arabian state.

The principles of the state's administration were laid down by the Prophet. Al-Medīnah, where the Prophet resided even after the conquest of Makkah, was the capital of the Islamic state (Ibn Hisham).

The Prophet was the head of the state assisted by his companions, who remained with him in al-Medinah. He was at all times within the reach of his people, leading a modest life and often seen mending his own clothes. At the regional level, Prophet Muĥammad appointed a leader or *imam* who was the religious deputy and the chief-of-staff for each province, and Qur'ān reciters who recited the Qur'ān to people and taught them the details of the new religion.

Sources of the Islamic Economic Thought

Islamic economic thought has evolved through the development of Islamic law, the Sharī'ah. The law incorporates the rules of life for Muslims economically, socially and religiously. It is a code for living. As such, the Sharī'ah and the development of its sources are worth studying before the economic issues are particularly addressed.

The Prophet's life could be regarded as an important factor in dividing the sources of Islamic law, the Sharī'ah, into two main sources: those that were established by the Prophet himself during his lifetime and the others which were derived by Muslims after his death. The first source incorporates the Qur'ān and the Sunnah, while the second encompasses the body of jurisprudence.

The Qur'ān

To Muslims, the Qur'ān is the word of God revealed to the Prophet Muĥammad by the Archangel Gabriel. It was revealed in fragmented texts over a period of twenty three years, the preaching period of the Prophet. The reason for the gradual revelation of the Qur'ān could be said to be threefold: firstly, to allow early Muslims to study it with deliberation. In this, the Qur'ānic verse says, "And it is a Qur'ān that We have revealed in portions so that you may recite it unto the people with deliberation", (Qur'ān, 17:106). Secondly, the texts contain several verses that ordain the change of the habitual pattern of consumption to which the individual was accustomed. It was recognised that the reform of an individual's consumption pattern might take time, and an individual would be permitted to rid himself or herself of any undesirable habits in phases (Al-Khun, 1984). This should be looked at in the light of the nature of life at that time, in which promiscuity, gambling and the consumption of alcohol occupied a high priority in the consumer's scale of preference. Thirdly, Qur'ānic verses, which aim to set the parameters governing the socio-economic structure of society, were revealed at various stages of societal development to accommodate changes in the Islamic community. It was necessary, therefore, to reveal those verses at intervals.

Turning our attention to the authenticity of the Qur'ān, Muslims have no doubt about the authenticity of the Book. Qur'ānic texts were written during the revelation by a team commissioned by the Prophet. The texts were divided into verses, given numbers, put in order and divided into chapters by the Prophet himself (Al-Qattan, 1992). Two years after the Prophet's death, the first Caliph, Abū-Bakr, ordered the manuscript of the Qur'ān to be collected and compiled in one copy. Abū-Bakr followed the method of dual-verification in compiling the Qur'ān, the written manuscript was checked with the text memorised by the memorisers of the Qur'ān and the Prophet's companions. In the third Caliphate, 644–656 A.C., Caliph Uthmān ordered copies to be made of the master copy and all other manuscripts to be burned. That copy is the copy that has been used by Muslims since (ibid.).

The Sunnah

The Sunnah represents what the Prophet is reported to have said, done and agreed to be undertaken during his lifetime. As a source of the Sharī'ah, the Sunnah therefore is divided into three main elements: the Prophet's sayings, his practice and his approval of others' practices. The Prophet's sayings, however, were not God's words, though he was inspired by God in what he said. They were said to clarify rules in the Qur'ān through man to man teaching and provide details of what has been generalised in the Qur'ānic verses. To avoid confusion between the Qur'ānic texts and the Prophet's sayings, the Prophet, while instructing his followers to write the Qur'ān, and indeed arranging for a group of writers to do so, ordered not to write his sayings and instructed that whoever had to erase what he had written and his sayings to be transmitted only verbally, (Khallaf, 1942). Muslims, therefore, differentiated between the divine texts, the Qur'ān, and the Prophet Sayings and practice, *Aĥādīth*.

The first attempt to collect the *Aĥādīth* in writing took place in the reign of the Umayyad caliph Umar ibn Abel-Azīz in the mid eighth century. Three reasons explain the collection: (a) the death of many *Ĥadīth* jurists and memorisers, (b) the dispersion of *Ĥadīth* memorisers in the country by the expansion of the Islamic state, which made it difficult to trace them for consultation on *Ĥadīth* verification, and (c) the intrusion of the newly converted Muslims and the political rejectionists with misinterpreted *Aĥādīth* to suit their purposes (Khallaf, 1942). Devout Muslims started, therefore, to compile the Aĥādīth from the memorisers, traveling to them in different parts of the country. To ensure the accuracy of the *Aĥādīth*, the compilers relied on a method called *isnad*, meaning that every *Ĥadīth* is supported by a chain of informants, mentioned by name, starting from the last one who reported the *Ĥadīth* to the first one who himself reported hearing or seeing the Prophet saying, doing or approving what is reported. This method is similar to that used by modern researchers in their reference to previous work and bibliography. Being aware of the problem of accuracy, the compilers scrutinised the compiled *Aĥādīth*, excluded those that were contradictory and assigned classes to them depending on the degree of reliability. In emphasising the authenticity of the *Aĥādīth*, the medieval jurist Abū-Yūsuf stated that for the Sunnah to be accepted as authoritative they should be:

1. in agreement with the Qur'ān,
2. received in such a manner as to exclude the possibility of doubt about their authenticity,
3. widely-diffused and generally accepted by the community,
4. transmitted by and/or known to, and accepted by, scholars and jurists,
5. transmitted by people well-known for their integrity and trustworthiness,
6. in harmony with the general spirit of Islamic teachings, and
7. representative of the normative conduct of the Prophet rather than that which is uniquely related to him (Ansari, 1979)

The following are the six well known books on *Aĥādīth* related to their compilers:

Imam al-Būkhari (810–870 A.C.), *Ŝaĥīĥ al-Būkhari*,
Imam Muslim (d. 875 A.C.), *Ŝaĥīĥ Muslim, with al-Nawawi's explanation*, Imam Muslim, *Ŝaĥīĥ Muslim: Sunnah of the Sayings and Doings of the Prophet Muĥammad*,

Imam Abū-Dawood (d. 888 A.C.), *Sunan Abi-Dawood,*
Imam al-Tirmizi (d. 892 A.C.), *al-Jāmi'*, *Sunan al-Tarmazi*
Imam ibn Mājah (d. 886 A.C.), *Sunan ibn Mājah,* and
Imam al-Nasā'i (d. 915 A.C.), *Sunan al-Nasā'i.*

Of these, two are widely used, Ŝaĥīĥ al-Būkhari and Ŝaĥīĥ Muslim. These books are available to all Muslims and represent, after the Qur'ān, the second source of the Sharī'ah.

The Jurisprudence

Jurisprudence is the product of changes in the Islamic society after the Prophet's death. As the Islamic state expanded rapidly Muslims faced new situations that did not exist during the Prophet's lifetime which necessitated taking certain actions not covered in the Qur'ān or the Sunnah. Early Muslim leaders, therefore, had to derive new rules from the Qur'ānic and the Traditional texts to accommodate the new situations. Hence, the word jurisprudence indicates in Arabic the effort made in order to form one's own judgment, *ra'y* (Khallaf, 1942). The religious legitimacy of this emanates from a situation when the Prophet sent one of his companions, Mu'az ibn Jabal, to al-Yemen as a judge. In guiding Mu'az, the Prophet approved the use of the power of reasoning to reach a ruling in the absence of a clear rule in the Qur'ān and Sunnah (ibid.).

Jurisprudence, therefore, relies on various sources and uses certain principles in deriving the required rules. The first of these is the Qur'ān and the Sunnah. Wherever there are explicit rules in the Qur'ān and the Sunnah, there is no room for self-judgment. But when either is void of an explicit rule, the general understanding of the Qur'ānic verses and their purposes and the interpretation of the *Aĥādīth* and their intention, the spirit of the law as we may say, should be used to guide the jurists in arriving at the required rule. No violation to the spirit of the Sharī'ah should be committed. The core of jurisprudence, therefore, is the Qur'ān and the Sunnah. It is important to realise that at this stage because many socio-economic issues in the Islamic economic thought emerged from jurisprudence.

The other bases on which Islamic Jurisprudence is established are: consensus of opinions, judicial reasoning, derivation, public interest and custom and usage.

Consensus of opinion, *ijmā'* is the common consent among leading Muslim jurists on a particular issue. Two points should be noticed: (a) the common consent does not imply the general agreement of all or the majority of Muslims, rather, it is confined to the general agreement among learned jurists and theoligists, the *fuqaha', or Ulama'* and (b) the consensus was applied only to secular matters. Ritual issues and rules of worship are explicit enough in the Qur'ān and the Sunnah with no need for personal judgment (Al-Zuhailī, 1989). The influential role of the consensus of opinion as a source of the Sharī'ah became weak at the end of the orthodox caliphate and the beginning of the Umayyad period. Muslims became divided politically and it was difficult to obtain common consensus among leading theoligists. However, the rules derived by consensus of opinion during the orthodox caliphate serve as a reference to jurists in forming their own judgment (Al-Qattan, 1986).

Judicial reasoning, *qiyās*, refers to the process of deducing a rule from what has been stated explicitly in the previous sources in a "best fit" case. The method helps fill in a gap that might exist in the application of the Sharī'ah. Deviation, or *istiĥsān*, indicates the deviation from a previous judgment reached by the *qiyās* in a certain case that is not explicit in the Qur'ān, the Sunnah or the consensus of opinion, for a more relevant reason. Public interest, *istislāĥ*, is a form of reaching an unprecedented judgment motivated by public interest to which neither the Qur'ān nor the Sunnah has an explicit reference (Zuhailī, 1989). Custom and usage, or the *'urf*, is the process of relying on the custom and usage of a particular society in deriving a judgment in a case, again, not explicitly mentioned in the Qur'ān, the Sunnah, or the consensus of opinion. The above principles of jurisprudence, though are weak in comparison with the prime sources of the Sharī'ah, the Qur'ān and the Sunnah, have been of considerable importance to Muslim jurists concerned with socio-economic issues. Within the boundaries of the Qur'ān and the Sunnah they derived several rules regarding secular issues, which contributed significantly to the development of Islamic economic thought, as will be seen in due course.

Economic Thought in the Qur'ān and the Sunnah
Basic Philosophy

Three main ideological concepts and three main principles, which have been well-established in Islam, could be said to have laid down the basic philosophy of Islamic economic thought. The three concepts could be classified as the concept of unity, the concept of vice-regency of human beings on earth, and the concept of free-will and responsibility (see for example, Ahmad 1980, and Naqvi, 1981), while the principles could be viewed as the principle of moderation, the principle of economic efficiency, and the principle of social justice.

Islamic Economic Concepts

The concept of unity, tawhīd

The concept of unity emanates from Muslims' firm belief in the oneness of God, "No God but One", which, with the belief in "Prophet Muĥammad as His messenger", constitutes the first pillar of Islam: the two Testimonies. The concept has various implications: the unity of the creator, God, the unity of His characteristics, *ŝifat*, the unity of His work and creation and, as a consequence, the unity of the universe as fully integrated in the unity of God. Nothing in heaven or earth could be viewed in separation of His will or work, nor could it be taken in isolation of His existence. The whole creation should be viewed as a "whole" and be seen as integrated in the holiness of the oneness of God. The consequences of the whole-ness of the universe indicates, if not commands, that any economic action taken by an individual or a group of individuals should not be harmful to the interest of others nor should it be damaging to other sources of goodness in the universe. No misuse or abuse of economic resources in pursuit of the "maximization" of benefits to some on the account of sacrificing the benefits of others. A well-defined balance should always be observed by the users of economic resources and should be constantly maintained. A deviation from this rule ought to be rectified, if not by the individuals themselves then by the state which has the right to step in to rectify the damage. If the harm is intentional and persistent the wrath of God is awaiting the wrongdoer and God's retribution is "promised" in return. Hellfire in the thereafter and heavenly punishment in life and hereafter is assured to the abusers if the rectification is not exercised. But if the abuser heeds the warning, or the advice, and rectifies his action, God is always forgiving, and he is generous in his reward for repentance. Further, earthly creatures other than human beings have the right to live on the goodness of the land, as they are meant to serve humans in survival. The maltreatment of animals for food or work is forbidden, and, equally, the misuse of natural resources is condemned. Finally, man is required, if not preordained, to civilize the earth, for his sake and the sake of other creatures.

The Concept of Vicegerency, al-khilafah

The concept of vicegerency on earth indicates that man is the centre of the universe and God's deputy on earth. This is the core of the Islamic ideology on which the Islamic economic thought revolves and to which almost all Muslim jurists, with the exception of the very few, adhere. Stressing that man is the centre of the universe, the Qur'ān states, "He it is who has created for you everything on earth", (Qur'ān, 2:29), and "has made subservient to you whatever is in the heavens and the earth and granted you His bounties, manifest and hidden", (Qur'ān, 31:20, see also 16:12–14, 17:70, 22:65 and 45:12–13). In stating man's viceregency on earth the Qur'ān declares, "When your Lord said to the angels: 'I am placing on the earth one that shall rule as My deputy"', "It is He who has made you vicegerents on earth", and "Have faith in God and His apostle and give in alms of that on which He has made you vicegerents", (Qur'ān, 2:30, 35:39 and 57:7 respectively). By the concept of deputizing, a deputy has to perform his duties in accordance with the instructions directed to him by his superior. The deputizing superior, God, has laid down His rules of utilizing economic resources in the manner He wishes it to be done. To put another way, whatever man has on earth of economic resources he has on the basis of trusteeship. It is a trusteeship between God, the superior creator and provider, and man, the user of what God has made available to him. The use of these resources therefore is controlled by the rules of trusteeship and any violation of these rules would render the entrusted party, man, guilty of the abuse and misuse of the subject of trusteeship, earthly economic resources. Man is, therefore, accountable to God and by the virtue of the rules of trusteeship, or stewardship, any violation of these rules would merit God's attribution and punishment. The degree of punishment, or even forgiveness to the repentant, is left to God alone as the creator of these resources and their ultimate owner. This concept, with the principles that are derived from it, has various implications for all economic functions on earth: consumption of economic resources, development of these resources, and the distribution of the added values among the contributors and the would-be contributors, as shown below.

The Concept of Free-Will and Responsibility, Amānah

Free will

This is the ability of human beings to choose, select and decide, which is clearly indicated in the Qur'ān, although the concept of destiny is also referred to. This might cause confusion, and indeed has done so, when the two concepts are looked at jointly and the question is asked of whether man is directed in his bevaviour by the divine force or by his power of reasoning. If it was the former, man should not be held responsible for what he does, while he ought to be accountable for his actions if the latter applied. Although such discussion will not be pursued here, it suffices to say that man has the freedom of choice as to good or evil and his destiny is only "known" to God through His wisdom and knowledge of the characteristics of the man He created. Man, therefore is free to choose, to act in harmony with God's code of conduct, the straight path, or to divert from it, and God knows that in advance. This faculty of freedom of choice has been emphasised in the Qur'ān in more than one passage, of which the strongest is perhaps the statement that man has accepted to bear the burden of God's trust on earth while no-one else dared to bear it. In a strong tone, the Qur'ānic verse states, "We offered Our trust to the heavens, to the earth and to the mountains, but they declined to bear it for fear of its burden. But man assumed it", (Qur'ān, 33:72). Also, man has been shown two paths, good and evil, and it was up to him to decide which to follow, "Have We not given him two eyes, a tongue, and two lips, and shown him the two paths?", (Qur'ān, 90:8–10). Free will is a reflection of the delegated authority given to man by God in the trusteeship relationship between God and man.

Responsibility

While authority, with the free will, represents one side of the trusteeship contract between God and man, responsibility portrays the other side of this relationship. It imposes limits to man's freedom of choice and makes man accountable for his actions. Economic resources which are owned by man on the basis of "ownership by trusteeship" should be managed in accordance with the conditions established in this contractual relationship; any violation of these conditions makes man accountable to the ultimate owner: God. Man's freedom may be called, therefore, operational freedom; it is not absolute but restricted and qualified. The restriction on man's freedom in utilising economic resources on earth is twofold: on the production side, he should seek efficiency, and on the distribution side he should strive for social justice (this is explained below).

A system of reward and punishment
This will have to be established to complete the operational machinery of trusteeship whereby the fulfillment of responsibilities will be evaluated in the Hereafter and judged accordingly. The Qur'ānic verses state, "And every man's augury have We fastened to his own neck: on the Day of Judgment We shall bring out for him (his) scroll, which he will see spread open. Read thine (own) record: sufficient is thyself this day make out an account against you", (Qur'ān, 17: 13–14).

Islamic Economic Principles

The Principle of Moderation, I'atidāl

The principle of moderation stipulates that human behaviour, the economic and even the non-economic, should be exercised in moderation with no tendency towards extremism. First, consumption should be in moderation and the real faithful, the believers, are described in the Qur'ān as those, who when they spend are neither excessive nor niggardly, but who are keeping a fine balance between, "O Children of Adam, take your adornment while going to pray, and eat and drink but not in extravagance, verily God does not like extravagance, (*al-musrifūn*, those who waste by extravagance)", (Qur'ān 7:31), and "Let not your hand be tied to your neck (in not spending) nor let it be stretched fully (in spending extravagantly) so that you may not end in poverty and regret" (Qur'ān, 17:29).

The concept of moderation is based on Islamic ideology and it extends to not only the materialistic use of resources, as we will see shortly, but also to religious devotion in obeying the divine force.

The Prophet, peace upon him, is reported to have advised three men who vowed, in pursuit of God's satisfaction to: (a) one to fast all his life, (b) the second to pray all night and (c) the third to abstain from marriage and the pleasure of women, that these acts of supposed sacrifice were wrong. In confirming the normality of life in Islam he emphasized to them, "I fast and break my fast, pray and sleep, and I marry" (Ŝaĥīĥ al-Bukhari and Ŝaĥīĥ Muslim). The principle of moderation has particular application to the consumption function as we will see shortly.

The Principle of Economic Efficiency

The emphasis on economic efficiency is a by-product of the previous concepts: unity and viceregency. Natural resources would have to be utilized in the most economically efficient manner to maximize, if we use a modern term, the value of output in relation to that of the input. The input has mostly been given by God in the form of natural resources, which with the addition of other factors of production lead to the increase in the treasure of the nation in the form of its gross national product, again to use modern technical terms. In the emphasis on the economic efficiency of the use of natural resources, either for consumption or production, we find Islam is differentiating clearly between two important notions: *isrāf* and *tabẑīr*. This has been mentioned in the Qur'ānic verses with a particular distinction between the two.

In consumption for example, *isrāf* could be interpreted as extending the level of consumption beyond the level of basic needs. This may lead to, and incorporates, the consumption of luxurious goods and services. In terms of the relationship between saving and spending, *isrāf* may also be widened to include sacrificing future consumption, saving, for the sake of immediate consumption, and spending; which is a reflection of the consumer's time preference in allocating his consumption between present and future income. In this case the balance between the two types of consumption, in both cases, first, the basic needs as compared with luxurious consumption, and second, future as compared to present consumption, which good Muslims are required to observe, may be impaired. This is not recommended; it is frowned upon and may even attract God's dissatisfaction. But the punishment for this behaviour, is not, as it seems from reading the Qur'ānic verses, as severe as the punishment associated with another level of consumption, *tabẑīr*.

Tabẓīr in an economic sense is the unnecessary use of economic resources, i.e. wastage of economic resources, large or small, and at all levels of consumption. *Tabẓīr*, is not confined to the level of extravagance, but goes beyond that to include even the level of necessities if the consumer was wasteful in satisfying his or her very basic needs of these essential physio-sociological wants. To put it another way, one may have a variety of suits, meals, electrical appliances, and may in that reach the level of extravagance, which, to remind ourselves, is frowned upon and may even attract a penalty subject to the ability of economic resources and the development state of the economy, but one may not waste fabric or food ingredients unnecessarily in having even one modest suit or eating one meal. Wastage, *tabẓīr*, even in fulfilling most basic needs is forbidden.

Therefore, while *isrāf* is the extensive use of resources, *tabẓīr* is the wasteful use of these resources; and there is a distinct line between the two. While the former may lead to further comfort, better appearance and, most likely, more pleasure in life, the latter leads to no purpose but wasting valuable resources to the community and the world by putting these resources to no use. The former may make one less of a perfect Muslim, but the latter would render a person irresponsible to the point of evil: a brother of Satan, "Verily resource wasters (*mubaẓẓirīn*) are brethren to Satan, and Satan is the worst unbeliever", (Qur'ān 17:27). *Tabẓīr* attracts the wrath of God, for which the penalty is His retribution. Those who practice *tabẓīr* are regarded as the brethren of Satan and cast away from Paradise and made to dwell in Hell as Satan and all the unbelievers. They are with Satan and those who do not believe in God in one category—the most damned sin that can ever be committed, a sin that can never be forgiven.

To introduce a new economic term to each one of these two concepts one may suggest the use of the term "extension" to *isrāf*, while the term "wastage" would be most suitable for *tabẓīr*. The differentiation between wastage and extension is a unique concept that is clearly stipulated in Islamic economics, in the prime source of the religion, the Qur'ān, and, more admirably, is a concept that has been with us for the last fourteen centuries or so. The concept can be widened to refer to any type of economic or non-economic activity, consumption, production or recreational, and at any level of analysis, micro or macro. The proper use of the notion of time and the consideration given to whether the use comes under the level of "extension" or "wastage" is demonstrably applicable. Both production and consumption functions in society are clearly affected by this basic principle in Islamic economics.

The Principle of Social Justice, adālah ijtima'iyyah

Social justice is embedded in Islam. People are equal in front of God, fear the day "when you come unto us alone (powerless, without wealth, companions or anything else), as We first created you, having left behind you what We have entrusted in you (on earth)", the Qur'ānic verse warns (Qur'ān 6:94), and "People are as equal as the comb's teeth", and, "The noblest of you are the best in character" (Ŝaĥīĥ al-Būkhari, and Ŝaĥīĥ Muslim).

Islam, however, recognizes the differences between people that may lead to differences in their ability to earn and, hence, in the amount of wealth they may accumulate. "To some of you God has given more than to others", (Qur'ān, 16:71). But Islam does not reward laziness or non-participation. It invites, or indeed ordains, every one to work hard in earning a living and to seek the utilization of the bounty of God. With the proviso that poverty is not the result of laziness or non-participation in economic activities, Islam does not accept a status quo of sharp demarcation between the rich and the poor. The rich has the duty of giving to the poor and needy, and to provide a balanced structure of relationships in the community, as what the rich are giving is regarded as what the poor are entitled to. The Qur'ānic message is very clear, "in their wealth there is a *right* given to the poor and the deprived", (Qur'ān: 51:19), and ". . . pay the *right* (italics ours) on it at the day of harvest", (Qur'ān 6:141). This emphasises the Qur'ānic fact that when the rich give they don't give with arrogance and air of superiority and when the poor take they don't receive with humiliation and humbleness, the giving and taking is well organized and ordained by the divine force. The rich, however, are not giving in vain, they are rewarded, and generously, by Him and Him alone, God, and the reward is bestowed in this life and life-after. This principle of social justice has particular implications for the distribution of income and economic justice as shown below.

Application of Basic Philosophy

The above set of Islamic ideological concepts and principles can be said to have one purpose in mind: the proper organisation of economic resources so as to satisfy the needs of God's creatures as revolving mainly around the needs of humankind and to preserve the surrounding environment in particular and the universe in general. The ultimate objective of the Islamic ideology cannot be resting therefore on a concept of "maximization" of any sort, utility, profit or wealth, as that might be, but on the concept of the preservation of the universe. A concept of maximization if adopted in Islamic economics would be in conflict with the basic concept of "moderation" that is embedded in Islamic ideology. Consequently, "maximization" per se renders itself alien to the spirit of Islamic ideology. We have seen above how the Prophet urged his followers to be moderate even in their core practice of God's worship. We can see further that God emphasises in more than one occasion in the Qur'ān that although He has ordained self discipline and full obedience He has not prohibited the enjoyment of His bounty in life. "And We have created you as a middle-of-the-road nation", (Qur'ān, 2:143). This is not to say that Muslim economists have not used the concept of maximization in their analysis, they have; though they have applied it to objectives other than profit or wealth. But a thorough scrutiny of the Islamic ideology would suggest a leaning towards "moderation" than "maximization". Among other things, moderation has a particular advantage over "maximization". It provides a "balanced" framework and a pattern of behaviour, including that involving economic decision making, while maximization is not free from skewness in this pattern that may not guarantee a form of normality.

Looking into the effect of the above basic philosophy on the economic issues in Islam, the analysis below, in line with the spirit of the religion, will focus on the economic resources that God has made available to His creatures with a view to seeing how humankind, as the trustees of these divinely resources, have been engineering these resources. The analysis will look into these resources from the following perspectives:

Economic Resources: definition and perception
Economic Resources: forms of ownership
Economic Resources: economic development and production

Economic resources: consumption
Economic resources: income distribution
Economic Resources: role of the state

The above classification, we hasten to emphasise, is not arbitrary. Instead, it is meant to reflect the stages of economic activities on earth and in reflection to the sequence of God's creation. First, economic resources need to be defined, or at least described. Second, a form of ownership of these resources can be established. Third, these resources need to be developed so as the fruit of development may be realised. Fourth, consumed, otherwise consumption without development would lead to the depletion of these resources. Fifth, within the embedded concept of social justice in Islam, the surplus, or value-added to use a modern economic term, should be distributed fairly among the participants to avoid injustice, and finally the role of the state as well as, not necessarily as opposed to, that of the individual need to be clarified. These issues are examined below.

Economic Resources: Definition and Perception

With some variation, the nearest analogy to Islamic economic resources in Western economic theory can be viewed as the factors of production. But factors of production emphasises the function of production in particular, looking at it from the specifically narrow angle of a certain use of these resources as related to the exact task of production. In Islamic economics, by the virtue of the Islamic ideology above, a classification of resources would need to be wider and more comprehensive so as to look at the resources first as a blessing bestowed upon humankind by the divine force and second by examining how these resources have been put to use. The line might be fine between the classification of the Western theory and the Islamic theory, but the demarcation line, fine as it might be, reflects the basic philosophy of the two systems. The economic resources are classified below into natural resources, labour and capital. The arrangements of these resources in this particular sequence, we hasten to emphasise, is not random. Rather, they reflect the sequence of God's creation of the universe: the resources were made available by Him first, then man was created and later labour and toil were needed to exploit the economic resources, and capital was developed later as a result of the combination of labour, natural resources and time.

Natural resources

As a factor of production, natural resources embrace more than land, the classical economic factor; they incorporate land, animals, minerals and the like, wind, water, and sea and river products. In the Qur'ān, reference has been made to these resources on several occasions in such a way as to: (a) cite to people the bounties of God so that they may be thankful to Him, and (2) encourage them to utilise these resources for the benefit of "self" and community. For example, the Qur'ān states, "He sends down water from the sky, and with it brings forth the buds of every plant. From these We bring forth green foliage and close-growing grain, palm-trees laden with clusters of dates, vineyards and olive groves and all manner of pomegranates", (Qur'ān 6:99).

With labour, or man, natural resources, which are provided by God, are the prerequisite for production. However, this is a general equilibrium perspective, looking at the economy as an integrated system. The process of production in such a system is achieved through the interaction between man and nature. However the time dimension should also be considered. Over time production requires the interaction of three main elements: natural resources, labour and capital. There is no inconsistency here if capital is regarded as stored labour, it is a product of the collaboration between labour and natural resources in the long run.

Labour

Labour has been emphasized in the Qur'ān and the Sunnah. The Qur'ān emphasises the importance of work, and the necessity for it, many times. In the Sunnah, work is so highly regarded that the Prophet is reported to have said that of the sins there are some that cannot be removed (forgiven) except by working to earn a living (Ŝaĥīĥ al-Bukhari). All types of legitimate work is encouraged, even that which may benefit birds and animals, "No Muslim has planted a plant or cultivated a branch, and a bird or an animal eats from it but has been given a divine reward for it" (Ŝaĥīĥ al-Bukhari). The examples of the Prophet and his companions making their living in the market and providing for their own needs are abundant.

Furthermore, the following points could be noted about the concept of labour in the Qur'ān and the Sunnah:

1. Labour is not confined to hired labour. Instead, it incorporates all types of labour including that which is embodied in capital and land. As such labour in the Islamic context may include entrepreneurship.
2. Work is regarded as a duty on the Muslim even if he/she is rich. There is no room for the idle rich.
3. Full devotion to worship is not an acceptable reason for not working; there is no monastery or nunnery in Islam. The Prophet is reported to have seen a man who had been spending all his time worshipping in the mosque, when he asked who was supporting the man and was told that some people did he said that those people were better than him.
4. Employers should be "fair" to their employees; paying them their wages in time, providing them with reasonable work conditions, assigning tasks to them according to their abilities and treating them as equal. The Prophet is reported to have said, "Your employees are your brethren whom God has made your subordinates. So he, who has his brother under him, let him feed him with what he feeds himself and clothe him with what he clothes himself and not burden him with what overpowers him. If you do so help him" (Ŝaĥīĥ al-Būkhari).

On the basis of the teachings on the previous point, setting minimum wages, as the wages that is sufficient to cover feeding and clothing in a manner similar to that of the employer, establishing a system for maximum working hours, creation of appropriate working conditions, enforcement of precautionary measures against work hazards and adaptation of technological innovations to reduce hardships would be fully in conformity with the spirit of Islamic teachings (Chapra, 1980).

Labourers are expected to do their best to meet work requirements; they should be honest, diligent and efficient. The Prophet said, "An employee who excels in his devotion to God and also renders to his employer the duty, sincerity and obedience that he owes him, for him there is double reward with God" (Ŝaĥīĥ al-Bukhari).

Capital

Capital has been regarded as stored labour embodied in commodities and used in the process of producing other commodities (Abū-Saud, 1965). The definition as such refers to economic labour as the base of creating capital. Capital however is not labour alone, rather, it is labour in conjunction with natural resources that compose the stored capital, which may require widening the definition to include both labour and natural resources in combination, though at various levels, in the process of creating capital. This would be more consistent with the Islamic view that begins with natural resources as bounties given by God in His divine wisdom to make the earth habitable added to labour which is highly regarded in Islam as an important factor in the production process, that aims, among other things, to increase the utility of the divinely provided natural resources. This is emphasised further by defining economic labour as the labour applied to nature in order to extract the consumer's utility or increase a production opportunity from natural resources (Bāqir-al-Sadr, 1968).

The Price of Capital

In Islam, the price of capital is not the rate of interest but the rate of return on capital, generated mainly from profit. Interest is prohibited in the Qur'ān and the Sunnah, referred to as Ribā, but trading is allowed in its place, "God has permitted trading but has forbidden Ribā" (Qur'ān, 2:275). Indeed the Prophet himself was a merchant. Therefore, the relationship between the lender and the borrower is twofold: (a) if the loan is for consumption purposes, it should be given free, and (b) if it is for business purposes, it should be given either with the intention of earning money on it, which in this case be a share of the business profit against bearing a share of the business losses, or, alternatively, with no intention of earning a return, and in this case it should be given free with the loan paid back at the agreed time. The business results will have no bearing on the repayment of the free loan. Given the controversy the issue of interest has raised it may be worthwhile to elaborate on the prohibition of interest below.

Ribā, defined as the lending of money at interest is forbidden in the Qur'ān in four references, with punishments being introduced in four stages.

The first reference is rather mild, though is still very discouraging, as it states that investment at interest does not increase in the sight of God, "That which you have acquired of Ribā seeking to increase your wealth by (charging) Ribā on people's holdings, is not an increase in the sight of God (not being blessed by God)" (Qur'ān, 30:39).

The second phase progressed further to state that the taking of Ribā is *forbidden* and will surely be *punished*, as it was forbidden to other nations and for which they were punished, "Because of their iniquity, We forbade the Jews good things which We formerly allowed them; because time after time they have debarred others from the path of God; because they practice Ribā—although they were forbidden it—and cheat others of their possessions. We have prepared a stern chastisement for those of them that disbelieve" (Qur'ān, 4:160, 161). Still, in these verses the reference is made indirectly to the Jews who practiced Ribā, which God had forbidden. By referring to that example as a sign of disobedience, Muslims by implication were ordained not to do the same, and should not get involved with Ribā. But the emphasis was still on prohibition by example.

In the third reference to Ribā, believers are instructed directly not to 'devour' Ribā doubled and multiplied, and should fear the punishment which was stated clearly as the Hell-Fire, "Believers, do not live on Ribā, doubled and multiplied and have fear of God, so that you may succeed in your life, and guard yourselves against Hell-Fire that is prepared for unbelievers" (Qur'ān, 3:131, 131). The instructions at this stage are direct and the punishment for disobedience is clear. But there may still be ambiguity related to the state of Ribā as being only the "doubled and multiplied". The fourth and final reference elaborates further to eliminate any ambiguity.

The fourth stage is the clearest, the most direct and the most punishing. It: (a) explicitly forbids Ribā, (b) threatens those who lend at Ribā with war from God and His apostle, (c) orders believers to repent and give it up, (d) states that if they repent they can take their money back in due time, and (e) defines what can be taken back as, and confines it to, the loan principle *Ru'aūs Amwalikum*. In explicit clarity, the verses state, "Those that live on Ribā shall rise up before God like men whom Satan has demented by his touch; for they claim that Ribā is like trading. But God has permitted trading and forbidden Ribā. He that receives an admonition from his Lord and mends his ways may keep what he has already earned; his fate is in the hands of God. But he that pays no heed shall be assigned to Hell-Fire and shall remain in it forever. God has laid His curse on Ribā and blessed almsgiving with increase. Believers, have fear of God and waive what is still due to you from Ribā, if your faith be true; or be warned of war declared against you by God and His Messenger. If you repent, you have the right to your principal, *Ru'aūs Amwalikum*, suffering no loss and causing loss to none" (Qur'ān, 2:275–279)

This escalation in the punishment for being involved in Ribā is not unusual in Islamic teachings, as a rule might be introduced in the Qur'ān to reproach a practice or restrict it, subsequently to be followed by another that overrules the earlier and ordains a complete abstinence from the practice. The prohibition of consuming alcoholic beverage is an example. It was introduced in the Qur'ān in two phases, the first ordained Muslims not to be drunk while praying, and the second overruled the first and stated that drinking alcoholic beverage is completely forbidden. In effect, the first rule would still partially limit unsocial behaviour resulting from drinking. As prayers are five times a day from dawn to dusk, it would be virtually impossible for a believer to become intoxicated during the day, leaving the only time for drinking to the time prior to going to bed. But the second phase of ruling is more decisive. The gradual prohibition of Ribā is completed in the Qur'ān by the rules of the verses 2:275–279. They are the most comprehensive set of verses in this respect. The verses state an important conclusion and answer a controversial question. The conclusion is that Ribā is no longer 'only' frowned upon by God but, more strongly, it merits the declaration of "war" from God and His Messenger. Moreover, the verses answer an important and controversial question regarding the meaning of Ribā, as shown below.

The meaning of Ribā

In the above Qur'ānic quotations it is noticed that the word Ribā has been quoted un-translated. By that, we meant to postpone the translation until such time when the meaning of the word is thoroughly discussed, an issue which has raised the interest of several writers. The difficulty arises because some argue that the word Ribā does not convey the meaning of interest as known nowadays, instead, it is the equivalent to usury, which connotes excessive interest (see for example, Maxime Rodinson, 1980). This argument does not seem to carry convictions for various reasons:

1. Linguistic meaning: the word Ribā in Arabic connotes the meaning of "increase", the verb of which is 'Yarbu', meaning it increases. This is the general linguistic meaning of the word which is not necessarily confined to the act of lending money at interest. But

when used in the Qur'ān, the word is used in a particular Qur'ānic reference to the act of giving money at a fixed increase, which is emphasised further by defining the word by the article 'al' meaning 'the'. Hence, the verb 'Yurabi' and the noun Murabi' to refer to the act of giving money at a fixed increase and the person who does such an act, respectively. These words are used in the Qur'ān specifically in this particular sense. The word Ribā is not the only word that has become confined to a specific technical Qur'ānic usage; there are many others that have developed in this manner. As in many sciences, including economics, words can develop into having a dual capacity, one linguistic and the other technical. Sharī'ah is no exception. It is not unusual to see scholars differentiating between the two functional roles of the word, one linguistic and another technical. The technical definition of the word Ribā' as such is emphasised further in the following Qur'ānic and Sunnah references.

2. Qur'ānic reference: this is demonstrated in two main areas:
   a. Verses 2:275–279 in which the rule, hence the definition, is explicit, "... if you repent you have the right to your principal, *Ru'aūs Amwalikum*". It follows that the principal or capital sums, *Ru'aūs Amwalikum*, is the only financial right which the lender has over the borrower. This defines clearly the meaning of Ribā, as the difference between the amount borrowed, the principal, and the amount due to be paid back, which includes the interest as it is called now.
   b. The Qur'ānic distinction between trading and Ribā. Although both, trading and lending at interest, Ribā, generate an 'increase' in capital, the former is permitted while the latter is forbidden, "God has permitted trading but has forbidden Ribā" (Qur'ān, 2:275). If both, Ribā and trading generate increase in capital and one is permitted while the other is prohibited, they cannot be of the same nature. The difference lies in the risk factor and the estimated balance between risk and gains in the allocation of both to the involved parties. While parties share both risk and gains in trading, risk lies solely on the borrowers in Ribā operations. In this sense, Ribā, distinguished from profit in trading operations, is the interest as understood today regardless of being excessive or otherwise.
3. The Sunnah: these have also made it clear that Ribā is any

increase that the borrower is asked to pay over the amount originally borrowed. The Prophet is reported to have said, "Loan Ribā is absolutely void. You own only your principal, *Ru'aūs Amwalikum*, without oppressing or being oppressed" (Ŝaĥīĥ Muslim).

From the above, it could be concluded that Ribā is equivalent to interest as known to us nowadays. This, hopefully, helps correct the misconception that surrounds the issue.

The reason for the confusion could be contributed to various factors:

1. The Qur'ānic use of the words "doubled and multiplied" in the third phase of prohibition. (see above) But this is ruled out by the ruling of the fourth and last phase of prohibition and by the Qur'ānic definition of debt as being 'capital sums, or, the principal', above which any sum becomes Ribā. Also, another interpretation of 'doubled and multiplied' is that Ribā, interest, even at a rate that is not doubled or multiplied may lead to increasing the capital 'enormously' over the years to that of the double and multiple of capital, which is what interest does over a long period.
2. The influence of Christian writers, especially Calvin, who differentiated between usury and interest: while the former is not permitted since it implies an "excessive" rate, the second is because it indicates a "reasonable" rate (Tawney, 1980). This in conjunction with "doubled and multiplied" might have influenced the writers' way of thinking.
3. The political climate to which Muslim writers might have been subject. This could influence some writers in trying to justify a non-Islamic financial policy favoured by the political authorities. This was particularly significant when Muslim governments suffered from decay during the medieval period and when governments in modern times tried to "Westernise" the economy under the notion of modernisation (Wilson, 1983).
4. The different interpretation of the prohibition of interest in Judaism and Christianity. While Judaism and Christianity are consistent in this regard with Islamic teachings, the Muslims' version of the Hebraic Bible is that the abolition of interest (usury) is meant to be not only between "the Israelite and his brother the Israelite", but also between the Israelite and the non-Israelite (Qur'ān 2:275–279). In Christianity, interest, though it is not mentioned

explicitly in the New Testament, is prohibited. Early Christian jurists were against it and any person obstinately declaring it was not a sin was to be punished as a heretic (see for example Tawney, 1980). Luther also persistently condemned it; Calvin was the first major Christian writer to accept interest as legitimate. In Calvin's view interest was lawful providing that it did not exceed a fixed maximum and the terms to the poor were interest-free. Calvin's advocacy of interest is ruled out, in the view of Muslims, by the teaching of early Christian jurists. Notably, Muslims believe in Judaism and Christianity as two divinely inspired religions.

Types of Ribā

Ribā can be classified into two main types: Ribā al-Qur'ān, or loan Ribā, and Ribā al-Sunnah, or commodity Ribā.

First: Loan Ribā

Loan Ribā is referred to in the Islamic literature in various terms that are used interchangeably:

Ribā al-Jahiliyyah: referring to *Jahiliyyah* as being the period before Islam, the period of ignorance,
Ribā al-Duyun, also Ribā al-Qurūd: *duyun* and *qurūd* means loans,
Ribā al-Nasī'a: meaning Ribā associated with the payment period, and
Ribā al-Qur'ān: Ribā that has been stated in the Qur'ān.

All these terms refer to the same type of Ribā, which is stated in the Qur'ān as discussed above with no need for repetition. The only loan that is acceptable in Islam therefore is the free-interest loan, *al-qard al-Ĥassan*, the benevolent loan, (*qard* in Arabic means loan, and *al-Ĥassan*, in this context, means benevolent,)

Second: Commodity Ribā, or Ribā al-Buyū'

This is the Ribā that has been stated in the Sunnah, not in the Qur'ān. It might arise as a result of exchanging commodities: (a) with or (b) without, a delayed period. This Ribā is divided into two types:

(a) Ribā that results from exchanging an object, or a commodity, with another object of the same type, or same commodity, with an immediate delivery for an increase in quantity. This type of

Ribā is called Ribā al-fadle—Ribā resulting from an increase in quantity of the same object in a transaction of an immediate delivery. For example, exchanging gold for gold or wheat for wheat. The exchange should not be at an increase. See further example below.

(b) Ribā that results from exchanging an object, of a commodity, with another object of the same type or another, same or another commodity, with a delayed delivery, future delivery. This type of Ribā is called Ribā al-Nasīʾa—Ribā resulting from an increase in quantity of the same or different object, commodity, in a transaction of a postponed, future, delivery. For example, exchanging gold for gold or wheat for wheat future delivery. The exchange should not be at an increase. Further examples are cited below.

Stating the prohibition of commodity Ribā, the Prophet is reported to have clarified the exchange conditions which should be satisfied in order to avoid this Ribā by saying, "Gold for Gold, equivalent for equivalent; silver for silver, equivalent for equivalent; wheat for wheat, equivalent for equivalent; barely for barley, equivalent for equivalent; salt for salt, equivalent for equivalent; dates for dates equivalent for equivalent; and whoever exceeds or asks for excess, he practiced Ribā. Sell gold for silver as you wish if it is hand to hand (prompt delivery) and sell barely for dates as you wish if it is hand to hand" (Ŝaĥīĥ Muslim).

From these sayings of the Prophet, and other sayings, the following general rules that govern commodity Ribā have been concluded (Al-Qusi, 1982):

1. When trading metal for metal and food for food (e.g. gold for gold or wheat for wheat), two conditions must be fulfilled: (a) the quantitative equality of both objects and (b) prompt delivery.
2. When trading metal for metal or food for food of two different kinds (e.g. gold for silver or wheat for barely) one condition should be met: the promptness of delivery (equality is not a required condition).
3. When trading metal for food (gold or silver for wheat or barely) neither condition is required. The transaction is fulfilled through free trade.

The rationale behind the above restrictions seems to lie in discouraging barter transactions in favour of monetary transaction. It is reported that the Prophet said to one of his companions, Bilāl ibn Rabāh, who exchanged two measures of low quality dates for one measure of high quality (dates), "It is exactly Ribā. Never do it, but if you want to buy such (high quality) dates you can sell yours for money and then buy the dates you want" (Ŝaĥīĥ Muslim). In addition to seeking the advantages of monetary transactions over the less advanced market mechanism of barter transactions, monetary transactions help eliminate the elements of ambiguity related to the process of estimating 'equivalence' in the objects traded.

The confusion surrounding the issue of Ribā is represented particularly in commodity Ribā, not the Qur'ānic Ribā. Some believe that the items in commodity Ribā are as "numerated" in the six commodities mentioned specifically in the Sunnah. As such, the rules of commodity Ribā should be confined to these while others suggest that this Ribā is "exemplified" in these six commodities and it should be applied to all types of commodities, even if not mentioned in the Sunnah (Al-Qusi, op. cit.).

The motives for the prohibition of interest in Islam are twofold: moral and economic. The moral motive revolves on the principle of not exploiting the poor and the needy through charging them interest on borrowed money. The economic motive emanates from:

1. the principles of justice, which is deemed as the fairness of dividing both gains and losses between the parties concerned in business deals,
2. the encouragement of hard work and the promotion of a positive contribution by capital owners to economic activities, and
3. alleviating the tendency for the concentration of wealth in the hands of the few. Islam is not against being rich, providing that, among other things, this is not achieved through idle and selfish activities such as the lending money for interest.

Economic Resources: Forms of Ownership

Basis of ownership

All that which is in earth and heaven is owned by God, "His is all that the heavens and the earth contain, to Him shall all things return", (Qur'ān, 3:109), "We shall inherit the earth and all who dwell upon it, to Us they shall return", (Qur'ān, 19:40) and "His is what the heavens and the earth contain, and all that lies between them and under the soil" (Qur'ān, 20:6).

The concept of ownership in the Qur'ān is established on these two main axioms: God is the ultimate owner of the universe and man is His representative on earth. The basis of man's ownership, therefore, is the "ownership by trusteeship". Man owns as a "trustee" to God who has delegated this ownership to him, which implies that the ownership must be exercised in accordance with the conditions laid down by the ultimate owner: God. Within the boundaries of this "trusteeship", man is free to exercise ownership rights. Three main principles organise the framework of this delegated ownership: free will (authority), responsibility, and a system of reward and punishment. These principles constitute the fundamental philosophy of Islamic economics (for example, Naqvi, 1981), as discussed above.

Types of Ownership

Based on the principle of "ownership by trusteeship", ownership is divided into two main types: private ownership and public ownership.

Private ownership

Private ownership is well recognised in the Qur'ān and the Sunnah. This recognition takes various forms:

Firstly, the Qur'ān ascribes private ownership to the instinct of man and in line with his human nature, "He (man) loves riches from all his heart" (Qur'ān, 100:8), and "Wealth and children are the ornament of this life", though "deeds of lasting merit are better rewarded by your Lord and hold for you a greater hope of salvation" (Qur'ān, 18:46). Also, the recognition of the importance of wealth, which man perceives, could be noted from the Qur'ānic verses that ordain Muslims to make sacrifices in the path of God and the Holy War. In these verses the word wealth always precedes the word "self" in making these sacrifices. For example, the Qur'ān states "Those that have embraced the faith and fled their homes and fought God's cause with the wealth and the persons are held in higher regard by God (Qur'ān, 9:20), and "Whether lightly armed or well-equipped, march and fight for the cause of God, with your wealth and your persons . . ." (Qur'ān, 9:41), also, "Those that believe in God and the Last Day will not beg you to exempt them from fighting with their wealth and their persons" (Qur'ān, 9:44). In fact, whenever wealth is mentioned alongside other matters of high value to man, such as self, children, parents and clan, wealth comes first. The only exception to that comes in one verse only where God says, "God has purchased of the faithful their lives and their wealth, and in return He promised them Paradise" (Qur'ān, 9:111). This sequence of order reflects the degree of priority given to the value of wealth by man over other values. There was a need for an emphasis therefore that man should give to God what man likes most, wealth, before considering other forms of giving. In other words there is an emphasis in the Qur'ān that the sanctity of giving is in giving what is worth more first, before considering giving what is worth less. The verse 9:111 above does not however contradict this analysis. The verse indicates what man is offering to, God. By man's inclination to hold on to what he values more to the last, man would offer himself first and then his wealth, in a descending order. The degree of uncertainty is driving the behaviour of man still. While giving away part of wealth carries a certainty of a reduction in the worldly value of wealth, giving away the self by taking part in military *jihād* may not necessarily lead to loss of life if the person survived the battle, and, even better, may lead to earning a gain as a share of the spoils of war. Therefore, offering self for battle, despite the probability of loss of life, was, by implication, done in pursuit of potential gains. It enhanced the drive for offering self further, compared to giving wealth in charity, the strong belief that being killed in battle in the sake of God and becoming a martyr guarantees a place in Paradise.

Secondly, the Qur'ān attaches high sacredness to private property to the extent that theft is punished by the amputation of hands. Qur'ānic verses rule, "As for the thief, man or woman, cut off their hands to punish them for the crimes (they have committed)" (Qur'ān, 5:38). Various conditions govern this rule. These are: the value of the stolen object is not trivial, the stolen object is normally kept out of the reach of the passer-by, the thief is not driven by hunger, the charge is decisively proven without any room for doubt, and the repetition of theft by the same person, so that the thief would have a regular source of income, (Qūtb, 1979). Also, the Prophet is reported to have said, "Whoever was killed while defending his property is regarded as a martyr", (Ŝaĥīĥ Muslim).

Thirdly, the Qur'ān and the Sunnah provide specific guidance for the inheritance of private property. Men and women, old and young, are all given shares of the legacy, though the amount of the share depends upon the closeness of their relation to the deceased, as will be shown later. This demonstrates the recognition of private ownership.

Private ownership is granted, however, on the condition that it should not be abused. Two conditions are stipulated: productivity and social justice. If the private ownership is abused the Islamic state has the right to step in and rectify the situation. (These issues are discussed below under economic development and income distribution).

Public ownership

As private ownership is acknowledged in the Qur'ān and the Sunnah, so is public ownership. The Prophet determined the scope of public ownership as being the ownership of water, pasture and fire; he is reported to have said, "People have collective ownership in three: water, pasture and fire" as being natural resources essential to life in the early environment (Qutb, 1979). The society as a whole has the right to the common use of these three types of economic resources depending upon how important they are to fulfilling the necessity of life. The reason for assigning the property of these resources to the society is, perhaps, obvious. They represented basic commodities to which people, particularly in Arabia, were badly in need and without which life would be difficult to sustain. These basic resources were deemed, therefore, to be excluded from private ownership. Although the relative importance of these resources to society varies from time to time and from one society to another, the rule boils down to the fact that in an organised society the state, representing the society, has the ownership of these resources when they are essential to society. The juristic principle of "public interest" may be resorted to in deciding whether a public ownership of a natural resource may be considered.

It may be worthwhile to stress that the society, or the state, assumes the ownership of these resources as being natural resources, but individuals may own their own water source (wells for example), pasture if it is planted by them or the source of fire. It is the condition of an economic resource of being a natural resource or otherwise, and how important it is to the society, that creates a reason for public ownership. Books of early Islamic history tell us about cases where Muslims owned their own water wells, some of whom gave their wells voluntarily for the benefit of the community.

This creates a main problem with respect to definition: when can an economic resource be regarded as serving the basic needs of the society as a whole and when can it be regarded as a natural resource? While the answer to these questions is not so difficult in a simple nomadic society, such as that of the early Islamic state, it is difficult to be determined in a more complicated society, such as that of contemporary Muslim states. This is one of the areas where the importance of jurisprudence appears; jurists derive new rules, from the Qur'ān and the Sunnah, to suit new needs. For example, after the excavation of minerals on a relatively large scale, some medieval Islamic jurists, such as Imam Mālik were of the opinion that the product should not belong to the owner of the land, instead it ought to belong to the society, i.e. the state (Al-Zarqani, 1990). The importance of this view becomes clear if we know that Sharī'ah has approached this issue with rules varying depending upon the type of ownership of the land and how the ownership has come to the holder, which may be summarised in the general rule that whatever is found buried in a piece of land is regarded as a treasure belonging to the owner of the land with only Zakāh on the discovered treasure, representing the right of the state on it (Al-Kalby, 1989). What is said about mines might be also applied to oilfields.

The issue of defining what should be put under the control of the state and included in public ownership, or that which could be left to the individual to embrace in private ownership, has been of interest to various jurists and scholars of different schools of thought. Public ownership has changed in terms of size and type of ownership throughout Islamic economic history, as will be discussed further later. We will, for example, see in the next chapter how the head of state second Caliph Umar ibn-al-Khattāb had assumed further control of land to ensure its most efficient use. Furthermore, conquered land was not to be distributed to Muslims, as had been the case before, but to be put under the ownership of the state for the use of all members in the community. Even further, those who had private land before the conquest, were asked to give to the state what was beyond their ability to cultivate.

Moreover, we will also see how the state, not the society, claimed the ownership of land in what became known as *sawāfī land* or Crown Estate. Moreover, the head of state, the Caliph, allowed himself the free disposition of this land to whom he saw fit in serving the state with devotion. Gradually this transfer of the ownership of Crown Estate to individuals, for their services led to consequences that were not known to Muslims in their early history: the development of feudalism, which became clearly manifested during the Umayyad and Abbasid caliphate.

But at this stage of our early discussion the following points may be emphasised:

(a) The Islamic approach to the ownership of economic resources is to allow both the individuals and the state the benefits of ownership with no supremacy to either,
(b) Nationalization of economic resources that does not give the individuals the opportunity of participation in the development of economic resources and the creation of surplus and wealth from these resources is an alien policy to Islamic ideology,
(c) The ownership of economic resources by individuals does not give them the right to the misuse of these resources,
(d) An unintentional misuse of economic resources by individuals may give the state a legitimate reason to step in and rectify the situation first through providing the necessary help to the individual and second, if this means is exhausted, through the redirection of the allocation of economic resources,
(e) An intentional misuse of economic resources may render the individual guilty of wrong doing and may attract the attention of the state to rectify the situation through the reallocation of economic resources,
(f) The reallocation of economic resources above does not lead to depriving the original owner from ownership, rather it reallocates the right to the utilisation of the economic resources without impairing the right to the ownership,
(g) In case of reallocation of utilisation, the original owner is to be given a fair share of the income generated from the reallocated economic resource,
(h) The state has the duty to provide assistance to those in need of help to utilize the economic resources they control. The role of the state is that of a facilitator and watchdog that aims to assist and educate on the one hand and to prevent waste and misuse on the other.
(i) Free competition is legitimate as long as the parties concerned observe the rules of the market with no harmful side effects for the others.

Economic Resources: Economic Development and Production

Economic Efficiency

Islam has a strong stand on economic efficiency. Uneconomic use of resources, or wastage, is emphatically condemned in the strongest possible language. Wasters, *al-Mubażżirīn*, are regarded as, "brethren to Satan, and Satan is the worst unbeliever" (Qur'ān 17:27). Wastage in consumption is reprimanded, and wastage of economic resources even in pursuit of quite a legitimate purpose, such as in the pursuit of economic development, is equally condemned. Wastage in this concept extends beyond the misuse of resources to stretch to the level of the excessive use of the resources even to achieve purposes that may be quite legitimate. In emphasizing the concept of economic efficiency, the reason behind equating wasters to being brethren of Satan, it seems, is that Satan has a mission to destroy the earth and its economic resources on which human beings are living. Humans, after all, are Satan's enemies. The enmity in Islamic and other religious ideology began when Satan refused to obey God in prostrating to Adam in Paradise; then he misled Adam, tempted him to eat from the Forbidden Tree, and drove him and Eve out of Paradise. Wastage, therefore, is a form of destruction of earth and its natural resources on which Adam and his heirs live.

Objectives of Production

Islam places great importance on the utilisation of economic resources. Indeed, the utilisation of these resources is regarded as one of the main sacred tasks which man is ordained to fulfill, "It is He who has subdued the earth to you, so walk about its regions (utilise them) and eat of His provisions" (Qur'ān, 67:15). Once more, this is tied up with the concept of viceregency of man on earth, "It was He who made you from the earth and gave you the right to utilise it" (Our'an, 11:61). Economic development with all economic activities it may incorporate could be said, therefore, to be the overall objective of production. The most eloquent example of the Prophet's sayings in encouraging Muslims to save no effort on economic development is, "If the Day of Judgment came to you while one of you has a small plant to plant, let him plant it", (Ŝaĥīĥ al-Bukhari).

The implication of the concept of ownership by trusteeship introduces a further dimension to the above objective of production: social responsibility. It refers to the societal responsibility of the producer towards employees and the surrounding community. The objectives of the producer, an individual or a group of individuals as it might be, could be, therefore, depicted as in figure 2.1. (see page 91). The producer aims, or should aim, to achieve three sets of objectives related to three groups: entrepreneurs, employees and society. In the course of realising these objectives the producer, or the entrepreneur, endeavours, or should endeavour, to achieve a "balanced" relationship between these three sets of objectives. The final reward is, as we might deduce, obtaining God's satisfaction. In examining the objectives of the entrepreneur, we must bear in mind the attitude of Islam regarding worldly needs: these should not be neglected. What is required, therefore, is a "balanced" relationship between the interests of these different groups. The concept of moderation might be also applied here. Using modern economic terms, the above relationship can be portrayed mathematically as follows:

$$\text{(maximise) } U = Ua\,(R),\ Ub\,[Ua(R),\ E,\ S],\ F\,(P) \qquad (1)$$
$$\text{Subject to } Y = R + E + S$$

where:

U = utility function
Ua = secular utility
Ub = ritual utility
R = entrepreneurs' financial rewards (profit)
E = cost of employment welfare (wages and the like)
S = social cost (cost of society welfare)
P = the degree of piety
Y = net value of production

It is noticed that the degree of piety is introduced in the equation. This is to show how the desire to obey God's rule and consequently to achieve the above "balance" by the entrepreneur varies from one person to another. Muslims vary from the level of merely satisfying the basic religious requirement to the level of entire devotion to God.

Bringing Western economic theory into the comparison a few observations may be made as follows:

Factors of production

While these are four factors of production in the Western economic theory: land, labour, capital and organisation, they may be viewed in Islamic economics as six: the environment, natural resources, the human factor which embraces labour and management, capital, society and divine guidance and blessing. It is not necessary to consider the factors of production in Western economics in this study given its focus, and these are in any case well known, but a recap might be useful in the case of Islamic economics.

The environment is the first factor determining production to be considered since man is ordained to make use of and preserve the environment as one of God's creation. The environment is the habitat of all God's creatures, which He made suitable for all to live in and grow in the balance, He maintains in the built-in mechanism of the structure of the environment itself. Man can make use of this environment in the process of production, but should not violate this balance. Destroying rain forests, for example, under the premise of increasing mass production, distorts the environmental balance and is not in line with the divine purpose of its creation. As this may hinder the process of economic development and adversely affect the quality of life in the long run, it cannot be permissible in the short run.

The second factor of production is natural resources. Man is allowed, and indeed ordained, to utilise the natural resources bestowed upon him by God in the process of economic development as God has made them available for that reason. The line between this factor and the previous one, the environment, may seem very fine but the difference between the two is that while natural resources are meant to be used up in the process of economic development, the environment, though is meant to be made use of, should be preserved in a manner suitable to all. To put it another way, natural resources are meant to be used, but need not be sustained if their use facilitates investment in diverse activities that may ultimately be more sustainable. Some natural resources are sustainable however, as although this may not be the case with mineral resources, other resources such as the soil, water, and the use of animals and birds should be sustainable.

The third factor is the human factor. This factor has been emphasised in the Qur'ān and Sunnah and discussed above with no need for repetition. What can be added perhaps is that in addition to labour the human factor includes management or organisation and entrepreneurship as mentioned in the Western theory.

The fourth factor is capital. Wealth, which embraces capital when it is allocated for purposes of economic development, has been emphasised in the Qur'ān and the Tradition as shown above, with no need for repetition. The price of capital has also been discussed above. Once more, the common area between the price of capital in Western economics and Islamic economics may be mentioned. While the two types of economics part significantly on the price of loan capital they meet on the price of equity capital. In both schools of economics the price of equity capital is the rate of return on equity, derived mainly from profit distributed as dividends. The price of loan capital in the Western theory is interest while in the Islamic theory loan capital has no price since loan capital, in line with other types of loans, has to be either converted to equity capital or given free.

The fifth factor of production is society. The reason that society may be included as a factor of production is twofold. First, society has an influential role in directing management and entrepreneurs when they design their production plans, as this input ensures that they best serve the community, which in its turn helps management maximize the benefits to their businesses. The international dimension of society may also be taken into consideration. Second, society provides businesses with the skilled human resources necessary for production. If society is taken into account as a factor of production, this will enforce the mutual relationship between business and the surrounding community in such a way as to create the feeling of need for, then the concern about, society in the process of production. Without such emphasis on the dependence of the production sector to society, the interrelationship between the two, business and community, may be neglected.

The above point is connected with objectives of economic development. The objectives of economic development in Islam is not to maximize value of production or profit per se but to enlarge, avoiding the term maximize, the welfare benefits from economic development to the individual and society. Western altruist economics and social economics are much nearer to Islamic economics on this issue than Western classical economics. This simply emphasises that moral issues and ethical values should be maintained in deriving the objectives of the function of production or of economic development.

The sixth factor is divine guidance and His blessing. As Muslims are ordained to observe God in whatever they do in their life and to take the Prophet's example as a pattern of behaviour, they seek guidance from God in pursuing economic development, refrain from what He prohibits and pursue the goodness of life He has predestined all to enjoy in seeking His blessing. In Muslim beliefs, no matter how well prepared a person may be, well arranged factors of production could be, and well thought of the plan is, no successful results may be obtained without relying on God's help, wisdom, guidance and blessing. The ultimate success is always perceived as from God. *Al-tawakkul ala Allah*, reliance on God, is a basic ingredient in the Muslim's way of thinking regardless of whatever that might be. This is applied to all activities in production, consumption or otherwise.

Economic Resources: Consumption

Islam and material needs

The Islamic ideology is not an anti-materialistic ideology. Goods are regarded as bounties from God. This has an important implication: wealth is not an evil, nor is the pursuit of materialistic needs a vice. Thus, being rich is not a sin, and being poor does not give per se an exclusive license to heaven since heaven is also open to the rich. The Qur'ān has stated, "Say: 'who has forbidden the enjoyment of God's bounties which He has bestowed on His people!'", (Qur'ān, 7:31), and "Believers, do not forbid the wholesome bounties which God has made lawful to you, but do not transgress, God does not like the transgressors. Eat of the lawful and wholesome things which God has given you, and heed God's orders, in whom you believe" (Qur'ān, 5:87–88). But the permission for the enjoyment of God's bounties is not unqualified; it is restricted by an important condition: moderation.

Behavioural considerations

In the conventional theory of consumer behaviour, the consumer is assumed to be "Homo-Economicus" whose ultimate objective is to maximise his consumption utility function of goods and services. According to the marginal analysis, the achievement of this objective will occur at the tangential point between the consumer's indifference and income curves. At this point the consumer is said to be in equilibrium.

This behavioural assumption is criticised by altruist economists who argue that more emphasis should be given to the social responsibility of the consumer, with considerable regard to the interest of the surrounding community. They suggest, instead, a social attitude where the consumer is a "Homo-Economicus-Humanus" with ethical values having a considerable impact on consumer behaviour in influencing the satisfaction he/she seeks to maximize (McKee, 1982). Among the sources of ethical values religion is considered as an especially rich source. How significant religion is, in relation to other sources of ethics to non-Muslim consumers, is an issue that will not be pursued here, but it suffices to say that to Muslims, and Muslim consumers, religion is a highly, if not the highest, influencing determinant of their attitude and behaviour. This is not to say, however, that all Muslim consumers will follow a unified pattern of behaviour in pursuit of their consumption satisfaction, some are more pious than others. The degree of piety is deemed therefore as an influential factor in shaping the utility function of the consumer and in determining his/her pattern of consumption.

Islam, as Muslims know, does not admit any separation between religious, political, and economic issues. For Muslims, it provides a comprehensive way of life. "Say, verily my prayers, sacrifices, life and death, are all for (the sake of) God (Allah) the sustainers of the universe, no equals are to Him, of that I have been commanded (by God), and I am the first of all Muslims", the Qur'ān is stating as God is addressing His Prophet (Qur'ān: 6:162). Islamic economic issues have to be viewed in the context of ethical values, however. This has been essential to the religion since it came in order to improve the system of life as a whole, boost spiritual development of individuals, and rectify the socio-economic imbalances in society by moving it towards social justice.

In the views of Islamic economists, looking at the consumer through Islamic social ethics would transfer him from "Homo-Economicus" to "Homo-Islamicus" (see for example Zarqa, 1980). Utilising this concept would require the consumer in the Islamic society to be expected to act in line with Islamic ethical values with regard to consumption, saving, and investment. In his mode of consumption, the "Homo-Economicus-Islamicus" consumer is dominated by four main factors: (a) the concept of ownership by trusteeship, (b) the belief in the system of reward/punishment in the hereafter, (c) the principle of moderation, and (d) the relationship between saving and investment (Kahf, 1980). While the concept of ownership has been outlined, the influencing role of the other remaining factors of consumption is discussed below.

The belief of the Muslim consumer in a system of reward and punishment, in life and the hereafter, is envisioned to be influencing the pattern of his consumption, the avenues in which he spends his income and, consequently, the utility function he seeks to maximise. His avenues of spending would cover not only secular aspects of satisfaction, physio-sociological wants, but also those aspects that would increase his reward in the Hereafter, mainly social-caring spending and spending in the cause of God. The utility function which the consumer seeks to enlarge, or maximize using the conventional terms, consists, therefore, of two main components: secular utility and Hereafter utility. His spending behaviour would be influenced by the weight he gives to each utility depending upon his religious scale of preference, i.e. degree of piety. Or in a mathematical presentation, his spending, as differentiated from his consumption, is a function of the satisfaction he gets from the consumption of goods and services, the moral satisfaction he obtains from feeling that he will be rewarded in the Hereafter, as a result of his religio-social-caring spending, and the degree of piety, subject, of course, to his income. This is shown as follows:

$$\text{(maximize)} \quad V = U(C, H), F(P) \qquad (2)$$

$$\text{S.t.} \quad Y$$

Where:

Y = income
V = spending function
C = consumption from goods and services
H = reward in the Hereafter from religio-social-caring spending
P = piety

Equation (1) would be analysed further in the light of the two remaining factors, the principle of moderation and the relationship between saving and investment.

The principle of moderation

Based on the teachings of the Qur'ān and Sunnah, Muslim jurists have classified human physiological needs into various categories, which should all be used in moderation. These are food, clothing, shelter, marriage, and some added, religion. Muslims are ordained to spend in moderation; they should be generous, but not extravagant, to themselves, their families and dependents. As said previously, moderation does not mean niggardliness and the prohibition of extravagance does not imply miserliness, the Qur'ān ordains neither, (Qur'ān 7:31, 17:29).

The principle of moderation applies to spending on consumable goods and services and spending on charity, on the one hand, and to the relationship between spending and saving, on the other. It necessitates maintaining balanced relationships among these types of economic decisions.

First, spending on consumable goods and services. Classical jurists divided the levels of consumption into three main levels: necessities, conveniences, and refinements (Imam al-Shātibī, n.d., Zarqa, 1980). Necessities are goods and services that are essential to survival as they sustain the fundamental principles of life; conveniences are less vital for survival but are still basics, while refinements are the goods and services that are beyond the level of convenience of what makes life more comfortable and enjoyable. The first level is classified by classical jurists as including: food, shelter, religion, mind, and marriage (ibid.), which covers the basic physio-sociological needs. The second level of consumption covers the commodities and services which are still counted as basic needs, though they are not (in terms of type, quantity, and quality) as badly needed as those of the first level. The third level, level of refinements which might include luxurious goods, is the level that is most targeted by the constraint of the moderate consumption. While a moderate consumption of goods and services at this level is acceptable a further consumption beyond that level may render the consumption extravagant.

In our modern times, the criteria that determine the level of moderation may, however, be difficult to establish. What are regarded as refinements in a society, or in a certain period of time, may be considered as conveniences in another society, or at a different period. Clothing, feeding, entertainment, education and spending on durable goods are some examples. Norms, therefore, would have to be established with the help of economic and social indicators such as the standard of living, the level of national income, the pattern of income distribution, the state of development and custom in differentiating between the various levels of consumption. Subjectivity does not seem to be avoidable in this matter, but it might be accepted as long as it projects the generally accepted conventions in a society at a particular time.

Second, spending on charity and spending on worldly needs. The Qur'ān states, "Do seek by means of that which God has given you to attain the Paradise to come, but do not forget your share of this world", (Qur'ān, 28:77). Also, in determining what could be spent in alms, the Qur'ān says, "They ask you what they should give in alms, say: what you can spare", (Qur'ān, 2:219). It is the surplus, after satisfying worldly needs, in moderation, and saving for dependent heirs to help them avoid poverty that should be spent in alms. Once more, even when it comes to spending on charity, a balanced relationship ought to be maintained.

Third, spending and saving. The consumer is ordained to achieve a reasonable relationship between his spending and his saving. Of the various purposes of saving, saving for bequeathing to dependent heirs is given high priority, even over spending for charitable purposes. The Prophet is reported to have discouraged one of his companions, Sa'd, from donating most of his wealth to social-caring purposes, and recommending instead to donate only one third, and to bequeath the rest to his heirs, and that "the one third is still too much; you would better leave your heirs rich than leaving them poor and dependent on others", (Ŝaĥīĥ Muslim).

The principle of moderation acknowledges a basic economic issue: scarcity. Scarcity of economic resources had been the main feature of Medieval Central Arabia, which characterised the life of the Bedouin at that time, as was shown in the previous chapter. It might be argued, therefore, that the Bedouin, with his scanty food and clothing, had no choice but to be moderate in his consumption with no need for Qur'ānic emphasis. But we must acknowledge the fact that the concept of moderation is not directed to the consumer as an isolated agent, rather it is intended to organise the consumption pattern of society as a whole. As such, the concept implies a voluntary redistribution of consumption between those who have and those who have-not. By the stipulation of spending in alms and social-caring purposes, the redistribution effect of the concept of moderation is reinforced further. In an environment with scarce economic resources, such as that of Arabia at that time, the emphasis on the concept of moderation was necessary. Furthermore, the Qur'ānic rules are meant to provide a framework for a long-term economic structure in the community, which, as happened later in the history of the Islamic state, might experience phases of affluence. In order for the framework to be comprehensive and conclusive, it should, therefore, provide rules to accommodate future changes.

With no need for repetition, it might be worthwhile to remind ourselves that in all levels of consumption/spending above, the principles of "extension", *isrāf*, as against "wastage", *tabẓīr*, should be thoroughly and continuously observed. While the former is acceptable within tolerable levels, beyond which it is frowned upon, the latter is always forbidden and at any level.

Linking the principle of moderation with the system of reward/punishment in the Hereafter, shows that at different levels of consumption there are different levels of reward or punishment. Subject to income availability, lack of spending on the first level of consumption, necessities, attracts punishment, but the more the consumer spends the less is the punishment, until he reaches the second level. The more the consumer spends on the second level, conveniences, the higher the reward he gets, until he reaches the third level. The third level, which might include luxurious goods, is the level where moderate consumption is most demanded which, when reached, gives the consumer the maximum divine reward. Beyond that level, is the level of extravagance, which is condemned.

Turning our attention back to the first level of consumption, the level of necessity, it might be argued that there is no need for the concept of reward/punishment at this level as the consumer will have to spend on these wants in order to survive. But when it is realized that the consumer is not regarded as responsible only for himself but also for his wife, even if she is rich, and dependents, including dependent parents, the need for the concept becomes clear.

Relating the above analysis to equation (2) implies that the reward of the Hereafter is in fact an outcome of two components of rewards: the reward from religio-social-caring spending, H, and the reward associated with the pattern of goods and services consumption, T. Thus equation (2) could be rewritten as:

$$\text{(maximize)} \qquad V = U(C, H, T), F\ (P) \qquad (3)$$

S.t. Y

(where other connotations are as above)

The relationship between saving and investment

The enlargement, or maximization, of the place of saving in the Islamic illustration of consumer behaviour would require looking at saving in the light of three main factors: the purpose of saving, "Zakāh", and the attitude of Islam towards profit and interest.

(i) The purpose of saving

As previously mentioned the reasons for saving could be categorized under four labels, (a) bequeathing to heirs, (b) precaution against unforeseen contingencies (uncertainty) (c) the postponement of consumption, and (d) the accumulation of wealth from the desire to be rich. The first purpose of saving, when it is for dependent heirs, is given high priority and when it occurs (within reasonable limits) it pleases God and renders reward in the Hereafter. The other (less important) purposes of saving are not condemned providing that they are in line with the moderation concept (leading a niggardly life in order to be rich is condemned).

Reflecting this on equation (3) shows it as follows:

(maximise) $V = U\,(C, H, T, Sa, Sb), F\,(P)$ (4)
s.t. Y

Where: $Sa = Sa\,(P)$
$Sb = (Y - (C + H + T + Sa)$
Sa = saving for bequeathing to dependent heirs
Sb = saving for other purposes
(other connotations are as above)

(ii) Zakāh

Zakāh is an annual religious levy ordained in the core of the Islamic teachings and regarded as a sort of worship which relates to the other four main pillars of Islam (the other four are the testimony that there is no God but one and Prophet Muḣammad is His messenger, prayers, fasting for the month of Ramadan, and pilgrimage, Hajj, for whoever can afford it). Although Zakāh has various characteristics, it suffices to point out at this stage that it has very special dual characteristics: the first as a type of worship, which places it at the heart of the religion, and the second as a financial levy that has economic implications for both its payer and receiver.

Further characteristics of Zakāh will be considered later in the examination of income distribution and economic justice.

By the nature of Zakāh (as above) accumulated wealth would be subject to a continuous decline unless it was invested at a rate of return at least equal to:

(Rate of Zakāh)/(1-the rate of Zakāh).

For example if the Zakāh rate is 2.5%, wealth will have to be invested at 2.5641% to maintain its value (assuming no inflation). The terminal value of wealth if it is not invested is calculated as follows:

$$NTV = \sum_{tz^1}^{T} W\ (1-Z)^t$$

Where: NTV = net terminal value

W = accumulated wealth
Z = Zakāh rate
T = number of years

Hoarding is not regarded, therefore, as a rational policy in consumer behaviour, which helps bring saving and investment together and assists in reducing idle capital in the society. Even if Zakāh encouraged consumption for some consumers, to avoid the payment of it, it would still bring that portion of income into economic activities and would thus discourage hoarding. The effect on consumption would have to be looked at, however, in light of what has been said about the purpose of saving and the concept of moderation.

(iii) The attitude of Islam towards profit and interest

As discussed earlier, while profit is recognised in Islamic teachings, interest is prohibited. Gains and risks should be shared by both parties: the provider and the user of capital. Fixed interest, which does not imply risk sharing as such, does not qualify as a means of yielding income. By contrast, profit does qualify. Thus saving would have to be invested on a profit-loss-sharing basis, not a fixed interest basis.

Looking at equation (4) in light of the above, it would become as follows:

$$\text{(maximise)}\quad V = U(C,T,H,Sa,Sb,Z,R),\ F(P) \qquad \ldots\ldots\ldots\ (5)$$

s.t. Y

Where: Z = Zakāh

R = returns on accumulated savings at the beginning of the period.

(other connotations are as above)

To sum up, the consumer behaviour from an Islamic perspective can be outlined as follows:

1. The utility function which the consumer seeks to maximise consists of two main components: goods and services consumption utility and religio-social-caring spending utility.
2. Both components of utility could be sought together and the ritual aspects of Islamic teachings does not necessitate the trade-off of goods and services consumption for the sake of religio-social-caring spending, subject to the conditions of the level of income and the fulfillment of fundamental needs.
3. A portion of saving, which is for bequeathing to dependent heirs, is mandatory in Islamic teachings; other portions of saving are induced by the force of the concept of moderation.
4. The institution of Zakāh promotes the religious feeling of religio-social-caring, provides the Islamic state with a flow of revenue to be spent on religio-social-caring purposes, and "penalises" idle savings, which helps narrow the gap between saving and investment.
5. Saving would have to be invested to, at least, maintain the terminal value of wealth. The investment would have to be on the basis of profit-sharing, not at a fixed interest rate, which might help encourage savers into becoming entrepreneurs in the long run.
6. With the restriction on credit sales, since credit sale would have to be granted by enterprises on an interest-free basis, and on bank loans, which would have to be given on the same basis, and by the condemnation of monopoly in Islamic teachings, it could be suggested that some inflationary pressure in the economy of a demand pull type might be alleviated.

Economic Resources: Income Distribution

Islam does not advocate an equal distribution of income. Instead, it recognises the differences between individuals' income and wealth which are related to the differences between their talents, earning ability and the amount of effort they put in to work. Being rich is not a sin and being poor does not give per se an exclusive license to paradise since paradise is also open to the rich. It is the person's behaviour, why he is poor (unwilling to work hard?) and how he uses his wealth that permits an entry to paradise or otherwise.

The recognition of income and wealth differences between individuals has been stated in the Qur'ān in various verses, for example, "God gives abundantly to whom He will and sparingly to whom He pleases" (Qur'ān, 13:26), "To some of you God has given more than to others" (Qur'ān, 16:71), and "God gives without measure to whom He will" (Qur'ān, 2:212). These differences arise because people are different as to: (a) their natural abilities and talents, for which God is responsible since He has made them so, (b) their endeavour to learn and acquire knowledge that helps improve their earning capacity, and (c) their readiness to work hard; some work harder than others.

Why people are created differently and have been given powers of discretion is a question that has been answered by God. The Qur'ān explains, "Had God bestowed in abundance upon His servants, they would have filled the earth with evil, but He gives them what He will in due measure, He knows and observes His servants. It is He who sends down rain for them when they have lost hope, and spreads abroad His blessings. He is the Glorious Guardian" (Qur'ān, 42:27, 28), and in a different example, "Had God not defended some men by the might of others, the monasteries and churches, the synagogues and mosques in which His praise is daily celebrated, would have been utterly destroyed" (Qur'ān, 22:40). The reason, therefore, seems to lie in the idea that legitimate discrimination may help achieve a sort of balance in the infrastructure of the community. (If all were rich, no one would be willing to do the jobs that demand less talent than others though they are very important).

However, illegitimate discrimination, by race or colour, is forbidden in Islam. The Prophet has stated emphatically, "People are as equal as the comb's teeth", and, "The noblest of you are the best in character" (Ŝaĥīĥ al-Būkhari). Furthermore, the recognition of wealth differences between individuals does not give a reason for any illegitimate discrimination in the society. The Prophet is reported to have said, "Certainly God does not look at your faces or your wealth; He looks at your hearts and deeds" (Ŝaĥīĥ al-Būkhari).

In warning Muslims against invalid discrimination by wealth, the Prophet, giving an example of improper bevaviour of previous nations, stated, "Communities before you strayed because when the high ranked committed theft they were set free, but when the low committed the theft the Law was enforced on him. By God, even if Fatimah, the daughter of Muĥammad (the Prophet's daughter), committed theft I would cut her hand" (Ŝaĥīĥ al-Būkhari).

What Islam advocates is the equitable distribution of wealth and income so as to reduce the gap between the rich and the poor. Three main approaches to wealth reallocation are adopted: the encouragement of voluntary alms giving, the enforcement of Zakāh and the inheritance law.

First: Voluntary Alms Giving—Charity.

Muslims are required to give alms to the poor and the needy, and are encouraged to do so in order to please God. In fact, whenever there is a mention in the Qur'ān that God has given individuals abundantly or sparingly, there is a mention that individuals should give alms. The verses that ordain Muslims to spend on alms are so many and the reward is very generous. In some expressions the reward is ten times as much and in others it is like ". . . a grain of corn which brings forth seven ears, each bearing a hundred grains" (Qur'ān, 2:261). The notable, and indeed moving, metaphor that has been used in the Qur'ān to stress the effect of alms is the one that regards giving alms as if it were as giving loans to God. The Qur'ān says, "Those that give alms, be they men or women, and those that give generous loans to God", and "Those who preserve themselves from their own greed will surely prosper. If you give a generous loan to God He will pay you back many times as much and will forgive you" (Qur'ān, 57:18; 64:16–17; respectively, also 73:20). To that effect giving alms is highly motivated.

There are conditions for alms giving and of the various conditions the following are the most notable: (a) alms should be given from what the giver would like to have for himself (Qur'ān, 3:92), (b) as expected, alms should not be followed by taunts or insults to the receiver (Qur'ān, 2:261, 262); a kind word in this case is better (Qur'ān, 2:263), (c) they may be given publicly, though it is more righteous to keep them privately (Qur'ān, 2:271), and more interesting (d) alms may be given to non-Muslims (Qur'ān, 60:8).

Second: Zakāh levy

Zakāh is an earmarked tax stipulated in the Qur'ān, operationally organised by the Prophet and politically emphasised as a state right by the first caliph Abū-Bakr (d. 634 A.C.). The Qur'ān stipulates the earmarking characteristics of Zakāh by specifying the manner in which its revenue should be spent, but without determining the tax base, the threshold or the rate. The Prophet organised the tax by clarifying the type of wealth on which it is levied, the threshold and the tax rate. The political dimension of Zakāh was stressed by the first Caliph when he successfully fought a group of Muslims over it after the Prophet's death; Zakāh has been known since as one of the state's prerogatives with no individual's discretion. It was not until the reign of the third Caliph Uthmān (d. 656 A.C.) when the state's revenues became very large that the Caliph decided that, with the exception of Zakāh on pecuniary wealth, individuals may pay their Zakāh, on the Caliphs behalf, to whichever extent they saw fit judged by their own religious conscience (Al-Neim, 1969). The new practice seemed to have opened the door for various state collection policies throughout history, ranging between compulsory state administrations to situations where the collection is organized by non-state institutions on a voluntary basis.

Special caution ought to be exercised when referring to Zakāh as tax. Muslim writers, in general, object to associating the term tax to Zakāh in defense of it, as it is one of the sacred five pillars of Islam. But if Zakāh is regarded as a tax, and in this case it will have to be regarded as a very special religiously motivated tax, it is a tax of the following characteristics:

1. It is a religious tax that is considered as a type of worship. (Zakāh is regarded as one of five pillars of Islam; the other four are: witnessing that there is no God but one and Muĥammad is His messenger, prayers, fasting the month of Ramadan, and pilgrimage for whoever can afford it).
2. It is an earmarked tax the proceeds of which should be spent in a certain manner specified in the Qur'ān, in which the beneficiaries are "the poor, the pauper, the people who collect it, the new convert, the liberation of slaves, the indebted, in the cause of God and the wayfarer" (Qur'ān, 9:60).
3. Zakāh has a broad tax base and a rate differential according to the type of economic activities, which are defined in the Sunnah.

4. It is levied on Muslims individuals only, which is implied in the features of Zakāh as a religious duty. Non-Muslims may be subject to a similar tax. (Historically, non-Muslims were subject to the Jizyah tax instead).
5. Zakāh is a capital tax imposed on total net accumulated wealth (net assets); all debts are deducted from total wealth when calculating Zakāh.
6. The wealth (the assets) is not subject to Zakāh until it meets the following conditions:
   a. Growth; with the exception of money items the assets must have the ability to grow, either by itself or someone's action.
   b. Quantity; it should be more than the minimum level (threshold) stipulated in the Sunnah. Also, the quantity owned must exceed the necessary amount of assets the income of which provides for the basic needs of the owner and his family.
   c. Period; with the exception of agricultural production, the ownership of the asset must remains with the holder for one year before Zakāh can be due. Agricultural production is Zakāh taxed at harvest.
7. The Zakāh rate is 2.5 percent on the net worth, which includes industrial assets and real estate. Agricultural production is taxed, however, at two different rates, 5 percent and 10 percent. The first applies to land irrigated operationally, while the second is applied to land irrigated naturally.

From the above, it could be noted that the effect of Zakāh is twofold: firstly, the social impact, where it helps reduce the gap between the rich and the poor, or the re-distributional effect of the tax, secondly, the economic effect, where it "penalises" the idle wealth. This wealth would have to be invested at the rate of: Zakāh rate/1-Zakāh rate per annum in order to merely maintain its value at the end of the period. Furthermore, it is interesting to note that Zakāh is regarded as the right of the poor to the wealth of the rich, "Of their wealth, there is a right for the poor and the beggar" (Qur'ān, 51:19). Zakāh is not regarded as charity, even if its revenue is spent in the manner mentioned above, mainly for the benefit of the poor and the needy. This differentiates it from alms; while alms are paid voluntarily, Zakāh is paid by force of law.

Third: Inheritance law

Contrary to other inheritance systems where the estate of the deceased might be passed on to the older male of the family, or the deceased's will might be enforced on all his estate, the Islamic inheritance law gives all relatives, males and females, a share in the estate. As for the deceased's will, this cannot be enforced beyond the third of the estate unless all heirs agree to it unanimously. The Qur'ānic verses, elaborated upon by the Sunnah, have determined that precisely. Although the verses that deal with the rules of inheritance might seem rather lengthy, they are worth quoting to summarise the whole picture. The Qur'ān stipulates as a general rule, "Men shall have a share in what their parents and kinsmen leave; and women shall have a share in what their parents and kinsmen leave; whether it be little or much, they are legally entitled to their share" (Qur'ān, 4:7). The orphans and the needy might also be given a voluntary share "If relatives, orphans, or needy (men and women) are present at the division of an inheritance, give them, too, a share of it, and speak to them kind words", think if your own children were left orphan and weak, what would you feel?, "Let those who are solicitous about the welfare of their young children after their own death take care not to wrong orphans. Let them fear God and speak for justice. Those that devour the property of the orphans unjustly swallow fire into their bellies; they shall burn in the flames of Hell" (Qur'ān, 4:8–10).

The shares of inheritor children and parents are determined as, "God has enjoined you concerning your children: a male shall inherit twice as much as a female. If there be more than two girls, they shall have two-thirds of the inheritance; but if there be one only, she shall inherit the half. Parents shall inherit a sixth each, if the deceased have a child; but if he leaves no children and his parents are his heirs, his mother shall have a third. If he has two brothers, his mother shall have a sixth; (the distribution in all cases is) after the payment of his debt and any legacies he may have bequeathed. You may wonder whether your parents or your children are more beneficial to you. But this is the law of God; He is wise and all-knowing" (Qur'ān, 4:11).

As for the inheritance between spouses, the Qur'ān continues to stipulate, "You shall inherit the half of your wives' estate if they die childless. If they leave a child (children), a quarter of their estate shall be yours, (all) after payment of their debts and any legacies that they may have bequeathed. Your wives shall inherit one quarter of your estate if you die childless. If you leave a child (children), they shall inherit one-eight, (all) after payment of your debts and any legacies you may have bequeathed." (Qur'ān, 4:12).

The half-brother, who might be in a weak position among the other full brothers, needs a further emphasis, "If a man or a woman leave neither children nor parents and have a (uterine) brother or sister, they shall each inherit one-sixth. If there be more, they shall share the third of the estate, (all) after payment of debts and any legacies that may have been bequeathed, without prejudice to the rights of the heirs" (Qur'ān, 4:12).

Furthermore, to complete the rules of inheritance, the Qur'ān concludes, "God instructs you regarding those that die leaving no descendants or ascendants as heirs: If a man dies childless and he has a sister, she shall inherit the half of his estate. If a woman dies childless, her brother shall be her sole heir. If a childless man has two sisters, they shall inherit two-thirds of his estate; but if he has both brothers and sisters, the share of each male shall be that of two females" (Qur'ān, 4:176).

From the above verses, it is noted that:

1. debts should be deducted from the deceased estate before distribution,
2. although the verses state that legacies that may have been bequeathed by the deceased should be enforced before distribution, the Prophet limited that to the third of the estate unless heirs agree unanimously, "No bequeathed legacy beyond the third",
3. the male's share is twice that of the female, though this should be looked at in light of the fact that the husband is responsible for his wife and the family financially; the wife's financial entity is separate from her husband's and she is not obliged to support the family financially even if she is rich, and
4. the wealth is distributed among a wide range of heirs, this helps prevent, or alleviate, the concentration of wealth in the hands of the few and works towards circulating the accumulated wealth among a greater number of individuals.

The encouragement of giving alms, the enforcement of paying Zakāh and the commandments of distributing inheritance are deemed as three important tools that help achieve socio-economic justice.

Economic Resources: Role of the State

In addition to what had been mentioned above, in relation to the type of ownership of economic resources and the role of the state in income distribution and economic and social justice, the following can be added to highlight the role of the state in organizing market forces. To begin with, the state has no role in influencing market forces through price fixation or similar devices providing that the market is operating normally. To put it another way, the term market equilibrium may be borrowed to emphasise this point further in ascertaining that as long as the market is in a state of equilibrium, the information is flowing without being distorted, supply is continuing without being interrupted and demand is meeting the supply without being hindered, the state has no legitimate right to interfere, or intervene. Market forces, guided by the ethical values in the belief of Muslims, should be let to operate freely without being influenced by exogenous forces such as those of the state. This has implications for three main issues: the state as an entrepreneur, market structure and state finance.

First: the state as an entrepreneur

Basically, the role of the state is a surveillance role: the state is to watch, plan and organise so as to provide the right environment for the free economic forces to operate. Nevertheless, the role of the state was widened during the Orthodox caliphate to include responsibilities and to cover tasks beyond that which existed at the time of the Prophet.

For example, the second Caliph Umar ibn-al-Khattāb had diverted from the practice before him in preference of the state having control over conquered land as a major economic resource. Furthermore, the efficient use of economic resources represented by land in particular seemed to have occupied the attention of Caliph Umar, so much so that he instructed those who had land beyond their means of cultivation to return to the state what they could not utilise, even if the land was given to them on the authority of the Prophet as a head of state (Al-Ťabarī).

Land management took a new turn when the state allowed itself to own and manage lands, which became known as *sawāfī* land or Crown Estate. Gradually Crown estates were transferred to individuals, which led to the development of feudalism that manifested itself clearly during the Umayyad and Abbasīd caliphate.

In addition we will see further how beginning from the mid eighth century the state under the Abbasīd caliphate assumed the role of entrepreneur in owning and running business enterprises when individuals were too risk averse to engage in these business activities and/or when the return potential from some of these businesses were too high for the state to want to sell its investments.

Second: Market Structure

The examination of market regulations as laid down in the Qur'ān and the Sunnah leads to an important conclusion: the Islamic market has the characteristics of a freely competitive market and that prices should be determined by the forces of supply and demand (Tuma, 1965). The Islamic market has, or should have, the following characteristics (Ibn-al-Ukhūwwah, 1939, Ibn-Taymīya, 1983):

(1) The condemnation of monopoly: all forms of monopoly are condemned in the Sunnah. The Prophet is reported to have said, "Those who practice monopoly are wrong-doers" (Ŝaĥīĥ Muslim), and in a stronger tone, "That who interferes in prices in order to increase them will be seated by God on a seat of fire on the Day of Judgment", also, "That who hoards food for forty days is God's enemy" (ibid). Hoarding food, or other commodities, is not always wrong, however, if hoarding is not for the purpose of controlling prices. Jurists have laid down conditions for monopoly, or hoarding, to be sinful (Al-Zuhailī, 1989):
   (a) The object hoarded is a surplus over what the person and his dependents need for a whole year, the person may hoard these needs for a maximum of one year.
   (b) The purpose of hoarding is to influence prices or with the intention of selling the object when prices increase.
   (c) The market shortage of the hoarded object.
   (d) It should be noted, therefore, that monopoly, or hoarding, per se is not regarded as a sin, rather, it is the purpose of hoarding and the consequences of monopoly that characterise a monopolist or a hoarder of being sinful or otherwise. For example, if monopoly appears as a result of one producer, or seller, becoming the only producer, or seller, of the product monopoly is not a sin providing that the producer does not use his monopolistic position to influence the market.

(2) Pricing: prices should be determined by market forces, demand and supply. The evidence of this rule is taken from the Sunnah where the Prophet is reported to have refused fixing prices, saying to the people who asked him to do so, "It is God who gives abundantly or sparingly, it is He who sets prices and I do not want to meet Him with someone's complaint of me in body or wealth" (Abū-Yūsuf). This is the general rule which, although accepted by all Muslim jurists, is conditioned by some. The Medieval jurist Ibn-Taymīya (1262–1328), for example, advocated that the Prophet's saying was based on the conditions of the stability of the market, but if the market becomes unstable for reasons not related to fair dealing, the state has to step in to fix prices. (The economic thought of Ibn-Taymīya will be examined in the following chapters).

(3) Information: the flow of information should be made available to both buyers and sellers. The Prophet is reported to have condemned meeting sellers outside the market place and finalising deals with them before reaching the market (Ŝaĥīĥ Muslim). This is to give the seller the opportunity to know the level of prices in the market place before finalising a deal and the buyer the chance of buying goods at prices not influenced by the middle man. Also, when a deal between the seller and the buyer is struck, other buyers should refrain from offering a higher price to the seller in order to change the deal (Ŝaĥīĥ Muslim). Before completing a deal, sellers and buyers are bound to follow the prices prevailing in the market.

(4) The condemnation of future contracts if the quantity of the object is not known: this is because the seller is uncertain of his ability to honour the contract. It is the ambiguity surrounding the quantity to be delivered that makes a future contract invalid. On the other hand, if the quantity is known, or could be agreed upon, future contracts may be allowed. For example, if a seller and a buyer completed a deal that the former would sell to the latter the total production of an activity during a future period at a certain time in the future (the crops of a field, the fish caught in a span of time, the output of a dive, the offspring of an animal or animals etc.) the deal is illegitimate (Al-Gizīrī, 1972). This is because the quantity of production that is subject to the contract is not known for certain. On the other hand if the subject of the contract was a determined quantity of future production (certain

measures of crops, fish etc.) the contract is regarded as legitimate. Thus it is what is called "sale of the uncertain", or "Buyu al-Gharar", which was condemned by the Prophet (ibid.).

It might be interesting to note that the awareness of market forces and their effect on prices by caliphs has been demonstrated more than once in Islamic history. During Caliph Umar's reign (634–644), as a result of a short of supply in al-Medīnah in around 639 A.C. the prices increased substantially. The second caliph did not try to fix the prices but instead instructed his viceroy in Egypt to send him supplies to bring the prices down, which he did (Tuma, 1965). Another example can be learned from the time when the caliph al-Mansūr was selecting a site for his new city, Baghdad, in 767 A.C. Al-Mansūr is reported to have said that he wanted a site where people could earn a living, where prices could not be high or supplies scarce, because if he resides where supplies could not be reached by land or sea there would be scarcity, high prices and hardship for the people (ibid.). This awareness of the Heads of State of the role of market forces reflect an early recognition of the role of demand and supply in determining prices with no need for state intervention. Even when the state intervenes in particular circumstances when the market is in a state of abnormality, a condition that requires intervention as Imam ibn Taymīya advocated, such intervention is not in negation of the recognition of the market forces. These forms of intervention, as Tuma suggests, are not in conflict with the competitive market structure or with competitive prices (ibid.) as long as they aim at stabilizing prices. But, when the market is stable, prices are determined in accordance with competitive market forces.

The state, however, has the duty of ensuring that the information given in the market regarding the quantity and quality of exchanged goods and services is sound and reliable. Without the reliability of information the parties in the transactions are likely to reach wrong conclusions and finalise transactions that may cause harm and lead to injustice. Furthermore, confidence in the market has to prevail if it is, with market forces, to function effectively and efficiently. The surveillance role of the state will add to this confidence and help enhance the exchange of economic activities. We will see later how the subject of accountability, business governance and public duties in Islam had attracted the attention of Muslim jurists in the early fourteenth century and had lead to the emergence of specialized writing in what became known as the institution of Ĥisbah, or public accountability.

Third: State Finance

The state revenue and expenditure have developed significantly during the history of Islam. During the life of the Prophet the state revenue was confined to mainly five *Fai*ʾ, one-fifth of the spoils of war, Zakāh, Jizyah, and private donations. Apart from the private donations, which were encouraged, the other types of revenue were specified in the Qurʾān as well as the manner of spending them. Furthermore, when there was confusion as to the definition of some type of these revenues, hence their expenditure allocation, this was also explained by Qurʾānic verses. Throughout the Islamic history, mainly as a result of Islamic conquests, these revenues expanded in types and size where more types were added to them both by necessity and innovation. We see the beginning of this notably during the reign of the second caliph Umar (634–644). Further expansion of conquests led to further expansion of types of revenues and that became particularly evident after the early caliphate during the Umayyad and Abbasīd caliphates, as will be examined in due course.

At this early stage of the Islamic state during the life of the Prophet state revenues, as stated in the Qurʾān, were as follows:

*Fai*ʾ *and Anfāl*

Although the line between the definition of *Fai*ʾ and spoils of war is very fine, the difference lies in that *Fai*ʾ was the spoils of war that were gained without the toil of actual combat, while spoils of war were gained from the enemy through actual combat (Qurʾān 59:6–8). The importance of that fine difference become significant when we know how each type was distributed among the warriors. *Fai*ʾ was to be put in full under the disposal of the Prophet, the head of state, with no share given to the warrior, while spoils of war was divided among them after deducting one-fifth to the state.

Anfāl also took the same rule of allocation; all to God and His messenger, which makes it identical to *Fai*ʾ in distribution. The difference between *Anfāl* and *Fai*ʾ is that while *Anfāl* resulted from actual combat *Fai*ʾ did not. *Anfāl* was however an infrequent case and that was when Muslims disputed over the spoils of the first battle of Badr in 624 A.C. and as a result, all spoils were put under the disposal of the Prophet who distributed them to all Muslims whether they took part in the battle or not (Māwardī).

Fai' was designated to the state during the Prophet's time by the force of the Revelation, (Qur'ān 59:6–8). The Qur'ān has emphasised various characteristics of al *Fai'*: (a) the event that gives rise to *Fai'* is the one in which the enemy surrenders before a military combat, "As for those spoils of theirs which God has bestowed on His Messenger, you spurred neither horse nor camel to capture them: but God gives His apostles authority over whom He will. He has the power over all things", (Qur'ān 59:6), and (b) the state has the right to the full value of the spoils with no share to the warriors and the revenue of *Fai'* has to be spent in a particular manner, "The spoils taken from the town-dwellers and assigned by God to His Messenger belong to God, His Messenger, his kinsfolk, the orphans, the poor and the wayfarers; they shall not become the property of the rich among you. Whatever the Messenger gives you, accept it; and whatever he forbids you forebear from it. Have fear from God; He is stern in retribution. A share of the spoils shall also fall to the poor Emigrants who have been driven from their homes and possessions; who seek God's grace and bounty and help God and His Messenger", (Qur'ān 59:7–8).

From the Qur'ānic verses it could be concluded that:

1. The Qur'ān differentiates between the spoils in case of surrender and the others in condition of actual combat, the latter which is called *Ghanīmah* has different rules of distribution, as will be shown shortly.
2. The reason why the warriors were not entitled to a share in the spoils of the *Fai'* was that due to the surrender of the enemy. The warriors did not use their effort, skill or risk their lives in acquiring the spoils, "you spurred neither horse nor camel to capture them: but God gives His apostles authority over whom He will. He has the power over all things", (Qur'ān 59:6).
3. *Fai'* was not a tax; it was revenue to which the state in its capacity as the ultimate political power was entitled in full.
4. It was earmarked revenue which should be spent in a particular manner specified in the Qur'ān. The main beneficiaries were: the Prophet and his kinsfolk, the orphans, the poor, the wayfarer, and the poor emigrants. The distribution in this case was more specific than that of Zakāh revenue, as will be seen later.

5. As the spoils were gained in a Holy war, *jihād*, which was ordained by God, determined by Him and conducted by His Messenger it was conceivable that God and His Messenger be assigned a share of the spoils; God's share to be spent on social welfare purposes and the Prophet's share to be spent on himself and his kinsfolk.
6. The orphans had and deserved a special mention in the distribution of *Fai'*, which was not the case in the Zakāh distribution. This was necessary because of the inevitable consequences of war on the loss of human life and the associated consequences for the orphans left behind. There would inevitably be an increase in the number of orphans in the community.

By implication, if the state still required funds to finance needs other than those mentioned in the *Fai'* verses it would have to seek other alternative sources.

The source, which was denoted to the state during the Prophet's time by the force of the Revelation, continued to be a source of revenue to the state during the Rightly Guided Caliphate and the dynastic caliphate. But that continued only when the state remained strong and able to conduct military expeditions.

One-fifth of the Ghanīmah, spoils of war

Ghanīmah, technically differentiated from *Fai'*, was the spoils of war that were gained during actual combat in military operations. By contrast to *Fai'*, warriors were entitled to the spoils of war, *Ghanīmah*, as they used their skills and effort, and they risked their lives in combat. However, the state was entitled to a share which was prescribed in the Qur'ān as one-fifth, which could be viewed as tax, "Know that to God, His Messenger shall belong one-fifth of your spoils", (Qur'ān 8:41). Furthermore, the verse specifies how the state share, or the revenue from this tax, should be spent, "Know that to God, His Messenger, the Messenger's kinsfolk, the orphans, the needy, and the wayfarers, shall belong one-fifth of your spoils: if you truly believe in God and what We revealed to our servant on the day of victory, the day when the two armies met", (Qur'ān 8:41). The revenue should therefore be spent in this particular manner as specified in the verse. Notably, apart from specifying the share of the Emigrants in the *Fai'*, the way the revenue from the one-fifth of the *Ghanīmah* and the revenue from the *Fai'* are spent is exactly the same. On the other hand the comparison between the distribution of the Zakāh revenue with that of the *Fai'* and the one-fifth of Ghanīmah shows some difference, as will be clarified after looking at the Zakāh as a source of state revenue.

Zakāh

As mentioned earlier, Zakāh as a religious tax has a unique feature that is not available to other types of taxes: its religious connotation—the tax is imposed in order to, spiritually, purify Muslims. The stipulation of the levy is in the Qur'ān, and the revenue of the tax is to be spent in a manner specified in the Book. The rate of tax is not determined by the Revelation, however. The Prophet, inspired by God's will, determined the rates, organised the tax base, and clarified the threshold.

The interesting feature of Zakāh as a source of revenue to the state is that in contrast to the previous sources of *Fai'*, and *Ghanīmah* it is of more contemporary relevance. Zakāh is more applicable to our modern time. The tax has existed through history and is still regarded as a prime source of state finance if and when the state resorts to it. Recently, with the move towards Islamic revivalism, various states in the Islamic world, such as Pakistan, Saudi Arabia, Sudan and Yemen have reintroduced Zakāh to their tax structure with a view to re-Islamising their taxation system (El-Ashker and Haq, 1995).

The Qur'ānic stipulation of the way in which the revenue of Zakāh is to be spent emphasises: (a) the earmarking feature of the Zakāh tax and (b) the difference between the distribution of its revenue and that of the *Fai'* and the one-fifth of *Ghanīmah.* The Qur'ānic verses stress that the distribution of Zakāh should be "to the poor, the pauper, the people who collect it, the new convert, the liberation of slaves, the indebted, in the cause of God, and the wayfarer" (Qur'ān 9:60). The revenue should therefore be spent on these items specifically. Comparing the Zakāh distribution with that of the *Fai'* and the one-fifth of the *Ghanīmah* reveals that when the expenses of collecting the Zakāh are excluded from the comparison, the net revenue is to be spent on items that are not particularly specified in the distribution of the *Fai'* or the one-fifth of *Ghanīmah.* If the poor and the pauper in the Zakāh verse are taken loosely to correspond to the needy in the *Fai'* and the one-fifth verses, the items that are specified in the distribution of Zakāh but not in the others become "the new convert, the liberation of slaves, the indebted, and in the cause of God".

These avenues of distribution are not mentioned in the verses of the *Fai*ʾ or the one-fifth of the *Ghanīmah*. On the other hand, the Qurʾānic verses of distributing the *Fai*ʾ and the one fifth of *Ghanīmah* have specified kinds of distribution that are not incorporated in the Zakāh distribution. No share has been specified to "God, His Messenger, the Messenger kinsfolk" in the Zakāh distribution nor has a share to the orphans been designated in it. These are covered from the revenue of the *Fai*ʾ and the one-fifth of the *Ghanīmah*, not directly from Zakāh revenue.

The difference between the distribution of Zakāh revenue on the one hand and that of the *Fai*ʾ and the one-fifth of *Ghanīmah* on the other seems to be related to the characteristics of the revenue of each. Zakāh has more general characteristics than the others. The "generality" of Zakāh is demonstrated in that its base is not specifically tied up to the consequences of military actions as in the case of the *Fai*ʾ and the one fifth of the *Ghanīmah*. Instead, it is based on the every day occurrence of economic activities that influences wealth and income and contributes in its turn to the amount of fund raised. As such, Zakāh guarantees an important prerequisite to the state revenue-continuity which, with stability, grants the state a reliable source of income. The two features of continuity and stability have influenced the way the revenue from the tax is distributed. They have made it so much wider than that of the *Fai*ʾ and the one-fifth of *Ghanīmah* that the removal of indebtedness and the liberation of slaves are included in it. In contrast to Zakāh, *Fai*ʾ and the one-fifth of *Ghanīmah* were the result of a specified action, war, and as such their revenues were generated from a source that was less general than that of Zakāh. The distribution would therefore reflect this attribute. Furthermore, as the spoils were gained in Holy war, *jihād*, which was ordained by God and conducted by His Messenger, it was conceivable that God and His Messenger be assigned a share of the spoils; the share of God to be spent on social welfare purposes and the share of the Prophet to be spent on himself and his kinsfolk. Also, the specific mention of the orphans in the distribution of *Fai*ʾ and one-fifth of *Ghanīmah* reflects the fact that in war the loss of life is almost inevitable and the avoidance of the resulting orphanage is virtually impossible. There was a need therefore for a special stipulation of the right of orphans to the spoils of war.

Jizyah

While Zakāh was imposed on Muslims, *Jizyah* was levied on non-Muslims. The imposition of the *Jizyah* tax has been established in the Qur'ān, as indeed has been the Zakāh. The tax was not to be charged on women or children, even if they were wealthy, old men who were not capable to work or had no wealth, or whoever converted to Islam. All these principles were laid down by the Prophet and exercised by his successors in the Orthodoxy caliphate. There were some modifications of the application of the *jizyah* tax, however, starting from the Umayyad caliphate as we will se in due course.

Islamic Economics in the Qur'ān and Sunnah and the Present Time

To say that the Qur'ān and the Sunnah did not provide for a comprehensive system of economics, as some critics suggest, is to fail to understand what the foundational source of a religion may provide and what it may not. The Qur'ān and the Sunnah did not come to provide a divine solution and a heavenly answer to every single economic problem that may face a community, now, or in the future. Rather, they have come to provide a foundational framework. From that solid base, an economic system, detailed as it might be, can be established. It is rather surprising to read some critics advocating that since the Qur'ān and the Sunnah have not, in their opinion, provided solutions to the economic problems of our time in such a well diversified industrial society, they, the sources, cannot be regarded as useful for contemporary economies. And how could they be divine while they cannot be regarded as complete and comprehensive; the argument continues. The early sources of the Qur'ān and Sunnah, some critics claim, were dealing with a primitive society with simple economic problems that may not be applicable to the industrial complexities of modern times; therefore they should be dismissed as obsolete. Moreover, how could these sources be regarded as divine while they had not anticipated all forms of our economic problems in the twenty first century and had not provided answers for them, the critics proclaim. But the opponents of Islamic economics, intentionally or unintentionally, seem to fail to understand two important points: first, the Qur'ān and Sunnah, and for that matter all God's Holy Scriptures, have not come to provide answers for every detailed economic problem. This is the case even if these problems coincided with the time of Revelation, let alone being the product of a society fourteen centuries after the birth of the religion. Even in contemporary legislations, no law can be perceived as able to do that. Laws are passed with a view to letting ministerial Decrees and court rulings fill in the necessary details through the practical application, which is often on a case by case basis. The divine sources provide a constitutional framework leaving details to the everyday law makers. (Can you imagine if the people at the time of the Prophet were told they would have TVs, mobile telephones, internet, and aircraft)! To put it another way, to see Fredrick Taylor's "Time and Motion Study", for example, absent from the Qur'ān and the Sunnah does not mean that Islam is unsuitable for industrial societies, nor does it imply that the method itself, or all scientific methods for that matter, are un-Islamic. Second, the Qur'ān and Sunnah have provided rules that have anticipated situations and pre-empted matters discovered subsequently centuries later. To quote but one example, the Qur'ānic debt verse, the longest in the Qur'ān, has organized the recording of the debt to a minor detail; it has differentiated between civil debt and mercantile debt, when a debt ought to be recorded and when it may not be, and when a testimony of witnesses could replace the recording and for how long and in what circumstances this may be done (Qur'ān, 2: 282); all of which has been anticipated and has indeed been included in modern civil and mercantile laws of Islamic and non-Islamic legal systems. The Qur'ānic attitude towards consumption is another example. "Don't ignore your share of this world", is a philosophy that helps achieve a balance between consumption and production and assists in keeping the economy revolving. Low consumption, as it has been demonstrated in theory and practice, while it may lead to an increase of savings and investment, may slow down production, reduce profitability, and may even lead to disinvestment. High levels of consumption may lead to the opposite effect: a decrease of saving and investment as a consequence of low saving, demand-pull inflation, an increase in the price of capital, and further cost-push inflation, and, in a global market, probably increase in the external debt and the financial risk as a consequence. Moderate consumption can be conceived as a desirable policy that helps avoid both extremes and assists in achieving a reasonable balance among the various sectors in the economy. And this moderation in consumption and saving is what Islam advocates, it is an Islamic policy, or a philosophy, that is well embedded in the Qur'ān and Sunnah.

Having looked at the framework of the Islamic economics in the Qur'ān and the Sunnah, we turn our attention in the following chapter to studying the development of Islamic economics during a much wider and richer era than that of the Prophet: the Rightly-Guided Caliphate.

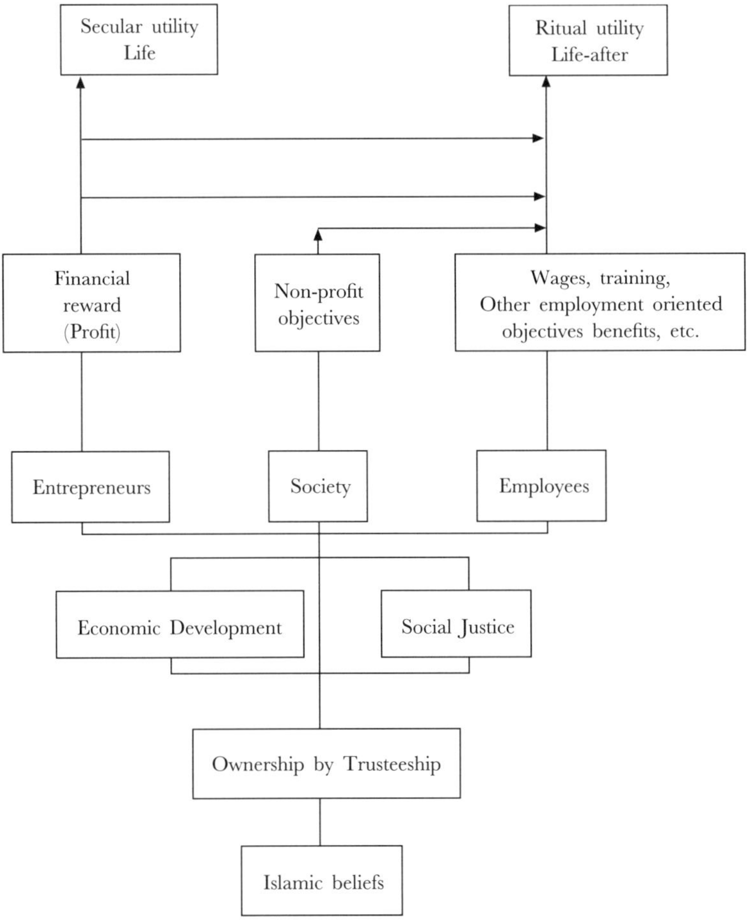

Figure 2.1: The objective of the Islamic entrepreneur (El-Ashker, 1987)

CHAPTER THREE

ECONOMIC THOUGHT OF THE RIGHTLY GUIDED CALIPHS (632 A.C.–661 A.C.)

Introduction

The rightly guided caliphate, *Al-Khilafah al-Rashīdah*, or the English version the Orthodox Caliphate, symbolizes a demarcation line between a period of asceticism and a stringent application of the teachings of the Qur'ān and Sunnah, and a period, from the Umayyads onward, of increasingly relaxed inclination towards these divine teachings and Islamic ideals. Rich in history, from an apostasy shortly after the Prophet's death, two separate assassinations of two distinguished companions and heads of state, one by a Muslim and the other by non-Muslims and the killing of a third by a group of Muslim rebels, a schism in the Muslim community that wrecked the ummah apart, in what became known as *al-fitnah al-kobra*, to military conquests on a scale that was never witnessed before and economic development and societal opening on two of the greatest civilizations of the time, the period is merited per se as a worthwhile scholarly study. In terms of religious liturgy, the period witnessed, for the first time, the birth of a coherent body of Islamic jurisprudence, *fiqh*, that served the Islamic jurisprudence that followed for centuries to come and contributed tremendously to the development of the judicial thinking, economic and otherwise, up to the outstanding four schools of thought. What concerns us in this study is the effect of those events, or the relevance of them, on the development of Islamic economic thought and the contribution of the Orthodox Caliphs to the progression of the subsequent coherent body of Islamic economic thinking.

Economic Islamic jurisprudence, *fiqh*, which was first witnessed at the time of the Orthodox Caliphate, was necessitated by the need to find answers to new compelling socio-economic questions that either did not exist during the time of the Prophet, or existed but not on the same scale (Khallaf, 1942). Conceivably, the answers were to adhere to the strict code of Islamic legislation, Sharī'ah, with no deviation from the Qur'ānic rules or Sunnah ideals—a difficult and ambitious task when the socio-economic changes were to appear well after the completion of the revelation and the death of the Prophet. But the Caliphs, the de facto economists and jurists of the day, carried out the responsibility and provided the ummah with the most needed self-exerted judgment that was based on the Qur'ān and Sunnah. This covered a wide variety of situations of different degrees of complexities.

The Caliphate

The year 632 A.C. witnessed one of the most dramatic changes in Muslims' life: the death of the Prophet. Although the death of Prophet Muĥammad was inevitable, and indeed expected, as the Qur'ān reminds Muslims that he is but a man and only a messenger preceded by others and warns them against any setback that might erupt after his "death" (Qur'ān, 3:144), Muslims were severely shocked. A close companion, Umar, later second caliph, believed that he had only gone away for a while, as Prophet Moses did, and will come back, and threatened any one who might dare to promote the "rumour" that the Prophet died (Al-Ťabarī). It was Abū-Bakr, the Prophet's close companion and father-in-law, who announced the passing away of Muĥammad. He reminded the Prophet's followers of the Qur'ānic verses, however, and preached, "Whoever worshipped Muĥammad, Muĥammad is dead, but whoever worshipped God, God would never die". Umar later said that when he heard Abū-Bakr reciting these verses, he felt as if he had heard them for the first time. The shock was severe but there was an eternal hope.

The death of the Prophet produced an inevitable problem which Muslims were to face for centuries to come: the caliphate, or who would succeed the Prophet as the head of state? In his capacity as the messenger of God, the Prophet was not to be replaced, that was well accepted, but in his role as the head of state, he would have to be succeeded, and the successor was not always agreed upon. From the day of the Prophet's death to the present day, even after the Kemalist Turks abolished the last titular caliphate in March 1924, which was last held by the Ottoman caliph Abd-al-Majid II, the political debate over the caliphate has been a crucial issue (Hitti, 1963). The debate over the caliphate started as early as the day of the Prophet's death. Before the Prophet's burial, two groups of Muslims disputed the right to the succession: the Medinese Supporters and the Makkahn Emigrants. The dispute ended by swearing the oath of allegiance to Abū-Bakr, the Prophet's close companion. The Immigrant Qurayshite, Abū-Bakr became the first successor, the caliph. Muslims, then, had time to prepare for their Prophet's burial.

Of the many caliphates that have come and gone over fourteen centuries or so, the Rightly Guided Caliphate is the most highly esteemed in Muslim minds. It is the correctly-guided caliphate, "*al-Khilafah al-Rashīdah*", as referred to by Muslims, and the only caliphate that is associated in Muslims' views with righteousness and highly spiritual values. The Orthodox Caliphate covered the years from 632 to 661 and embraced four correctly-guided Caliphs: Abū-Bakr (632–34), Umar (634–44), Uthmān (644–56) and Ali (656–61). All were the Prophet's close companions with the last one, Ali, also being the Prophet's first cousin. All had marriage relationships with the Prophet; Abū-Bakr and Umar, were the Prophet's fathers-in-law, and Uthmān and Ali were his sons-in-law. All but one, Abū-Bakr, had tragic deaths: Umar and Ali were assassinated while praying and Uthmān was killed while reciting the Qur'ān. All caliphs contributed to the development of the Islamic economic thought, though at different levels and to varying degrees.

The period of the Rightly Guided Caliphate was a crucial period in Islamic history. It witnessed (a) the psychological shock caused by the death of the Prophet, (b) tribal revolt which had to be defeated militarily, (c) active Islamic conquests that reached as far as Khurasān in the east, Georgia and Armenia in the north, Egypt and the North-African coast in the west, and Yemen and Ĥadramawt in the south (d) rapid and dramatic changes in Islamic society in a way that was never experienced before, and, towards the end of the period, (e) internal schism which reached the level of bloodshed. In other words there was a sharply contrasting combination of events, ranging from a wide Islamic expansion to a deep Islamic, or perhaps non-Islamic, schism. What concerns us in this study is the effect of those events, or the relevance of them, on the development of Islamic economic thought and the role of the Orthodox caliphs in the development of Islamic economic concepts. As mentioned previously, Islamic jurisprudence, which incorporated economic issues, was first witnessed at the time of the Orthodox Caliphate and was necessitated by the need to find answers to new socio-economic problems, that either did not exist during the time of the Prophet or existed but not on the same scale. Various Caliphs contributed to the development of economic jurisprudence in several ways and at different levels, as shown below.

The First Caliph Abū-Bakr (632–634)

Caliph Abū-Bakr, the Man

Caliph Abū-Bakr was tender hearted, gentle natured, approachable, generous and pious. As far as precedence in Islam is concerned, he was the first man, or one of the first three men, to have embraced Islam. "Al-Siddiq", the believing, he was nicknamed as he unconditionally believed in the Prophet and in what he said without any shadow of doubt, particularly after the Prophet's proclamation of visiting Jerusalem and Heaven and returning to Makkah in one night (the Night Journey). After embracing Islam, he spent his wealth in the cause of God generously, buying Muslim slaves and setting them free to save them from torture. He also participated in the preparation for Holy War to the full extent of his wealth. "I left them God and His Messenger", was Abū-Bakr's answer when he was asked by the Prophet about what he left for his family after donating all his money in God's cause. He was one of the closest associates of the Prophet and the man who was chosen by Muĥammad to accompany him in his secret emigration to al-Medīnah—a great honour. The next notable honour came when the Prophet chose him to lead Muslims in congregational prayers during his final illness (Al-Suyūti, d. 1511 A.C.).

Despite his short caliphate, the first caliph succeeded in establishing his leadership in the early crucial period of Islam after the death of its Messenger. He had the ingredients for a charismatic leader which helped him to gain the general acceptance of Muslims. This was due to his closeness to the Prophet during his life, his early response to the Islamic call as the first man to have embraced Islam, his complete devotion to the Islamic movement since its early days, his deputyship to the Prophet in congregational prayers, Ŝalāh, during the Prophet's final illness, and the fact that he has been referred to in the Qur'ān on more than one occasion (Al-Ťabarī). All this gave Abū-Bakr the pre-requisite for a charismatic Islamic character. His work afterwards confirmed the genuineness of his image.

Caliph Abū-Bakr, nevertheless, was not innovative; and he did not seem to want to be otherwise. In his first speech to Muslims as a caliph he said that he was not innovative but obedient to the word of God and the Sunnah of His Prophet and that people should obey him as long as he obeyed them (ibid.). Nevertheless, his control of the first problem that faced his caliphate, the Apostasy with its economic and political implications, was remarkable.

The Apostasy and the Establishment of Islamic Taxation

Shortly after commencing his Caliphate, Abū-Bakr faced the first test of his leadership: the apostasy revolt "al-Riddah". No sooner had the Prophet been declared dead than several tribes revolted and rebelled against the payment of the Islamic tax, Zakāh. The revolt, which seemed to have been triggered off by the death of the Prophet, did not necessarily imply a return to paganism, although some claimed false prophethood, but it aimed essentially to break away from the control of the Medīnah government (Al-Ťabarī). For Abū-Bakr this was not acceptable; the movement was a threat to Islam: a threat to the unity of Muslims and a threat to the integrity of the religion. While the threat of the revolt to the political unity of Muslims is understood, that to the integrity of Islam needs to be explained. In Abū-Bakr's view, Islam was indivisible: the five pillars of Islam (witnessing the oneness of God and of Muĥammad as His Messenger, Ŝalah, Zakāh, fasting and pilgrimage for whoever can afford it) must be accepted as one inseparable set of rules with no differentiation between Zakāh and others. Abū-Bakr sought support for his view from the Qur'ānic verses in which Zakāh and Ŝalah (congregational prayers) are always mentioned together. He therefore viewed the refusal to pay Zakāh as an illegitimate attempt to divide the essential values of Islam by, conveniently, accepting some and rejecting others. Furthermore, it was a breach of a prior commitment that the rebelling tribes made to the Prophet before his death. For all, that was not accepted.

Was Caliph Abū-Bakr justified in deciding to fight the rebels even if they were Muslims? The answer could be negative especially as we know that the Prophet stated that his followers should fight the unbelievers until they would witness that there was no God but one and that Muĥammad was His messenger. Only by saying this they could save their blood and possessions. Relying on the Prophet's saying, Umar strongly opposed Abū-Bakr, "How could you fight those who witness that there is no God but one and that Muĥammad is His messenger?" "I swear to fight those who separate Zakāh from Ŝalah", said Abū-Bakr. The argument between the two men continued for sometime but Umar eventually accepted Abū-Bakr's view, "By God, when I realised that Abū-Bakr is determined to go ahead and fight the rebels, I came to believe that it was the guidance from God" (Al-Suyūtī). The awareness of the two men of each other's characters helped promote mutual understanding, as would be expected, and speeded up an agreement on that issue as well as others. Abū-Bakr was renowned for his particular tenderness in character with no inclination to violence, both before and after embracing Islam, while Umar was known of his inclination to violence and his desire for physical challenge, particularly before accepting Islam. With his tender character and soft nature, Abū-Bakr would have avoided a military action with the Muslim rebels if possible. But since a caliph of that nature insisted on fighting the rebels, the fight must have been inevitable, and with the piety of Abū-Bakr it could only be legitimate. That seemed to have been how Umar perceived Abū-Bakr's insistence on the military confrontation.

The decision of the first caliph to fight the rebels although they were Muslims should be viewed from various perspectives:

Firstly, the religious factor as indicated above. Abū-Bakr viewed the rebels as aiming to divide the basic values of Islam as a religion.

Secondly, there was a need to unite the Arabian Peninsula, particularly in the transitional period of the Islamic state, and to transfer the Bedouins into a coherent political entity (Al-Nabrawi and Mihanna, 1982). This was necessary in order to prepare the Arabs for the next stage to come. As previously stated, the Bedouin, as a result of the nature of the land, were free in the vast desert with no particular loyalty but to their families and kinship. Or, as Hitti says, the Bedouin were never able to raise themselves to become a social being of an international type or to develop ideals of devotion to common good beyond that of the tribe (Hitti, 1963). Forcing the Bedouin to bow down to the will of the state was a necessary step in Abū-Bakr's view to tame his temperament and widen his loyalty so that he might fit in with the new organisational structure of the Islamic state. True, the Bedouin bowed to the will of the Prophet and to the Prophet's Islamic state, but Abū-Bakr was not the Prophet. To the Bedouin, it was the Prophet in person, with his spiritual charisma that emanated from the divine revelation, that deserved full obedience, not an elected successor. The example of the Bedouin who prayed, "O Lord, have mercy upon me and upon Muĥammad but upon no one else besides", (ibid.) could be repeated. Abū-Bakr, therefore, needed to emphasise the concept of the state in a purely civil sense to the Arabian mentality (Al-Nabrawi and Mihanna, 1982).

Thirdly, the fight was inevitable to emphasise the special role of Zakāh as an allocative tool in the process of wealth distribution and social caring. Zakāh is an earmarked tax the revenue of which is to be spent in a particular manner specified in the Qur'ān, in which the beneficiaries are "the poor, the pauper, the people who collect it, the new convert, the liberation of slaves, the indebted, in the cause of God and the wayfarer" (Qur'ān, 9:60). The allocative role of the tax as such needed to be emphasised and the role of the state in assuming the responsibility of making sure that the system worked had to be stressed. This should be looked at in conjunction with the following point.

Fourthly, the state's financial resources were very limited at that time. The Islamic state at the beginning of the Orthodox Caliphate was not particularly rich and with a great number of Muslims in need of the state's financial support there was a need for a policy of public finance in which revenues and expenses were well controlled. Furthermore, the Holy war, *Jihād*, that aimed to establish the authority of Islam in Arabia and beyond was imperative, an expedition was on the way to south Syria and a scheme of large scale expeditions to Syria and Iraq was envisaged, and that required a well state-organised policy of public finance.

The apostasy wars ended in 633 A.C. and Caliph Abū-Bakr was victorious: he established the political domain of the central government in al-Medīnah, the political unity of Muslims, the integrity of the religion and the institution of Zakāh. By forcing the rebels to pay Zakāh, the caliph established an important principle in Islamic taxation: the Islamic tax, Zakāh, is one of the state's rights with no individual's discretion. The compulsory element of the tax was therefore fulfilled but in a convenient manner as it was collected on harvest and/or after one year of owning the capital. The principle of certainty was already introduced in the Qur'ān and the Sunnah, as the rate of tax was known in advance, as well as that of equity, as Zakāh had a threshold and different rates. Hence Zakāh obtained its main tax characteristics from this early period.

Caliph Abū-Bakr died in 634.

The Second Caliph Umar (634–644)

To save Muslims from a similar dispute over the caliphate to that which took place after the Prophet's death, Abū-Bakr recommended Umar as the second caliph after his death. Muslims, however, would have to approve the choice of Abū-Bakr by paying allegiance to Umar. In 634, on the death of Abū-Bakr, Umar ibn al-Khattāb became the second caliph.

Caliph Umar the Man

The biography of Umar is significantly different from that of Abū-Bakr. In his personality, Umar did not have Abū-Bakr's tenderness, natural gentility, approachability or affability. With his courage, physical strength, boldness and fortitude, he was a source of both fear and respect. Muslims feared him before he became Muslim and esteemed him after he was one. In terms of precedence in Islam, Umar was not among the early Muslims. His acceptance of Islam came as late as the sixth year after the birth of the religion. Worse still, he resented Prophet Muĥammad and regarded him responsible for the division in the Makkahn community and punished new converts including members of his own family. But the Prophet was keen on Umar becoming a Muslim, "O Lord, reinforce Islam by one of the two Umars, Amr ibn Hesham or Umar ibn al-Khattāb", he prayed. It was to be Umar ibn al-Khattāb. He changed from a man who had, literally, the intention to kill the Prophet to a man who went to him to witness that "there is no God but one and Muĥammad is His messenger" in one day (the story of Umar's acceptance of Islam is one the most intriguing stories, which has been widely reported (see for example Sirat-ibn-Hishām). After embracing Islam, Umar became one of the strongest supporters of the religion and one of the most, if not the most, distinguished leaders in Islamic history after the Prophet. He was exemplary for his piety, simplicity, high regard to justice and fairness. Sound judgment and intellectual ability are much respected by Muslims.

One main factor in Caliph Umar's life seemed to have influenced his state policies: his late conversion to Islam. There was perhaps a sense of deep regret in his mind that he was not one of the early believers in the new religion. That was reflected in his high appreciation of those who embraced Islam early before him especially Caliph Abū-Bakr, who was, as already mentioned, the first man to have believed in the Prophet and his message. In Caliph Umar's words, "Abū-Bakr was always ahead of me in Islam, even when I thought I guaranteed a step ahead of him by donating half of my wealth in the cause of God, I discovered that Abū Bakr donated all his wealth", (Al-Suyūtī). "Precedence in Islam", became one of the main criteria which Caliph Umar used in evaluating Muslims morally and financially. After he became the second caliph, or Amir of the Faithful, we find caliph Umar, for example, using the same criterion, "precedence in Islam", and the degree of closeness to the Prophet as two main bases, among others, in allocating stipends to Muslims. Those who embraced Islam earlier than others are better and, therefore, should be paid more. "I do not make those who fought the Prophet equal to those who fought with him", was the most quoted Caliph Umar's defense (Al-Ťabarī). For example, when Umar's son objected to him that the father and the caliph allocated to him less stipends than that allocated to somebody else without justifiable reasons, Umar's reply was that the father of that person was more loved by the Prophet than his father (Umar himself). Caliph did the same when he distributed 2,000 Dirham more to the Prophet's wife Aisha over above the rest of the Prophet's widows because of her being closest to the Prophet, though Aisha declined the privileged payment (Al-Ťabarī). Another example was that when some Muslims remarked that he gave other Muslims more stipends than them even when the others were not in any way higher than them in rank, position or tribal history, they only accepted the ruling when they were told by the Caliph that the distribution was according to precedence in Islam (ibid.). By contrast, Abū-Bakr's approach to the distribution of the stipends was completely different, he gave to people equally, saying, "Precedence in Islam is to do with God and He rewards for it, but stipends are to do with this life and are meant to help people in their living" (ibid.).

The quality of Caliph Umar's mind was particularly remarkable. He was able to foresee consequences others, with the exception of a very few, were not able to predict, and he could analyze situations other Muslims found difficult to understand. He disagreed with the Prophet and Muslims on some political issues, and his views turned out to be what the Revelations supported later. The issue of the prisoners of war who were taken from the leading Makkahns at the battle of Badr (the first battle between Muslims and Makkahns) is an example. The prisoners who included rich Makkahn leaders were ransomed in favour of having a financial support that might help the new Islamic community. Caliph Umar strongly disagreed advocating that if they were ransomed they would return to fight Muslims with more power and greater strength; they should be killed instead as that would weaken the enemy. Later, the Revelations strongly denied the taking of ransom and rebuked the taking of it, "for seeking the chance of gain in this world while God desired for them the world to come", (Qur'ān, 8:67). Another example could be taken from Caliph Umar's perception of the prohibition of alcoholic beverages. Alcoholic beverages were prohibited in phases in the Qur'ān, starting with the phase of ordaining Muslims of not being drunk while praying. But Caliph Umar was not satisfied with the partial prohibition praying to God that it would be completely abolished. Eventually, verses were revealed to stipulate a complete prohibition. Furthermore, Caliph Umar is reported to have been among the very few who envisaged the form of the prayers' call, the "Ażan". This has given the Islamic call its uniqueness differentiated from that of other religions. Moreover, he is reported to have recommended to the Prophet the covering of the Prophet's wives and their segregation from male Muslims in general meetings. Revelation came later in support of that recommendation. The establishment of the Islamic calendar is, also, attributed to him, after he became caliph, who adopted the date of the Prophet's emigration to al-Medīnah as the start of the calendar (Al-Suyūtī). With the help of the calendar Muslims were able to historise events, which was impossible to do so with precision before then. Those qualities of mind which the second caliph had, helped develop Islamic jurisprudence in general and Islamic economic thought in particular. Indeed it had characterised Umar's thinking and made him more of an innovator than a follower. The originality of the economic thinking of the second caliph is examined below after looking at the expansion of the state under his reign.

The Expansion of the Islamic State under Caliph Umar

The expansion of the Islamic state must have been in the Prophet's mind before his death. He is reported to have prophesied the conquests of Byzantine and Persia and that the Arabs would rule over those countries (Sirat-Ibn-Hishām). At his death, an expedition was on its way to the south of Syria and had to be stopped at the outskirts of al-Medīnah on hearing the shocking news. The expedition was dispatched by Abū-Bakr as planned by the Prophet. At the death of Abū-Bakr, Muslims were experiencing early victories in Iraq and the south of Syria. But the Islamic conquests reached a high peak at the time of Umar. The second caliph started his caliphate by completing the task which his predecessor had started: the invasion of Syria and Iraq. That was done successfully. On the Byzantine front, Damascus fell in 636 after a series of battles, Jerusalem surrendered in 638, Caesarea fell in 641, and Ascalon was capitulated in 644. Meanwhile, Muslim troops marched into Egypt and defeated the Byzantines near Heliopolis in 640 which resulted in the fall of Babylon. Almost a year after the fall of Babylon, Alexandria fell and a peace treaty was concluded between the Patriarch Cyrus, the civil governor of Egypt, and the Muslim commander, Amr ibn al-As, in 641. The Byzantine Empire was not entirely destroyed, however, as Anatolia and the Balkans remained with the Byzantines. On the Persian front Muslims had a similar success. Despite tough resistance and an early defeat in 634 Muslims achieved a decisive victory in the battle of Qadisiya in 636 and a final victory in 642. The 642 victory was called the "victory of victories". That put an end to the Persian resistance in Iraq and forced the Persian king to retreat to Istakhar, the old Persepolis, (Al-Ṭabarī). As a result of the severe resistance of the Persians, Umar did not want to pursue the Persians any further and wished, "that a barrier was built between us and them". It was not until 652 AC, under the Umayyads, that the remaining resistance of the Persians was demolished and the Persian king was killed.

The expansion of the Islamic state, or the empire as it might be called, brought with it changes in Islamic society that necessitated a fresh outlook in dealing with economic issues. The contribution of the second caliph in this respect was particularly admirable.

The Economic Thought of the Second Caliph Umar

Umar's policies were a reflection of his own mind. They sometimes coincided with the policies of the Prophet and Abū-Bakr while, at other times, they deviated from those policies quite notably. But the difference was a difference of opinion not a diversion of principles. The spirit of Islam as a religion and an economic system was always observed. Umar's economic thinking can be explored as follows:

The Ownership of Economic Resources

The most notable example of the novelty in Umar's economic thinking is demonstrated in his attitude towards the ownership of land as a factor of production. After the Islamic conquests, the majority of Muslims advocated that, in accordance with the rules of the Sharī'ah, the conquered land of Iraq and Syria should be distributed among the warriors. Umar disagreed. He was of the opinion that the land should be kept in the hands of the state, or nationalised, and a tax would be imposed on the original owners, from which Muslims would be paid stipends. To understand the dimension of this problem, and Caliph Umar's approach to solving it, we should look into the system of dividing the spoils of war among the warriors as stated in the Qur'ān and the Sunnah. We recall that spoils of war are of three types: *Anfāl*, *Ghanīmah* and *Fai'*. The Qur'ān states different rules regarding the allocations of these types of spoils to Muslims. As we saw previously, about *Anfāl* the first verse of Chapter 8 of the Qur'ān states, "They ask you about *Anfāl*. Say, 'the *Anfāl* belongs to God and His Messenger'. Therefore, have fear of God and end your disputes. Obey God and His Messenger if you are true believers". The verse was revealed after the battle of Badr, the first battle between Muslims and Makkahns in which 300 Muslims achieved a complete victory over 1000 Makkahns in 624 A.C. Muslims, reports say, disputed over the spoils of the battle and as a punishment for such behaviour all the spoils were put, by Revelation, under the disposal of the Prophet who distributed them among Muslims who either participated in the battle or otherwise, (Māwardī). The allocation of *Ghanīmah*, which was different from that of *Anfāl*, was ordained as in the Qur'ān, "Know that to God, His Messenger, the Messenger's kinsfolk, the orphans, the needy, and the wayfarers, shall belong one fifth of your spoils: if you truly believe in God and what We revealed to Our servant on the day of victory, the day when the two armies met" (Qur'ān 8:41). In this distribution, the warrior would keep four fifths of what he gained in the battle and pay the Prophet, or the state, one fifth which would be distributed among Muslims as above. As for the *Fai'* and *Anfāl*, the distribution has also been ordained in the Qur'ān (8:1, 59:6–8), as mentioned previously with no need for repetition (see state finance in the previous chapter).

Muslim warriors, therefore, demanded the implementation of the Qur'ānic rules regarding the distribution of conquered Iraqi and Syrian land. They claimed the right to four fifths of the spoils, including land, with one fifth to be paid to the state—the *Ghanīmah* distribution. Umar disagreed. He differentiated between two types of spoils: mobile and immobile. For mobile spoils the Qur'ānic rules were to be applied; one fifth to the state and the rest to the warrior. But for immobile spoils, particularly those of land, they were to become the property of the state. With the right of ownership resting with the state, the land would remain in the hands of the original holders who would utilise them and be liable for the payment of land tax, "Kharāj". Caliph Umar's council was divided. Some found merit in what the caliph suggested but others viewed the proposal as violating the Qur'ānic rules. The opposing members of the council insisted that Muslim soldiers in Syria and Iraq should have the right to their specified shares of all spoils, including land, as specified in the Qur'ān. Their argument carried conviction. The issue was concluded when ten noble members of the Supporters, *Ansārs*, five from each of the two main tribes, were invited to the debate by Umar to discuss the views of each party and Caliph Umar put his points of view as follows (Abū-Yusuf):

Firstly, economic reasons

(1) Assigning the conquered land to Muslim soldiers might turn Islamic society into a feudalistic society, which Umar opposed strongly. He might seem to have diverted in this issue from the practice of the Prophet who distributed some conquered lands (for example those of Khayber) to Muslims during his life. But the land distributed by the Prophet was very small and not comparable to that of the new conquests.

Even further, a story is told that when a Muslim purchased a piece of land on the bank of Euphrates, Umar ordered him to return it to its previous holder and to get his money back: "these are the owners of the land (pointing to Muslims), did you ask them if you could buy it from them?"; the dialogue between Umar and the buyer was concluded (Abū-Ubaid).

(2) The distribution of land to Muslim soldiers was bound to create class distinctions in Islamic society. In this Umar referred to the Qur'ānic verses of spoils distribution which concluded that the method of distribution, which Umar adopted, was meant to prevent, or alleviate, the circulation of wealth only amongst the rich (Qur'ān, 59:7).

(3) The welfare of future generations should not be sacrificed for the sake of the well-being of the present one. "If I distributed the land, nothing would be left for those who will come after you and who will find that the land had already been distributed and inherited", Caliph Umar explained.

(4) The distribution of the new land would limit the ability of the state to establish the system of social security which Umar seemed to have envisaged. If the land was distributed "what would be left for the descendants and the widows of this land and for the people of Syria and Iraq?" Umar exclaimed.

(5) Umar seemed to have favoured a form of socialism based on Islamic teachings where, while private ownership is allowed, public ownership is permissible for the sake of society. "I have distributed whatever property they acquired as booty amongst those who deserved but I have taken out the fifth and have allocated this on the prescribed basis. I believe that I should nationalise these lands and impose on them taxes, and on their occupants a poll tax which they should pay. This would be a permanent booty for the Muslim cause to help the soldiers, their descendants and for those who come after them," Umar stated in the general debate.

Secondly, military reasons

(6) The need of the state for individuals to protect the conquered areas and to pursue the Islamic Holy War, *Jihād*. "Don't you see these frontiers? It is necessary to appoint men to defend them", Caliph Umar continued.

(7) The need of the state for a regular source of finance to spend on defense and new expeditions. That source would be generated from land tax, Kharāj, if the land was kept in the hands of the holders with state ownership. "Have you seen these great cities like Syria, Jazira, Kufa, Basra and Egypt? It is imperative to appoint military governors there and to fix their stipends. From where will these be paid if I distributed all the land and mules?" Caliph Umar defended his view in the debate.

Thirdly, religious reasons

(8) Umar viewed as general the verses that put the spoils at the disposal of the Prophet, or the state, to allocate them to Muslims in the way he saw fit and the other verses that determined the right of the soldier to four fifths as specific. His main argument was that the distribution of spoils should not lead to the circulation of wealth only among the rich (Qur'ān, 59:7).

The debate ended with the approval of the proposal of the caliph.

Economic Development

If the policies of the second caliph regarding the conquered land are analyzed in a broad economic context, they will depict the caliph's awareness of two main economic issues in the early Islamic state: economic development and wealth distribution. The efficiency of using economic resources in general and the productivity of land in particular seemed to have been a primary target in Umar's economic development. His attitude regarding the conquered land was an economist's attitude towards land as a means of production. In that example, the land was left in the hands of the original holders who were more capable than the Arabs of cultivating it. Furthermore, in imposing land tax, Kharāj, the base of tax was the cultivable land regardless of the land being cultivated or otherwise. That was deemed to increase the utility of land as a means of production.

The emphasis of the second caliph on the efficiency of using land as a means of production was demonstrated further in the next two cases: the case of reclaiming barren land and the case of owning more land than what one could afford to look after. In the case of reclaiming barren land, Umar, in line with the Islamic teachings, instructed, "Whoever revives dead land becomes its owner" (Abū-Yūsuf). When no one had ownership over the barren land, no argument was likely to arise, but a dispute might erupt if the land had an original owner. Then came the second case: "If the owner of land had not utilised it fully for three years and someone else, or a group of people, came along and utilised the abandoned part he, or they, may claim the ownership of that part", Umar warned, (Abū-Ubaid). The second caliph emphasised, "there is no right to the holder after three years of no utilisation" (Al-Māwardī). Umar was so strict in the implementation of these rules that he confiscated land belonging to one of the Prophet's close companions, Bilāl, despite the fact that the land was given to the companion by the Prophet himself. When Bilāl protested, "How could you take from me what the Prophet gave me?" Caliph Umar's counter argument was decisive, "The prophet gave you the land to utilise not to deprive others, keep what you can afford to look after and give the rest back to Muslims" (Al-Māwardī).

It is clear from the above that the second caliph attached a great importance to natural resources as a means of production and endeavoured to maximise the benefits generated from these resources. Umar's policies, with regard to ownership of means of production, were neither capitalistic nor communistic, to use modern economic terms, but a reflection of Islamic economic teachings. Private ownership, as stated in the previous chapter, is highly regarded in Islam provided that it is not abused. If it is abused the state has the right to step in and rectify the situation. After all, the ownership is ownership by trusteeship between a man who is delegated to own and God who owns everything. Nationalisation was not therefore one of the state's general policies, it was only a necessary step taken to rectify a situation and prevent the misuse of economic resources.

The second caliph's awareness of the need for the full use of economic resources did not stop at the level of land as a means of production; it went further to reach human resources and capital. Labour, as previously mentioned, occupies a prominent place in Islamic economic teachings (see chapter 2) and Caliph Umar's policies on labour emphasised these teachings. He encouraged people to have an occupation, to learn and train, to give up laziness and false religious devotion, and to strive through work for the sake of God, "To die while striving in my work hoping for the bounty of God is even better to me than being killed in Holy war for the sake of God", Umar stated, (Al-Shaibanī).

Also, labour to Umar was not only a duty on the worker to the state but also a right to the individual by the state. In directing his deputy Umar is reported to have said, "God has deputised us on his servants (people) to protect them from hunger, to clothe them, and to facilitate finding occupations for them" (Al-Ghazālī). Furthermore, the second caliph seemed to have realised the relationship between unemployment and civil unrest as early as the mid seventh century. In his directions to the same deputy he stressed, "God has created hands to work, if they cannot find work in obedience they will find plenty in disobedience, so keep them busy in compliance before they get you busy with defiance" (Al-Ghazālī).

Civil unrest in some countries in recent history seemed to lend support to Umar's view about the relationship between unemployment and deprivation on the one hand and civil disturbances on the other.

Besides land and labour, capital as a means of production also occupied the attention of the second caliph. Umar stressed the importance of rationalising consumption for the sake of increasing saving and investment. His recommendation to his subjects was not to consume all their income, but to divide it into two parts: one for consumption and another for investment (Al-Balażrī). In his stand on the rationalisation of consumption for the sake of saving, the second caliph had advocated the concept of moderate consumption. We recall from the previous chapter that although Islam does not condemn seeking the satisfaction of materialistic needs, it ordained that it should be done in moderation. We also recall dividing consumption into several levels, varying from the level of merely sustaining the fundamental principles of life to that of extravagance, with moderate consumption lying somewhere between. Umar seemed to have narrowed the level of moderate consumption so much that he brought it very close to the level of necessity, with anything above that level as lying in the extravagant category. He is reported to have reproached one who seemed to him to have bought a large quantity of meat, "Do you buy all that you desire?" exclaiming twice. He preached, "Beware of overeating, it is harmful to the body and wasteful with the money, be moderate in your eating, it saves your money, keeps you in the right path and brings you nearer to God", His recommendation was to divide income into two distinctive parts, the first for consumption and the other for reinvestment. Furthermore, to help members of the community with starting capital the caliph took the initiative of distributing barren land to those who were capable of utilising it and granted them its ownership as well as offering financial help to those who were in need for help to cultivate it (Abū-Yūsuf).

Wealth Distribution

Turning our attention to wealth distribution, the other factor in economic welfare, we find that this was taken care of by two main means. The first was the institution of Zakāh, which was already established in the Sharī'ah, while the second was a system of stipends that was introduced by Caliph Umar. Revenues of Zakāh were to be spent in a particular manner specified in the Qur'ān in which the beneficiaries are "the poor, the paupers, the people who collect it, the new converts, the liberated slaves, the indebted, in the cause of God and the wayfarer" (Qur'ān 9:60). A further reinforcement to Zakāh revenues came from that of Khums, one fifth of spoils of war. Qur'ānic verses stipulate that it is for "God, His messenger, the messenger's kinsfolk, the orphans, the needy and the wayfarer" (Qur'ān, 8:41). The earmarking characteristics of Zakāh and Khums that implied taking from the rich and giving to the poor, would help, therefore, alleviate misdistributions of economic resources in the community. Furthermore, in distributing those revenues to the poor Umar emphasised further an important concept in distribution: the poor should be given to enrich, if possible, not merely to meet his basic needs. "If you give, enrich", Caliph Umar recommended (Abū-Ubaid). The story is also told that the second caliph gave a poor man three camels, stating that he would continue to give even if it amounted to a hundred camels to one person (ibid.). There was an emphasis of the function of the tax in re-allocating economic resources. But poverty was not accepted by Umar at face value. He is reported to have reprehended those who were poor because they did not strive to earn their living or because they spent all their time in the mosque, even though it was for worshipping God and reciting the Qur'ān, "Would not these people know that heaven does not rain gold and silver!" exclaimed the caliph (ibid.).

The second tool of wealth distribution in the community was a stipend system which was introduced by Caliph Umar. The caliph was able to use Kharāj revenue in establishing his system in which he granted Muslims two types of allowances: monetary allowances and allowances in kind. All Muslims were entitled to those allowances including children whose allowances would increase with the increase in their age. In allocating allowances in kind to individuals he followed a novel idea: he gathered a group of men (thirty) and fed them to their full satisfaction for a few days. Then he used the results of that experiment in deciding how much allowances in kind would be given to the individual every month (Abū-Yūsuf). Not all of Umar's monetary allowances could be classified, however, under social-caring spending. The second caliph distributed stipends to everyone though differentiating in distribution between individuals depending upon the closeness of their relationship with the Prophet and the person's precedence in Islam. It is noted that Umar's principle of monetary distribution was different from that of Abū-Bakr. While Abū-Bakr did not differentiate among Muslims in allotting spoils of war, as they were all given equally, Umar discriminated in allotting stipends depending upon the precedence of the person in embracing Islam. In defending his approach, Umar argued that he would not make the one who fought against the Prophet equal, in terms of distribution, to the one who fought on his side (Abū-Ubaid). To Abū-Bakr, however, the precedence in accepting the new faith was entirely in the hands of God and He would reward for it, but the distribution of the spoils was a worldly matter in which equity was far better than any discrimination. Hence there were two contrasting approaches by the two caliphs: Abū-Bakr who was the first man or amongst the first three men to have embraced Islam refused to consider the principle of precedence in Islam as a basis of distribution, while Umar, who came to Islam six years after its emergence, refused to consider otherwise. Their devotion to Islam was, nevertheless, beyond doubt.

Tax Structure

Five types of taxes existed at the time of Umar's reign: Kharāj, Ushūr, Zakāh, Jizyah and Khums. The first two taxes were introduced by Umar while the other three were already established in the Sharī'ah.

As stated above, Kharāj tax was introduced by Umar to replace the system of distributing conquered land among Muslim warriors. With the approval of Umar's proposal in the general debate, Kharāj became the first tax to be introduced to the Islamic tax system outside those which were stipulated in the Qur'ān and the Sunnah. The new tax had the following characteristics:

(1) It was imposed on land not on individuals. This implied that the tax was not affected, increasingly or decreasingly, by the number of people living on the land. By contrast, Jizyah, or poll tax, was imposed on individuals.
(2) The base of tax was the cultivable land. This would encourage the tax payer to maximize the productivity of land, as uncultivated land would still be treated as being cultivated as long as it was cultivable.
(3) The tax rate was a proportional rate though it varied depending on the degree of the fertility of land, the market value of the produce and the difficulty of irrigation.

(4) The tax was an annual tax, though it could be paid by installment.
(5) It was paid in kind or in money.
(6) The liability of tax lay on the occupiers of land, either Muslims or non-Muslims.
(7) The revenue of Kharāj was not to be mixed with that of Zakāh, because the revenue of Zakāh was to be spent in a manner specified in the Qur'ān, while the state had the discretion as to the way the Kharāj revenue would be spent.

A discussion has arisen among historians as to whether Kharāj was the same as Jizyah. Hitti, for example, argues, "The differentiation between the two forms of taxation implied in Jizyah and Kharāj was not made until the time of the late Umayyads" (Hitti, 1963). The importance of the discussion, therefore, is that if Kharāj were in fact the Jizyah as imposed by the Qur'ān and the Sunnah, it would mean that Caliph Umar could not have introduced it as a new tax to the Islamic tax system. It suffices to say that Hitti, and others, seemed to have overlooked what Umar is reported to have said in the debate between him and Muslims regarding the distribution of conquered land. Caliph Umar said, "I impose Kharāj on them for the land they hold and levy a Jizyah on their persons" (Abū-Yūsuf, Māwardī, and Abū-Ubaid). The second caliph, differentiated clearly between the two types of taxes: Kharāj and Jizyah. He specifically related Kharāj to land but Jizyah to persons. As mentioned above, the ownership of the land rested with the state. The state in its turn entrusted the original owners or keepers with the utilisation of land—a form of ownership by trusteeship. Kharāj was, therefore, a financial reward charged by the state from the keepers for delegating the right of utilising the land to them. Furthermore, in levying Kharāj the second caliph called for the measurement and registration of the lands. At the instruction of Umar, as Abū-Yūsuf said, "Uthmān ibn Hanif surveyed the lands and imposed ten dirhams per jarib on grapes, eight dirhams per jarib on sugar cane, four dirhams per jarib on wheat, and two dirhams per jarib on barely" (Abū-Yūsuf). It does not seem conceivable to regard Jizyah as Kharāj while Jizyah was imposed as a fixed sum per head and Kharāj was levied on a measure of produce (jarib). It reinforces this further to quote the rest of Abū-Yūsuf's report, ". . . and twelve dirhams, twenty four dirhams and forty eight dirhams per head (according to their capacity)", (Abū-Yūsuf). Bearing that in mind and taking into account what has been mentioned above, with no need for repetition, it can be said that Umar could be but aware of the differences between Kharāj and Jizyah and had the intention of differentiating between the taxes when introducing the land tax Kharāj.

The other tax which caliph Umar introduced to the Islamic tax system was the Ushūr or custom duties. At the recommendation of one of Umar's governors, Abū-Musa al-Ash'ari, the tax was initiated as a reciprocal tax to that which Muslim merchants paid to foreign states on crossing their borders. The rate of the tax was one tenth, or "Ushr" the plural of which is "Ushūr", which was determined at the same rate that was imposed by foreign countries on Muslim merchants. In the words of Abū-Musa in his letter to Umar, "Muslim traders from our dominion go to the country of the enemies and they levy Ushr (one tenth) on them", to which Umar replied, "Take Ushr from them just as they charge from the Muslim traders", (Abū-Yūsuf). In his application of the tax, the second caliph, nevertheless, did not stop at charging non-Muslim merchants crossing the Islamic borders; he also extended the tax base to cover all goods crossing the borders with concessions given to Muslims and the żimmis (Christians, Jews and Sabians). ". . . and charge from the żimmis half of Ushr and from the Muslims one dirham for every forty dirhams", the second caliph continued his instructions to his governor, (Abū-Yūsuf).

The difference between the Ushūr tax treatment of Muslims, żimmis and people of other un-tolerated religions was that while merchants of religions other than Islam, Judaism or Christianity were liable to ten percent of the value of the goods transferred, Muslim merchants paid two and half percent and Jewish, Christian and Sabian merchants paid five percent. Also, the concessions given to Muslims were higher than those given to żimmis. The tax discrimination in this regard, as well as in other aspects of taxation, should be viewed in the light of the fact that the burden of defending the state was allocated more heavily on Muslims than on non-Muslims. Most notably, non-Muslims were exempt from taking part in wars which were both defensive and expeditionary. Also, the differentiation in the rate of tax was due to constitutional reasons: (a) the rate on Muslim merchants was deemed as the equivalent rate of Zakāh tax on trade assets, which by being stipulated by the Prophet could not be changed, (b) the tax on Christians, Jews and Sabians (the People of the Book) was regarded as equivalent to the Kharāj tax, which was introduced after the death of the Prophet, while (c) the rate on others was an outcome of the reciprocal treatment which the subjects of the Islamic state received from other states.

Other characteristics of the Ushūr tax were that the tax had a threshold, 200 dirhams, it was levied once a year on the same goods transferred regardless of the number of times they crossed the borders and it was imposed on external trade with no levy on the transfer of goods among the state provinces (Abū-Yūsuf).

Turning our attention to Zakāh, we recall that Caliph Abū-Bakr established the right of the state to collecting Zakāh as one of its affairs. That practice continued in the reign of Umar. The second caliph, however, initiated two issues in Zakāh: (a) he postponed the collection of the tax, as well as other taxes, when the Islamic state experienced severe economic problems, such as those that happened in the years of the famine, and (b) he modified the manner in which Zakāh revenue was to be spent by taking non-Muslim chieftains off the list of beneficiaries, stating that Islam was strong enough to defend itself with no need to buy someone's peace or loyalty. The modification made by caliph Umar was an example of a man who was not simply copying those before him, but who questioned the wisdom of the law and the purpose in the stipulated rule even if it was stipulated in the Qur'ān and exercised by the Prophet and Abū-Bakr before him. The second caliph demonstrated, in this example and several others, the purpose of revealing a verse. This is an important principle in understanding the Qur'ānic rule that relates to socio-economic activities and deriving rules from it. The principle is widely acknowledged among jurists.

Jizyah tax which was imposed on non-Muslim men, not on women or children, had three different rates: forty eight dirhams, twenty four dirhams and twelve dirhams depending upon the ability-to-pay. Exemptions were given to the destitute to whom charity was given, the blind who had no provision or any work, persons receiving charity, disabled unless they were prosperous, monks living in monasteries and people living in synagogues unless they were prosperous, women and children even if they were well off, old men who were incapable of doing work and had no wealth, the insane and the żimmi if he converted to Islam (Abū-Yūsuf). The tax was an annual tax and it was personal in the ultimate sense, which meant that if the person died before paying it his heirs were not responsible for it, nor would the deceased inheritance be reduced by the unpaid tax (ibid.).

In addition to the above taxes, there were two other sources of public finance: Khums and the revenue of *sawāfi* land. The Khums, one fifth, was the share of the state of the spoils of wars gained by Muslim warriors (with the exclusion of lands in the reign of Umar as detailed above). It also included the share of the state of the treasure (and the minerals) that might be extracted from earth. Swafi land was the land which was deserted by its owners who fled the country after the Islamic conquest in pursuit of their masters. That land was put under the direct control of the state and managed by state employees.

State Expenditure

Turning our attention to the expenditures side of public finance, we find that avenues of expenditures varied depending upon the source of revenue. Revenue of Zakāh and that of Khums, one fifth of war spoils, were to be spent in a certain manner specified in the Qur'ān. Revenue of Jizyah was general since neither the Qur'ān nor the Sunnah specified the way it was to be spent. As for custom duties, Ushūr, these were introduced at the time of Caliph Umar and as such they were to be spent on general purposes of state affairs. But the bulk of revenue was that of Kharāj. An examination of the types of public spending at the time of the second caliph reveals that those could be divided into three main types: social-caring spending and stipends expenditure, current expenditure and investment expenditure. The first category was stated above with no need for repetition. The second category of state expenses related to those expenses which were necessary for running the every day affairs of state administration, or current expenses. Stipends paid to Muslim soldiers, governors, local treasurers, judges and clerks lay in that category. Investment expenditures were of a more permanent nature: building bridges, road maintenance, digging canals and rivers, and helping those who needed capital to set up entrepreneurial ventures (Abū-Ubaid). Umar was conscientious about the need for public facilities and road maintenance so much so that he is reported to have said that if a mule stumbled in a road as far as the Euphrates embankment he would be responsible for not paving the road for it.

State Administration

During the reign of caliph Umar's predecessors, the state was run by the central government in al-Medīnah, though during Umar's time the state became much wider and the administration grew more complicated. Province governors were given certain authority by which they would run the regular affairs of the province without necessarily having to wait for orders from the capital. Tax policies were designed and determined by the central government; no governor had the right to impose new taxes or change tax rates. But governors were given the authority to spend of the tax revenue on the affairs of the province, leaving the surplus to be sent to the central government. For example, one third of the tax revenue in Egypt was allocated to maintaining roads, building bridges and digging canals in the province (Kettani, 1979). Zakāh revenue was to be spent on social-caring spending in the province first and the rest to be sent to the government in al-Medīnah. Hence the Islamic administration at the time of Umar could be called a flexible-central government. Governors were under the continuous surveillance of Umar and any misuse of power was severely punished. The second caliph introduced the principle of questioning the governor for any extra wealth he might have achieved as a result of his position. At the end of the governor's service he was to explain the reasons for any substantial increase in his wealth between the date of assuming his post and the date of his retirement. Pecuniary gifts to governors given by foreign or influential local delegates were to be regarded as gifts to the state, even if they were given in personal capacity. In one example when a governor differentiated between what was given to him as a personal gift and what was given to the state he was reprehended by Umar who regarded all that had been given as state property: "Would he see if he was not a governor and sat in his father's and mother's house instead, what gifts would be given to him!", angrily exclaimed the caliph (Al-Suyūtī).

The state finance was administered through local treasuries and a central treasury. A local treasury was established in each province and was headed by a treasurer, who was not the province's governor, appointed by the head of state. The treasurer was responsible for the province's revenues and expenditure and was accountable to the head of state in the state's capital. A central treasury was established in al-Medīnah, the state's capital, and was headed by a treasurer, not the head of state. The function of the central treasury was twofold: to act as a local treasury to al-Medīnah and its surrounding area and to act as an organiser among local treasuries. Those treasuries that had surpluses were to forward their surplus to the central treasury to meet the needs of other local treasuries that had deficits, or to receive instructions from the central treasury to transfer from their surpluses what could meet others' deficits.

Also, state registration, *Dīwān*, was introduced by Umar, on the advice of his council (ibid.) and perhaps influenced by state registration in conquered lands in Syria and Iraq. The most notable of these were stipends registration and Kharāj registration. The first included registration of the people, their names, tribes, places and how much stipends they were allowed. The second included a survey of Kharāj lands, their occupiers, degree of fertility, products, the amount of Kharāj levied and how much was spent on the land of public money—a detailed register of the main source of state finance.

After ten years of his caliphate, the caliph who rendered great services to the organisation of the Islamic empire tragically died. In 644 he was assassinated while leading congregational prayer by a poisoned dagger of a Christian Persian slave. On knowing who stabbed him he thanked God that he was not stabbed by a Muslim (ibid.) for fear of schism among Muslims. Schism was to come however in a decade or so after him. The sudden death of Caliph Umar ended a great period of a successful Muslim leader.

The Third Caliph Uthmān (644–656)

Caliph Uthmān ibn Affan was one of six men whom Umar managed to name in the short time before his death as prospective caliphs from whom Muslims would choose one. They were all the Prophet's companions who gained his approval and blessing and who were renowned for their piety and tremendous support to Islam. The selection was narrowed down to that between Ali and Uthmān but the latter was eventually given the oath of allegiance. In his early seventies, Caliph Uthmān was probably too old to resist the political greediness of his kinsfolk—an ingredient for later Islamic revolt.

Caliph Uthmān, the Man

In terms of personal temperament, Caliph Uthmān was much nearer to Abū-Bakr than to Umar. He was known for his tolerance, approachability, gentle nature and modesty with a touch of shyness. In terms of precedence in embracing Islam, again Caliph Uthmān was nearer to the first caliph than to the second; he was one of early Muslims and above all he was one of few people chosen by the Prophet to write Qur'ānic verses when they were revealed. But the third caliph had something which none of his predecessors had: wealth. Wealth to Uthmān the Muslim was a blessing but to him as caliph it was, nevertheless, otherwise. When the Islamic movement was poor, Uthmān spent on the Islamic cause generously, so much so that he is reported to have financed as much as one third of the cost of an Islamic expedition on his own (Al-Ṭabarī). The wealth turned into a curse, however, after Uthmān became a caliph. He was accustomed to good living and he continued to do so and perhaps more after he was selected as a head of state. When comparing his style of living with that of Caliph Umar whose food and dress were scanty, the Muslim community had many questions and objections. Caliph Uthmān's defense was that it was from his own wealth he spent on himself not from Muslims' money in the state treasury. But the effect Caliph Umar left on Muslims and his incomparable example of self-denial was too deep to eradicate. At least it was much too soon to change the style of leadership. The weakness of the old caliph in facing his kinsfolk who were eager to be appointed to elevated political positions as province governors did not help the matter either. Caliph Uthmān was accused of nepotism (ibid.). But despite all that, the third caliph had the opportunity to complete the compilation of the Qur'ān and to administer further Islamic expansion. By the time of his death, the Islamic state extended to Sigistan in the east, Georgia between the Caspian Sea and the Black Sea in the north and further in the North African coast in the west. Further expansion produced further wealth for the Empire.

Caliph Uthmān and Financial Administration

The third caliph was not particularly innovative. He was, as he affirmed, a follower of those before him. His general economic policies, therefore, were a continuation of those of his immediate predecessor. Indeed, Caliph Umar left after him a solid body of economic and financial policies that would be difficult to change without justification. It is not surprising therefore to know that the general policies of Caliph Uthmān coincided with those of Caliph Umar. To Caliph Uthmān's credit, it should be pointed out that as a member in Caliph Umar's council Caliph Uthmān must have participated in the process of decision-making. Caliph Uthmān was one of Caliph Umar's supporters in his debate over the ownership of conquered lands (Abū-Yūsuf).

The main sources of public finance at the time of Caliph Uthmān were as laid down by Umar. Those were revenues from Zakāh, Khums (one fifth of spoils of war), Jizyah, Kharāj, Ushūr (custom duties) and state property, the ownership of which was transferred to the state as a result of not having private owners. Public expenditures were also of three main types: social-caring and stipends expenditure, current expenditure and investment expenditure (Muĥammad, 1986).

However, a marked development in the ownership of agricultural land took place during the reign of the third caliph, which was to have a dramatic effect on the structure of land ownership for many years to come. Until the reign of Uthmān the state had owned agricultural land which it inherited from the previous owners who fled Iraq and Syria after Islamic conquests. Although the land, which was called *sawāfi* land, had been regarded as belonging to Muslims in general, a view which the second caliph Umar seemed to have always maintained, and as such the land was kept under the direct administration of the state, Caliph Uthmān was of the view that the land could be transferred from the state to individuals to look after on a rental basis. The development started with a request from the governor of Syria Mu'awiyah, who seemed to have been able to introduce many novelties to the administration of the Islamic state, though not always favourable, asking the caliph to give him the land from which the Byzantine governors fled after the Islamic conquests (Al-Ťabarī). Mu'awiyah based his request on the argument that his salary was not sufficient to cover his expenses which included gifts of which a considerable part was meant to impress the neighbouring Byzantine Empire. Since that portion of his personal spending was politically beneficial to the state it was only reasonable, from his point of view that he should be compensated for these expenses and the compensation, as he saw it, should be in the form of the requested *sawāfi* land. With his shrewd power of persuasion, influential role in Syria, and, some say, his kinship to the caliph, Mu'awiyah gained the approval of Uthmān. But the caliph was accused of nepotism.

Although the third caliph Uthmān opened the door for a marked change in land ownership, which led later on to the appearance of Islamic feudalism, his views seemed to have been based on plausibly economic argument. He was of the view that: (a) the land was given to individuals on a rental not ownership basis, with the rent being based on the principle of sharing while the full ownership still resting with the state, (b) the new system would capitalise on the personal incentive of the keeper, which would enhance the productivity of the land and increase the revenue generated from it to the state, and (c) the assignment of land to individuals would alleviate the state public expenses as it would cut down the state administrative cost from operating the land, (d) with the extra revenue expected through the introduction of the personal incentive and the reduction of the state administrative expenses, the net revenue from this land would increase (Mohammad, 1986). This argument found support from the substantial increase in the state revenue from this source which increased from a range between 4,000,000 and 9,000,000 to 50,000,000 dirhams during the reign of the third caliph (Al-Māwardī).

On the other hand, Caliph Uthmān's introduction of the new system marked the beginning of feudalism in the economic history of Islam, a change that was far from being expected by him. The new policy led to various adverse consequences: (a) it opened the door to what could be viewed as nepotism on a large scale, (b) what started as giving away only the right of utilisation ended in giving up the full right of ownership, (c) as the policy gradually transferred a considerable amount of the state revenue and ownership to individuals the policy led to widening the base of the private sector and reducing the base of the public sector, and (d) with the burning of the registers of those lands during the civil disturbance that took place during the Umayyads in 82 H an important source of information to the state was lost, which led to false claims of ownership and the ability of individuals to join lands they did not actually own (Al-Māwardī). Consequently, despite Caliph Uthmān's genuine intention, his policy seemed to have carried with it the seeds of Islamic feudalism.

Using modern economic, or political, terms one would say that the third caliph Uthmān was more in favour of privatisation and less of the economic role for the state. By contrast, the second caliph Umar was more in support of an economic role for the state and of less for privatisation. Uthmān was rich but Umar was poor.

The reign of Caliph Uthmān ended, as mentioned above, with a military revolt that besieged the caliph's house and killed him in 656 A.C.

The Fourth Caliph Ali (656–661)

Imam Ali ibn Abi-Taleb, the Prophet's first cousin, his son in law and the father of his beloved grandson's al-Ĥassan and al-Ĥusayn, was elected as a caliph after the death of caliph Uthmān. But the election did not last long: rivalry to Caliph Ali's successorship arose in al-Ĥijaz, lead by two influential leaders and reinforced by the Prophet's young wife Aisha "the mother of the believers" (Al-Ťabarī). The days of communal spirit and self-denial seemed to have long gone. The rivalry developed into a military confrontation which took place between Caliph Ali and the coalition of the three rivals in 656 outside al-Basra in Iraq in a battle called "the battle of the camel" which referred to the camel ridden by Aisha in the battle. The result of the battle established the position of Caliph Ali, as the coalition was defeated, the two rivals were killed and the rider of the camel was captured. Imam Ali mourned his rival friends, buried them honourably and sent the Prophet's wife Aisha back to al-Medīnah in a dignified manner that suited her position as the Prophet's widow. Although that rivalry was defeated, another, but much longer and more bitter one followed in Syria which was lead by the governor of Syria, Mu'awiyah ibn abi-Sufyan, the kinsman of ex-caliph Uthmān. Mu'awiyah, who was among those dismissed from office by caliph Ali in the latter's attempt at removing the reasons of discontent among Muslims, withheld his homage from Caliph Ali. He declared that he was the avenger of Uthmān's blood and cunningly stated that if Caliph Ali could not execute the assassins of the murdered caliph he should be regarded as an accomplice and therefore should be disqualified from the caliphate. The issue was a political one. The armies of the two men met in 657 and when Caliph Ali's forces were about to achieve victory Mu'awiyah they resorted to arbitration by lifting the Holy Book on the tips of spears (Al-Ťabarī). The result of the arbitration was chaotic, caliph Ali's representative walked into a trap designed by Mu'awiyah's shrewd representative that lead to disqualifying the caliph by his representative and reinstating Mu'awiyah by his referee. The results of the arbitration were disastrous to Caliph Ali. It made things worse, a few thousand men of his supporters rose against him for accepting the principle of arbitration and formulated a new group called Khawārij, (seceders), who were neither on caliph Ali's nor on Mu'awiyah's side. Despite their military defeat by Caliph Ali, they succeeded to gather again and continued to be a source of annoyance to the caliphate for decades to come. In 661 while Imam Ali was on his way to congregational prayers early in the morning he was assassinated by a Kharijite. In contrast to the person who assassinated Caliph Umar, the assassin of Caliph Ali was a Muslim. In the same year Mu'awiyah in Syria declared himself as the new caliph.

Caliph Ali, the Man

Three main features characterised Imam Ali distinctively: righteousness, knowledge and bravery (Al-Suyūṭī). He was pious; the examples of his piety are numerous in history books. He was knowledgeable of the Sharī'ah, "Ali is the gateway of knowledge", the Prophet testified. He was also brave, he slept in the Prophet's bed at the night of the Prophet's emigration to elude those who besieged the Prophet's house and he would put himself forward for a duel before the start of the battle against well-known knights with far more experience than him. For his bravery he was nicknamed by the Prophet "the lion of God". The fact that Ali was brought up by the Prophet since he was a child must have influenced his character, promoted his piety, deepened his knowledge and reinforced his sense of bravery. Moreover, as a caliph, he was approachable, lenient and affable.

Economic Thought of the Fourth Caliph Ali

Caliph Ali's economic thought is best summarised in a comprehensive document that took the form of instructions to his newly appointed governor of Egypt, Mālik al-Ashtar. Compared with instructions given to governors by previous caliphs in similar occasions, Caliph Ali's document was rather lengthy and more comprehensive. It reflected the thought of the fourth caliph in a comprehensively constitutional manner that covered economic and administrative matters in the state. From the document (Al-Sharief al-Radhie, *Imam Ali's Nahg al-Balāghah*), Caliph Ali's thought can be depicted as follows:

General function of government

After praising God, the caliph laid down the general function of government as being to "seek the goods of people and to make cities prosperous". How that could be generally done was by the fulfillment of God's obligations, the protection of human rights without distinction of religion or community, the care of the destitute and the poor, the provision of succor to the low and the down-trodden, the establishment of peace and security, and the prosperity and well being of the people.

There were four main issues in his general guidance: the moral issue, justice, peace and security, and economic prosperity. To Caliph Ali, it was important that the four issues were to be integrated together to achieve general prosperity in the community.

Structure of society

After laying down the general objective of governorship, the caliph went on to furnish more details. He went on to divide the community into seven sectors: the army, judges, executive officers and clerks, cultivators, traders, industrialists and the poor, the destitute, the penniless and the disabled. He emphasised, however, that all sectors are dependent on each other.

The army and the subjects

"The army is the fortress of the subjects and the means of peace, without which the subjects cannot exist, while the army can only be maintained by the funds fixed by God in the revenues of the subjects".

Judges

"These (the above) two classes cannot exist without the judges, the executives and the secretaries who pass judgments about contracts, collect revenues and are depended upon in special and general matters".

Trade and industry

"These (above) classes cannot exist except with traders and men of industry, who provide necessities for them, establish the markets and make it possible for others not to do all this with their own hands".

The poor and needy

"The lowest economic class in society is the class of the needy and the destitute the support and help of whom is an obligation laid down by God".

After highlighting the general structure of society and the importance of its integration, the fourth caliph continued to discuss each sector individually.

Agriculture

He stressed the importance of the agricultural sector stating that on its prosperity depended the prosperity of other sectors. The governor should "keep an eye on the cultivation of land more than on the collection of land tax because revenue cannot be raised without cultivation and whoever asks for revenue without looking after cultivation ruins the area and brings death to the people". Catering for the needs of cultivators and the removal of their distress "is an investment made in them . . . (this) brings confidence in them because of the justice extended to them".

Traders and industrialists

These are equally important to society and its prosperity because "they are sources of profit and the means of the provision of useful articles. They bring them from distant and far-flung areas throughout the land and sea, plains and mountains, from where people cannot come and to where they do not dare go". The state has a responsibility towards traders and industrialists by giving them professional advice and information, "give them good counsel whether they be settled (shop-keepers), traders or craftsmen". But traders and industrialists may abuse their economic power through monopolistic activities which might harm the community, "they hoard goods for profiteering and fix high prices for goods, which is a source of harm to the people and a blot on the officers in charge". In such a case the state would step in to rectify the situation, "stop them from hoarding because the Prophet has prohibited it". But the punishment for the offence should not be too severe, "whoever committed hoarding after being prohibited give him exemplary but not excessive punishment". As for market conditions, "the sale should be smooth, with correct weights and prices, not harmful to party, the seller or the purchaser". In summary, it was a self-regulated market with government surveillance.

Civil service sector

The sector was represented in the caliph's view in judges, executive officers and the clerical establishment. Judges were to be selected carefully from those who should be "most ready to stop (to ponder) on doubtful points, most regardful of arguments, least annoyed at the quarrel of litigants, most patient at propping into matters and most fearless at the time of passing judgment". They should be reasonably rewarded with no power over them from other administrative ranks. Executive officers should be tested before being appointed and should not be appointed on grounds of partiality and favouritism to avoid injustice and unfairness. Also, they should be generously rewarded so that they may not "have an eye upon the funds in their custody". But they should be observed by the state and be under the surveillance of trusty observers as that would urge them to preserve trust and competence. The importance of the clerical establishment lies in its role in smoothing and speeding up governmental communications. Secretarial workers should be chosen with care because they were entrusted with government documents which contained policies and confidential information. The selection of those members of staff should not be only on the basis of the impression they might project, but they should be also tested and reference from previous employment should be considered. To organise their work the establishment should be divided into departments and one chief should be in charge of each department. Finally, the work of that establishment should be viewed with great care since if any defect of the secretaries was overlooked, the government would be held responsible for it.

The prosperity of society

This, in the views of the fourth caliph Ali, therefore, depended upon three main issues: moral values, economic development and just distribution of economic resources. Moral values based on the teachings of Islam were essential to the prosperity of the community to avoid the misuse of economic prosperity and to preserve a sound social structure. Economic development relied on the acknowledgement of the importance of various sectors in society and the need to achieve economic integration among those sectors. The fourth caliph looked at society as being divided economically into various interrelated sectors each of which should be of the focal attention of government in the process of development. The classification brings to mind Plato's classification in his Republic, though at the time of the fourth caliph Greek philosophy was not yet translated by the Arabs. Although the role of the agricultural sector in economic development was particularly emphasised in Caliph Ali's thought, anticipating in that the thought of the physiocratic school, the important role of trade was also stressed, foreseeing in that the thought of the mercantilistic school. The service sector, including the army, had also an important role to play in economic development and the role of government in the development was particularly important. A just distribution of economic resources was also of paramount importance in the process of development. The economic development for the fourth caliph, and indeed for caliphs in general, was not confined to the development of production but it would also extend to cover the distribution of the value of production among the population. To use modern economic terms, it was not only the increase in the value of national product, or national income, that concerned him but also how the national product was allocated to the individuals in the community. He used an interesting expression to refer to the equitable distribution of national income. To him, the optimally just distribution of income in the process of economic development was the one in which the increase in an individual's wealth was not accompanied by a decrease in another's. Such a concept of optimal distribution is very near, if not identical, to Pareto's concept of efficient distribution.

Without doubt, the economic thought of the fourth caliph Ali was particularly rich. As early as the mid seventh century he tackled economic issues and anticipated economic ideas that became of interest to economists subsequently.

By the death of Caliph Ali in 661 the Rightly-Guided Caliphate, al Khilafah al-Rashīda, came to an end, giving way to a new era of Islamic government: dynasties. The first of these was the Umayyad dynasty that lasted for ninety years.

CHAPTER FOUR

THE DYNASTIC CALIPHATES THE UMAYYADS AND THE REFORMS (661 A.C.–750 A.C.)

Introduction

The period under examination in this chapter is a particularly interesting period for various reasons. First, the period marked the change of the Islamic caliphate to a dynastic system; second, it witnessed a move toward Islamic urbanisation on a large scale; third, the period witnessed a further expansion of the political borders of the Islamic state which led to a substantial increase in the size of trade, and fourthly, during that time the Islamic state reformed monetary policy and streamlined the administrative system. The Umayyad period seemed to have paved the way for the development advances in the Abbasīd caliphate that followed.

The Caliphate and the Dynasty

No sooner had the fourth Rightly Guided Caliph Ali been assassinated in 661 than Mu'awiyah, who established himself as the head of the province of Greater Syria, al-Sham, declared himself the new head of state. Before long, al-Ĥassan, the older son of the Caliph Ali, who was regarded by Ali's followers as his spiritual successor, abdicated. The lack of a similar military support to that of Mu'awiyah, a desire to prevent a further bloodshed and perhaps less inclination towards politics, persuaded al-Ĥassan to retire.

The ascension of the Umayyads to power marked a dramatic change in the system of the caliphate: the transfer of the caliphate from an elective into a hereditary system. The mastermind behind the change was Mu'awiyah, the founder of the Umayyad state (Al-Ťabarī). Without denying the right of Muslims to elect their own caliph, Mu'awiyah introduced his son, Yazīd, to the Muslim community as his legitimate successor claiming that while this would help avoid bloodshed over the new successorship it would not breach the basis of the elective system since an oath of allegiance would still be required by Muslims to approve of the new Caliph. That was the theory, but the reality was different. During his life, Mu'awiyah secured the approval of his son Yazīd as the prospective Caliph by persuading the notable Muslim leaders to pay homage to him. The few who did not agree were regarded as rebels and were left for Yazīd's sword to silence in due course. On the ascension of Yazīd to power after his father's death, a revolt erupted in Iraq and another in al-Ĥijaz. The Iraqi revolt, which was headed by al-Ĥusayn, the younger son of Caliph Ali, was easily crushed after the withdrawal of the Iraqis' support and the massacre of al-Ĥusayn and his family by the Syrian soldiers in 680 A.C.. The revolt in al-Ĥijaz led to an assault on al-Medīnah in 683, resulting in it being looted by the Syrian soldiers for three days. Makkah was also besieged and attacked by catapults, which resulted in the burning the Ka'aba itself. Eventually, peace was established in al-Ĥijaz in 692 by forcefully eliminating the last opposition. When local disturbances erupted they were crushed with vigorous force. With an attitude like that of the province governor al-Ĥajjaj who threatened, "I see heads ripe for cutting and I am the one who is going to collect them", and "I will beat you as straying camels are beaten", (Al-Ťabarī), peace, as an outcome of fear, was eventually restored.

Mu'awiyah's innovation of the dynastic caliphate became the rule rather than the exception and from the Mu'awiyah's caliphate onwards the caliphate became a dynasty.

A further change, though not as dramatic, was also notable in the caliphate: the Caliph no longer mixed with the public (or slept under trees as a foreign delegate once found caliph Umar), they kept themselves aloof, surrounded by a court, appearing in congregational prayers escorted by guards and establishing ceremonial practices. To Muslims, the Umayyad caliphate marked the beginning of a kingdom, "Mulk", rather than a caliphate (Hitti, 1963).

After ninety years in power, the Abbasids—yet another dynasty that descended from al-Abbās, the Prophet's uncle, overthrew the Umayyads. Rivalry over the caliphate, or the kingdom, gave way to the growing influence of the Abbasids who developed their influence in the eastern side of the empire in Khurasān and Iraq, making an alliance with the Alids, the long-time rivals of the Umayyads (Al-Ťabarī). The founder of the Abbasids was the Caliph Abū-al-Abbās

(750–754) who is nicknamed al-Saffāh, the generous or, with reference to the way he treated his enemies, the bloodshedder. At the peak of the Abbasīd reign, particularly during the time of al-Rashīd (786–809), the Islamic empire reached its golden age.

The Abbasīd caliphate, however, suffered a number of setbacks, which started with the civil war between al-Rashīd's two sons over the caliphate. Some regard the dispute as between the Persians, supporting al-M'mun whose mother was Persian, and the Arabs, supporting a l-Amin whose mother was an Arab (Ĥassan, 1959). When the Abbasīd Caliph became weak, separatist movements arose in the east and west of the empire and some succeeded in establishing independent dynastic governments. This led to the dismemberment of the empire and the further weakness of the central government. Interestingly, although those local dynasties were independent of the central caliphate, they kept their symbolically spiritual link with the Caliph who by that time became only a figurehead. "Is it not ironic that revenues are collected in the name of the Caliph while the Caliph does not get from that a penny!" exclaimed the powerless Caliph al-Mu'tamid, 870–892 (ibid.). From time to time, a Caliph would rise to restore the political power of the caliphate but that was not always consistent as it depended on the relative power of both the commander of the Turkish army, the Sultan, and the power of the caliph (Lapidus, 2002). Eventually attacks on the Islamic empire came from outside, the first of these was the first Crusade in 1096. But the final blow came from the Mongols who captured Baghdad and killed the last of the Abbasīd Caliphs in 1258. Despite the political disturbances in the Islamic empire, particularly during the last phase of the Abbasīd regime, the period witnessed much progress in education, science, culture, and economic development as shown below.

Islamic Expansion and the Need for Administrative Reform

The Islamic territorial expansion during the Umayyad reign went in three main directions: north, west and east. On the northern front, the development of the Islamic fleet enabled the state to compete with the Byzantine in the Mediterranean Sea and put the Byzantine capital, Constantinople, under siege from the direction of the sea. The capital was put under siege three times between 661 and 714.

However, it never surrendered. Indeed, it was not until 1453 that the Byzantine capital was taken and Byzantine rule in Constantinople was overthrown by the Turks under Muhammad II "the Conqueror". Under the Umayyads the Muslim army, nevertheless, had succeeded in putting some strategic islands under its control: Cyprus, Rhodes and Crete, which helped put the Mediterranean trade route under the partial control of the Islamic state (Hitti, 1963). On the western front, Muslims had more long-term success than that in the north. By 682 the Byzantines were defeated in North Africa and the Islamic army penetrated the North African coast as far as the Atlantic. However, a revolt by the inhabitants of the area, the Berbers, erupted, which led to the taking of North Africa out of the control of the Umayyad government for some years. By 705 the North African coast was regained by the central government and the Umayyads restored their control over the area permanently (ibid.).

The control of North Africa and the successful recruitment of the Berbers in the Islamic army helped extend Islamic rule towards the Iberian Peninsula, Spain. In 711, the Muslim expedition crossed the Mediterranean strait into the peninsula, which, with further reinforcement, led to the fall of the Visigothic kingdom to the Berber Arab army (Ĥassan, 1959). However, Charl Martel interrupted the advance of the Muslim army between Tours and Poitiers in 732. On the eastern front, the Umayyad Caliph continued their expansionist plans. After subjugating the revolt in Iraq successfully, they dispatched two troops to the east: one marched from Khurasān to the valley of the Indus and the other went to the northeast borders of Khurasān, the countries of "beyond the river". By 713, the Islamic conquests reached the lower valley and delta of the Indus, capturing Multan, Lahore and Kangara in the north, and al-Daybul on the Indian Ocean. On the "beyond the river" front, Balkh fell in 705, Bukhara was conquered in 709, and Samarqand, Khwarism and Farghanah were put under the Arab domain by 715. By the occupation of Tashkand in 751, under the Abbasids, Muslims established their authority in Central Asia (ibid.). The removal of political barriers helped, and with the security of trade routes and development, this aided administrative and economic reform and promoted trade between the provinces of the empire, as will be examined shortly.

Administrative and Economic Reforms

The Umayyad period was significant for its administrative reforms. Despite his unpopularity among early historians as the man who transferred the spiritual caliphate into a hereditary kingdom and the first head of state who set himself remote from the reach of ordinary Muslims, Mu'awiyah is credited for a few creditable administrative initiatives. The establishment of the institution of postal service, *al-Barīd*, the establishing the bureau of registry, which developed subsequently during the Umayyad and the Abbasīd regimes to well-organised systems of state bureaux, the Arabicisation of state administration, and monetary and other reforms are some notable examples.

The Institution of Postal Service

Although the institution of the postal service was meant to serve the state primarily by linking the Caliph with his provincial governors in a speedy and an organised manner, the service was extended to the public at substantial cost. Postal points were built across the routes at interval distances of twelve miles where fresh animals, mules and horses in Persia, and camels in Syria and Arabia, were ready to transfer the post. Pigeons were also used in what might be called the airmail service. The postal service became of vital importance to the state, so much so that the Umayyad Caliph Abd-al-Mālik (685–705) is reported to have said to his chief-of-staff, "I fully delegate to you the administrative affairs of what comes to my door except for four: the caller of prayer; he is the caller of God, the night caller; a need must have driven him to call otherwise he would have slept until morning, the post; the delay of the post might spoil people's planned journeys, and the food when it comes" (Ĥassan, 1959). During the Abbasīd reign, the postal service was further organised and plans of routes were kept in the postal headquarters in the capital Baghdad. This proved useful to travelers, merchants, pilgrims and, later, geographical researchers. The postal service had a further function as not only transporting mail but also transferring to the caliph the news of any potential political disturbances and/or governor's negligence. For the importance of the postal service a special government department, *dīwān*, was established in the Abbasīd government to organise the service. The head of the postal department,

Sahib-al-Barīd, seemed to have occupied an important role in the government as not only the postmaster-general, but also the chief of the intelligence service, *Sahib-al-Barid wal-akhbar*. He was accountable to the Caliph, while accountable to him were the local postmasters who were to report to him on the state of the service in their provinces and the conduct of provincial governors. Government expenditures had increased accordingly to cover the cost of the service and special allowances had to be made in the state budget under the heading of the postal bureau, *dīwān al-Barīd*.

The Establishment of the State Bureau

The establishment of the state bureau could be said to have been initiated by the second Caliph Umar. After conquering Iraq and Greater Syria Caliph Umar established a registry office to organise the allocation of state revenue from the land tax, al-Kharāj, to Muslims (Al-Ťabarī). At the top of the registration list came the Prophet's kinsfolk, followed by Muslims who embraced Islam first and ended by Muslims who converted to Islam at a later stage. The payments varied in a similar fashion, "I do not equate those who fought with the Prophet with those who fought against him", were Umar's famous words as mentioned in the previous chapter. With the complexity of the state administration during the Umayyads and the Abbāsids as a result of the expansion of the state there was a need to establish a new system of administration. Besides the postal bureau, as mentioned above, new administrative offices were established: the bureau of correspondence, *dīwān-al-rasa'il*, and the bureau of seal, *dīwān-al-khātim* (Al-Ťabarī). The main functions of the bureau of correspondence were: (a) to supervise the correspondence between the Caliph and his province governors, (b) to keep copies of the caliph's outward-mail in special files for control and future reference, (c) to supervise the state archive, and (d) to organise public announcements and declarations issued by the Caliph to his subjects (ibid.). The head of the bureau occupied an important role in the state administration and was accountable to the Caliph directly. Given the importance and sensitivity of information coming from the provinces that might be reflecting the conditions of law and order in the state and the pre-warning of any potential discontent among the subjects, the postal service could be viewed as analogous to the intelligence centres of our modern state. As in the case of the bureau of correspondence, Mu'awiyah established the bureau of seal, *dīwān-al-khātim*, for the purpose of controlling the state documents. It aimed to: (a) prevent the misuse of the caliph's stamp of approval, (b) ensure that the caliph's letters were sealed and stamped by a special stamp, and consequently, (c) prevent the carrier from opening up the letters and changing their content. The head of this bureau was also accountable to the Caliph directly because of the sensitivity of his job (Al-Ťabarī).

The system of administration was reorganized further under the Abbasids. While the functional classification of the administration was still maintained, the postal service bureau, the correspondence bureau, the stamps bureau, as well as the army bureau, finance bureau, caliphate residency expenses bureau, were divided further into provincial bureau and central bureau. While the provincial bureau aimed to help the governors' administrative control over the affairs of the provinces, the central bureau was designed to help the state in the capital to monitor the affairs of each province (Ĥassan, 1959). Each bureau in the capital and the provinces was divided further into two main sub-bureau: administrative bureau, *dīwān-al-asl*, and financial control bureau, *dīwān-al-zimam*. While the former was related to administrative matters such as the administration of the collection of taxes, the latter was concerned with the financial and accounting control aspects of these activities. An independent head accountable to the caliph's deputy was in charge of each sub-bureau. This indicates that the government of the day recognised the importance of the need for skilled and specialist employees for different types of jobs.

The introduction of a central auditing bureau or what is known in modern time as the Central Auditing Office, was a notable development in the organisation of the financial control of the state that took place during the time of the Abbasīd Caliph al-Mahdi (775–785). The establishment of the new bureau was attributed to al-Mahdi's assistant Umre ibn-Bari'a who was appointed to supervise the work of the financial control bureau (Al-Rayyis, 1977). Ibn-Bari'a is reported to have thought of an independent bureau that would be accountable to him directly, which would help him exercise tight control over the work of the financial control bureau. He therefore established *dīwān-al-zimmah*, plural of *zimam*, or the equivalent to a modern

Central Auditing Office. The head of *dīwān-al-zimmah* was accountable to him, the caliph's deputy, directly, which, with the direct link, guaranteed the autonomy of the bureau and its employees at both the central and provincial levels and their independence from the administrative authority at both levels. In effect, there were two types of financial control in the state: internal control, or internal auditing, and external control, or external auditing. While the internal control was for the benefit of the province governors and carried out by their officers, the external control was for the benefit of the central government and was undertaken by officers under the direct command of the central government. Interestingly enough, accounting and financial control systems of modern times are based on a similar system of dual control: internal and external control systems. While the former is exercised for the benefit of the internal users of information, who are mainly the organisation managers, the latter, the external control, or auditing, is carried out for the benefit of the external users of information, who are mainly the owners and shareholders.

The Arabicisation of the State Administration

The Arabicisation of the state administration is attributed to the Umayyad Caliph Abd-al-Mālik (685–705) and his son al-Walīd (705–715), (Al-Ṭabarī). The process was twofold: changing the language of the public registers from Greek and Persian to Arabic, and the creation of an Arab body of state officials. The changing of language in the official registers helped to: (a) reinforce the Arab characteristics of the state administration, (b) reduce or eradicate the reliance on non-Muslims or non-Arab Muslims in administering state records, (c) promote the Arabic language among non-Arab Muslims, (d) promote Arabic writing and calligraphy, and (e) transferred administrative posts to the Arabs and the Arabic speaking Muslims.

Caliph Abdel-Mālik, and al-Walīd after him, arranged for the tax registers to be translated from Greek and Persian into Arabic. The changeover was made in 697 in Iraq, in 700 in Syria and Egypt, and shortly afterwards in Kurasan (Lapidus, 2002). The Arabiciation move was also directed towards state officials. In the first decades of the Arab state the administration had been undertaken by Greeks and Persian-speaking officials serving in the new occupied land being inherited from the two older empires. However, by 700 a new generation of Arab-speaking officials came to power and with their descendants formed the secretarial vertebral column of the Arab-Muslim empire until the tenth century (ibid.).

Monetary Reform

The study of historical monetary changes reveals that the changes are, invariably, a result of the growing perception of the heads of state of their political autonomy and their need for a means of demonstrating the economic independence of their states. Various factors, however, would play an important role in developing such a perception. During the Prophet's time the unification of Arabia under a religio-political banner with a view to expansion into the Byzantine and the Persian borders seemed to have occupied the Prophet's attention so much so that he accepted the prevailing pre-Islamic Roman and Persian money as a means of exchange. An additional reason could be that the early state of Islam was not yet of the size or complexity that would necessitate a coinage of its own, nor did the state have the international recognition of the time that would make its coin acceptable in the Persian and Byzentine lands. With the development of the state during caliph Umar's time, Umar took the first attempt towards changing the form of money by superscribing Arabic and Qur'ānic writing on the prevailing coinage and it was not until the reign of the Umayyads that the Arabic coinage started to appear (Al-Ṭabarī). Abd-al-Mālik, the Umayyad caliph, was the first to have struck the Arabic golden dinar and the silver dirham in 695 (ibid.) as part of the wide process of Arabicisation of state administration.

The monetary change, or reform, at the time of Abd-al-Mālik, which was a reflection of the establishment of a consolidated state by the Umayyad Caliph, had both political and economic consequences. The following are most notable (Hitti, 1963):

a. the reinforcement of the sovereignty of the state as reflected in its own independent coinage,
b. the collection of taxes at a unified monetary unit instead of the Persian coin in Persia and that of the Romans in Syria and Egypt,
c. the further emphasis on the need for money-changers, who were

more able than others to realise the value of the new money in relation to the existing currency,

d. the emergence of a form of banking operations, and
e. the spread of financial instruments such as the "*ruq'a*", an order of payment, the "*sakk*", drawn on the banker with whom the drawer had an account; hence the word cheque in the European language, and the "*ĥawālah*", a form of a bill-of-exchange by which the debtor would transfer the debt to his own debtor, or to another person able to pay the debt to the original creditor, (Goitein, 1967), as discussed below.

Islamic Urbanisation

The first feature of the Islamic urbanisation could be said to have started with the building of the mosque in al-Medīnah after the emigration of the Prophet. The mosque was not only a place of worship but also a centre of learning and a gathering place where Muslims discussed their affairs in war and peace. The mosque in Islam also developed a further function by using it as a depot of spoils of war until distribution. The differentiation between the mosque in Islam, and the temple and church in Judaism and Christianity is based on the same differentiation between Islam on the one hand and Judaism and Christianity on the other: while Islam is a religious and a political community, Judaism and Christianity are religious communities. The mosque, therefore, represented the nucleus part of the Muslim city upon which, with the market and, later on, the government office, "Dar- al-Khilafah", the city was established. Islamic conquests introduced an early need to establish new cities, the first of which were founded in the reign of the second Caliph Umar. With a view to keeping the army apart from the inhabitants of the conquered land and causing the least possible disruption to the inhabitants, Caliph Umar ordered the building of special cities to accommodate the soldiers and their families (Al-Ṫabarī). The most important of these cities were al-Kufa, which was built on the Euphrates River near al-Hira, al-Basra, which was strategically founded on the head of the Persian Gulf for easy communication with the central government in al-Medīnah, and al-Fustat, which was established below the delta of the Nile in Egypt. Umar's initiative was followed by Caliphs after him and during the Umayyad reign al-Mosul and al-Wasīt were established in Iraq. Al-Qayrawan (Tunisia) was also founded in North Africa to serve as a military base for the Islamic expansion in the North African strip. However, in other areas, such as Iran, the Muslim army settled on the outskirts of existing towns and cities (ibid.).

During the Abbasīd reign the foundation was laid in 762 for the establishment of the city that would occupy a prominent place in history for centuries to come: Baghdad. The new city, which was chosen as the capital of the Abbasids, was located at the intersection of three river routes and two land routes, which made the site, as the Abbasīd Caliph al-Mansūr said, "excellent as a military camp", besides "here is the Tigris to put us in touch with lands as far as China and bring us all that the seas yield as well as the food products of Mesopotamia, Armenia and their environs, then there is the Euphrates to carry for us all that Syria, al-Raqqah and adjacent lands have to offer" (Al-Ťabarī, Hitte, 1963). In the mid ninth century, Baghdad, the "city of peace", was larger than the Imperial Rome and Constantinople together at that time, and as big as Paris at the end of the nineteenth century (Hitti, 1963). The establishment of new cities helped promote economic development in and around the cities. Soldiers needed to be fed and clothed and weapons needed to be made. Efforts were made to encourage agriculture, trade and crafts. The swamps around al-Kufa were drained and brought under cultivation, the salt marches to the east of al-Basra were reclaimed, and the irrigation systems in Iran were improved, which helped encourage agriculture, enhance trade and stimulate economic growth (Lapidus, 1988). Moreover, the economic growth of the cities attracted non-Arabs with various crafts and skills to settle, which helped integrate the Arab and the non-Arab dwellers and transform the city society into a more cosmopolitan structure. In addition, settlement helped transform the Bedouin into a more sedentary person. For example, as al-Basra developed into an important administrative capital, a centre of cloth manufacturing and a trading city connected with Iran, India, China, and Arabia. Arab settlers became merchants, traders and artisans (Lapidus, 1988).

Agriculture

Agriculture occupied a paramount position in the economic chart of the Islamic state from its early days. The Qur'ānic verses that refer to the bounties God has given us from land and agricultural produce and the need to work continuously to preserve and develop such production are numerous. The Prophet's encouragement of agricultural development is reflected in the Sunnah in which he is reported to have said: "He who sows grain or plants a plant will have as his alms all whatever is eaten from it be it by a person, beast or bird" and his reply when he was asked which kind of property was the best, "A field! As long as the rain pours down upon it, and the owner cultivates it, and gives the due Zakāh on it on the day of harvesting" (Ŝaĥīĥ Muslim). The Prophet also laid down two main principles of land ownership, which were to be followed by successors after him: firstly, "The original rights of ownership in land belong to God and His Prophet and then to you. But he who revives dead land has the right of ownership to it", and secondly, "If one neglects (enclosed) land for three years, it belongs to him who revives it afterwards" (ibid.). Islam, after all, found a great support in the sedentary community of al-Medīnah. There are however other *Aĥadīth* attributed to the Prophet which if misinterpreted would lead to the misconception that the Prophet discouraged settlement in land through agriculture, but these *Aĥadīth* should be viewed as particularly related to the discouragement of giving up the pursuit of Holy war, *jihād*, under the false premise of being engaged in agriculture (Al-Rayyis, 1977).

During the reign of the second Caliph Umar when the Islamic state experienced political and an economic expansion that was not experienced before, the Caliph was active in emphasising the following three aspects of state agricultural policy (ibid.):

(a) on the ownership of existing land, "Whoever revives unowned dead land becomes its owner" and "There is no right to the holder of the land after three years of no utilisation",
(b) on the ownership of newly conquered agricultural land, the ownership was to rest with the state, representing the community, and the farming of the land was to be left to the actual cultivators even if they were not Muslims, and

(c) the state had the duty of digging canals and establishing bridges to help develop agriculture and related economic activities, "If a mule stumbled in Iraq Umar would be responsible for it".

The second Caliph demonstrated that the agricultural productivity of the land was his main concern. By qualifying the ownership of existing land Umar provided an incentive to the owner to look after it and by leaving the conquered agricultural land in the hands of its keepers he recognised that:

(a) the original farmers were more able to cultivate the land than the Arabs
(b) the keepers would have more incentive to work hard than the case would otherwise be, and with a fair system of land taxation this would help
(c) improve the agricultural productivity of the land and the revenue to the state.

Agriculture continued to occupy an important position in the state economy during the dynastic caliphate of both the Umayyads and the Abbasids. On the instruction of the heads of state, province governors paid considerable attention to the agricultural sector. Of these governors, al-Ĥajjaj, the governor of Iraq under the Umayyads, is a distinguished example. Despite his unpopularity among historians for his cruelty and ruthlessness, al-Ĥajjaj is reported to have been active in developing the agriculture sector. His policy was twofold: (a) preserving the existing land in its most suitable form and (b) establishing new communities on newly reclaimed land. He embarked on digging up rivers and canals in Iraq, reclaiming agriculture land and building up towns in the reclaimed areas (Al-Ťabarī). To help establish new communities on the new land he brought thousands of working cattle (buffalos) and agricultural labourers from other areas, either from the same province or from other provinces, and encouraged them to settle on the reclaimed land (ibid.). Force, which was not strange to al-Ĥajjaj, was resorted to when the need arose to reinforce his ideas of agricultural development. By force he forbade the internal emigration of agricultural workers to the main cities, and although this might be regarded as harsh, it reflected al-Ĥajjaj's awareness of the economic consequences of the problem. Similar actions are not unknown to be taken by modern governments when faced with similar problems. The policy however was abandoned when it was criticised as not being particularly Islamic. This was another example of al-Ĥajjaj's economic ideas, which were often discussed in histories of the period as a mixture of ruthlessness and shrewdness. The irony was that in which he forbade people from slaughtering cows for food when an economic hardship was experienced (Al-Ťabarī). Although that sounded ironic, as expressed by the poets of the time, "when we complained to him of land destruction, he forbade us from beef ingestion" (Al-Ťabarī), it was indeed a necessary step to stop people from eating up an important means of production. Besides being a source of labour, cattle were also needed as an important source of fertilizers.

In Egypt, a similar policy to that of al-Ĥajjaj in Iraq was followed where families were brought from other provinces to develop areas in Balbees in Lower Egypt. As a result, the number of families in the area increased during the Umayyads time and by the end of their reign this reached three thousands families (Al-Maqrizi, 1324H, Hitti, 1963), which was a considerable number by the standard of the day.

The importance of agriculture as a main economic activity and source of finance continued during the Abbasīd reign. Special schools were established to provide the necessary study, research and training as to the types of plants, suitability of soil, fertilisation and methods of irrigation. Irrigation, which was based on the general policy of making water free for all, was well organised. It took the form of a comprehensive network of irrigation canals in Egypt, Iraq, Yemen, Persia and other areas. A special team of engineers was responsible for the maintenance of canals and dams. Also, a special bureau, the bureau of water '*dīwān al-maa*', was also established to register the quantity of water supply in each area, observe the changes in water levels and classify the cultivable land in accordance with the availability of water and the system of irrigation for the purpose of taxation. With ten thousand workers (Ĥassan 1959), the bureau seemed to have been of a considerable size.

Trade and Commerce

With the expansion of the Islamic state from India in the east to Spain in the west, political barriers were removed, which, with security, urbanisation, and the diversity of agricultural and manufacturing products, helped promote trade in the Islamic world. Several types of commodities were traded: food products, animal stock, timber and the products of the forest, metals, and textiles, products of stone and soil, fish and sea food, writing materials, medicinal products, and slaves (Goitein, 1963). Trade routes connected Europe with the Islamic world mainly via Syria, Egypt, Tunisia and Sicily. The main commodities that were imported from and exported to Europe were timber and foodstuff respectively. Egypt seemed to have enjoyed a particularly important location on the Indian trade route which stretched from Indonesia and Samarta in the east, passing through the ports of the Red Sea and Old Cairo in Egypt, to North Africa and Spain in the west. As indicated in Cairo Geniza documents, Old Cairo served as terminus both for the Mediterranean and the Indian trade (Goitein, 1963). The commodities that came from or through India and other countries of the Indian Ocean were mainly spices, though other commodities were also included. In the Geniza papers, a provisional list of goods coming from the Indian direction showed that the goods consisted of (Goitein, 1963):

> Spices, aromatic, dyeing and vanishing plants and medical herbs (47%),
> Brass and bronze vessels (15%),
> Indian silk and other textiles made mainly of cotton (10%),
> Iron and steel (8%),
> Tropical fruits, such as coconuts (7%),
> Pearls, beads, cowry shells and ambergris (5%),
> Chinese porcelain, Yemenite stone pots and African ivory (4%),
> Shoes and other leather-works (3%), and
> Timber (1%).

The eastbound goods, as shown in the same list, consisted of (ibid.):

> Textiles and clothing (35%),
> Vessels and ornaments of silver, brass, glass and other materials (22%),
> Chemicals, medicaments, soap, paper, books (18%),
> Foodstuff, such as cheese, sugar, raisins, olive oil and linseed oil for lamps (10%),
> Household goods, such as carpets, mats, tables, frying pans (7%),
> Metals and other ingredients for the copper industry (7%) and
> Coral, (1%).

This is only an example of one shipment, which is not necessarily an exhaustive list of the Indian trade. Moreover, short and long distance routes connected the Islamic provinces internally such as the routes between Syria and Egypt, Egypt and the North African coast, Egypt and Arabia, Iraq and Syria, and Iraq and Arabia. It is also interesting to note that merchants were of different religious persuasions: Muslims, Jews, Christians and Hindus, and business relationships between those of different religions were amicable. In the Geniza letters, merchants of various religions address each other with the same honouring and amicable epithets as the writer's own brethren (Goitein, 1963).

Generally, merchants consisted of various categories: producers and dealers, retailers and wholesalers, travellers and the stationary, and brokers and auctioneers. However, the line between each group in the category, and sometimes between one category and another, was not always clear-cut. For example, the producers of manufactured goods, who were mainly artisans, sold not only their own products but also the products of others and the wholesaler in textiles sold single pieces. Furthermore, the degree of diversification in the traded commodities seemed to have been rather wide. The merchant would deal in a wide range of commodities such as flax, silk and other textiles, olive oil, oriental spices, dyeing materials, metals, books, perfumes, jewelry, glass, corals, foodstuff, hides and leather, pitch, and a wide variety of household goods (Goitein, 1967). This was meant perhaps to reduce the level of business risk involved through diversification. Specialisation, nevertheless, existed and some traders became specialists in one type of goods. The cheese dealer, "*al-gabbān*", the milk dealer, "*al-labbān*", the perfume dealer, "*al-attār*", the indigo dealer, "*al-nīlī*", and the date dealer, "*al-tammār*", are examples of the cases where the family names of the dealers became associated with the type of goods in which they traded (ibid.).

Cooperation between merchants in distant countries seemed to be generally accepted as the "custom of the trade". Two merchants in different trading centres would buy and sell on behalf of each other in a very informal way with no commission paid but mutual services would be expected (Goitein, 1967). Besides selling and buying, the services also included the supervision of collecting business debts in the foreign country. The distant trade and the attempt of minimising costs made such cooperation worthwhile. In addition, a great deal of trust between the two merchants was necessary for the success of such cooperation. However, one would think that the information obtained by the merchant about the distant market, no matter how historical such information might be, would serve as a guideline to the merchant and a safeguard to the continuation of the cooperation, especially when both merchants know that such information was difficult to obtain. A dispute might arise, as the Geniza papers show, if the merchant thought that his counterpart did not act in his interest, which would put the cooperation into jeopardy. Trust, which would be enhanced gradually by the repetition of operations, the reputation of the merchant and the flow of information via travelling fellow merchants, made the system workable. Or, as Goitein (1967) says, "The fact remains that the Mediterranean trade, as revealed by the Cairo Geniza, was largely based, not upon cash benefits or legal guarantees, but on the human qualities of mutual trust and friendship".

Agency was also common as a means of running the business. The merchant would have a representative in the far market to render services to him for a fee or a commission, which varied depending upon the level of services. The representative, "*wakīl*", had three different interrelated tasks: (a) to represent the merchant in legal disputes, which explains why professional experience in law was required in representatives, (b) to provide storage facilities, which were provided on premises owned by the representative, and (c) to serve as a depositary for the merchants and a neutral arbiter between them (Goitein, 1967). The warehouse of the representative served also as a bourse for auctioning the goods and a postal address for merchants.

Legal Forms of Business

Turning our attention to the legal forms of business, we find that businesses, as shown in Figure 4.1 (see page 154), consisted of three main types: sole proprietorships, partnerships, commenda and state enterprises. The sole proprietor had the full authority of running the business, within the general rules of the Sharīʾah, and was liable for the business debt up to his own private fortune. Partnership was based on the conditions laid down by early Muslim jurists. The jurists divided commercial partnership into two main types: "*mufāwadah*" partnership, which could be translated as unlimited-authority partnership, and "*inān*" partnership, which could be translated as limited-authority partnership. The relationship between partners in the "*mufāwadah*" partnership is based on mutual surety and mutual agency, while it is based on the principles of mutual agency only in the "*inān*" partnership. This differentiation affects various aspects of the partnership: similarity of religion, level of authority, bases of profit sharing and financial liability. While the similarity of religion is necessitated in the "*mufāwadah*" partnership, it is not so required in the "*inān*" partnership. The partnership is operational as long as the non-Muslim partner observes the Sharī'ah in trade dealings otherwise it becomes invalidated. In addition, while the authority of the partner in the "*mufāwadah*" partnership is unlimited, that of the "*inān*" partnership in conditioned. Profit is allocated to the partners on the basis of their capital contributions to the business. However, a greater portion of profit might be allocated to the partner who manages the business in compensation for his work and effort. Nevertheless the losses have to be shared in proportion to the capital contributed by the partners, even if they agreed on different bases of allocating the profit. The reason behind the flexibility in allocating profits and the rigidity of allocating losses is that since, in case of a loss absorbing total capital, as in the event of liquidation, the loss would have to be born by the partners in proportion to their capital, the loss that does not absorb total capital should, therefore, be borne by the partners on the same basis. As for the financial liability of the partners, while this is unlimited in the "*mufāwadah*" partnership, it is generally limited in the "*inān*" partnership.

The commenda was another form of business operations. It is an arrangement in which an investor or a group of investors entrusts capital or merchandise to an agent-manager, who is to trade with it and then return to the investor(s) the principal and a previously agreed-upon share of the profit (Udovitch, 1970). As rewards for his labour, the agent-manager receives the remaining share of the profits. Any loss resulting from the exigencies of travel or from an unsuccessful business venture is borne exclusively by the investor(s); the agent is not liable for a loss of this nature, loosing only his expended time and effort (Udovitch, 1970). The commenda, which existed in Arabia before Islam, is referred to in Arabic by three different terms: *Mudārabah*, *Qirād* and *Muqāradah*. The three terms, however, mean the same thing; the difference is semantic and is related to linguistic derivation influenced by geographical locations. The pre-Islamic commenda was approved by the Prophet and became an Islamically acceptable form of business. In addition, religious differences are no barrier in the commenda; both Muslims and non-Muslims may engage in a commenda contract providing that the rules of the Sharī'ah be observed.

The Cairo Geniza papers show that the following points had to be taken into account when concluding a partnership or a commenda contract (Goitein, 1967):

1. The number and status of the contractors
2. The object of the contract and the aims pursued in it
3. The nature and extent of the contribution of the partners (capital, goods, premises and work) and the specific rights and privileges granted to each partner
4. The partners' share in profit and loss and their responsibility for the capital invested
5. Conditions governing expenditure for the partnership and living expenses of the partners
6. Conflict of interest; whether the partners could enter into other partnerships and commendas of similar objects
7. The duration of the partnership, except in the case of specific commercial ventures
8. The date of rendering accounts when interim accounts were required
9. Specific conditions of any kind
10. Eventually, in the absence of a certain condition, the generally accepted rules of the custom of the trade and current practice would be applied

With the wide geographical area of trade, several financial instruments were either introduced or modified from their Persian origin. The "*ruq'a*", which means in Arabic a piece of paper or writing material, referred to an order of payment, and the "*sakk*", which means an issued deed or document, was an order of payment drawn on the banker with whom the drawer had an account. The "*suftaja*" was another instrument, which originated from Persia, the use of which had been conditioned by Muslim jurists. Suftaja could be defined, according to the jurists, as the process of transferring a loan of money to be paid in a different place, or a different country, to avoid the risk of transport. Because of the risk involved in transporting the money, which was born entirely by the debtor without any financial reward, such as fees or wages, Muslim jurists viewed the suftaja as harmful to the debtor. On the other hand, it might be for the interest of the debtor to pay the loan back in another place or another country. Muslim jurists, therefore, conditioned the use of suftaja: first, if it benefited the creditor and harmed the debtor it is prohibited; second, if it benefited the debtor without any benefit to the creditor and the condition of the payment in another country is established by the creditor, it is allowed; and third, if it benefited both debtor and creditor, it is allowed (Al-Misri, 1984).

"*Al-Ĥawālah*" was another form of *suftaja*, where the debtor would transfer the debt to his own debtor, or to another person able to pay, to pay the debt to the original creditor. It involved three persons, or more, instead of two, which resembled the modern bill of exchange and from which the French word "aval", endorsement on bill of exchange, was originated. Also, *suftaja* were issued "payable to bearer". The use of *suftaja* was fairly well developed, especially inside Egypt itself, between Egypt and its immediate eastern neighbours, and between international centres such as Cairo and Baghdad (Goitein, 1967).

State Finance

The structure of state finance during the dynastic caliphates resembled that of the Rightly Guided Caliphate, though the magnitude of finance varied depending upon the political power of the state, its ability to keep law and order, the eruption of the separatist movements, and the state of economic prosperity. Minor changes were however noticed in the type of taxes imposed and the application of existing taxes. The Umayyad caliphs were more concerned with the reorganization of finances in various regions than introducing new taxes. Caliph Umar II (717–720) proposed a major revision of the rules and principles of taxation in order to achieve uniformity and equity to the taxation system. The caliph Hishām (724–743) followed the policies of his predecessor and tried to apply Umar II's taxation reforms to Khurasān, Egypt and Mesopotamia (Lapidus, 2002). During the Abbasīd caliphate, more types of taxes, such as market tax, were introduced, though these were of a minor magnitude. In addition, the application of some taxes witnessed some variations during the two dynastic caliphates. Non-Muslim clergymen were no longer exempt from Jizyah tax, though the poor and the old were still exempt, a change which was necessary after the increase of the wealth of the clergy (Al-Maqrizi, Hiti, 1963). Al-Kharāj, which was the main type of tax, occupied the attention of both the Umayyads and the Abbāsids. More surveys of the Egyptian land and a population census were carried out between the years 726 and 728 in order to exercise more control over the Kharāj revenue (ibid.). Other Sources were also developed during the Umayyad and the Abbasīd reign, such as revenue from publicly owned business enterprises.

Given the importance of state finance, as the topic that attracted the attention of writers in their first specialised work on Islamic economics in the late eighth century, it is worthwhile to shed more light on it. The framework of state revenue would show the state revenue divided into two main types: non-tax revenue and tax revenue, with each type divided further as shown below.

First: Non-Tax Revenue

Faiʾ

As mentioned earlier in chapter two, historically *Faiʾ* referred to the spoils of war, which were gained from the enemy when the enemy surrendered without any actual military combat. All the spoils of war in that case would go to the state with no share to the warrior. The definition of *Faiʾ*, as above, does not necessarily imply that in order for the spoils to be classified as *Faiʾ* the surrender would have to take place without any initial military action undertaken by the Muslim army. What was required to satisfy the conditions of *Faiʾ* was that the surrender would take place prior to any actual military engagement even if the enemy contemplated a battle. Surrender after a siege for example would still be regarded as submission without actual combat and accordingly the spoils would be categorised as *Faiʾ*. The importance of the definition lay in that it qualified the magnitude of the share of the state in the spoils. In case of surrender without fight the state had the right to all the spoils with no share for the warriors, but in circumstances of surrender after engagement, or defeat, the state had the right to only one-fifth of the spoils. Further discussion of the *Faiʾ*, the difference between *Faiʾ* and spoils of war and the way the revenue of the *Fai'* was to be spent was provided earlier in the second chapter and hence there is no need for repetition.

Sawāfi land, crown estates or fiefs

The term referred to the land, the ownership of which was transferred to the state because of several reasons. These are mainly: (a) the original owners deserted the land after the Islamic conquest, (b) the death of non-Muslim landowners in wars against Muslims without leaving heirs, and (c) the death of the landowner, Muslim or non-Muslim, without leaving heirs (Abū-Yūsuf). The first large scale appearance of *sawāfi* land took place during the Islamic expansion under the reign of the second caliph Umar when a large number of Persian and Byzantine owners abandoned their lands in Iraq and Syria. The state managed those lands on an economic basis and with revenue reported as ranging between 4,000,000 and 9,000,000 dirham (Al-Rayyis, 1977), which was a considerable sum by the standard of the day, *sawāfi* land seemed to have been of a great importance to the Islamic Treasury.

Although the land had been viewed as belonging to Muslims in general, a view which the second caliph Umar maintained, a change took place during the reign of the third caliph Uthmān which transferred the ownership of *sawāfi* land from the state to individuals. As said previously, the development started with a request from the governor of Syria, Mu'awiyah, to give him the land from which the Byzantine governors fled on the argument that his salary was not sufficient to cover his expenses.

Although the third Caliph Uthmān opened the door for a marked change in land ownership, his views could be based on the following sound reasons (Muĥammad, 1986):

i. the land was given to individuals on a rental, not ownership, basis,
ii. the new system would enhance the personal incentive of the keeper, and increase productivity
iii. it would alleviate the state public expenses as it would eliminate the state administrative cost from operating the lands,
iv. as a result of the above two factors, the net revenue from this land would increase.

This argument was supported by the substantial increase in the state revenue from this source, which increased from between 4,000,000 and 9,000,000 to 50,000,000 dirham during the reign of the third caliph (Al-Māwardī).

Nevertheless, Caliph Uthmān's introduction of the new system marked the beginning of feudalism in the economic history of Islam.

Therefore, what started as a request from the governor of Syria to the caliph, which was granted on the condition that the land would be rented not owned, led to the accumulation of land by Muʾawiyah and the caliphs after him, who developed a great passion for land ownership (Al-Ťabarī). This led to a considerable increase in the size of fiefs, which grew even further as a result of the application of the principle that a person could claim the ownership of barren land if he or she revived it. Although the rule was useful for agricultural development in principle, the adverse application was that when the Umayyad and Abbasīd caliphs revived vast areas of land they claimed the ownership of the land for themselves instead of adding it to that of the Treasury. Consequently, this increased the size of the royal fiefs.

The history of the Umayyad always finds an exception in the person of the outstanding Caliph Umar ibn-Abd al-Azīz, Umar II, (717–20) whose piety nicknamed him the fifth Rightly Guided Caliph. Denying the right of the preceding caliphs to give as gifts or inherit as legacies lands that belonged, or should have belonged, to the state, Umar annulled the transfer of such land to him or to other members of his family and transferred the ownership to the Treasury (Al-Ťabarī). But Umar was an exception. After him, caliphs reversed his decisions, took back their, or what they thought was their, land and resumed a policy that was temporarily interrupted. After the eclipse of the Umayyads and the rise of the Abbāsids, the policy of accumulating *sawāfi* land continued, but with new owners: the Abbasids who had a similar passion for land ownership. Inheriting all that the Umayyads left; they owned the existing fiefs and increased their size even further (Al-Rayyis, 1977).

Business Public Sector Revenue

Small as it was in comparison with *sawāfi* lands; a business sector was owned and run by the state. It was represented mainly in public baths, small shops, grinding mills, and lands on which shops were erected, all generating revenue to the state either through direct management or in the form of rent. These enterprises, and the revenue generated from them, seemed to have increased during the reign of al-Walīd ibn-Abd al-Mālik (705–15). During al-Walīd's reign a special bureau, *Dīwān al-Mustaghallat*, was established to run and supervise the activities of this government business sector (Al-Rayyis, 1977). The establishment of a special bureau to monitor the operations of this sector would indicate that the activities of this sector were of a significant size in comparison with other sectors.

Secondly: Taxes

One-fifth of the Ghanīmah, or the Khums (kums means one fifth)
The one-fifth levy, *khūms*, on the spoils of war, *Ghanīmah*, is stipulated in the Qur'ānic verses as revenues that would be put under the full disposal of the Prophet as the head of state. As mentioned earlier in chapter two, the manner of spending this revenue was also defined in the Qur'ān. Although the size of this source of state revenue was rather limited during the early period of the Islamic state during the Prophet's time, the source became more significant from the reign of the second caliph Umar (634–644) with the major expansion of the Islamic state.

Zakāh
We learned previously from chapters two and three that although the political dimension of the tax was emphasised by the first caliph Abū-Bakr in his treatment of the apostasy, the third caliph Uthmān decided that with the exception of Zakāh on pecuniary wealth Muslims may pay Zakāh, on behalf of the caliph, to whichever extent they saw fit judged by their own religious conscience. This policy continued during the Umayyad and the Abbasīd caliphates (Al-Ťabarī).

Jizyah
As stated earlier, while Zakāh was imposed on Muslims, Jizyah was levied on non-Muslims. This has been established in the Qur'ān. However, the tax was not charged on women or children, despite the state of their wealth, old men who were not capable to work nor had any wealth, or the new convert to Islam. All these principles,

which were mentioned earlier, were laid down by the Prophet and exercised by his successors in the Rightly Guided Caliphate. However, there were some modifications of the application of the Jizyah tax starting from the Umayyad caliphate. As a result of the increase in the wealth of non-Muslim clergies, the clergies were no longer exempt from the Jizyah tax, though the poor and the old were still exempt, (Al-Maqrizi, Hitti, 1963). In addition, the increase in the number of Christians converting to Islam was said to have raised the concern of the state, as that led to a notable reduction in the revenue of Jizyah. Suspecting that the conversion, or part of it, could have been an attempt to evade the tax, some province governors continued to collect the Jizyah from the new converts (ibid.). However, the Umayyad caliph Umar ibn-Abd-al-Azīz, Umar II, (717–720) decided to give the newly converts the benefit of the doubt and ruled that no Jizyah tax would be levied on converts regardless of the degree of originality in their conversion, "We were sent as Islamic preachers, not tax collectors", were his famous words (Al-Ťabarī). Interestingly, on the assumption that the new convert converted on the false pretence of accepting Islam, this convert would have to pay Zakāh instead.

This point could perhaps have been exaggerated as the financial benefit to the new convert would be represented in only the marginal difference between Jizyah before conversion and Zakāh after conversion. In addition, the new convert would have to take part in military activities after conversion, either in defending the borders or in launching new conquests. He was exempted from these activities as a non-Muslim. Conversion would not be appealing per se, therefore, for the possible risk of loss of life, unless the share in the spoils of war was particularly encouraging so much so that the risk involved was justified by potential gains. Adverse collection policies of collecting the jizyah by governors and their agents must have existed during that time in order for medieval historians to give the matter their attention. However, in order to highlight their dissatisfaction with injustice in the collection policies of some governors, or particular governors, historians had a justifiable reason to focus on the bad practice of these governors. For example, al-Ĥajjaj, the governor of Iraq (692–715) serving under the Umayyads (under Caliph Abd-al-Mālik, 685–705, and his son Al-Walīd, 705–715) is always a prime target for historians to attack and criticise, sometimes amusingly. Because of his oddity, shrewdness, cruelty and ruthlessness, and his biased devotion to the Umayyads against the rest of Muslims, al-Ĥajjaj, who no doubt provided historians with rich material, mostly adverse, had invariably, though consistently, been criticised by historians. In some cases the material provided about him becomes a source of a peculiar mixture of entertainment and bitterness, though it is still cited for condemnation. For example, to dissuade new converts from what he saw as false pretence of conversion, al-Ĥajjaj, oddly enough, is reported to have charged the new converts both Jizyah and Zakāh!, (ibid.).

Kharāj

Kharāj was a significant source of state finance. It was the tax imposed on the agricultural land that was left in the hands of the non-Muslim keepers on Islamic conquest. We recall from chapter three that a debate had arisen between the Muslim warriors and the second caliph Umar over the allocation of the conquered land to them as spoils of war. We recall that while the warriors demanded that the land should be distributed to them as *Ghanīmah*, after deducting one-fifth, *Khūms* to the state, the second caliph was in favour of keeping the ownership of the land in the hands of the state. The actual keepers of the land were its existing owners, but the ownership was that of the state, leaving the keepers to pay a Kharāj tax on the land according to its cultivability, "I impose Kharāj on them for the land they hold and levy a Jizyah on their persons" (Abū-Yūsuf) .

Kharāj land should not be confused with *sawāfī* land or Zakāh land. Kharāj land was the land that was left in the hands of its original non-Muslim owners at the time of Islamic conquest for the payment of kharāj. *Sawāfī* land was the land whose original non-Muslim owners had deserted, or died without leaving an heir, at the time of conquest, and as a result, the land was put under the direct administration of the state. Zakāh land was the land owned by Muslims, which was mainly in the Arabian Peninsula prior to Islamic conquests. The lands took their names from the tax or revenue generated from them. Kharāj land was the land on which Kharāj was imposed, Zakāh land was the land on which Zakāh was levied and *sawāfī* land was the land from which profit was generated. To the state, the revenue from each type of land was categorized accordingly: Kharāj, Zakāh and Sawāfī revenues (Abū-Yūsuf).

Initially Kharāj land, which was especially surveyed to determine various tax parameters, was taxed at a proportional rate that depended upon the type of produce, the difficulty of irrigation and the fertility of the land. The tax was modified later on, during the reign of al-Mahdi (775–785), when the crops sharing method replaced the proportional rate method (Abū-Yūsuf). On the other hand, Zakāh land was taxed at two rates, one higher than the other, depending upon the difficulty of irrigation, as stated in the Sunnah and shown previously. Furthermore, revenue from Zakāh land was not to be mixed with other types of land tax or revenue, as the revenue from Zakāh was to be spent in a particular manner specified in the Qur'ān, while the spending of the revenues form the other sources was not particularly specific.

Other types of taxes

Ushūr, or custom duties, was first imposed, as previously stated, at the time of the second caliph Umar, initially as a response to a similar tax imposed by foreign countries on the subjects of the Islamic state but later to be extended and applied to all goods crossing the borders by Muslims and non-Muslims. The tax continued during the Umayyads and the Abbāsids.

New taxes were introduced during the reign of the Abbasids. These were mainly (Al-Rayyis, 1977):

1. Market tax, which was first introduced in 784 under the reign of the caliph al-Mahdi (775–785) and was imposed on shops in the market. The rate seemed to have reached as high as 33 per cent, which led to a revolt in Egypt that lasted for two years.
2. Stamp duties on the sale of estate property imposed on the seller at a rate that reached 2 per cent.
3. Inheritance tax, the rate of which reached as high as one third. This tax seemed to have been introduced as late as the year 1252 under the reign of al-Mūsta'sim, the last of the Abbasīd caliphs.
4. Fishery tax, which was imposed on fish and other sea products. The tax seemed to have been directed at fishermen who would otherwise be able to avoid other types of tax. The tax revenue was used to maintain and improve the harbours.

After having looked at the development of Islamic society from the pre-Islamic period to the mid eighth century, examined the Islamic economic teachings in the Qur'ān and the Sunnah, synthesized the

Islamic economic thought of the Rightly-Guided Caliph and investigated the socio-economic environment of the first dynastic caliphate, we are now in a position to examine the first specialised work on Islamic economics. This is the beginning of our next chapter.

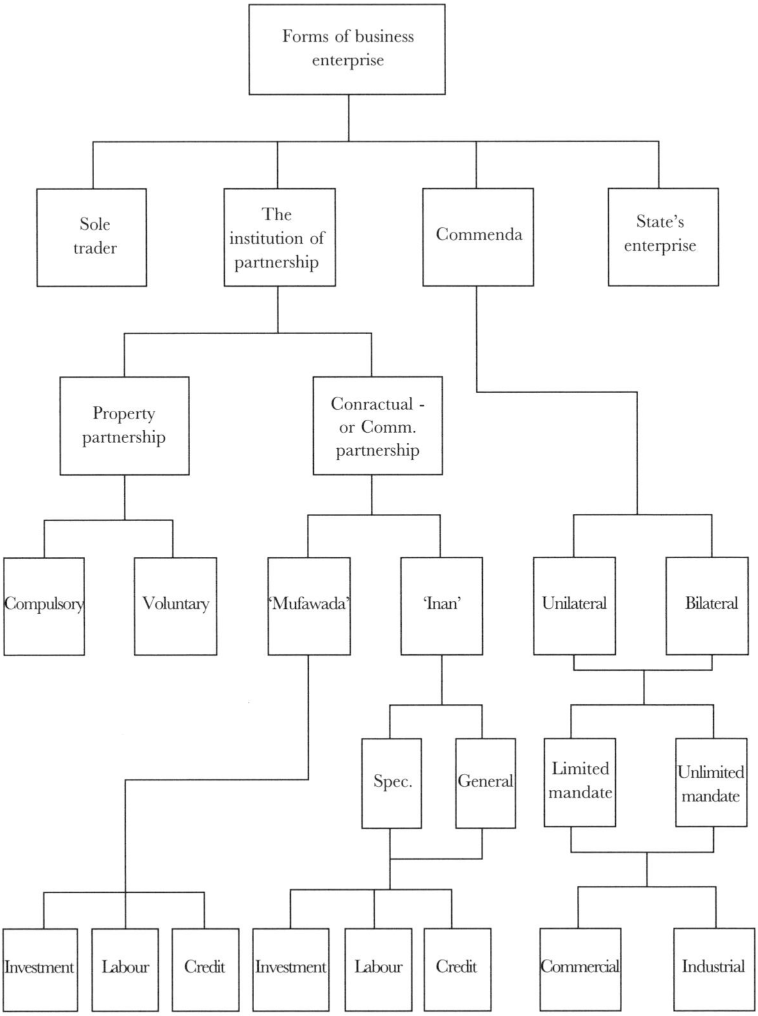

Figure 4.1: Legal Forms of Islamic Business (from El-Ashker, 1987)

CHAPTER FIVE

THE ABBASĪD'S GOLDEN AGE THE FLORESCENCE OF ISLAMIC ECONOMICS (750 A.C.–1000 A.C.)

Introduction

The period under examination in this chapter is that from the mid eighth to the late tenth century. It is a particularly interesting period for several reasons. Firstly, the period witnessed the change of the caliphate from the short lived Umayyad dynasty to the much longer surviving Abbasīd dynasty. Secondly, during that period the Islamic empire reached its widest and most consolidated formation. Thirdly, it witnessed an enormous scale of Islamic urbanisation and trade that stretched from India in the east to Spain in the west. Fourthly, during that time the Islamic empire reached a high level of state administration and cultural development. Fifthly, it was the period when Islamic writing on economic issues appeared in specialised work for the first time. Finally, the period ended with the decline of the Islamic empire and the beginning of the Crusades. More interestingly, the period provides a sharp contrast between the East and the West. It was the time when the West was primitive, backward and primarily rural, while the East maintained and developed the traditions of wealth, cultural and artistic achievement.

Leading Specialised Work on Islamic Economics

The first general observation about the leading specialised work on Islamic economics is that the work was broadly on state finance and taxation. This could be attributed to various factors: (a) the complexity of the subject, which had increased as a result of the further expansion of the state, (b) the changing of the structure of tenure and ownership of agricultural land between Muslims and non-Muslims, (c) the continuing dominance of agriculture as a prime source of state income and the concern of writers with land taxation, (d) the nature of the subject as a device that is able to project justice, conceptually and practically, which explains why some of the early writers were judges and jurists, (e) the special nature of taxation as a subject that embraces per se other subjects related to state economic policies, (f) the political dimension of taxation, an issue that is deeply rooted in Islam as a religion that does not admit separation between religion and politics, and (g) the encouragement of some caliphs and heads of state who commissioned work rather similar in nature to a modern "committee of inquiry".

The second general observation is that the work, which contained important views on the running of the state finance, was not undertaken by caliphs as heads of state but by jurists and professional judges. This was in contrast to the case prior to the Umayyad and Abbasīd caliphate. For example, we saw how the Rightly Guided caliphs were able to formulate their juridical views, constitute their policy and accordingly reach a decision, economic and otherwise. In particular, we saw the second caliph Umar formulating his own opinion in relation to the arrangements of the conquered lands in Iraq, debating this view on juridical as well as political grounds and successfully defending his policy. The significance of Caliph Umar's example is that not only did he use political reasons, as a statesman, in defending his economic policy but also he argued the juridical evidence from the Qur'ān and Sunnah—the task of a jurist. The fourth caliph was another example. In his comprehensive letter to his province governor of Egypt, we saw him concerned to assert his views on various matters related to agriculture, trade, industry, public services, employment, state administration, taxation, policing, and so on, as was shown in chapter 3. This judicially remarkable ability would not have been possible without a profound understanding of Islamic law, Sharī'ah. This does not seem to be particularly traceable in the dynastic caliphates.

Furthermore, the increasing reliance on men of jurisprudence and the desire of heads of state for these men to be seen close to the royal court could be the product of the change in public's perception of the royal entourage. With the exception of Caliph Umar ibn-Abd-al-Azīz, Umar II (717–720), from the Umayyad caliphate onward there seemed to have been a sense of feeling among Muslims that their caliphs were no longer the piously infallible, divinely inspired, or judicially exalted men of God. The dynastic caliphate was no longer a series of individual reigns deeply dependent on the personal religious or political qualities of the caliphs, but, instead, the state as an institution was made the focus of ideological loyalty (Lapidus, 2002). As statesmen and military leaders they lacked neither courage nor fortitude, and some, like the first Umayyad caliph Muʾawiyah, were renowned for their political shrewdness. However, as exalted jurists, they were neither renowned nor qualified. Four reasons could have contributed to that: (a) the Islamic expansion, (b) the schism in the state, (c) the time lapse, and (d) the increasing complexity.

First, the enormous expansion of the state with the intensity of military combat during the Umayyads and the Abbasids must have occupied the full attention of the caliphs and left them with less opportunity to study the complexities of the Sharīʾah.

Second, the schism in the Islamic state, first between the last Rightly-Guided Caliph Ali and the first dynastic caliph Muʾawiyah, then between the Umayyads and the Abbasids, must have engulfed the leaders of the sate in the intricacy of politics too much to be concerned about leaving jurisprudence to specialists.

Third, the continuous widening of the time gap between the Prophet's time and that of the caliphs with the inevitable consequences of the reduction in the number of people who surrounded the Prophet as his companion who were prime candidates for the caliphate.

Fourth, the increasing complexity of life in general and the affairs of the state, in particular in the post Rightly-Guided caliphate era, which must have suggested the need for specialisation in Sharīʾah. To clarify the last point further, the Islamic intellectual thinking witnessed a particular development within the science of jurisprudence that led to the appearance of more than one school of thought in the Sharīʾah with its implications on economics subjects. For example, we see the Ĥanafī jurist Abū-Yūsuf regarding what Caliph Umar did in his administration of the lands of Iraq and Syria, as not necessarily binding on Muslims after him. Caliph Umar, Abū-Yūsuf argued, was not the Prophet and apart from what the Prophet did or approved doing, to which Muslims should adhere to, Caliph Umar's practice in administering the state's finance could be deviated from as the need might be (Abū-Yūsuf). Caliph Umar's practice was the result of his own opinion reached by his self-exertion, *ijtihād*, not that of the Prophet. Other jurists would disagree with Abū-Yūsuf, advocating that the practice and the opinions of the

Rightly Guided caliphs ought to be considered as part of the general consensus, *ijma'*, in the science of jurisprudence. They base their arguments on Prophets' *Aĥadīth* in favour of the judicial ability of caliphs Abū-Bakr, Umar and Ali (see for example, Al-Qattan, 1986).

The first wave of the specialised work on Islamic economics was therefore surrounded by economic and intellectual changes in the fabric of the Islamic state. To fully appreciate the role of these changes, in stimulating the need for the work and the shaping of its dimension, it might be worthwhile to look into these changes, briefly. This is shown below with particular emphasis on the economic and intellectual changes during the period under examination.

Main Changes in the Economic Features

The Increasing Wealth of the State

The increase in state revenue from the time of the Rightly Guided caliphate to the Abbasīd rule was enormous. History books tell us how the second caliph Umar found the figure of the revenue reported to him by his envoy to Iraq beyond comprehension, "You are probably confused as a result of your tiring journey, go to sleep and report to me tomorrow" said the sympathetic caliph (Al-Ťabarī). Little did Caliph Umar know that the revenue would far exceed his expectation during the time of the Abbasīd caliph al-Rashīd. Comparing the state revenue at the time of the third Rightly Guided caliph Utman, around 650 A.C., when the caliphate reached its peak of prosperity, to that at the time of al-Rashīd, around 796 A.C., when the Abbasīd caliphate reached what it is known as the golden age, reveals that the revenue increased dramatically. From a total of about 200,402,000 dirhams, (Abū-Yūsuf, Al-Balażrī, Al-Mawirdī, Al-Rayyis, 1977), the revenue reached a sum of 530,312,000 dirham (Al-Jahshiyari, 1938, Al-Rayyis, 1977). By the standard of the day that was a considerable sum. The increase reflects not only the growth in the state revenue but also the budget as a whole including expenditures, which would determine the size of the state administration. Caliphs, particularly in matters related to a highly sensitive subject like taxation, liked to be seen as fair and just, while, simultaneously, they had their concern about the size of the tax revenue.

Consequently, questions related to the administration of tax would require immediate attention. Tax rates, the tax base, the efficiency of the collection of tax, the allocation of the tax burden, the efficiency of the distribution of tax revenue, fairness, and so on, are some examples of complex questions that may require inquiry by specialists to provide their most plausible answers. And when the required answers had to be in conformity with the Sharī'ah, it would be inevitable that Muslim jurists were the prime authority for the task. That was the case with the caliph al-Rashīd who asked his chief justice Abū-Yūsuf to write him a treatise on state finance. But Abū-Yūsuf was a *Ĥanafī* jurist, following the *Ĥanafī* school of thought although that was not the only school available. As Abū-Yūsuf wrote his book from a *Ĥanafī* point of view, there would be a need for writing another from a different point of view reflecting the opinion of another school of thought.

The Variety of Products and Diversity of Economic Activities

Al-Jahshiyari's list of the state revenue (the authenticity of which is strongly emphasised by himself in his *Futūh al-Bildān*, and other lists compiled by other historians such as ibn-Khaldūn and ibn-Qudamah), had four distinctive features: (a) it recorded in detail the state revenue reported by region, (b) the size of the region was considerable, the region was, not surprisingly, the size of a country as we know it today, e.g. Egypt, Iraq, Cyprus, etc., showing each as a region, (c) the number of regions was large, 36 regions/countries in the list, (d) the tax paid was in monetary units and/or in kind (Al-Rayyis, 1977). From the list, two important conclusions can be reached: (a) the geographical area for which the detailed revenue was to be managed by the state tax administration was particularly vast, from India to North Africa, and (b) the taxable activities in each region were of a wide variety. In addition, although the main amount of tax revenue was largely in monetary units, the payment in kind was also quite considerable. Furthermore, because of the variety of produce across the regions, tax in kind was well diversified throughout the regions. This suggests that each region had its own main distinguishing products in addition to the agricultural produce. With a range of about fifty distinguished products, in the list, between raisins, spices, salt, silver, carpets, garments, elephants and slaves, that size and variety of production activities seemed to have been huge.

The diversity could be attributed to two main reasons: the vast geographical location and the active trade. The vast geographical locations of the state allowed the incorporation of a wide variety of seasons and weather conditions, which allowed in its turn a wide variety of agricultural produce. To give a few examples, al-Jahiz (d. 869) explained that as many as 360 different types of dates could be found in the market of al-Basra, while al-Ansari stated that in 1400 A.C. in the near vicinity of a small village on the North African coast there were 65 varieties of grapes, 36 types of pears, 28 kinds of figs, 16 categories of apricots, and so forth, (Watson, 1981). What seems to have been certain, as Watson says, is that the range of useful plants available to cultivators was greatly increased in the early centuries of Islam by the widespread diffusion of new plants and the development of new strains (ibid.). Trade was another reason. The expansion of trade between regions as well as with other countries, helped create the conditions for diversity of products and activities.

This would make the task of imposing and collecting the tax in kind, as well as in monetary units, rather complex, which must have created a need for a complex tax system that ought to be well controlled and administered. For example, complexity in relation to issues such as tax rate, quantification of the tax base, threshold, direct and indirect tax, ad valorem tax, and consumption of produce before taxation, would suggest the need for good ministerial solutions that had to be not only efficient but also in conformity with the Sharīʾah. The need for expert jurists and the need for writing on taxation would therefore become obvious—and need is the mother of invention.

The Change of the Structure of Land Ownership

Three issues lay at the heart of the structure of land ownership between Muslims and non-Muslims, first, the right of Muslims to purchase land from the non-Muslims, a right the exercise of which became more notable during the Umayyads and Abbasids, second, the right of the caliph to grant Muslims land in appreciation of services, again, a right that was used during the two dynastic caliphates on a much greater scale than that of the Rightly-Guided caliphate, and, third, the right to the ownership of the previously neglected ownerless land by whoever revived it. These three major factors seemed to have played a considerable role in changing the structure of land ownership in the Islamic state particularly during the Umayyads and Abbasids. During the Umayyad and particularly the Abbasīd caliphate, land granted in reward for services, known as *qata'i*, singular *qati'a*, grew in size and economic significance and it became one of the main features of agricultural activities (Al-Rayyis, 1977). What is notable, therefore, is that the pendulum of ownership during the late Umayyad and Abbasīd period seemed to have swung towards Muslims, who developed an interest in acquiring agricultural land (Cahen, 1970, Lapidus, 1981). The relevance of this development to the writing on state finance in general and land taxation in particular is that the change of the religion of the owner of the land, the tax payer, may, in the views of some jurists, change the type of tax from Kharāj to Zakah, *ushr*, tax. This is not always the case, however, as in the opinion of other jurists the nature of the tax should not be changed by the change of the religion of the owner. Historically, government policy during the Umayyads varied between the change of tax to *ushr*, to reverting to the old status, Kharāj, even with a change in the owner's religion (Al-Rayyis, 1977). The claim was that this was meant to discourage tax evasion when Kharāj was higher than Zakāh. The issue was therefore debatable as it would raise practical as well as judicial considerations; hence the appearance of more than one book on *Kharāj*.

The Introduction of Intermediaries in Tax Collection

Furthermore, a further feature appeared with regard to the collection of tax. An intermediary agent would present himself to the Treasury as being responsible for the payment of the total tax levied on the region, pay the tax either when it is due or in advance, and then collect that from individual tax payers. Although the system was convenient to the Treasury it was not without problems. There was always the possibility of the intermediary agent charging tax payers more than what was due. This would create injustice and severity to the ultimate payers. Abū-Yūsuf as we will see was strongly against it.

Intellectual Development

The intellectual development that surrounded the writing on Islamic economics during the period under examination depicted some distinctive features. The spread of the religio-political philosophy, the critique of the Greek philosophy, the development of the Islamic juridical philosophy, and the establishment of a coherent school of mysticism are most prominent. These are highlighted below.

Islamic religio-political philosophy

The Islamic religio-political philosophy developed so rapidly that in a short period it reached a stage of a considerable diversion and high complexity. Very often a philosophy would be introduced, from which another would be developed, which would breed a third, from which a fourth would be generated, and so on. Various sects in Islamic religious philosophy existed, some very often contradictory, and many with political implications. Allegations went as far as accusing some of these sects, such as some Isma'ilite sects, of heresy, communism and unacceptable religious practice.

Interestingly enough, the thinking of Muslims on religio-political philosophy during that period seemed to have shaped the thinking of Muslims for many years to come. The Mu'atazilah, the Ash'ariah, Ŝūfīsm, Asceticism, Mysticism, theosophy, pantheism, Fraternal order, the Rosary, the cult of Saints, Shī'ah, Isma'īliyyah, Batiniyyah, Qarmatiyyah, the Assāssīns, Nusayris, Druzes, Takhtajis (woodcutters) of western Anatolia, Ali-Illahis of Persia and Turkestan, Qizil-bash (redheads) of the east of Anatolia, and the Baktashis of Turkey and Albania and the Zaydis of al-Yemen, are the main sects and concepts that developed in Islamic religious philosophy over the period from the early ninth century to the early eleventh century (Mahmoud, 1986).

Religious sects were severely criticised by Muslim scholars. For example, we find the eminent scholar al-Ghazālī (1058–1111) condemning them and regarding them as those described as being on the wrong path. In his criticism, al-Ghazālī condemned those who changed the concepts, perception and meaning of Islamic phrasing and terminology. He elucidated that *Fiqh*, instead of being the science of the knowledge of the meaning of the Qur'ān and the Sunnah, had become the science of the unusual legal cases, mystery of the minutest details of jurisprudence and excessive debates over them. *Ilm*, the science of the knowledge of God and His verses, became the science of those who could well debate the cases of jurisprudence with their adversaries, and those who could not do that were described as weak and were not included in the category of eminent scholars. Tawhīd became the knowledge of the methods of argumentation, the manner of confronting adversaries, instead of being the belief that all things come from God with no intermediary agents. Circuits of Zikr, remembrance of God and His creation, turned into meetings of preaching, lecturing and story-telling. Poetry, the use of which was restricted as it was confined mainly to religious purposes, became unrestricted. Subjects varied from personal eulogy as well as defamation, to description of wine drinking circuits. Hakim, a word used to describe a wise man, was used to describe physicians, astrologers and palm readers (Al-Ghazālī, Vol. I).

Critique of the Greek philosophy

The interest of Muslims in Greek philosophy could be said to have developed at the reign of the Abbasīd caliph al-Ma'mūn (813–833). Ibn-Khaldūn tells us that al-Ma'mūn, who himself had a desire for science, sent ambassadors to the Byzantine emperors to explore the Greek science, and "have them copied into Arabic writing; he sent translators for that purpose", (Ibn-Khaldūn). The mission seemed to have been successful as we learn from the same source that, "As a result, a good deal of material was preserved and collected", (ibid.) Prior to al-Ma'mūn's endeavour, the Muslim caliph was restricted to mathematics. Al-Ma'mūn's great grand father, the caliph Ja'afer al-Mansūr, went to the Byzantine emperor and asked him to send him "translation of mathematical works", (ibid.). The Byzantine emperor who seemed to be happy to oblige, sent him Euclid's book.

Muslim thinkers developed a special interest in the Greek sciences and achieved a notable skill. Some were keen to develop some philosophical work, with an Islamic version, in parallel to that of the Greek philosophers, such as al-Farābī in his City in parallel with Plato and his republic. Others provided a critique of the Greek work, and contradicted the First Teacher (Aristotle) on many points and surpassed their predecessors in intellectual sciences (ibid.). Consequently, the Greek intellectual sciences succeeded to some degree in penetrating Islam, and "seduced many people who were eager to study those sciences and accept the opinion expressed in them" (ibid.). Therefore, in a period where writing on philosophy and the political theories dominated the intellectual activities, there was much less writing on Islamic economics.

Development of Islamic Juridical Philosophy

The first wave of Islamic writing on economics was preceded with, and later on surrounded by, an active movement in the thinking of Islamic jurists who devoted particular attention to the socio-religio side of Islam. By the time the first specialised work on economics appeared there were two distinct well established schools of Islamic thought, developed over a period of two centuries or so, and, a third was beginning to make itself evident. While an independent body of Islamic economic literature was taking a distinctive shape, a fourth school of thought (the Ĥanbalī) was firmly founded. These schools had a considerable influence on the thinking of the jurists' writing on economics who were themselves followers of one school or another. For example, while the chief justice Abū-Yūsuf belonged to the Ĥanafī school, Yahya ibn Adam al-Qurashi belonged to the Ĥanbalī school. When considering the effect these schools have had on the development of Islamic economics, it may be worthwhile to explore briefly the development of the Islamic juridical thought on the eve of, and during, the first appearance of specialised work on Islamic economics.

The events of the first civil war in Islam (656–661) that took place between Caliph Ali and Mu'awiyah left Muslims divided into three religio-political groups: the Khawārij, the Shī'ah and the Jama'a or Sunnī. As mentioned in the previous chapter, the Khawārij were those who, although were fighting with Caliph Ali against Mu'awiyah at the beginning, disagreed with him after the arbitration that lead through deceit to his removal (Al-Ťabarī). The religious sincerity of the Khawārij and their devotion to the religion is difficult to question. They were courageous, puritans and prepared to die for their beliefs but they went to the extreme of claiming that by accepting arbitration Caliph Ali became an unbeliever.

The Shī'ahs stood at the opposite end of the Khawārij, they supported Caliph Ali in his dispute to the bitter end. The Shī'i support reached the level of believing that the Message of Islam was meant to be descended on Caliph Ali but by mistake on the part of the Arch Angel Gibra'il it went to the Prophet Muĥammad. The name of Caliph Ali was then added to the name of Prophet Muĥammad in the Shī'i Muslims' call for prayer. After Caliph Ali's death and the retirement of his elder son al-Ĥassan from politics, the Shī'iah instigated al-Ĥusayn's revolt against Mu'awiyah's son

Yazīd I (680–683), promising him their military support. However, their support did not materialize and the Prophet's grandson and his family were massacred by the Syrian army in Karbala' in the south of Iraq (Al-Ťabarī). (This explains the sense of guilt some Shi'is feel nowadays and the self-inflicting injuries they exercise at the anniversary of al-Ĥusayn's death, or martyrdom). Relying on Hadiths and their interpretation of certain verses in the Qur'ān the Shi'ī emphatically maintains that Caliph Ali was the only legitimate caliph after the Prophet and therefore the caliphate, or the Imamah, should be confined to Imam Ali' decedents.

The Jama'a or Sunnis were the middle of the road group, though they were not particularly enthusiastic towards Mu'awiyah or his son Yazīd, they regarded them as de facto rulers who should be obeyed. The pivotal difference between the three groups, therefore, was based on the concept of the caliphate, *Imamah*, and the legitimacy for it, though other differences on secular matters were further developed.

The term Sunni, with reference to Jama'a should be viewed with caution. It does not imply that the Sunnis are the only group who followed the Prophet's Sunnah. All Muslims are ordained to follow the Sunnah, which is embodied in the Prophet's deeds and sayings, *Aĥadīth.* But the difference between the groups lies mainly in the debate over the Islamic legitimacy of the caliphate, or *Imamah.*

Of the above three groups the teachings of the Sunnis developed more widely than others. That was perhaps because they were the largest group of Muslims, the more tolerant and the less politically inclined. Their basic political and theocratic philosophy is based on the principle of following the general consensus of the ummah, *jama'*, as that is, in their view, what the Sunnah recommends. Their theological study contributed significantly to the development of jurisprudence. As mentioned in chapter two, jurisprudence started with, and was the product of, changes in the Islamic society after the Prophet's death. In line with the spirit of Islam, the early Rightly Guided caliph in consultation with the Prophet's companions resorted to their opinion in dealing with situations that either did not arise at the Prophet's time or did not exist to the same degree. The apostasies during the reign of the first caliph, Abū-Bakr, and the ownership of the conquered land during the time of the second caliph, Umar, are the most obvious examples. The body of opinion constituted by the early caliph and the companions, the consensus of the companions' opinion, served as a third basis of jurisprudence after the Qur'ān and the Sunnah. By the incrcasing complexity of the affairs of the state during the Umayyads and the Abbasids there was a need for further development of jurisprudence. With the absence of a clear-cut secular rule in the Qur'ān, the Sunnah or the consensus of the companions' opinion, Muslim theologists, in line once more with the spirit of Islam, resorted to other means of formulating a view: analogical reasoning, *qiyās*, juristic preference, *istiĥsān*, and public interest, *istislāĥ*.

Various leading scholars placed different emphasis on one means or another which led to the development of two schools of legal philosophy: the school of opinion, *ahl al ra'y*, which flourished in Kufa in Iraq, and the school of *Aĥadīth, ahl al Ĥadīth*, which was influential in Makkah and al-Medīnah in al-Ĥijaz. While the first school widened the concept of juristic preference, *istiĥsān*, and analogical reasoning, *qiyās*, with less reliance on *Aĥadīth*, the second relied more heavily on *Aĥadīth* and less on *istiĥsān* or *qiyās*. An important Tradition lends support to the use of one's opinion in reaching a rule in relation to a situation that is not specifically specified in the Qur'ān or the Sunnah. It is an important dialogue that is reported to have taken place between the Prophet and Mu'aż ibn-Jabal when the Prophet appointed him as a judge in al-Yemen. The Prophet asked Mu'aż how he would decide when a question arose. Mu'aż answer was, "According to the book of Allah". "And if you find naught therein?" the Prophet asked. Mu'aż's answer was "According to the Sunnah of the Messenger of Allah". Then came the crucial question, "And if you find naught therein?" Mu'aż's answer, to which the Prophet gave his approval, was, "Then I shall apply my own reasoning". This tradition provides the much needed legal support for the school of opinion, *ahl al ra'y*, in developing their approach to Islamic law, Sharī'ah (Al-Qattan, 1986).

Various factors could be said to have affected the move of each school towards its own direction: (a) the lack of hadiths in Iraq compared to that of Makkah and al-Medīnah, (b) the high degree of complexity in the Iraqi society as a result of its closeness to Persia and the Persian civilisation compared with the much simpler life in al-Ĥijaz, (c) the suspicion of the Iraqi scholars that the Khawārij and the Shi'ī who dominated Iraq could have injected false hadiths in the Sunnah to serve their political claims, and (d) the delay in the appearance of Hadiths canonical books, a task which was undertaken for the first time by al-Būkhari (810–870), followed by Muslim-ibn-al-Ĥajjaj (d 875), Abū-Dawūd (d 888), al-Tarmażī (d 892) and al-Nasa'i (d 915).

Jurisprudence Schools of Thought

By the late ninth century, there were six main schools of law, though the surviving schools became four: the Ĥanafī, the Mālikī, the Shafi'ī and the Ĥanbalī. These are highlighted briefly as follows:

THE ĤANAFI/SCHOOL. The founder of the school was Abū-Ĥanīfah (699–767), al-Nu'man ibn-Thabit, who relied on juristic preference, *istiĥsān*, and analogical deduction, *qiyās*, in arriving at juristic rules (Al-Qattan, 1986). Without perhaps realising that he would be forming a juridical school, Abū-Ĥanīfah became the founder of the most tolerant school in Islamic jurisprudence. The teachings of Abū-Ĥanīfah flourished in Iraq, Kufa and Baghdad, and the jurist had many followers among who were Abū-Yūsuf whose book "al-Kharāj", public finance, was the first to appear in Islamic economic writing. Presently, the school has the largest followers in the Muslim world.

THE MĀLIKĪ SCHOOL. This was founded by Mālik-ibn-Anas (715–795) in al-Medīnah, who paid particular attention to the Sunnah, and the customs of al-Medīnah during the Prophet's time and the consensus of opinions during the reign of the four Rightly Guided caliphs (ibid.). His book "al-Muwatta'", the levelled path, is the oldest surviving book on the codification of Islamic law. To Mālik the theory of public interest, *istislāĥ*, is attributed. The main followers of Mālik are in North Africa and Eastern Arabia. The difference between the Ĥanafī approach and that of the Mālikī is the difference between the approach of opinion and that of the Tradition.

THE SHAFI'Ī SCHOOL. Founded by Muĥammad Idrīs al-Shafi'ī (767–819) who was born in Ghaza, the school strikes a balance between the Mālikī, the upholders of Sunnah, and the Ĥanafī, the upholders of opinion. Al-Shafi'ī, who was a disciple of Mālik, adopted a balanced approach between those of his predecessors: Sunnah can only be accepted through unbroken narrators and analogical deduction should be used as a last resort and should be restricted as to exclude arbitrary opinions (ibid.). His major treatise on the principles of jurisprudence, *Kitāb al-Risālah fi Usūl al-Fiqh*, is a landmark in the books of jurisprudence. The Shafi'ī were mainly in Lower Egypt, Syria, Jordan and Lebanon, although they were subsequently to become influential in South East Asia.

The Ĥanbalī School. The founder of the School was Ahmad ibn-Ĥanbal (784–855) who strictly adhered to Sunnah to the letter narrowing the margin of the consensus of opinion and analogical approach and rejecting any form of human reasoning. Although he was a student of the moderate al-Shafi'ī he adopted an uncompromising approach to Islamic jurisprudence. His approach, it seems, was a reaction to the Mu'tazilah movement, which resorted to reasoning in developing the science of theology during the Abbasids period and were in favour with Caliph al-Ma'mūn (813–833). In vain were the efforts of the Abbasīd caliph al-Ma'mūn, which reached imprisonment, to force him to change his mind. His book "al-Musnad" which contains forty thousand *hadīth* of the Sunnah is a major work in the subject. His followers are mainly in Saudi Arabia (ibid.).

The development of the Islamic legal thought was by no means the only aspect of intellectual development in Islam under the Umayyad and the Abbasīd reign. Islamic histories tells us about the development of medicine, astronomy, mathematics, astrology, alchemy, geography, fine and industrial arts, architecture, philosophy, Arabic grammar, history writing, poetry, music, belles-letters and calligraphy, (see for example, Hitti, 1963). In law, theology, philology and linguistics, Muslims, Arabs and non-Arabs, also carried on original thinking and research (ibid.). Learning is almost regarded as sacred and Muslims are ordained by the Qur'ān and the Sunnah to learn and seek knowledge, "even as far away as in China", as the Prophet instructs his followers (Ŝaĥīĥ Muslim). Jihād is a term that is not confined to Holy War; it also incorporates the hardship borne in seeking knowledge, where Muslims are ordained with regard to learning, "the best of you are those who learn and teach what they learn", (Ŝaĥīĥ Muslim). Knowledge as such, or science, is divided into two types: religious science, *Ulūm al-Dīn*, and secular science, *Ulūm al-Donia* and both are equally important. Islamic economic science is par excellence a mixture of the two types of science, religious and secular, and the contribution to it is a contribution to both.

Now we turn our attention to the early work on Islamic economics: treatise on Kharāj.

The First Specialised Books on Islamic Economics

Writing on Kharāj
Meaning of Kharāj

The word Kharāj claims an Arabic etymology. The word has been mentioned in the Qur'ān indicating the meaning of payment, or regular payment, "And they said, 'Dhul-Qarnayn, Gog and Magog are ravaging this land, would you build a rampart between us and them and we will pay you a kharāj". The Qur'ānic verses, 18:94, inform us about an encounter between one of God's prophets with some people who were suffering from the people of Gog and Magog. On another occasion God rhetorically exclaims with a view to comforting the Prophet Muĥammad in his encounter with the unbelievers, "Or do you ask them for a kharāj, verily your Lord's Kharāj is far better" (Qur'ān, 23:74). And as the Qur'ān confirms on more than one occasion that its definitive meaning is in, "an Arabic tongue" the word by inference must be an Arabic word. Linguistically, it means a payment, a regular payment, or a return. However, in taxation terms, several writers affirm that as a land tax it was known in Persia before the coming of Islam. But under the same term Kharāj, early Islamic writers referred to it in their books as land tax. Technically, the term could have a dual meaning: it may be used in a general technical term to mean public finance as a whole, including all taxes and the way revenues are distributed, as the early writers did, but when used in a narrowly specifically technical manner the term would refer to the revenue from land tax in particular. As such, one can say the state's Kharāj, meaning state's total revenue, as invariably used by early historians, and land Kharāj to refer to revenue from land tax (Al-Rayyis, 1977).

Books on Kharāj

In his examination of taxation in Islam, Ben Shemesh cites a number of books on Kharāj during the eight century or so. However, the only surviving books are the three mentioned below.

Abū-Yūsuf's "Kitāb al-Kharāj", book of al-Kharāj. In the peak of the Abbasīd period, under the reign of the strong caliph Harūn al-Rashīd (786–809) and in the midst of an impressive cultural renaissance, the caliph asked the jurist Abū-Yūsuf (731–798) to write a comprehensive treatise on the collection of tax. Abū-Yūsuf, the Ĥanafī, wrote the book "al-Kharāj" which is the first extensive book on the subject.

Yahya ibn-Adam's "Kitāb al-Kharāj". Yahya ibn Adam al-Qurashi (757–818) compiled a book on al-Kharāj with a view to providing a collection of the Prophet's sayings and deeds. The book also contains references to the opinions of other scholars, including Yahya's contemporaries. Occasionally, however, Yahya gives his opinion, but by contrast to Abū-Yūsuf, this is very limited. In terms of size it is about half the size of Abū-Yūsuf's kitāb al-Kharāj, or less, and is not as comprehensive or as diversified. However, the book contains some fundamental legal principles with regard to landed property, which are still in operation in some Muslims countries in modern times (Ben Shemesh, 1967).

It is interesting to note that in the middle of his compiled *Aĥadīth* in taxation and the like, Yahya has devoted a section, very short nevertheless, on the merits of trade, agriculture and palm tree cultivation as professions. He quoted the Qur'ān and cited the Sunnah to encourage pursuing the three different economic activities without emphasising any particular preference between them. The relevance of this point becomes clear if we know that some Muslims, relying on a certain *ĥadīth*, held the view that trade was superior to other activities and that agriculture was the most inferior of all. But the citation of the Qur'ānic verses and the Prophet's *ahadīth* by Yahya is an indication of the plausibility of these activities. The book is the second extant book on the subject.

Qudama ibn-Ja'afer's "Kitāb al-Kharāj". Abū al-Faraj Qudama ibn Ja'far al-Katib (864–932) wrote his Kitāb al-Kharāj, which is the third surviving book on al-Kharāj from that era. Although the topics treated in his book are not beyond that covered by his predecessors, Qudama's book should be viewed with three things in mind: (a) at the time of his writing, all juridical schools of thought were well established and maturely formed, which was not the case for those before him, (b) the six books of *ĥadīth* were complete and well authenticated, (c) it was almost one hundred and fifty years since Abū-Yūsuf's well known treatise on al-Kharāj appeared, which might have merited a new contribution, and (d) Qudamah lived at a period when the rise of the Islamic state began to be reversed, starting from the beginning of the decline of al-Muktafi caliphate (902–908). These circumstances could have urged the writing of his book.

In terms of the size of the work, the depth and variety of treatment, and the comprehensibility of topics, it might be justifiable to focus our examination on Abū-Yūsuf's work, leaving the other, similar, two to a more specialised work.

Abū-Yūsuf (113–182 A.H., 731–798 A.C.)
Kitāb al-Kharāj, Treatise in al-Kharāj

The Author

He is Abū-Yūsuf Ya'qub ibn Ibrāhīm al-Ansari (113/731–182/798), a student and a friend of Abū-Hanīfah the founder of the Ĥanafī school of thought. As a Ĥanafī belonging to the school of opinion, *ahl al-ra'y*, Abū-Yūsuf would resort to reasoning in matters related to secular issues when a Tradition either did not exist or existed but, in the scholar's opinion, the circumstances in which the Prophet took action, were different from the prevailing circumstances in which a ruling was needed. Juristic reasoning was not, however, free from restrictions. According to the school of opinion reasoning was resorted to only when there was no clear-cut rule in the Qur'ān, the Sunnah or the consensus of the opinion of the Prophet's companions. Furthermore the opinion should be based on the principles of analogical reasoning "*qiyās*", juristic preference "*istiĥsān*" and public interest "*istislāĥ*", as said previously.

The Ĥanafī approach, or generally the approach of the school of opinion, is reflected distinctively in Abū-Yūsuf's writing of his Kitāb al-Kharāj. When discussing a controversial matter we invariably find Abū-Yūsuf expressing a ruling which would be either preceded or be proceeded with the expression "in my opinion". We also find him using the term "if this leads to the betterment of the people" when suggesting a course of action to his Caliph that might differ from previous courses, which shows the effect of the principle of public interest "*istislāĥ*" in reaching a ruling.

But Abū-Yūsuf would disagree with Abū–Ĥanīfah, his teacher, in support of a course of action that was different from that of his master. This is expressed in Abū-Yūsuf's book on several occasions where we find him after stating Abū-Ĥanīfah's point of view disagreeing with him and preferring another. The difference of opinion between Abū-Yūsuf and his master does not, however, make him less Ĥanafī.

Although it helps define Abū-Yūsuf's independent thinking, the difference, by the degree of intensity and frequency, does not create a gulf or cause controversy between the student and the teacher. The tactful student Abū-Yūsuf would conclude his statement with, "Allah knows best", when there was an interlocking difference of opinion between himself and his teacher. As for the caliph, it was up to him, the ruler, to take the action he saw fit, "I have elucidated the matter to you, commander of the faithful, and it is up to you, with your wisdom, to take the action that will be beneficial to Muslims", we see Abū-Yūsuf invariably stating.

The independence of Abū-Yūsuf's thinking, as demonstrated in the occasional disagreement between him and his teacher, was perhaps related to, or more a product of, his profession. As a judge, and later the chief justice to the Caliph Harūn al-Rashīd, he must have developed independence of thinking that was necessary for the achievement of fairness and neutrality required by a judge. Also, as the chief justice Abū-Yūsuf must have acquired through practice the ability to listen to different points of view, some coming from well practicing judges, weigh the argument for and against, evaluate the opinions of others and then finalise his own.

This approach, the approach of a judge, is distinctive in Abū-Yūsuf's book of al-Kharāj. In his book he poses the question, examines what has been stated in the Qur'ān and the Sunnah, surveys what has been done by the Rightly Guided caliphs, portrays what has been told by other jurists, reaches a ruling and formulates an opinion with an explanation of the basis of his ruling and the support of opinion. In this respect the book is particularly educational. With his vast knowledge in ritual precepts, he wrote other books on prayers, fasting and Zakāh, and his competence in Islamic law, Abū-Yūsuf with Abū-Ĥanīfah were declared to be the most learned men in religious law (from Al-Suyūtī's Tabaqat al-Huffaz quoted in Ben Shemesh, 1969).

Abū-Yūsuf seemed to have enjoyed the respect of his caliph. This is inferred from two points in the introductory chapter of his book. First, when he referred to the act of being commissioned for the task by his caliph we find Abū-Yūsuf using the verb "ask", rather than "order", hence, "the Commander of the Faithful has asked me", and "has requested" from me. It was only towards the end that "ordered" appeared. Respect, courtesy, politeness, and the fine art of diplomacy, are shown to the caliph throughout the book, no doubt, but that did not stop Abū-Yūsuf from referring to himself as being asked. A credit to a jurist who returns credit to a caliph. Also, that could perhaps be the managerial style of al-Rashīd, a great caliph in whose reign the state reached, as history books assert, its golden age in science and politics, towards his highly appreciated judge. Or it could be that caliphs treated their judges in general and chief justice in particular with due affection. Jurists were the men of Islamic precepts and law. It emphasises this point further to know, as mentioned earlier, that caliphs during the Umayyad and Abbasīd caliphate were more of political leaders than exalted jurists.

Second, Abū-Yūsuf seemed to have assumed the role of advisor, counsel, and almost preacher to the caliph in his book. We see that throughout the introductory chapter of the book where he is constantly reminding the caliph of his responsibility, duties and obligations towards his subjects, God's commands and the commands of his Prophet with regard to "the shepherd, the folk, and the owner of the folk", and God's reward and punishment in all matters related. In 17 pages out of 217 (the edition on hand), the warning tone of preaching does not stop. Even more interestingly, Abū-Yūsuf in these compelling pages seemed to have had the courage to quote the Umayyad caliph Umar ibn-Abdel-Azīz, Umar II (717–720), as a role model of piety. An Umayyad caliph quoted for an Abbasīd Caliph as an example to follow could be a recipe for a disaster! But Umar II was special, so was Abū-Yūsuf, and must also have been Harūn al-Rashīd the caliph. This helps demonstrate Abū-Yūsuf's writing as politically impartial and academically objective.

The Book

The General Approach

The book was a commissioned work, to an audience of, initially, one. This is shown in the second paragraph of its introductory chapter, "The Commander of the Faithful, May Allah strengthens him, has asked me to write *for him* (italics ours)". It was, therefore, as a result of Abū-Yūsuf being commissioned by the caliph Harūn al-Rashīd (786–809); to prepare an extensive report, that the book on Islamic economics was born. In parallel to the practice of government of today, the subject must have been of state concern, as the caliph was interested in getting the issue examined, and the commissioned writer must have been capable of carrying out the task.

The subject of the book was to provide a comprehensive study, on "... the collection of the Kharāj, tithes, alms, Jizyah, *and other matters* (italics ours) of what he (the caliph) ought to look into and act upon", and the objective was to "avert oppression from his subjects, and benefit their interests". The "other matters" in the above statement suggests that the book was not meant to be exclusively on taxation, or, even, purely on land taxation as it has been conceived and presented by some writers. It was wider than that, even if land taxation was one of its main components. This will become clear when we look into the structure of Kitāb al-Kharāj.

The book is written in the form of answering questions posed by the Caliph. Whether the Caliph actually asked these questions or if Abū-Yūsuf used them as a stylistic approach to his writing is not clear. It could be assumed however that when the Caliph asked Abū-Yūsuf to write for him a treatise on taxation and state revenue with a view to answering potential questions, Abū-Yūsuf presumed implicitly that the Caliph would ask these questions. It is also important to note that in his book, which is directed to the Caliph himself, Abū-Yūsuf gives Sharī'ah rulings, advice and opinions, not decisions. The decisions were left to the Caliph, "It is up to you, O Commander of the Faithful, to decide which view to follow"; Abū-Yūsuf invariably ends his ruling.

Abū-Yūsuf's approach to writing on the subject of al-Kharāj was a pragmatic approach. He looked into the prevailing practice, examined past applications, studied the problems arising from present and past policies, scrutinised the Qur'ānic rules, the *Aḥādīth* and jurisprudence to insure conformity with the Sharī'ah, and then reached an opinion which would provide in his view a plausible answer. The deductive approach he used was for the purpose of proving a point, debating an issue, defending an idea, or criticising a judgment. But the pragmatic approach was the general scientific approach he followed. In that sense it can be said with Yusri (1992) that Abū-Yūsuf was the first writer to have taken Islamic economics towards the "scientific" nature of the subject as a proper subject for scientific research.

Structure of the Book

For convenience of discussion, but not necessarily in the strict sequence in which Abū-Yūsuf's book appeared, the structure of the book could be rearranged as follows:

Introduction
Expenditures and distribution of revenue
Taxation
  Land Taxation
  Kharāj
  Ushr
  Administrative Reform in Land Taxation
Other taxes on derived products
  Zakāh
  Jizyah
  Custom Dues
Public administration, "law and order"
Other issues
  Leasing of land
  Public Goods and Externalities
  Pricing, scarcity and value

The above will be discussed below with different emphasis depending upon level of complexity.

Introduction

The introduction is devoted to the preaching of the Caliph, praising him and reminding him, in a highly spiritual manner, of his duties towards his people, as explained above.

Expenditures of the state and the distribution of revenue

The distribution of the spoils of war was the starting point of Abū-Yūsuf's treatment of the topic. This merited a discussion by Abū-Yūsuf for perhaps two reasons: (a) how the share of the Prophet, and his kinfolk who were not entitled to receiving from Zakāh revenue, be distributed after the Prophet's death, and (b) whether a variation from that of the Rightly Guided caliphs, particularly that of Umar, could be adopted. On the first question he maintained that the Prophet's share should be distributed to his relatives, and on the second he, after clarifying some of the problems that had arisen after the Prophet and the Rightly Guided caliphate, proposed a distribution that varied slightly from that of Caliph Umar's.

On the issue of the distribution of Zakāh revenue, which came under the Zakāh section in his book, Abū-Yūsuf stressed three points: (a) Zakāh revenue should not be mixed with revenues from other taxes, and (b) revenue from Zakāh should be strictly distributed as stipulated in the Qur'ān, and (c) this revenue should be distributed to local beneficiaries in the town, city, or region from where the revenue was collected. There was one exception: the stipulated share of "in the cause of God", this may be allocated generally, and a local surplus may be distributed to other localities. Notably, this, from the economic point of taxation, would help reduce transportation costs and consequently decrease the administrative burden of tax.

Also, the collectors of Zakāh should be given their shares from its revenue, as stated in the Qur'ān, but if the revenue was not sufficient to give them, the general pool of Zakāh or even other pools could be used to pay them their needs. Payment to these administrators ought to be in moderation but without deprivation and should be determined by the caliph himself. Interestingly enough, Abū-Yūsuf seemed to have had in mind two points; not to overburden the administrators with more than what they were paid to do, and, perhaps, to reduce the possible immoral hazard that might incur on the part of the administrators if they were particularly underpaid.

With regard to the wages of judges and officials, Abū-Yūsuf emphasised that they should be paid from the central Treasury, *Bait-al-Māl*. This, in his view, would guarantee that the services rendered would not be restricted to the revenue collected from the region and, therefore, all, the rich and the poor regions, would get the required services. He further emphasised that public servants should not be paid from the revenue of Zakāh, unless the officials were working exclusively for the collection of Zakāh, whose share in this case is specified in the sacred book as one-eighth. Private services provided by these judges, such as management of trust funds or legacies, may be paid privately by those benefiting from the service, but judges should not overcharge their agents lest the legacy should be eroded in the long run. It is interesting to note that Abū-Yūsuf's view coincides with an important point in the concept of fairness in taxation. Fairness, as has been established in tax literature, is not to be perceived as being based on the benefit approach. The benefit approach to taxation suggests that the tax should be collected from the tax payers in line with the benefits they receive from public services. To Abū-Yūsuf, the state has a responsibility to provide the services needed by both the poor and the rich, and more so by the poor, regardless of the amount of tax collected from them.

Land taxation

For convenience of presentation land taxation is divided below into Kharāj tax and ushr tax, followed by the administrative reform of land taxation. But to avoid a potential confusion of terms, a clarification of the term *ushr* and *half ushr*, and *ushūr*, may be needed. In linguistic terms *ushr* means one-tenth, i.e. ten per cent, and *half ushr* is, hence, five percent. Applying this to land taxation would lead to classifying lands according to the tax imposed into *ushr* land and Kharāj land. *Ushr* land was mainly the land in the hands of Muslim owners, while Kharāj land was the land under the occupation of non-Muslims, which came to being after the Islamic conquests. A misconception is created by referring to *ushr* land as Muslims' land and Kharāj land as non-Muslims' lands. But this is not necessarily the case as lands in hands of non-Muslims could be, and were, taxed at ushr, ten per cent. These were the lands of the People of the Book in Arabia, i.e. Christian and Jews, and of others outside Arabia who had a peace treaty with Muslim armies stipulating the *ushr*, ten per cent, provision. Furthermore, Muslims land could also be taxed at the Kharāj rate. This would be the case if Muslims purchased lands from the owners who were taxed at the Kharāj rate. To extend the clarification further, the *ushr* rate was not always ten per cent; the rate could be halved to one fifth, five per cent, depending upon the burden of irrigation, as stipulated in the Sunnah. But the tax, and the land, would still be referred to as *ushr* tax and *ushr* land. A further and last point: *ushūr*, plural of *ushr*, is often confused with *ushr* land tax. *Ushūr* are custom dues. The reason for the confusion is that custom dues were charged at the rate of ten per cent, *ushr*, but that was the only common factor between the two types of taxes. However the ten per cent rate on custom dues could be halved to five percent.

Kharāj tax

In his book, Abū-Yūsuf introduced a new method of Kharāj taxation. Before Abū-Yūsuf, the manner of taxing conquered land was dominated by the practice of the second caliph Umar when the land of Iraq, *al-Sawad*, was conquered: a fixed rate with a threshold. In his treatise, Abū-Yūsuf deviated from Umar's ruling and proposed another method which was based on crop-sharing, *muqāsamah*.

Abū-Yūsuf went to some length to introduce his method. Before introducing his suggestion he provided a synthesis of what Caliph Umar had done and the opinion to which he resorted. "I have looked into the taxation system in the territory of Iraq, *al-Sawad*, and the ways it was collected, and have obtained the opinions of the experts and others and discussed this issue with them. They pointed out that it was impossible to continue with the systems laid down during the reign of Umar", Abū-Yūsuf stated, preparing for his favourable pragmatic approach to solving the problem. Abū-Yūsuf's recommendation for a different tax system had come, therefore, as a result of his thorough examination and consultation with the experts on the subjects.

But deviating from Caliph Umar's practice could not have been an easy task. Caliph Umar's view was a focal point in the core of the consensus of opinion in jurisprudence from which jurists should not depart in reaching a juridical ruling, a *fatwa*. It would be worthwhile therefore to look into Abū-Yūsuf's argument in defending the new system in his proposed treatise.

First, to safeguard his opinion against potential criticism he stressed that it was the outcome of intensive examination of the problem and consultation with others. A public relation exercise perhaps that was inevitable to begin with in order to ensure that he was not alone on this matter.

Second, Abū-Yūsuf proceeded to discuss his proposal from a crucial juridical question, as summarised below:

1. Caliph Umar was assured at the time that the land was able to bear the Kharāj tax which was imposed on it. This may be inferred from the next point.
2. After the return of Ĥużaifah and Uthmān, Caliph Umar's administrators, from surveying the land and levying the tax, Umar asked them, "How did you levy on the land? Perhaps you imposed on the inhabitants more than they could bear?" Ĥużaifah replied, "I left a surplus" and Uthmān said, "I left twice as much as I could take if I wanted to". Umar said, "Beware not to levy tax on the land beyond what it could bear". By asking his officers these questions, Caliph Umar was perhaps in doubt whether his fixed-rate

tax reflected the complete fairness he wanted to achieve. But by the assertion of the two administrators that they had not charged the land with more than it could bear, the land must have been able to pay the tax imposed. Abū-Yūsuf in putting this point forward seemed to have wanted to stress the point of the condition for complete fairness in taxing the land, which although it could have been achieved during Caliph Umar's time it might not have been realised afterwards. The following point clarifies this further.

3. At the time of Caliph Umar the cultivated lands were much greater than the uncultivated lands which were very minor. While the fixed rate system on cultivable land, either cultivated or uncultivated, worked in forcing the keepers to cultivate the land, there were lands left uncultivated for one hundred years or so after Caliph Umar's time. These could not be developed and cultivated without the heavy expenditures and investment that lay beyond the ability of the peasants. Therefore, the cultivation of these neglected lands in the near future was virtually impossible. The principle of complete justice could not, therefore, exist without a change in the system.
4. Consequently, a fixed rate of tax could be harmful to the ruler, the Treasury, and the taxpayer. To the ruler, if it happens that the corn is very cheap in a certain year, with the fixed measure of crops the revenue from the collected tax will not be sufficient when converted into cash to cover the state expenses. On the other hand, if the price of crops rises the ruler will not be ready to give up what is collected of crops which might be regarded as excessive (in monetary terms) by the taxpayers. Moreover, the fixed tax rate, in cash or in kind, is harmful to the taxpayer because the possibility that they may entail unjust distribution of the taxes and the oppression of the weak by the strong.
5. If what Caliph Umar imposed on the land was final it would not be lawful to increase or reduce the tax. But Umar did not say that what he imposed of Kharāj was final or that it was not permissible for him or for a Caliph after him to reduce or increase it.
6. Caliph Umar's question to Ĥużaifah and Uthmān "Perhaps you levied on the land more than what it could bear?" furnishes an argument that if they had informed him that the land could not bear such taxes he would have reduced the Kharāj tax. As Caliph Umar's question implied, the tax was imposed on what the land could bear and this could be changeable.

7. Uthmān's and Ĥużaifah's answer to Caliph Umar's question that they left excess which they could have taxed if they wished and the approval of Umar of this answer reinforces the argument that the tax could be increased or decreased depending on what the land could bear.
8. By changing the taxation system from the fixed tax system to the proportional crop-sharing system, *muqāsamah*, Caliph Umar's rule of not charging the land more than it could bear would be more observed.
9. The ruler has the right to decrease or increase the Kharāj tax but he should avoid over-burdening the land taxpayers with the tax.
10. The argument in the previous point was reinforced by that which Caliph Umar levied on the people of *al-Sawad* one bushel and/or dirhams on every *jarib* (a survey measure) of cultivated or uncultivated land and eight dirhams on each *jarib* of palm trees, but he later cancelled the tax on the palm trees that were growing in areas otherwise cultivated to make the tax more bearable to the tax-payer. Also, when Caliph Umar sent his administrator Ya'la ibn Umayyah to Najran, he instructed him to hand over the land to them on a proportional crop-sharing tax system: two-thirds of tax on the yield of corn and the yield of palm trees in naturally irrigated land and one-third in artificially irrigated land. These two examples, al-Sawad and Najrān, show that the ruler has the discretion to impose on people what is bearable in accordance with the capacity of the taxpayers.
11. When the Prophet conquered Khyber by force he did not levy a Kharāj tax on the land in the form of a fixed monetary tax. Instead, he gave it to the keepers of the land, the Jews, on a *musāqāh* agreement whereby half of the yield was to be taken in the form of tax.
12. Caliph Umar ibn Abdel-Azīz, the pious Umayyad Caliph, ordered one of his governors, Abdel Hamid ibn Abdel Rahman, to survey the land and instructed him not to treat the barren land as the land under cultivation, or vice versa. The barren land should be surveyed, and a levy applied that was related to what it was capable of producing if it was improved and became worth cultivating. For the land on which the Kharāj was to be exempted the matter should be resolved leniently to the satisfaction of the people on the land. No Kharāj was to be imposed on the houses,

or the income earned by female workers or those who embraced Islam.

In the light of the above Abū-Yūsuf recommended that the best taxation system for the Treasury, and the most adequate one to prevent injustice to the taxpayer, was a just proportional crop-sharing tax system, *muqāsamah*. To him, the system would benefit the Treasury and at the same time alleviate injustice to the taxpayer.

On the rate of *muqāsamah*, the sharing proportion, Abū-Yūsuf proposed a variable rate depending upon the ability of the land to pay and the burden of cultivation. He suggested the rates to be as follows:

1. Two-fifths, 40%, on wheat and barley of the lands that were irrigated naturally, i.e. by rainfall and the water of natural springs.
2. One-and-half-tenth, 15%, and three-tenths, 30%, on crops from the lands that were irrigated artificially, depending upon the amount of toil endured and the methods of irrigation required. The low rate in this category compared with the previous one was meant to allow for the cost of irrigation.
3. One-third on palm trees, vineyards, vegetables and orchards, but only one-quarter would be taken from summer crops.
4. One-tenth on the lands of *qata'i* that were irrigated naturally and one-twentieth on the artificially irrigated. *Qata'i* lands were, as explained previously, the lands granted by the caliph to those rendering distinguished services to the state and Islam. They were not always of high quality and some required the construction of bridges and canals.
5. One-tenth, 10%, and Zakāh on the lands of Ushr, owned by Muslims, if the land was irrigated naturally and half-tenth, 5%, if irrigated artificially.

From the administration point of view, Abū-Yūsuf confirmed that a proper means of valuation should be followed and nothing should be taken on the basis of a guess or a mere conjecture. A market value, determined by market forces, should be reached where the whole produce was sold in the market and then the entire sale proceeds were divided into the specified shares, or, in the absence of a market value a valuation should be based on a just appraisal that was not overcharging the taxpayer nor damaging the interest of the authority. In both cases, whatever was easier to the taxpayers was to be used.

Also, perishable commodities, such as vegetables, melons, cucumber, pumpkins, eggplants, carrots, herbs, aromatic plants, and similar, and wood for fuel, were all exempt from the tax. The simple administrative criterion of differentiation was that the non-perishable commodities were those which were normally measured in bushel, *qafīz*, and weighed in *rutl* (a weight) such as wheat, barley, maize, rice, sesame, hemp, almonds, hazel-nuts, walnuts, peanuts, saffron, olives, safflower, coriander, caraway, cumin, onion, garlic, and similar crops (all these examples of produce were given by Abū-Yūsuf in his Kitāb al-Kharāj).

A threshold was also given. The tax was to be imposed on five *wasaqs* or more. If the land produced less than five *wasaqs* no tax was to be charged. In calculating the thresholds, quantities of different produce were added up. If the land produced two and half *wasaqs* of wheat and two and half *wasaqs* of barley (total of five *wasaqs*) or if the produce consisted of one *wasaq* of wheat, one of barley, one of rice, one of dates, and one of raisins (total of five *wasaqs*) the tax was imposed. If the total was not five *wasaqs* no tax was imposed except for expensive produce such as saffron which was taxed at the above rates even if the produce was less than five *wasaqs* as long as the value of the produce was equivalent to the value of five *wasaqs* of cereals which was the cheapest yield of the land. If the value of the saffron was less than the value of the cereals no tax was charged. This was a distinct differentiation that considered the ability of the produce to pay.

Furthermore, in leniency to the tax payer, if the yield was found to be less than the threshold, five *wasaqs*, because the owner had consumed part of the produce or fed his family, neighbours and friends, or part of it was stolen, the tax will be calculated on the balance after deducting the above. In allowing a threshold, Abū-Yūsuf differed from his teacher Abū-Ĥanīfah whose view was that nothing should be exempt from the tax even if it was of the smallest quantity. In permitting the reduction of the produce used for feeding the family and friends from the tax base the threshold was in effect greater than it was under Abū-Ĥanīfah's and was effectively a surplus over the personal use. Also, allowing a similar deduction for feeding friends and neighbours would make the threshold even greater. This last allowance may have been deemed as being in line with the culture of generosity of the day as well as being a contributing factor towards strengthening the relationship and harmony between members of the community.

To clarify the unit of measurement, the above was based on the following measures: a *wasaq* (bushel) consisted of sixty *sa'*, specified as the Prophet's *sa'*, five wasaqs therefore contained 300 hundred *sa'*. The *sa'* contained five and a third *rutl*, and the *rutl* was a pound in weight of grain of wheat (Al-Rayyis, 1977). To put it another way, the threshold in weight was about 1,600 pounds of wheat. If there are 2.2 lb in one Kilogramme, the threshold would be the equivalent of approximately 727 kilogrammes of wheat in today's terms.

The base of Kharāj tax was widened further by including the lands conquered after the reign of Caliph Umar. Having looked at the land of Iraq which had seen Caliph Umar's rulings, Abū-Yūsuf turned his attention to other lands which were not yet under Caliph Umar's administration. Once more the role of jurisprudence became useful and the pragmatic conviction of the Ĥanafī in the principle of public interest provided practical answers. In Abū-Yūsuf's view the land of Basra and Khurasān were like the land of al-Sawad, "in my opinion", as he says. Those lands which were conquered by force are Kharāj lands and were subject to Kharāj tax which could be increased or decreased, in variation from Caliph Umar's rates.

There was one exception to the permission suggested by Abū-Yūsuf to increase or decrease the rate of Kharāj and that was related to lands under peace treaty. These lands should be taxed in accordance with the terms of the peace treaties, which should never be altered. The only factor that would cause a change was that if the people of the lands under the treaty embraced Islam. In this case one-tenth, *ushr*, or half of that depending upon the state of irrigation, would be imposed on their lands. So "my opinion is that you should leave them in their present condition (in accordance with the terms of the treaty), and this is the verdict upon which your action should be taken", says Abū-Yūsuf.

The economic implications of muqāsamah

Compared with the fixed rate of tax, *muqāsamah* may lead to reducing, or eliminating, the excess burden of taxation through reducing the dead loss of tax. The figure below shows this effect. Assuming that the conditions of demand and supply are as projected in the figure, imposing a fixed monetary tax on a commodity would increase the price per unit by the amount of tax; from P_1 to P_2, the difference being equivalent to the tax per unit. In the absence of external effects and with the market operating under perfect conditions, the supply curve S will shift upward to SS reflecting a higher social opportunity cost of the commodity. But the new level of supply will reduce the quantity demanded and supplied from Q_1 to Q_2. This will generate to the state tax revenue correspondent to the area P_1 P_2 A E, i.e. Q_2*(P_2-P_1). The consumers however will lose the benefit of consumption that is equivalent to P_1 P_2 A C. The consumers' loss is therefore greater than the benefit to the state from the tax. The area AEC is an excess tax burden, or dead loss (James, 1983). The same could be applied to reflect the mirror image from the producer point of view. The dead loss in this case will be the area BEC. The total dead loss, as a result of imposing the tax, is represented in the area ABC.

Abū-Yūsuf's Muqāsamah taxation system will not suffer the same disadvantage. The price of the commodities will be free from the possibility of incurring an increase, other things, as economists say, being equal. Moreover, Abū-Yūsuf's suggestion implied that the share of the state from the produce will be sold alongside that of the tax payer, which is more likely to help determine the price by market forces. After all, the Islamic approach to economics calls for not fixing the price and leaving it to free market forces, as Abū-Yūsuf confirmed on this occasion in reiterating the saying of the Prophet.

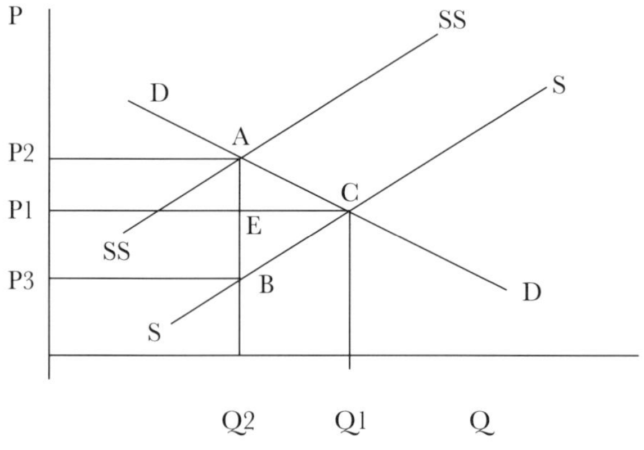

Ushr *Tax*

Still under land taxation, the *ushr* land tax was the land tax, the rate of which was one-tenth, or half of that, one-twentieth, depending upon the state of land and irrigation. The base of tax included four types of land: (a) land in the hands of Muslims, (b) lands in the hands of the People of the Book in Arabia, Christian and Jews, (c) lands of *qata'i*, and (e) revived lands. In terms of the tax rate and the justification for the variation from that established before him, Abū-Yūsuf's proposal is outlined below.

Lands in the hands of Muslims

The tax base was the land owned by Muslims before the Islamic conquests, i.e. lands in Arabia, and outside Arabia if purchased after the conquests. The latter type was a development that was witnessed during the Umayyads and the Abbasids but was not approved of during Caliph Umar's time. We notice that during Caliph Umar's reign the purchase of land by Muslims outside Arabia was not permissible as the conquered land was regarded as collectively owned by all Muslims. "These are the owners of the land, have you purchased it from them?!", said Caliph Umar while pointing to Muslims sitting at a meeting, in reproach of someone who purchased land in Iraq (Abū-Yūsuf). But the rule seemed to have been relaxed after Umar's time.

The tax rate was one-tenth, ten percent, if the land was irrigated naturally, by rainfall or canals. Half of that, five per cent, would apply if the irrigation was undertaken artificially such as by using labour and machinery, or if the land was in need of extra toil in digging and tilling, which would incur extra expenses. As the rate was determined by the Prophet during his life, that was not to be changed. However, the rate could deviate from that, in Abū-Yūsuf's view, on Muslims' land outside Arabia. And this is where the Ĥanafī approach to jurisprudence became operational. He believed that the Prophet's ruling covered only lands in Arabia, as other lands were not conquered during his time, and it was wrong to include villages of Persia under the terms of the Arabian villages. He advocated that land of Iraq should be treated differently, be taxed at a higher rate than ushr, and the ruler would be legitimately acting if he deviated from the practice of the Prophet in this particular regard. Practically,

Abū-Yūsuf's view would put all lands outside Arabia, either owned by Muslims or not, on an equal footing. The argument against that is that Muslims would still have to pay Zakāh on their possessions, which might be higher than the *jizyah* imposed on non-Muslims depending upon their state of wealth.

Lands in the hands of the People of the Book in Arabia

Arabia was singled out in its tax treatment because the rate imposed was determined by the Prophet. In support of this view, Abū-Yūsuf stated that with regard to the land of Ĥijaz, Makkah and al-Medīnah, the land of Yemen and the other lands of Arabia which the Prophet had conquered, the tax was not to be increased or decreased. This was something on which the Prophet had issued his orders and no one could change them, and that was the tax rate of only one tenth, *ushr*, or half-*ushr* depending upon the state of irrigation. In taxation terms, these lands were, therefore, regarded as *ushr* land. But in contrast to others, the Arab pagans who did not have a monotheistic religion were treated differently in that no Jizyah was to be accepted from them and they would have to either accept Islam or to be put to sword. On them Kharāj tax was not, therefore, applicable. The people of Yemen, still in the lands of Arabia, were the People of the Book and as such they were allowed to retain their religion for the payment of *jizyah*, the poll tax for non-Muslims and the one-tenth tax, *ushr*, or half of that, on their lands.

To sum up, in the Arabian Peninsula, where people were only either Muslims or Christians and Jews, the land was taxed by the Prophet, and remained so, at the rate of *ushr*. In retrospect, the question that could be asked would be: would the Prophet have adopted a different attitude towards the taxation of land in Arabia that was similar to that advocated by Abū-Yūsuf outside Arabia? We do not know. On economic grounds, the fertility of lands in South Arabia could not have been less than that of other conquered lands outside the Arabian Peninsula. We saw in previous chapters how these regions had developed an advanced civilization based on agriculture and how trade routes between the south and north continued to be particularly active up to the emergence of Islam and after. Did the Prophet aim to achieve equality of treatment in taxing the land in general, and as such should this equality have been maintained throughout the Islamic state? Or did he want to tax the land in Arabia in that particular manner, but allow land outside Arabia to be taxed differently? We do not know the answer to either question, and a variety of answers are possible. But, on the whole, the argument of the Ĥanafī chief justice seems to carry "legal" conviction.

Lands of Qata'i

Abū-Yūsuf then turned his attention to an important tax base which by the standard of the day must have been of a sensitive nature: the fiefs, or *sawāfī* lands; the terms are used interchangeably. He began by clarifying, or rather, stating a condition for the land to be regarded as such. The condition was that these lands were crown lands which belonged to: (a) the Persian king, or his family, (b) a man who had been killed in war without heirs, (c) one who had fled to the land of the enemy, (d) the under-water lands, (e) post office buildings, and (f) all the lands that did not belong to anyone or had a right of inheritance on them, or had a sign of any development on them.

When this land, or part of it, is given to someone in appreciation of his services the land under the new owner is called *qata'i*. In that, Abū-Yūsuf argued that the ruler had the right to give rewards out of *sawāfī* land to those who had offered valuable services to Islam, and a just ruler would do that without undeserved preference between them. In that, Abū-Yūsuf differed from those jurists who held the view that the lands belonged to all Muslims and therefore should not be distributed to anyone. Instead, he took the opposite view that contended that the ruler might grant this land to someone, as the Prophet did with the land of Banū-al-Nadhīr and the other lands that were in his disposition. One could argue, however, that the land given by the Prophet was modest in size in comparison with lands allocated after him. Abū-Yūsuf, however, did not elaborate on this and briefly based his opinion on the Prophet's Sunnah.

Was Abū-Yūsuf trying to please his caliph by giving him a free hand in distributing this land, or did he really believe that a degree of flexibility ought to be guaranteed in order to improve the efficiency of the land by putting it in charge of able persons? The answer is perhaps both. However, judging by how Abū-Yūsuf was able to address his caliph objectively, or daringly, in his introduction, one would argue that it was more likely that Abū-Yūsuf's main aim was to put that land in to good use.

Keen to see stability in land ownership and in related business transactions, and with a view to curbing the freedom of the ruler to changing this relationship, Abū-Yūsuf stressed that the decision of the ruler of granting the land should not be annulled by any other ruler after him. The land could not be taken back, providing that it was not beyond what the holder could manage to look after. Further, the holder had the right to transfer the allocated land by sale or inheritance. In confirming that, Abū-Yūsuf went even further as to state that if the land was taken back then it would be like robbing someone and giving the stolen property to someone else.

With regard to the tax rate levied on those *qata'i*, Abū-Yūsuf was of the view that *qata'i* lands be taxed at one-tenth, *ushr*, for it was like *ushr* lands in the hands of Muslims. He proceeded, however, by suggesting that a heavier tax could be imposed at the discretion of the ruler: double the ushr, one-fifth, or a Kharāj tax. By advocating a heavier tax, Abū-Yūsuf seemed to be allowing for the fact that the land was granted with no financial sacrifice in return; no capital was paid in the acquisition. On the other hand, looking at it from the tax payer's point of view, and possibly in reflection to the reported low efficiency of these lands and the need for the extra care to improve its productivity, no increase beyond the one-tenth, *ushr*, was charged if the granted land had to bear the expenses of digging canals, erecting farm buildings, and drilling the land. "The matter", however, "rests with you, you should act upon what you see fit", Abū-Yūsuf addresses his caliph.

Revived lands

On the relationship between tax and economic efficiency, in relation to land, Abū-Yūsuf turned to answer an important question: what was the most suitable tax policy to be adopted regarding uncultivated and unused lands? Focusing on barren lands he began with a definition, or condition: these were the lands where there was no sign of any construction or cultivation or that the land was used for public utility for the people of the towns such as public parks, grave yards, forests, a pasture for cattle and sheep, and it is not in the possession of anyone. Then he proceeded with the following opinion: (a) as a general rule, whoever revives such land, or any part of it, becomes its legitimate owner, and (b) the caliph may grant from this land to whom he wishes, lease of it, or do anything beneficial with it, but (c) a permission was required from the Caliph when reviving the barren land in order to claim its ownership otherwise, in the absence of permission, the land may be taken away from the reviver. In agreement with Abū-Ĥanīfah, but in contrast to the Sunnah, Abū-Yūsuf explains the reason for the permission as being necessary in case there was a conflict of interest or competition over the land. However, Abū-Yūsuf was of the opinion that if there was no damage or harm to someone, or dispute over the land, no permit was necessary and the general practice of the Prophet would hold. In taxing the revived land after cultivation, the *ushr*, one-tenth, should be imposed if the land belonged to the category of *ushr* land, and Kharāj tax should be levied if it was Kharāj land. Also, if the revived barren land was part of the conquered land which the Caliph decided to distribute to the conquerors (Muslims), after deducting the state's one fifth, Khums, the reviver would pay the *ushr*, one-tenth, or half the *ushr* depending upon the state of irrigation. On the other hand if the land was part of the conquered land which the Caliph decided to leave in the hands of its owners (non-Muslims), the reviver would pay the Kharāj tax on the revived land.

Administration of land tax

On the administration of Kharāj, Abū-Yūsuf believed that no Kharāj administrator or a governor was entitled to release someone from the Kharāj tax without permission from the Caliph. Similarly, no one was to be allowed to accept a release from the Kharāj tax imposed on him knowing that no permission had been given from the authority to release it. Release from the Kharāj tax may be granted to someone if this was for the benefit of the community.

Also, it was not permissible for anyone to convert Kharāj land to *ushr* land or vice versa. The conversion was permissible only when a man who possessed land of *ushr* bought land of Kharāj in the neighbourhood and joined the two lands together, and then he paid *ushr* on it. The conversion was also permissible when a man who owned Kharāj land purchased land of *ushr* and added it to his own land; he would pay Kharāj tax on it.

Furthermore, Abū-Yūsuf was against intermediaries between the Treasury and tax payers in paying land tax, or taxes in general. The practice of an intermediary holding himself responsible for the required payment, paying it to the government on time, or even in advance, and collect that from the tax payers was a notable feature of land taxation during the Umayyad and Abbasīd caliphate, as mentioned earlier. It was easier for the Treasury, and even more beneficial, if the tax was paid by the intermediary agent in advance. But that method had adverse consequences as the agent very often charged the real tax payer more than the due tax. In effect it was a feature of injustice. Abū-Yūsuf was entirely against it, "in such a system lies the devastation of the country and the destruction of the subjects". He strongly recommended that the system of intermediary be abolished.

Other Taxes on Derived Products

These products could be mainly divided into three categories: (a) products derived from agriculture, (b) products extracted from the ground, and (c) what is produced from the sea. For the produce derived from agriculture, Abū-Yūsuf turned to products such as honey, nuts and almonds and clarified how these were to be taxed. Notably, he suggested that nothing should be levied on cane, fuel-wood, grass, straw, nor on palm-boughs; except for sweet rush because it is a useful plant even though it is not edible, and sugar-cane which is edible. Also, nothing was to be imposed on petroleum, tar, mercury, or asphalt, found in the land. With regard to sea products, one-fifth, *Khums*, was suggested on whatever was brought out from the sea such as ornaments and amber. With respect to other sea products, Abū-Yūsuf was in disagreement with his teacher Abū-Hanīfah who believed that nothing was taxable, because they were like fish which was not taxable. Relying on evidence from the practice of the second caliph Umar, Abū-Yūsuf believed that one-fifth, *Khums*, should be imposed on all sea products. One wonders what Abū-Yūsuf's opinion would be on the taxation of the excavation of oil and other minerals on such a large commercial scale today.

Zakāh

Abū-Yūsuf's treatment of the tax base and tax rate did not stop at land taxation; it went beyond that to look into Zakāh. However, he confined his treatment of the subject to Zakāh on animals. In examining the base and rate of tax, Abū-Yūsuf, reiterated the rules of the Sharī'ah which have been established in the Qur'ān and laid down in the Sunnah. A threshold is given and a form of a near proportionate rate is applied.

But Abū-Yūsuf emphasised some important issues in his book in relation to the administration of Zakāh. First, when Zakāh is imposed on animals three points should be taken into account: (a) the base of tax should not be enlarged by the collectors unnecessarily by gathering together the scattered herds that are not meant to be together, or reduced by the tax payer by dividing the herd—to benefit from the threshold allowances, (b) Zakāh on jointly owned herds will be apportioned equally between the partners, (c) no Zakāh is to be imposed on animals used for cultivation; the idea of exempting from tax assets used in production and (d) other matters related to caring for animals in the process, taking the average animal not the best or the worst, not taking animals that were providing milk to their offspring, not taking newly born animals that are relying on their mothers for feeding, taking care of animals in transportation and so on. Animal care seemed to have been of the concern to administration. This is not surprising if we know that there are *Aĥadīth* that urge Muslims to be kind to animals.

Second, the necessity of observing efficiency of administration in the collection of Zakāh and distribution of its revenue: (a) an honest man was to be chosen by the caliph and put in charge of the administration of Zakāh as a head of his team (minister of Zakāh ?), (b) this honest head man should choose an honest man in every city whom he trusts for the collection of Zakāh in the city, (c) the administration of the collection of Zakāh should be separated from that of other taxes because Zakāh revenue ought not to be mixed with the revenue of other taxes and this is because other taxes are meant to generate revenue for all public purposes, while Zakāh revenue should be distributed in a particular manner specified in the Qur'ān, (d) Zakāh revenue, coming from different Zakāh sources in the region, should be joined together and specifically spent on: the poor, the destitute, those who collect it, those whose hearts are to be won over, the emancipation of captives, those who are in debt, in the cause of God, and the wayfarer, (e) Zakāh collectors should be paid what was sufficient to sustain them even if it was more than the specified one-eighth of the revenue. Also, the Zakāh share of "in the cause of God" may be spent on the improvement of public roads.

The shares of the poor and destitute must be distributed to those entitled to receive them from the people who live in the town where the Zakāh was collected, and should not be given to those of other localities.

Interestingly enough, Abū-Yūsuf treated the administration of Zakāh under a separate chapter, "The increase, decrease and loss of Zakāh revenue". By doing that, Abū-Yūsuf emphasised the need for the proper administration of Zakāh.

The administration of both Zakāh and Kharāj would have had several implications on compliance costs, the administrative burden, and the net benefit of the tax. In the absence of the state discretion with regard to the tax rate or base, the net revenue of tax can be increased by minimising administrative costs and potential waste of revenue through efficiency; hence, maximising the tax net revenue. This brings to mind "efficiency" as one of the four emphases in Adam Smiths' cannons of taxation of which the other three are certainty, fairness and clarity (Adam Smith, Wealth of Nations). In fact, bearing in mind all that Abū-Yūsuf wrote in his book on taxation, it can be said that Adam Smith's four cannons of taxation are certainly included in Kitāb al-Kharāj.

Jizyah

In addition to investigating Zakāh taxation on Muslims, Abū-Yūsuf examined the Jizyah taxation on non-Muslims. In a similar fashion he reiterated the ruling of the Sharī'ah regarding the base and the tax rate, emphasising that although it was a tax per head the ability-to-pay of the tax payer was to be taken into consideration: 48 dirhams per annum on the wealthy, to be halved to 24 on those on middle incomes, and this to be halved to 12 on the labourer unless he had wealth. Children, women, the poor and recipients of charity, monks unless they were wealthy, were exempt. In case of dispute over the level of wealth and in the absence of hard evidence an oath taken from the man according to his sacred book would be sufficient. Other rules stating that Jizyah was not a debt on the deceased to be deducted from his legacy, conversion to Islam before and after the expiry of the one-year-period, and the importance of exercising leniency in collection were stressed. *Aĥadīth* reporting the Prophet as saying that he would be the advocate of the oppressed Jizyah payer in the Day of Judgment were quoted.

On the administration side, once more Abū-Yūsuf emphasised the need for observing efficiency in the administration, parallel to that of Zakāh. One would notice that leniency was particularly emphasised by Abū-Yūsuf in the administration of Jizyah. As non-Muslims were the ethnic minority it was conceivable that a chief judge and a writer on the affairs of the state would stress the importance of these points to ensure equality and societal harmony in the community.

Custom Dues

Abū-Yūsuf started his chapter on custom dues by an emphasis on administration, "in my opinion, you should entrust it to honest and God-fearing officials who should be clearly warned not to wrong the subjects by charging more than what is due. You should also investigate their doings, dismiss the wrong-doers and return what they overcharged to the wronged subjects, and reward those who carried out their duties honestly and justly". Then he proceeded to highlight the charged rate, the tax base, the threshold, and the tax incident that would prompt the charge. Exemptions were stressed: animals not meant to be for trade such as sheep, cattle and camels if they were not pasturing animals, cereals meant to be for sowing and not for sale, and other agriculture produce and dates if they were not purchased for trade. Interestingly enough, it was sufficient for an exemption to be granted that the person would take an oath, according to his religion, to state that these goods were not for trade. One would add to that that the officials would perhaps need to be vigilant as to what quantity of goods could pass as being for personal use. Subjective criteria would possibly be relied on, hence the emphasis of Abū-Yūsuf on fairness and God fearing officials. A threshold was also established, and, in contrast to modern practice, the tax was applied annually. One wonders what sort of documentation was used by the state officials to ensure proper financial control. But this is another subject.

Custom dues were introduced by the second caliph Umar when he noticed that other countries charged the dues on the trade passing their borders. In a way, it started as a form of a reciprocal treatment.

Public Administration "Law and Order"

Various chapters of Abū-Yūsuf's treatise could be categorised under this heading. Examples of these are: the arrangements regarding the conduct of religious festivals of the People of the Book, the building of churches, synagogues, and monasteries, people of no recognised sacred books, crimes of houses of disrepute, theft, and moral offenses, apostasy, and spying. Although all these issues were not related to taxation or public finance they were important, as Abū-Yūsuf saw them, to the legal framework of the state. This shows further that Abū-Yūsuf's work was not exclusively on "land taxation" as is often perceived.

Other Issues

There are other issues relating to the economy of the state, which can be categorised, as below.

Leasing

On leasing, Abū-Yūsuf focused on leasing of fields and palm orchards, with a particular reference to the cultivation of barren land on a lease basis. Abū-Yūsuf explained that the jurists in al-Hijaz (the Mālikī) had a different view from that of the jurists in al-kufa. In al-Ĥijaz and al-Medīnah, jurists, did not allow the lease of barren land on a sharing basis, one half or one third, as they argued that barren land was not like orchards and other gardens for which they allowed sharing leases. Some of the jurists in al-Kufa allowed sharing in orchards and other trees and permitted sharing of crops in barren land at a half and one-third ratio, while others did not allow sharing in orchards or other fruit trees and did not permit sharing of crops in a barren land. Abū-Hanīfah was against the validity of the lease.

Those jurists who did not allow the transaction relied on the juridical argument against uncertainty; the yield from the lease of the barren land was uncertain and any involvement in such a transaction could be harmful to either partner. On the other hand, those who allowed leasing depended strictly on the practice of the Prophet when he let the lands of Khyber to the inhabitants of Khyber on a yield sharing basis.

Abū-Yūsuf's view was that all such leases were allowed and valid. He regarded them as sharing in partnership contracts in which one partner participates in the partnership with his capital and the other with his labour and expertise. The profit, even if it was still unknown to them, were divided on the basis of profit-and-loss-sharing. This form of partnership is unanimously acceptable by jurists. In Abū-Yūsuf's view, leasing of barren land, orchards and other trees was like a partnership: the land was similar to the capital in the partnership contract. To enforce his view, Abū-Yūsuf relied on the precedent of the Prophet in the lands of Khyber. The *Aĥadīth* in support of permission were more reliable and general than the *Aĥadīth* in support of inhibition, he argued. Abū-Yūsuf elucidated different forms of lease contracts in which he clarified the relationship between the partners in the contract, and the tax position of each. It is apparent from his classification that Abū-Yūsuf widened the scope of leasing by allowing several structures. He perhaps had in mind a special consideration for public interest without sacrificing the basic principle that the partners should be clear before the start of the transaction as to the conditions of the contract. His thought on the classification coincides with the classification as known in modern time and the differentiation between a financial lease and other types of lease.

Public goods and externalities

Abū-Yūsuf stressed the importance of public works undertaken by the state in improving the conditions of agriculture. The state should be digging canals, building bridges, and maintaining roads. This would have a threefold effect: (a) helps reduce the area of uncultivated lands, (b) helps increase the productivity of cultivated lands, and consequently, (c) helps increase the tax revenue. To emphasise this point further he stated that public works are one of the main duties of the state as they involved substantial expenses beyond that of what land owners could bear.

In reaffirming the Islamic principles he referred to the public ownership of three distinctive types of goods: water, fire and pasture. No private ownership of these goods could be allowed to deprive others from their use as long as no harm would fall upon the owner as a result of allowing others to use the goods within his ownership.

Pricing, scarcity and value

The general rule of determining prices by market forces is affirmed by Abū-Yūsuf. Price fixing was rejected by the Prophet in an example given when people asked him to fix prices, as previously stated.

But while discussing pricing of goods, Abū-Yūsuf made a pertinent remark. His thought on this was that supply does not affect prices: goods supply can be high and the goods abundant, but prices can be high, while supply can be low and goods not in abundance and prices can be low. He applies the same to money supply. Abū-Yūsuf does not elaborate on this, however, nor does he refer, explicitly, to the relationship between demand and supply as illustrated in Adam Smith's example of the scissor blades. He seemed to have focused on the supply side only. Could the demand side be inferred from his statement to complete the equation? We do not know. But what we do know is that he reached what became a plausible argument after him that the supply side on its own does not make the prices what they are. Conceivably, he seemed to have assigned a greater role to demand in affecting prices than supply.

Furthermore when dealing with pricing, Abū-Yūsuf touched on a very important point in economics, on the relationship between economic goods, scarcity and value. Discussing the issue of whether one could charge for a good that is regarded as readily available commonly and the conditions for the charge, he, using the example of water, stating that while the water from a running river may not have a value, it would have a value if it was brought to a different location where the river was not running. He referred in particular to three important factors that would create a value for a good, the water in his example: scarcity, the cost of equipment and transportation costs. This analysis conforms to the fundamental analysis of value in economics.

The above were the main points in Abū-Yūsuf's book of al-Kharāj. We have given Abū-Yūsuf a considerable amount of thought in this book. This is for various reasons: (a) it was the first book to be published on Islamic economics, (b) it was necessary to look, in some detail, into the work to gain an insight into the thinking of the first Muslim writer in the field, especially as (c) the book was a first serious work on Islamic economics, particularly when (d) the book provided a comprehensive framework, almost a constitution, on the state finance and public administration, of (e) a considerable magnitude, and (f) the book could still be regarded as a reference book by the standards of today. For that, Abū-Yūsuf deserved a special treatment. Not all the writers following Abū-Yūsuf will enjoy the same expanded coverage. Due space will however be given when the need arises, as we will see later.

Following Abū-Yūsuf's Kitāb al-Kharāj, the writing of specialized books on Islamic economics took an interesting turn. It moved away from Abū-Yūsuf's area of public finance, into a much more entrepreneurial area with more of, to use a modern term, a micro economic approach to economics. Borrowing a nineteenth century term, we could say without much exaggeration that it was the beginning of writing on political economy. An example of this is the treatise of al-Shaibānī on "Earnings".

Al-Shaibānī (132–189 A.H., 750–804 A.C.): From Macro-Economics to Micro-Economics: Kitāb al-Iktisāb, Book of Earnings

The significance of the work of al-Shaibānī is that his book is purely on micro economics. No public finance or state taxation; instead it concerns consumption, production, value and distribution. In addition, he wrote his book on his own initiative without being commissioned by a government authority or a caliph's request—at least there is no evidence to suggest otherwise. In that sense it can be said that with al-Shaibānī's writing, economics was beginning to develop as an independent body of literature. More important, his ideas on economics seemed to coincide, partially, with some of the economic thought that came a few centuries after him.

The Author

He is Muĥammad ibn-al-Ĥassan al-Shaibānī (132–189 A.H./750–804 A.C.). Like his predecessor Abū-Yūsuf, al-Shaibānī, whose life span overlapped with that of Abū-Yūsuf (731–798 A.C.), he was a jurist and a judge, though he did not reach the position of chief justice. He was another Ĥanafī who received his juridical education from Abū-Hanīfah, the founder of the school, then he became one of Abū-Yūsuf's followers after Abū-Hanīfah's death in 150 A.H./767 A.D. He was highly regarded by his contemporaries. Financially, he seemed to have been well off. His inheritance from his father was said to be 30,000 dirham, most of which is said to have been spent on learning as he devoted most of his time to education (Arnoos, 1986). This seemed to have been reflected in his views as demonstrated in his book. But this wealth did not lead to vanity. We see him emphasising in his book that the rich are in need of the poor as the poor are in need of the rich.

The Book

What has come to us of al-Shaibānī's Earnings of a Clean Living, *al-Iktisāb fi al-Rizk al-Mustatāb*, is about a 20,000 word summary of his original book, by one of his followers, Muĥammad ibn-Sama'ah. The book itself does not seem to have survived the ravage of time. Moreover, the summary includes some commentary notes by another consecutive scholar, al-Sarkhasi, who died in 483 A.H. (ibid.). How big the original book was, we do not know but with a summary of that size the original book must have been substantial.

The general scientific approach of the book is the deductive approach. The author raises the issue, examines the Qur'ānic verses and the Prophet's sayings and, then, states his findings. Representative examples from real life were also given. And when the issue is controversial the author is persuasive: he discusses the question, extracts evidence from the Qur'ān and Sunnah, uses analytical reasoning and then reaches a conclusion which very often has a compelling effect. Again, an analytical approach of a judge—a Ĥanafī judge.

Consumption and Earnings

Al-Shaibānī associated consumption with earnings and, as expected, the divine ruling. In what seems to be an austerity approach to physiological consumption he divided consumption into three levels, the first is the level of subsistence, or necessities, the second is the level of moderation, or enhancement, and the third is the level of extravagance, or refinement. Concerning the first, the consumer is compelled by the divine rule to satisfy this level. This might sound like stating the obvious as the consumer is driven to the satisfaction of these needs by nature's forces. But three points would clarify the need for al-Shaibānī's emphasis: first; to him the consumer is not only the consumer per se, rather he is the household consumer that includes in addition to himself his wife and dependent children and parents, and, second; the level of physiological needs also includes clothing and housing, or as he put it, "eating, drinking, clothing and sheltering from the cold and the heat", and third; there is no room in his mind for abstention from satisfying these needs, in full, under any false religious pretense. The level of consumption here is therefore extended horizontally to include the household (the family including parents if they have no means of support), and vertically to embrace a bundle of necessities. Satisfying this level, in his mind, is a divine duty of the first degree. The implications of characterising this level as such are twofold: (a) not satisfying this level would render a divine punishment on the consumer: the less is consumed, the higher the penalty, and the more that is consumed, the higher the divine reward, and (b) the consumer should endeavour to seek a means of earnings to cover these needs and this endeavour is regarded as a compulsory divine duty of the first degree.

Bearing in mind the same concept of the consumer as being the household, the second level of consumption, is the level of moderation. In al-Shaibānī's words, it is the level of *ma'rūf*, which he defines as the level that is below the level of extravagance and above the level of niggardliness, *doon al-saraf wa fawq al-taqteer*. The types of goods in this category are as inclusive as before but the quantity and variety can be greater and the quality may be higher. In relation to earnings, the consumer, should seek earnings to satisfy these needs also. However, no divine punishment would be incurred if he did not do so providing that there is a legitimate reason for not trying to earn more, such as spending time seeking knowledge and becoming educated, and spending time, in the cause of God. This is in contrast to the previous level where not seeking earnings to satisfy attracts a penalty.

The third level is the level of extravagance, and this is forbidden. It is the level above the level of moderation. But in relation to earnings, this does not imply that the consumer should not endeavour to work hard in pursuing earnings beyond what is needed to satisfy the second level, the level of moderation, he should work hard, providing that his earnings are not spent on extravagance. The extravagant are Satan's' brethren, the Qur'ān states. The extra earnings can be directed to helping others, leaving to dependent heirs, providing capital for production, seeking education, spending in the cause of God, and so on. But earnings should not stop at that level or be spent on futile pursuits, as extravagance is sterile spending.

Al-Shaibānī's analysis of the levels of consumption has served as a valid starting point for many Islamic economists after him, including those in modern time, who looked into the theory of consumer behavior from an Islamic perspective (see Chapter 9). One would point out, however, that these levels of consumption are bound to vary from time to time and from one society to another. While the necessity level might not be as changeable, this is the level that keeps body and soul together, the moderation level and the line between that and the level of extravagance would be more changeable depending on time and societies. Al-Shaibānī, perhaps, would not have been in disagreement with that modification to his analysis. We find him clarifying that there might be situations where one would exceed the level of consumption beyond the expected moderate level, such as in festival seasons and religious occasions, which is still acceptable providing that it does not lead to vanity and self-admiration.

Furthermore, the question of utility was examined by al-Shaibānī throughout his analysis of the above levels of consumption, confirming that utility diminishes with extra goods consumed—the law of diminishing utility as we know it today.

Production and Earnings

On the sources of earnings, hence the categories of productive activities, al-Shaibānī classified them into these four: hiring-out, industry, agriculture and trade.

Hiring-out

It is interesting to see al-Shaibānī specifying hiring-out as a separate category of production activity. Normally, this is included in other sectors: agriculture, trade and industry. The justification for identifying this sector separately by al-Shaibānī could be related to the issue of the ownership of means of production. In that, he is more precise in relating the activities, and their rewards, to the ownership of these means. Looking at the classification of activities as an informative device, his classification helps provide more detailed information than the classical classification, and his arrangement is more in line with the need for information, as has been increasingly emphasised in recent time. More precisely, hiring-out has an effect on each of two particular issues: the financial performance of business and value-added statement. In modern financial analysis of accounting statements, it is emphasised that in addition to looking into the relationship between sources of funds on the one hand, and the income generated in relation to these funds on the other, the careful analyst is advised to look into the question of hiring assets. The effect of hired assets on the revenue generated by the business and the result of that on the rate of return on capital-employed need to be particularly examined in order to neutralize such favourable or adverse effect from the overall performance of the business assets. Revenue generated from hiring assets, or expenses incurred from hired assets, are bound to distort the indicators of business results if the hiring of assets is concealed. In this process revenues generated from hired assets should be highlighted, otherwise the rate of return could be exaggerated.

Hiring assets will have a similar distorting effect on the information generated from the value-added statement. On the breakdown of the value-added statement, which is the basic statement in calculating gross national product, the statement is found to be consisting of four well-known items: rent, wages, interest and profit. Specifically, rent is shown on its own as the reward for, or the cost of, hired means of production. And if the statement was to be broken down further the figure of net profit could be shown exclusive of all the rent incurred from hiring assets which are means of production. When that is done, the statement fully matches al-Shaibānī's direction in his classification. Turning our attention to labour, if labour is regarded as human capital, wages in the statement would reflect the cost of hired capital. This fits in with his intention even further. Al-Shaibānī's classification includes labour by implication, as he does specify the exclusion of labour from hiring-out. In fact, his focus on hiring-out in his classification helps shed more light on the contribution of this sector to the value of production and the creation of gross national product. The assertion of this by a writer in the mid eighth century can only be viewed as extremely foreseeing. It looked as if al-Shaibānī had anticipated our needs for information and had preempted our thinking.

Industry

On the outset, al-Shaibānī viewed all production activities as equally important. Looking into industry, he ridiculed the ideas of his contemporaries who claimed that industry was a demeaning type of production activity in comparison to trade. Examining the claim from a religious perspective first, he named about a dozen Prophets and

Messengers who had vocational occupations and argued that these occupations could not have been inferior to others and, on the contrary, they must have been blessed by God. On a more worldly ground he went on to explain how each sector of production activity is important to fulfill the purpose and functions of the others, which would lead to making these sectors of the economy well integrated. Production sectors are complimentary with each other, he stated. To appreciate the novelty of al-Shaibānī's thinking his view should be seen within the context of the prevailing thinking at the time. As a source of earnings, and a production sector, trade was regarded as superior to any other profession, it is the profession that is referred to in the Qur'ān and stressed favorably by the Prophet.

Still on industry, al-Shaibānī stressed the importance of specialisation and division of labour. By specialisation, he stated, skill could effectively be gained and the profession be better performed. Looking at it from a micro angle he stressed that if one endevours to learn all required skills, one would come to the end of his life without achieving that; life would have gone but the skills would not have come. People should learn a skill related to what they feel they can do best, depending upon their ability given by God, and should rely on the skills of others in meeting their needs. With this, the variety of skills of individuals and the variety of gifts bestowed on people by the divine force, jobs would be better performed and the community becomes more integrated. Believers to each other, in a quotation from the Sunnah, are "like one building in which parts strengthen one another". When al-Shaibānī's argument is extended to the macro level, it could be established that specialisation speeds up the process of gaining skill, or technology, and helps increase integration among sectors of the economy.

Agriculture

In contrast to his contemporaries, al-Shaibānī defended agriculture vigorously. Even further, for him it is the far superior production activity to all others; hiring-out, trade and industry. His defense of agriculture should be viewed within the context of a *ḥadīth* reported about what the Prophet said when he saw some tilling articles in a house. He was reported to have said that these instruments would only bring humiliation to their people. In interpreting the *ḥadīth*, al-Shaibānī elucidated that the *ḥadīth* was meant to discourage Muslims from settling in rural areas and deserting military expeditions, *jihād*.

The religious counter-argument is based on various other *aĥādīth* that encourage cultivation so much so that the cultivator is rewarded for even the bird eating from his field, and that, "The cultivator is a trader with God". The religious argument was vital, particularly, at that time when the whole economic system was based on divine law.

The reason why al-Shaibānī regarded agriculture as relatively superior to other production activities is, to him, fourfold: first, it is the sector on which other production sectors are based. It provides the industry with raw materials and trade with traded agricultural produce, and when the subject of trade is manufactured goods this would not have been possible without raw materials. Second; agriculture is more widely beneficial to people in general than other sectors, as it is particularly important for sustaining lives. And when the *ĥadīth* says that the best of you is the most beneficiary to others, this leads to deducing that cultivators engaged in agriculture are superior to others. Third; agriculture, and its derived activities, is the main provider of the needs of other living beings, birds and animals, which may be edible or otherwise. Fourth; by contrast to other vocational occupations, agriculture provides a source for Zakāh from within as compulsory alms, as Zakāh, on agriculture is stipulated in the Qur'ān. All said al-Shaibānī confirmed that all sectors are inseparably useful, and cooperation among the sectors is indispensable, but that the superiority of agriculture is, however, a relative superiority.

Trade

For the creation of wealth, or income, and the relationship between agriculture and trade we find al-Shaibānī providing a very interesting statement: agriculture provides what is necessary to the individual but with trade and exchange, wealth is developed. Although this is a simple statement, it has a very important implication, which is that al-Shaibānī has indeed preempted the Physiocrats' thinking almost ten centuries later.

The similarity, and dissimilarity, between the thinking of al-Shaibānī on agriculture and the Physiocrats may merit a brief comparison. Appearing in France in the eighteenth century, the Physiocrats concentrated on agriculture as the only sector that is capable of producing a net product, *produit net*, and as such, they contributed to discarding the mercantilist's belief that wealth and its increase were due to exchange. Having discovered the origin of surplus, *produit net*, they went on to add, in Quesnay's '*Tableau economique*', an analysis of its circulation among different classes of society (Roll, 1973). They advocated that those who worked in industry and trade depended ultimately on the amount of subsistence raised by those working in agriculture above the needs of the latter. In other words, they understood that that degree of productivity of labour, which made a surplus possible, made its first appearance in agriculture (ibid.) Therefore, agriculture was the only form of surplus, and any measures of fostering the industry were useless. Because of this limitation, no value was related to trade, or exchange. It was not until Turgot that exchange-value was introduced, *valeur-exchange*, which Turgot called valeur *appreciative*, and said it was determined by the average of the estimated value of the parties to the exchange (ibid.).

Al-Shaibānī did not go as far as Quesnay's '*Tableau economique*', but what could be attributed to him, in contrast to the Physiocrats, is that (a) he did not argue for agriculture as being the only productive sector with other sectors being sterile; to him all sectors were productive but agriculture was superior to the others, and (b) from the start he acknowledged the exchange value attributed to trade, "Trade does not provide subsistence but with trade, wealth, or income, *Māl*, develops", he states. Though he did not examine the topic as extensively as the Physiocrats, he introduced fresh thinking and new ideas in the subject, which were capable of being developed further in parallel with the Physiocrats. In that sense it could be said that he preempted Turgot in his findings on the exchange-value, *valeur-exchange*.

Other Issues

In addition to the above topics, al-Shaibānī discussed other issues in detail.

He criticised severely those opting for voluntary unemployment, particularly the *Ŝūfīs*, a religious group appearing during that period who called for the full desertion of worldly matter and complete devotion to God's worship—the analogy of monks in other religions. How could they accept to feed themselves from the offerings made to them by the others who worked to make these offerings possible, while they simultaneously frown upon work, he exclaimed. In appreciation of the value of work for earning a living and linking that with worship he ascertained that work is important for enabling the person to fulfill worship duties, hence work is a divine duty of the first degree. What he said about the *Ŝūfīs* was also applied to those able to earn and do not seek means of earnings. Further, he attacked those who were able to work but received charity instead.

He valued education highly and stressed the need for it. Education, he confirmed, is valuable for different aspects of life: learning about the religion as well as trade and occupations. Education to him helps specialisation and division of labour, which helps, in turn, to improve efficiency. Emphasising the importance of education is not surprising from a man who is reported to have spent most of his inherited fortune pursuing education.

On the institution of Zakāh as alms, al-Shaibānī argued an interesting case. He stated that the rich, the giver of charity, is in need of the poor, the recipient. Without the poor, the rich would not be able to fulfill his religious duties nor would he get a divine reward from giving to the poor. Therefore, the rich needs the poor to accomplish his religious commitments otherwise they would remain incomplete and the reward for that would not be attained. The poor has therefore rendered the rich a benefit! As such, providing that the receiver of Zakāh, or any other form of charity, is deservedly in need for it, he is preferred to the rich! In this al-Shaibānī reiterates the Islamic principle that the poor have a right to the wealth of the rich. However, if the beneficiary of the religious charity is able to earn and is claiming the right to it falsely, this, besides being religiously unlawful, makes the rich preferred to the poor. Al-Shaibānī's conclusion, however, that both the poor and the rich are in need of each other is a very interesting suggestion.

Without doubt, al-Shaibānī's writing on Islamic economics was a notable landmark in the development of the subject.

The next writer is a major writer in that era; the jurist Abū-Ubaid al-Qasim ben Sallam. His book, Kitāb al-Amwāl", the Book of Wealth, is still until today a major reference on the subject. The Abū-Ubaid's book of wealth can be regarded as a text on macro-economics.

Abū-Ubaid (d. 224 H., 838 A.C.)
Kitāb al-Amwāl, Book of Wealth

By the time Abū-Ubaid came to write his book, almost three times the size of Abū-Yūsuf's Kitāb al-Kharāj, (622 pages, the Arabic edition in hand), there were already two well established judicial schools of thought and a third beginning to make its mark. The Ĥanafī, founded by Imam Abū-Ĥanīfah, was well established in Iraq where the capital and the caliphate headquarters were, the Mālikī, founded by Imam Mālik, was very stable in al-Medīnah, and the Shafi'ī, instituted by Imam al-Shafi'ī, was beginning to make its presence obvious in al-Sham and Egypt (see earlier sections). By that time two major books of Kharāj, Abū-Yūsuf's and Yahya ibn-Adam's, were in circulation. Two main reasons could have perhaps motivated Abū-Ubaid to write his book, besides his own personal drive as a jurist: (a) to fill in the gaps in the work of his predecessors, as shown below, and (b) to assess the issue from the contemporary, but different schools of thought.

The Author

He is Abū-Ubaid al-Qasim ben Sallām (d. 224 A.H./838 A.C.). Like previous writers, he was also a judge, though he did not reach the position of Abū-Yūsuf as chief justice. He was highly appreciated by his contemporaries for his piety, and his knowledge of jurisprudence, Sunnah, history, and Arabic literature (Harras, 1986). From his Kitāb al-Amwāl, it does not appear for sure to which of the then existing schools of thought he could be attributed; he would look into what "the people in Iraq", *ĥanafī*, had done and what Imam Mālik said, and derive an opinion of his own, leaning to one or another, or state his own. In that sense he was an innovator more than a follower. He wrote many books on the Qur'ān, Sunnah, jurisprudence and poetry (ibid.). During one stage of his life he seemed to have been able to devote all of his time to his writing, being helped in that by the financial support of a wealthy governor who is reported to have said after seeing his work, "The possessor of such brain that produced such work should not be distracted by the burden of seeking a living" (ibid.). This was the utmost expression of admiration by an able, noble and knowledgeable supporter for an able scientist.

The Book

In a work almost three times the size of Abū-Yūsuf's Kitāb al-Kharāj, Abū-Ubaid wrote his Kitāb al-Amwāl, "the Book of Wealth". The book has three distinctive features that previous books on al-

Kharāj do not have. First, it does not focus on one type of wealth; rather it incorporates all types that may be generated from agriculture, trade, or other sources. For example, in contrast to previous work, it looks into the wealth generated from trade, as well as agriculture, and the rules regarding the tax imposed on it. In that sense it is more comprehensive in providing a blend of macro and micro economics than previous works.

Second, it is much better documented than any of the others. Not only do we see clearly *isnad*, the citation of a chain of informants of the Prophet's sayings and deeds, but also we read letters sent by the Prophet and caliphs after him to their officials and leaders of their adversaries, and examine the treaties between Muslims and non-Muslims—all well documented. In that sense, Abū-Ubaid spent more time to provide documented proof of what was practiced in the past and, presumably, ought to be practiced at his time. One would not suggest that the writers of previous works were not aware of these documents, but Abū-Ubaid is given the credit for incorporating them in one volume presented in a well documented form. The focus of each writer is, however, equally appreciated.

Third, the book provides a greater variety of opinions on the treated subject. This was perhaps made possible by the fact that Abū-Ubaid's writing came much later than that of the others, probably between thirty and forty years after Abū-Yūsuf's. During that period a wider variation of opinion would have been developed, enhanced, by the further variation in the juridical schools of thought.

A further feature could perhaps be added to the above three. Although the book can serve the purpose of the state in shaping its finance, it can also be useful to the reader in general. It shows Muslims and non-Muslims their duties, rights and commitments with regard to both what is levied on them as financial right of the state, which they need to follow as good citizens, and what is imposed on them by the divine right, that they need to observe as pious Muslims. Further, for lawyers, advocates, or those defending their case, the book is a valuable legal text that provides rules and case law in a manner that helps reinforce the submission for and against.

Abū-Ubaid's Kitāb al-Amwāl is a manual in public finance. Details of practice are well explained, as well as being well documented, in a manner that would serve officials in dealing with what ought to and ought not to be taxed, who should and should not be taxed, the factors that justify the imposition of taxation, and how revenues should be distributed between the categories of expenditures. Overall the book shows that Abū-Ubaid's thinking in finance is very instructive.

The Contribution of Sūfism to Islamic Economic Thought

Development of the Sūfī Movement

Whenever Ŝūfīsm is mentioned, two names are the first to come to mind: Rabi'a al-Adawiyyah of Basra, and al-Ĥallāj of Baghdad. Rabi'a (d. 185/801) loved God for the sake of his love and chanted her love to Him in the following most celebrated manner (translation by Nicholson, 1993):

> Two ways I love Thee: selfishly,
> And next, as worthy of Thee.
> 'Tis selfish love that I do naught
> Save think on Thee with every thought;
> 'Tis purest love when Thou dost raise
> The veil to my adoring gaze.
> Not mine the praise in that or this:
> Thine is the praise in both, I wis.

Al-Ĥallāj (285–309 A.H., 898–922 A.C.) died on the cross in Baghdad after a brief inquisition by the Traditional Ulama'. He refused to recant his belief or retract his claim that he and God were two in one, "I am the Creative Truth", *ana al-Ĥaq*, meaning God. Yet when he saw the cross and the nails, he turned to the people and uttered a prayer ending with the words, ". . . and these Thy servants who are gathered to slay me, in zeal for Thy religion and in desire to win Thy favour, forgive them O Lord, and have mercy on them . . . (because they are ignorant of what you have revealed to me) . . . Glory unto Thee in whatsoever Thou doest, and glory unto Thee in whatsoever Thou will." (Arberry, 1990).

But the crucifixion of al-Ĥallāj was almost two centuries after the emergence of Ŝūfīsm. Ŝūfīsm started as the creed of some Muslims who resented the exorbitant extravagance of lifestyle that was beginning to make itself obvious from the Umayyads onward. The Islamic state during the Umayyads, and more so during the Abbasids, witnessed a wide expansion that took the borders as far away as India in the east and the Iberian Peninsula in the west. With that came economic prosperity and a style of life to which Muslims were never accustomed. Muslims, mostly the Bedouin inhabitants of the Arabian Peninsula as we recall from the first chapter, found themselves exposed to the two greatest civilizations in the world at that time and to a lifestyle the Bedouin would never have dreamed of. The imitation of the Persians' and Byzantines' life style, with all the comfort it had with it, was difficult to resist.

Nothing was un-Islamic; the argument was no doubt maintained, in benefiting from the bounties that God had bestowed on Muslims after the great conquests and in indulging oneself in the comfort that was brought by His will. But that was not acceptable to some. It added to the image of exorbitant extravagance the luxurious type of life with which the Umayyads surrounded themselves within the royal court and in their personal life. Against the majority of Muslims who must have enjoyed the new comfort which the new era had brought to their life, a minority stood to express grave concern. To this minority the new style of life represented a drift from the Islamic norms and ideals and that was in contrast with the ascetic model proclaimed in the teachings of Islam. Islam, as we recall from the previous chapter, is not against the enjoyment of life as long as this is within the level of moderation. With a royal court that was not dissimilar to that of the Persians or the Byzantines, the principle of moderation, at least to this minority of Muslims, seemed to have been violated. With the memories of the ascetic lifestyle of the Rashidīn still fresh in mind, the contrast between the Rashidīn society, or the society of Medīnah, and that of the Umayyads was too sharp to remain unnoticed.

The danger, it seemed, lay in the perception that such a new opening to luxury may lead to a break away from the basic spirit of Islam; a matter which had lain in the minds of sincere Muslims and devoted Ulama'. The recent schism in the Muslim community resulting from the dispute over the caliphate and the growing bitterness of the Shī'ah over the loss of the caliphate and their readiness to amass the blame over the Umayyads must have fuelled the resentment further.

However, the resentment was not taking a political uprising against the Umayyads; that came later with the Shī'ah's uprising and claim to the caliphate. Rather, it was taking an inward direction towards the inner self in an endeavour to purify it and return the self to the puritan teachings of Islam. Having resigned politically to accepting the dominance of the Umayyads, those Muslims, who later became known as Ŝūfīs, turned towards the self in an attempt to purge it from the worldly influence that caused spiritual corruption and led to religious distortion (Armstrong, 2000). It was probably a case of despair that was felt by some as they saw Muslims killing Muslims, a Muslim governor defying a caliph to the level of bloodshed, the Prophet's wife heading an army at the back of a camel with some of the Prophet's companions fighting the new caliph. The psychological shock to those who lived through it and those who came after them must have been tremendous. The, psychological, answer to some could have been, "reject all worldly life and turn to God"—a call for inner salvation.

The term Ŝūfī claims two etymological sources. The first which is widely known originates from the habit of the Ŝūfīs of deserting the soft clothing of cotton and similar material to the wearing of the harsh surface wool, *suf* in Arabic. The second means purity, *safa'*, which is claimed by Ŝūfīs themselves who explain, "The Ŝūfī is he who keeps his heart pure, *safi*, with God", and, Ŝūfīsm is the being chosen for purity, *istifa'*: whoever is thus chosen and made pure from all except God is the true Ŝūfī", (said by Bishr al-Hafi, the barefooted, who died in 841–42, and Junayd of Baghdad who died in 909–910, respectively, both are cited in Nicholson 1993). A complete denial of self and renouncement of worldly life with an intense focus on worshiping God: that was the message. The line between Ŝūfīsm and asceticism may be very fine but it still exists. While asceticism is the desertion of materialistic wants for the sake of pleasing God and attracting His reward, Ŝūfīsm renounces the same but for the sake of pleasing Him, motivated by their love to Him, with no particular expectation for a compensatory reward or avoidance of His punishment; it is the love of God for the sake of loving Him (the great Ŝūfī Suhrawardī, cited in Nicholson, op. cit.). Ŝūfīs, by conviction, worked and earned very little, accepting modest labour and vocation to earn only enough to keep them alive for the sake of worshiping the Almighty. No political ambitions or cut-throat competition over worldly positions; their ultimate aim was to worship the divine deity with absolute love and devotion.

Some names have been cited as the early initiators of what developed over the first three centuries of Muslim history into the Ŝūfī school of thought. The first of those was Ĥassan al-Baŝrī (d. 110 A.H./728 A.C.) who preached the return to asceticism and the renouncement of the personal pursuit of worldly life for the sake of God. He was brought up in Medīnah in a close proximity to the Prophet's family and lived there until the death of the third caliph Uthmān. Later he moved to Basra in Iraq, where he became renowned for preaching the ascetic life of the Prophet's model and the renouncement of worldly desire for the sake of God. He criticised the lavish lifestyle of the Umayyad court and, although he accepted the Umayyads as the new caliphs, he regarded them as accountable for their actions. Ĥassan al-Baŝrī did not claim that he was a Ŝūfī, however, and probably the term Ŝūfī itself was not commonly used until, according to Qushayri (d. 465 A.H./1072 A.C.), towards the end of the second century of the Hijra, 815 A.C., (cited in Nicholson, 1993). That was about a century after al-Basari's death.

Ibrāhīm ibn Adham, who was a Persian belonging to the royal family of Balkh, Abū Ali Shaqiq, also of Balkh, Fudayl ibn Iyad, a converted captain of banditti, Sufyan al-Thawri, of Kufa, and Rabi'a al Adawiyyah, from Basra of the tribe of Adi, are all names associated with the early history of Ŝūfīsm. They all died between the middle and the end of the second century of Hijra (767–815 A.C.). Ibrāhīm ibn Adham gave up his wealth and royal lifestyle for the sake of God, living in a cave for a few months. Shaqiq emphasized the concept of tawakkul, a full reliance on God and a complete trust in Him in all one's deeds and actions. Fudayl proclaimed, "To abstain for men's sake from doing anything is hypocrisy, while to do anything for men's sake is idolatry". Sufyan founded a school of jurisprudence and suffered maltreatment for refusing public office. And Rabi'a declared, "love of God has so absorbed me that neither love nor hate of any other thing remains in my heart". By the mid third century of Hijra, mid ninth century, a few more names were added to the list such as Dhu al-Nun al-Misri from Egypt (d. 246 A.H./861 A.C.).

Looking at the development of the school of Ŝūfīsm, we find the real founder of the school in Baghdad and the man who first wrote a book on Ŝūfīsm was Abd Allah al-Ĥārith ibn Asad al-Muĥāsibī (d. 243/857). In his book *al-Ri'āyah li-ĥuqūq Allah*, the Observance of God's Rights, he laid down the foundations of the 'science' of mysticism, Ŝūfīsm, which became a model for later writers (Arberry, 1990). What distinguishes al-Muĥāsibī from the other Ŝūfīs, particularly in the context of economics, is that he defined the line between Ŝūfīsm and the choice of living in poverty. He is not an advocate of poverty; we find him in his book *Risalat al-Makāsib wa'l Wara'*,

Treatise on Earnings and Asceticism, declaring that the full reliance on God and the complete trust in Him, *twakkul*, does not mean that a man should refrain from taking lawful means to earn a livelihood, nor does it mean to live in idleness at the expense of others (Smith, 1977). There is a distinction in al-Muĥasibi's mind, therefore, between monks in monasteries and ascetic Muslims living in poverty in reliance on others, on the one hand, and what the genuine Ŝūfīs should really be, on the other. There is a clear cut distinction between the two groups. To him, there is no idleness under the ostensible premise of abstaining from the worldly desire in pursuit of God's love. Even taking up the sword in the cause of God is part of the spirit of Ŝūfīsm, he emphasises.

For his emphasis on ascetic lifestyle and, simultaneously, on the necessity of earning a livelihood by all lawful means, al-Muĥāsibī is cited among Muslim economic thinkers with his thought included as a phase in the history of Islamic economic thought (see for example, Aidit Ghazāli, 1992, Siddiqi, 1992, and Yusri, 1987). The emphasis has been on his teaching of the ascetic consumption and the lawful pursuit of earning a livelihood. In that sense al-Muĥāsibī's writing was the first work to have appeared in a published form on the subject of austerity and ascetic consumption. Needless to say, al-Muĥāsibī did not intend to have his work classified under economic writing, if there was any. Rather, he intended to focus on the purification of the self, the refinement of the soul, the renouncement of the worldly desire and the desertion of wealth (as he did himself); all for the sake of God, which comes with it the call for austerity and ascetic consumption. Therefore, although he was simply writing on Ŝūfīsm, not economics, he produced a treatise on Earnings and Asceticism, from within Ŝūfīsm, in which he fervently contended that the religiously desired *twakkul*, the reliance on God while pursuing means of earning, does not coincide with the undesired concept of *twaakul*. Notice the difference in spelling, which is the reliance on God with no self-exertion in chasing means of gaining an income. For his influence on the Ŝūfī thinking and his fervent endeavour to correct their thought on such an important economic issue, his Earnings and Asceticism is examined later.

After al-Muĥāsibī came al-Junayd (d. 289/910), a disciple of al-Muĥāsibī, who followed his master's footsteps in consolidating the Ŝūfī school of thought. With the introduction of new concepts such as *fana*ʾ, self-naughting, *baqa*ʾ, eternal survival in unity with God and *mithaq*, covenant with God, and other concepts introduced later by those after them, the school was beginning to take a coherent conceptual formation. It was the time when Ŝūfīsm, Sunni by conviction and non-political by choice, began to contribute to the prevailing culture of religio-philosophy or theosophy.

The Economic Implications of Sūfīsm

Looking at Ŝūfīsm from an economic perspective, the problem, it seems, is that if the Ŝūfīs reject the accustomed lifestyle and apply austerity to their own model of consumption and earning, as individuals, this will not raise an economic concern at the macro level. But when the call for the return to asceticism is publicly declared as the ideal way in which God ought to be served, and to which all pious Muslims should adhere, Ŝūfīsm is bound to raise a few concerns from the economic point of view. This can be highlighted as follows:

First, while austerity is advocated, and sometimes advised, as an economic policy in the case of inflationary economy it is not recommended in the case of deflationary economy. Austerity helps curb the demand-pull forces in an inflationary economy that is caused by the effect of the increase in aggregate demand for the goods and services available. Nevertheless, when the economy is in a state of deflation, as a result of not having sufficient demand for the supply of goods and services available, the deflationary effect, other things being held constant, is expected to be worsened in a Ŝūfī economy. By contrast, as a means of creating, or increasing, aggregate demand, governments, more often than not, pursue a policy, or policies, that activate demand including the direct injection of voucher money that is aimed particularly at increasing consumption, not saving.

Second, with limiting the aggregate demand for goods and services, sales will decrease, leading to decreasing entrepreneurial profits and/or generating losses. If that persists, enterprises will be forced out of business as a result of not being able to cover their costs and of the rate of return on capital being less than the cost of capital. This leads to loss of production. Production, after a period of piling up, will decrease as a result of decreasing sale, and total production in the economy will decrease as a result of both the productive enterprises being forced out of the market and the surviving enterprises decreasing their production. The aggregate supply of goods and services will, therefore, decrease. Prices may come down as a result of the decrease in both aggregate demand and aggregate supply, but that would be a case of low prices in an economy of poverty.

Third, if the society is limiting its earning capacity to the level that is merely sufficient to keep soul and body together, as most Ŝūfīs advocate, the level of production will be lowered further, leaving very little room for economic development, let alone growth.

Fourth, with very little revenue, if at all, to the Treasury, as a result of the Zakāh base being almost non-existent, the Islamic state will not have sufficient funds to spend on education, health and other public services and infrastructure that are deemed necessary to the survival of society. Defense will be almost non-existent, as a result of a zero, or meager, defense budget; which will make the Islamic state vulnerable to any take over attempt by neighboring non-Islamic, or non-Ŝūfī Islamic, states.

Fifth, even from a religious point of view, not having enough to spend on one's food and basic needs would make one vulnerable to illness and weakness that may prevent one from exercising the love of worshiping God fully.

Sixth, in brief, Ŝūfīsm cannot stand on its own as an economic model. If Ŝūfīsm is advocated as an esoteric way of life, it is only suitable as a sect within other sects of a more worldly outlook to life so as the rest of society can provide for the needs of society, including those of the Ŝūfīs.

It is not surprising therefore to find someone like al-Shaibānī (750–804), as we saw earlier, criticizing the Ŝūfīs' views on consumption and earnings. Nor should it be surprising to see al-Muĥāsibī, the renowned Ŝūfī, adopting a different view from that of the Ŝūfīs in his Earnings and Asceticism as we see below.

Abdullah al-Ĥarith bin Asad al-Muĥasibī, (d. 243 A.H., 857 A.C.) *Kitāb Risalat al-Iktisāb wa al Wara'*, *Treatise on Earning and Asceticism*

The author

Abdullah al-Ĥārith bin Asad al-Muĥāsibī was a Ŝūfī by choice, not by necessity. He was born to a wealthy father with a considerable fortune that provided the family with an affluent life style that was in a sharp contrast to that which he adopted later in life. On his father's death, al-Ĥārith would have inherited a sizeable fortune that would have ensured riches and fame had he accepted to be the prosperous heir. But he rejected all of that wealth and opted for a course of action that placed him among the poor and made him the renowned Ŝūfī we know. The father's Qadarite sect was not acceptable to al-Muĥāsibī the son, al-Ĥārith, and in that he came to the conviction that he had no right to enjoy the life style, or later at the father's death, the inheritance of a father who he believed was not on the right religious path (Al-Khisht, 1983). A strong conviction of a fervent believer, and that was how al-Ĥārith al-Muĥāsibī was.

To us, al-Ĥārith's desertion of his father's wealth on the basis of the differences in their religious convictions has a special meaning. First, it demonstrates that he was a man who genuinely followed his own conviction, even at the expense of a materialistic loss of a substantial magnitude. In that sense he substantially narrowed down the gap between theory and practice, as he practiced what he preached. Second, he was a scholar who followed his own thinking. Not influenced by his father's doctrine, albeit his father's well known stand among the sect followers, nor had he been affected by the stream of religio-philosophical thought at his time, al-Ĥārith followed his own thinking. He studied the teachings of the Khawārij, Mu'tazilah, and Murji'ah and the others, he followed his own thinking and was later to criticise these religious sects fervently. His criticism, however, was objective; he would cite the points of disagreement between himself and others, explain them well and then criticize them vehemently. Between the advocates of the power of mind over the text, such as the Mu'tazilah, and the proponents of the authority of the text over the mind, such as the Khawārij, he adopted a middle of the road approach; no denial of the power of mind but no overruling of the necessity of the text. To him, there was no contradiction between the two, as the textual rules, cited in the Qur'ān and the *Ĥadīth*, are in full agreement with the sound reasoning and inference of the sound mind. This approach has been demonstrably applied to his teachings of Ŝūfīsm and in the writing of Earnings and Piousness, (or Asceticism) a book among thirty three books he is reported to have written (Al-Khisht, 1983).

To add to his biography, he was born in al-Baŝra, in Iraq, hence his nickname al-Baŝrī. His exact year of birth does not seem to be known for certain, though a recent biography by al-Khisht, 1983, suggests that he was born in the last third of the second century of Hijra. His year of death is referred to in the same study as the year of 243 H, approximately 857 A.C. (Al-Khisht, 1983).

The Book

The full title of the book on hand is, the book of "*al-Makāsib wa al-Wara' wa al-shubuhāt wa bian mubāĥaha wa maĥzuraha wa ikhtilāf al-nās fi ṭalabiha wa al-radd ala al-ghāliteen fih*", that can be translated as, "Earning and asceticism, and the suspicion surrounding earnings, a clarification of what is permissible and not permissible and of the different means of obtaining earnings with a reply to those discussing it.", a long title that is abbreviated to and widely known as, "Earnings and Asceticism". The size of what has come to us of the teaching of al-Muĥāsibī in this book is about 10,500 words, hand written in about 43 pages, of twenty lines per page with an average of 12 words per line (Al-Khisht, op. cit.). The printed form of the book reaches about 133 pages. In citing his references, we find al-Muĥāsibī specifying that he relied on the Qur'ān, the Sunnah, consensus of opinion, deduction, *istinbat*, and comparability of rules, *qiyās*, whenever that was permissible. This highlights a new approach in his writing; the deductive approach in the absence of a clear text.

To understand the full dimension of the importance of the Earning and Asceticism we have to realize that it was written at a time when the Ŝūfī thought was mainly concentrated around the concept of abandoning the strive for earning a living and concentrating instead on the worship of God. God would provide for those who honour him through the devotion of worship, the Ŝūfī argument goes, and no matter how much one would strive to earn, one would not earn more than what God has destined for one to earn. Al-Muĥāsibī, a devout Ŝūfī, came with a different view, though still lying in the heart of the Ŝūfī teachings. The belief in that, although earnings come in accordance with fate and destiny, this should not overrule the premise that one has to strive in order to obtain them. This is shown below. Earnings do not come alone, God commands humankind to seek a means of earnings, so that his bounty can reach everyone. Earnings come, through pursuit of means of earning, *or ĥarakah*, is the message al-Muĥasbī emphatically emphasised.

Earning and Asceticism is divided into an introduction and fifteen chapters. This is shown as follows:

Introduction
Chapter 1: full reliance on God, *tawakkul*, and earning
Chapter 2: pursuit of means of earning, *al ĥarakah*, the good of that and the bad
Chapter 3: desertion of pursuit of means of earning, desertion of *ĥarakah*, the good of that and bad
Chapter 4: meaning of piousness, the disagreement of *Ulama'* in defining piousness, *wara'*, piousness, *wara'* in eating and clothing
Chapter 5: helping and receiving help from the oppressors
Chapter 6: inheritance of oppressing fathers
Chapter 7: disagreement between Ulama' regarding *shobha*
Chapter 8: the meaning of the Qur'ānic verse, "do not cooperate on injustice and aggression"
Chapter 9: the permissible and forbidden
Chapter 10: disagreement among Ulama' regarding prizes of the rulers, Sūltān
Chapter 11: pursuit of blessed food
Chapter 12: pursuit of hunger and reply to those claiming it is part of worship
Chapter 13: enquiry about the source of a living
Chapter 14: land of *Fai'* and Kharāj
Chapter 15: prayers in the *maghsub*, the taken unjustly by force

Not all the above are bearing the section of "chapter" however. For reasons that are not clear to us, the sections after chapter four do not bear the term "chapter", the Arabic *bab*. Instead, they are written without such classification. The topics however seem to have a distinctive separation, and that is why they are mentioned above as separate chapters.

Now we turn our attention to the content of the above chapters with different emphasis given as the need arises.

The introduction seems to be a necessary start. It emphasizes various points in relation to earnings with particular reference to Qur'ānic verses, as shown below:

First, it refers to the creation of the universe, heaven, earth and what is between and beyond. A logical start in a book of earnings, as earnings relate to what God has made available to his creatures.

Second, it provides an emphasis on the quest of the mind and how the believers are ordained to think in, and reflect on, His great creation. A necessary pre-requisite that implies: (a) a reply to the prevailing religious sects at that time which overruled the mind in pursuit of the text, and (b) as thinking and reflecting involve an effort made by human beings in appreciating God's creation, there was a need to make a similar effort by Ŝūfīs to gain a living as part of the pursuit of worship.

Third, it adds a further emphasis on the intention of God in the creation of human beings who have physiological needs in order to thrive and survive, once again this reads like an implicit early warning to his fellow Ŝūfīs.

Fourth, it gives further stress on what God has guaranteed through the provision of an amount of earnings to each one of his people which he/she is destined to gain so that people's hearts may remain confident in God and may not be too preoccupied by distress over earnings to worship Him.

The introduction seems to be conveying a very clear message: God has destined the earnings so that His creatures may make the effort to gain them. This is in a direct clash with the views of other Ŝūfīs.

The first chapter deals with a crucial issue in the heart of Islam in as far as the relationship between man and God is concerned in general, and in earning a living in particular. This is the difference between *twakkul* and *twākul* (or *twaakul*); notice the double 'k', *twakkul*, in the former and the 'ā' or double 'a', *twākul* in the latter. The difference in spelling, minor as it might seem in English, is of a paramount importance in Arabic. *Twakkul* means the full reliance on God in all that one does in one's life, including earning a living, on condition that one strives hard in pursuit of what is needed to be obtained. Al-Muĥāsibī refers to the pursuit of earning as *al-ĥarakah. Twākul* on the other hand, although means, yet again, the full reliance on God in what one does including earning a living, it stops short from working hard, or for some, working at all, in order to earn a living, or obtain what is needed, and relying instead on praying for God's help, hope and assistance. In al-Muĥāsibī's expression, this boils down to defining *twakkul* as believing, with work *ĥarakah*, while *twākul* refers to belief, but without *ĥarakah. Ĥarakah*, once again, is defined as the effort made by the individual towards earning a living, or obtaining whatever the individual wishes to obtain. The two meanings and intentions are very different. God has ordained his people to rely on Him in pursuit of earnings but such reliance does not overrule the genuine attempt and sincere effort demanded by

God in search of these earnings. This might sound logical to the mind of today, but, at a time when Ŝūfīs turned beggars while devoting all their lives to the worship and the love of God, the point carried a strong message.

Al-Ĥārith's argument in his first chapter is strong and convincing. It carries the same approach of criticizing those in disagreement with him: explaining their points of views, thoroughly supported with reference to the Qur'ānic verses that confirm the provision of God for everyone's needs but also contending these views eloquently, yet with strong support from the same source: the Qur'ānic text. Using the power of reasoning, he continues to explain to his opponents, yet fellow Ŝūfīs, the purpose of the Qur'ānic text, the intention of the divine rule, and the variation that might sound like a conflict of commands. In contention with fellow Ŝūfīs, who advocated the desertion of the chase of earnings for the sake of worship, we find him referring to the Qur'ān and *Ĥadīth* in stressing that while God has permitted the pursuit of earnings, He organized that by a mandate that this should not lead to diversion of God's rule or His worship, not the other way round. The psychological approach to his argument also seems obvious in this chapter which reflects a deep understanding of self and others.

In his second chapter of Earnings and Asceticism al-Ĥārith is devoting a considerable part to the discussion of the ethical basis of the pursuit of earnings: the permissible and the forbidden. In general, the permissible is the type of pursuit that does not imply a breach of God's rules or commands. The forbidden by contrast is what deviates from the commands of God. A further clarification of the responsibility of the individual in earning a livelihood is added: ones responsibility towards one's own family. This seems a further reinforcement in argument against the fellow Ŝūfīs, who regarded worship as superior to earning a living. The message is that devoting one's life to worship without supporting one's family would leave the family devastated. And this is against God's command. The argument is reinforced in this chapter with examples from the lives of the Prophet and his companions and their practice and ethical means of earning a living.

The argument against the other Ŝūfīs on the subject takes a specific turn in the fourth chapter. It focuses on a renowned Ŝūfī from Khurasān, Persia, mentioned by name as Shaqiq, Shaqiq ibn Ibrāhīm ibn Ali al-Azdi al-Balkhy. Al-Ĥārith cites Shaqiq's claims and replies to them. The contended claims are mainly: (a) if one strongly believes in God, and in that God will provide for one's needs, as God has stated, and one still strives to earn a living, this would imply that one has doubts about the ability of God to provide, and this is *kufr*, disbelief, (b) in striving for a living of something God has destined for one to have, one would be interfering in the timing of God and this would be like hurrying God in obtaining what one is destined to get at a certain time, in God's knowledge, and this is also not permitted, and (c) the pursuit of a living emanates mainly from a weakness in faith as the real faith would imply that the believer should be content with what God has given him and ought to wait until God's bounty reaches him. This sounds like a plausible argument that might seem convincing to some Muslims who are seeking the blessing of God by any means, or the weak-hearted in facing the hardship of making a living. Al-Ḥ̂ārith exposes these claims and replies to them logically and coherently with evidence from the Qur'ān, the Sunnah and the practice of the early companions. Of the reasons he mentions for the invalidity of these claims, one reads, with interest, his statement that by the Ŝūfī accepting offerings from others he might be accepting donations from the sources of which may be forbidden in the sight of God. A means that does not justify the end!

The remaining part of Earnings and Asceticism is purely an ethical treatise on earnings and how it can be used. It addresses various ethical issues with regard to earnings; the generation of earnings and the use of its revenue in fulfilling one's needs. Written by a Ŝūfī, the book, in this part, projects the Ŝūfīsm's views on such an important economic issue. It is distinguished from other ethical writing on economics in that it projects a puritan view as seen by a sect that, despite the extremity of some of its followers, has always been regarded as having highly spiritual values. The particular puritan distinction of the Ŝūfī can be seen throughout the book when a special emphasis is placed on the necessity to leave out what may not be forbidden in case it is not decisively permissible. This is a theme that can be seen to be stressed in the writing of the Earnings and Asceticism. The section begins with the definition of asceticism, *wara'*, in views of al-Ḥ̂ārith and other teachers of Ŝūfīsm of his contemporary as well as those before him. Asceticism, which is still difficult to define with one comprehensively precise definition, is "the avoidance of what may not please God, of saying, of action, of inner thought, or of an inner desire, and the avoidance of missing out on what God has ordained either by action or by thought or feeling." God-fearing in all aspects of life explicit and implicit, is the concept of asceticism in al-Ĥārith's views and the views of his fellow Ŝūfīs. Beyond that, and without that, the Muslim is said not to be practicing *wara*ʾ. This is not necessarily what the non-Ŝūfī view is, as Muslims are accountable only to what they have actually said or done. For what the Muslim has in mind but has not brought out in the form of a behaviour, this is left to God to penalize for it or otherwise; He may or may not forgive at His own discretion as the Qurʾānic verses 2:285–286 are telling us. But for the Ŝūfī, asceticism, piousness, or *wara*ʾ, addresses the inner soul and thought of the individual not merely his or her acted behaviour.

Giving up the doubtful, *shubuhat*, for the sake of what is certain is a main feature of *wara*ʾ. There may be a need, for example, to abandon a lawful means of earnings if it may lead to a forbidden means of earning to others. The example of a Muslim burning out his vineyard for fear of it being used by a buyer to trade in alcoholic beverage is cited by al-Muĥāsibī as an example of piousness. This may sound like taking religion to extreme, as the person is only responsible for what he/she has done, as the Qurʾān is telling us (2: 286), and it may be an extreme example of God-fearing, but it is still, nevertheless, a case of a puritan avoiding the doubtful un-forbidden for the sake of the certain permissible. In very brief, as al-Muĥāsibī is telling us, in the market place earning a living, or otherwise, one ought to be conscientious of God's existence; observing His commands in action and in heart.

The importance of the treatise of al-Muĥasibi is threefold: (a) it shows the views of Ŝūfīsm on an important economic issue, earnings, (b) it criticises the claims made by Ŝūfīs concerning economic behaviour, mainly in the pursuit of earnings and consumption, and (c) it is rich in ethics and the ethical treatment of economics. In that sense, Earnings and Asceticism can be regarded as a great contribution by the puritans to economic issues. Al-Muĥāsibī is said to have influenced great writers after him such as Imam al-Ghazālī whose great master piece, "Iĥya' Ulūm al-Dīn" is examined in the following chapter.

Now we turn our attention to examining the development of Islamic economic thinking during a difficult period in the history of Islam that was marked by political fragmentation. This is the start of the next chapter.

CHAPTER SIX

POLITICAL FRAGMENTATION AND CULTURAL DIVERSITY (1000 A.C.–1400 A.C.)

Introduction

For more than one century, from the time when Abū-al-Faraj Qudama ibn-Ja'afer (864–932) wrote his Kitāb al-Kharāj until al-Māwardī wrote al-Aĥkām al-Sūltāniyyah (972–1058), there was a complete absence of writing on Islamic economics. Two contributory factors could be suggested: (a) the decline in the political power of the caliphate, and (b) the preoccupation of Muslim thinkers with other areas of intellectual civilities, most of all philosophy, which overshadowed the subject of economics. A further factor could be added: the sharp division in the schools of religious thought and ideology that led to the appearance of several politically motivated religious factions of conflicting ideologies and contradicting directions. These factors, the political decline and the intellectual development, are outlined below with a view to looking into their implications for the writing on Islamic economics.

Political Fragmentation

Historians observe that the political decline of the caliphate started from the time of al-Mūtawakkil (847–861). One of the reasons for such demarcation is that he was the first Abbasīd caliph to have been murdered by his own bodyguard. But the decline could be traced to a decade earlier when the caliph al-Must'asim (833–842) was overpowered by his Turkish bodyguards who were originally imported to counter-balance the increasing influence of the Persian soldiers.

The period was marked with the growing power of three different forces: (a) the Alid movement, (b) the Arab separatist movement, and (c) the non-Arab separatist movement. Not all of these movements had the same implications for the development of science, art and literature. While some had devastating consequences, others, amazingly, had very favourable effects. A brief discussion of these main movements and their impact on the intellectual life of Muslims is given below with a view to exploring the environment within which Islamic economic writers initiated and completed their work.

The Alid Movement

The Alids, who sided with the Abbasids in overthrowing the Umayyads, had hoped at best that the caliphate would be restored to them as legitimate heirs, and at worst to be given a role in running the affair of the state. The outcomes were quite the opposite; there was to be neither. The Alids who felt betrayed regarded themselves as caliphs in waiting and never missed an opportunity to establish their own political entity in the face of their cousins the Abbasids.

Of the few Alid attempts to establish an independent state, within the Abbasīd state, is the Fatimid. The Fatimid movement, named after Lady Fatimah the Prophet's daughter and Caliph Ali's wife, was the most influential and the longest lasting. The Fatimid movement was based on the Ismāīlī, or Shī'i Seveners movement that was named after the seventh Imam Ismāīl the descendant of Caliph Ali. The Ismāīlī spread their missions throughout the country preaching the return of al-Mahdi, Muĥammad the son of Ismāīl, who, in accordance with a Prophet's prophesy, would return to restore justice, remove the oppression (caused by the Abbasids in the interpretation of the Ismāīlī), and apply equality. They found success in Yemen in 901, and in 908 they established their rule as the Fatimid caliphate in Tunisia. From Tunisia they extended its domain, taking over Egypt in 969 and then Syria in 1003 (Hitti, 1963). What is particularly noted about the Fatimid movement is that it was the only movement that represented a challenge to the Abbasīd on their own grounds: the issue of the caliphate as being based on the kinship to the Prophet. Therefore, it was not an independent state, within the Abbasīd caliphate, which would still pay homage to Baghdad, but an independent caliphate that did not acknowledge the religious legitimacy of the caliphate in Baghdad. It was based, instead, on the Shi'ī conviction that the caliphate had belonged to them since the death of the Prophet.

The centre of power was, therefore, shifted from Baghdad to Cairo, the capital of the Fatimid caliphate. The Fatimid caliphate lasted until 1167 when the last Fatimid caliph was displaced by Saladin,

Ŝalah-al-Dīn, at the outbreak of the Crusades, with a view to uniting the country, under his leadership, and to providing political power in the face of the Crusade armies.

The Fatimids paid considerable attention to learning and education. The caliphs in Egypt developed great scientific and learning centres where scientists found the right environment to flourish and develop their work. In 972 A.C. al-Azhar mosque was built, and used as a centre of learning as well as a place of worship. Al-Azhar became one of the oldest surviving universities in the world and continued to be so in Egypt until the present day. Dar-al-Hikmah or Dar al-Ilm (hall of wisdom or of science) was established in 1005 with a specified fund to be used for books and research. Special attention was given to the writing, maintaining and repairing books, and from the Fatimid Egypt came the earliest-known Islamic bookbinding which many assigned to the eighth or ninth century. A Royal Library was established, during al-Mustansir caliphate (1035–1094), which contained as many as 200,000 books (Hitti, 1963). Therefore, although the Fatimid move was a breakaway from the central state it did not lead to the weakening of the scientific and cultural activities during the period. Under their reign, scientists, with the support of the newly formed caliphate, had introduced to the world some of the finest reference work that served for many years after them.

But despite the notable development of science, art and industrial art, and the encouragement of learning by the Fatimids, there does not seem to be any specific writing on Islamic economics during the Fatimid period. It was only towards the middle of the eleventh century that al-Māwardī wrote his *Al-Aĥkām*, with no evidence to suggest that he was under the patronage of the Fatimids. Even further, al-Māwardī was not a Shī'ī scholar but a Sunni Shafī'i. It was as if the Jurists of the day were more concerned with the promotion of the Shī'ah theology than the advance of economic literature.

The Arab Separatist Movement

To the north and northeast of the Islamic Abbasīd empire lay another independent state. It was a religio-politically driven state with another dynasty that lasted for about half a century. The Shi'ī Ĥamdānīd state was first founded in northern Mesopotamia with al-Mawsil being its capital (929–991). In 944 the Ĥamdānīds stretched their boundaries to North Syria and by taking this part from the Ikhshīdids, who presided over Egypt, they came in direct rivalry and confrontation with them. By contrast to other sundry states, the Ĥamdānīds were of an Arab stock. They were descendants of Taghlib tribe, and in religious conviction they were Shi'ī. As such, the Ĥamdānīds were the second Shī'ah independent state, which preceded the Fatimids, but came after the Idrisids in North Africa. They lasted until 1003 when the last of the dynasty gave way to the Fatimid caliphate that by that time crushed the Ikhshīdids in Egypt in 969. It was perhaps a case of Shi'ī political amalgamation between the small Ĥamdānīd dynasty in the north and the major growing caliphate in the south.

The intellectual life of the Ĥamdānīd court was very rich. In contrast to the non-Arab sundry dynasties, they encouraged learning and prided themselves on attracting a distinguished learning circle. Sayf-al-Dawlah, the sword of the dynasty, (944–967), himself a poet, is renowned in history for his patronage of learning. The literary circle included the highly celebrated philosopher-musician al-Farabi, the distinguished historian of literature and music al-Aŝfahānī, whose autograph manuscript al-Aghanī is a celebrated reference on the subject until today, the eloquent court preacher ibn-Nabatah whose elegant sermon in rhymed prose fired the zeal of his hearers for prosecuting the holy war against Byzantine, and the celebrated poet laureate al-Mutanabbi, whose bombastic and ornate style with its flowery rhetoric and improbable metaphors made him to the present day the most popular and most widely quoted poet in Arabic language (Hitti, 1963). Added to the list, was the poet-philosopher Abū-al-Ala' al-Ma'ari (973–1057), who projected the skeptical pessimistic feelings of an age of social decay and political anarchy in Islam (ibid.).

The Non-Arab Separatist Movement

The Persian Separatist Movement

The north western region of the Abbasīd caliphate was the main domain of the non-Arab Persian and Turkish quasi-independent states.

The first, to the east of Baghdad, was the Tahirids, named after the general of the caliph al-Ma'mūn (813–933) who helped the caliph in his dispute with his brother al-Amin (809–813) over the caliphate. He was a Persian slave. Extending their domain to the Indian borders, the Tahirids remained in power from 820 to 872 (ibid.).

The Saffarīds, yet another Persian dynasty, founded by a head of a gang of outlaws, ruled all of Persia to the Indian frontiers from 867 to 908.

The Samanīds, founded by a Zoroastrian aristocrat, started by taking away Khurasān from the Saffarīds in 900 and later expanded their domain further, were the next dynasty of Persian power. In sharp contrast to their predecessors the Samanīds had a considerable interest in learning and their court attracted both Arab and non-Arab scholars such as al-Razi in medicine, ibn-Sina in literature and others. It was the period when Arabic literature was first translated into Persian and the capital Samarqand almost outshone Baghdad as a centre of learning and art (Hitti, 1963). It would not be an exaggeration to say that the interest of the Samanīds in learning could be interpreted as a reflection of the quality of their aristocrat founders, who were in sharp contrast with slave founders of other non-Arab separatist movements.

The Samanīd period was the period that witnessed the growing power of the Turks, starting with that of the Turkish slaves who were recruited in the Samanīds' army. In what seemed to have become almost a usual occurrence, the Turkish slaves, with whom the Samanīds filled their army, rose to power and overcame their masters. That was the beginning of the influence of the Ghaznawids that started from 962 and grew to become an empire. By 1186 their reign stretched to cover Afghanistan and Punjab. The real founder of the Ghaznawid Empire was Subuktigin (976–997), a slave and a son in law of Alptigin who was a governor under the Samanīds (ibid.)

That was the beginning of the major Turkish influence in the Islamic world. The Ghaznawids glory finally came to an end in 1186 at the hands of the Ghurids of Afghanistan.

The Būwayhīd dynasty marked the influence of the Shi'ī Persians on the caliphate. At the time of the Abbasīd caliph al-Mustakfi (944–946) ibn-Buwayh entered Baghdad in 945, and was received with honour by the Caliph who seemed to have been pleased to see the Turkish guard fleeing on his arrival. He was designated the title "commander of the commanders" and "the one who makes the state mighty". The Būwayhīd had a free hand in Baghdad and tended to govern with or without the caliph, though they maintained the concept of the caliphate as a figurehead caliph. In a certain instance there was an attempt to forge a coalition between their political and military power on the one hand, and the religious legitimacy of the caliphate on the other. To cement the coalition in 980 the Būwayhīd, Adud-al-Dawlah (949–83), married the daughter of the caliph al-Tai' (974–91).

The Būwayhīds had a tight control over the caliphate. Those caliphs who dared to oppose were deposed, humiliated, and in some cases blinded and forced to beg for alms. In 946 al-Mustakfi was blinded, deposed by ibn-Buwayh and a new caliph was appointed. The fate of the two predecessor caliphs was not any better. They were blinded and seen begging for alms in the streets of Baghdad. Throughout their century or so of supremacy (945–1055) the Būwayhīds made and unmade caliphs at will (Hittis, 1963). By that time there were three assumed caliphates: the puppetry Abbasīd in Baghdad, the Fatimid in Cairo, and the Umayyad in Cordoba.

What is worth noticing about the Būwayhīds is that they embarked on a programme of economic and administrative reform. They repaired canals and repaired and built mosques, hospitals, public buildings, a library with 10,000 books and an observatory, and they extended their patronage to poets and men of literature (ibid.). More important to Islamic economics, it was the period when al-Māwardī wrote his *al-Aĥkām al-Sūltāniyyah*, the ordinance of the state. Interestingly enough the title of al-Māwardī's book is derived from the political title given to the Būwayhīd ruler by the ailing Abbasīd caliph. "Al-Ŝulṭān" was a title given for the first time to a ruler and adopted later for a book. Worth noting is that the title has an Arabic connotation, which would provide evidence against a possible suggestion that it could have been 'imported' from other cultures. It is derived from the noun 'Ŝulṭān', meaning power, ability and authority. But the word is not an adjective or a proper noun. It could be a case of a linguistic distortion necessitated by the need to look for an exceedingly exalted title to be given to an exceedingly exalted army general. Or, on the other hand, it could be a word implying that the person with such a name was the person with such power: the person with power, Sultan, or for simplicity, the Sultan. Al-Māwardī's *al-Aĥkām al-Sūltāniyyah* will be discussed shortly.

The family quarrel and the Sunnis' resentment of the Shi'ī Būwayhīds led to the fall of the dynasty. In 1055 the Saljuk Turk Taghril Beg entered Baghdad and put an end to the Būwayhīd rule.

The Turkish Separatist Movement

The influence of the Turks began when the Caliph al-Mūsta'sīm (833–842) surrounded himself with 4000 strong Turks from Transoxiana to counterbalance the influence of the Persian hegemony in the army. The Persian influence was an inevitable consequence of the dispute between the two sons of Harūn al-Rashīd over the caliphate. Al-Ma'mūn (813–833), whose mother was Persian, sought the support of the Persians against his Brother al-Amin (809–813) whose mother was an Arab (Al-Ťabarī). With the victory sealed for al-Ma'mūn the Persians felt that the caliph owed them his victory. But importing the Turks guard had an opposite effect. The predominantly Turkish guards soon overpowered the caliph so much that in 861 the Caliph Al-Mūtawakkil was murdered by his guards at the instigation of his son.

The Turkish separatist movement was first witnessed in Egypt. Prior to the Fatimids, the Tulūnīd dynasty was founded by Ahmad ibn-Tūlūn, whose Turkish father was a slave sent in 817 by the ruler of Bukhara as a present to al-Ma'mūn (813–833). The dynasty lasted from 808 until it reverted to the Abbasīd caliph in 905. At its zenith, the Tūlūn dynasty ruled Syria in 877, when Ibn-Tūlūn annexed it without considerable resistance, and for the first time since the Pharaonic time a government in Egypt, Ahmad ibn-Tūlūn, ruled both provinces of Egypt and Syria, and for many centuries to come Syria continued to be ruled from the valley of the Nile (Hitti, 1963).

The Tulūnīd Egypt witnessed some favourable economic and artistic activities. Realising the importance of agriculture to the economy of Egypt, the Tūlūnids paid particular attention to the irrigation system and public works. Arts, architecture and craftsmanship also developed. Ahmad ibn-Tūlūn's mosque is standing in Cairo today as an architectural sight and a tourist attraction. The Tūlūnid dynasty was, however, short-lived. It consisted of only two generations; the founder father, a successor son, two grandsons, and the founder's son. The dynasty did not have the deep political or traditional roots that would strengthen its existence in the Egyptian soil. Relying mainly on a recruited bodyguard-cum-army imported from foreign origins, with no theological philosophy based on religion, even if controversial, the dynasty did not have the much needed support of the masses. With no broad genealogical base and a distinctive approach to theology on the part of the rulers, there was perhaps a mutual sense of alienation between both the rulers and the subjects. Apart from a strong governing imported army, a superficial allegiance to an ailing caliph in Baghdad, and a fertile agriculture land, there were no strong ties between the rulers and the inhabitants of the land. The problem with the strong imported bodyguard-cum-army is that its loyalty, in the absence of amalgamation with society, becomes confined only to the power of the military leadership which when changed, forces a change of loyalty in a similar direction. That was once again an example of a history repeating itself as in the case of the Ikhshīdids who followed the Tūlūnids.

The Ikhshīdis, who were yet another Turkish dynasty, followed the Tūlūnids in Egypt and ruled the country with quasi autonomy from 935 until they were crushed by the Fatimids in 969. Like his Tulūnīd predecessor, the founder was appointed by the caliph over the province of Egypt, and like him he annexed Syria and ruled it from Egypt, but, unlike his predecessor, he incorporated both Makkah and al-Medīnah into his domain. Notably, and in contrast to their predecessors, the Ikhshīdids left no artistic marks or sign of public works after them, nor did they have a literary life of their own (op. cit.)

Again, neither during the Tūlūnids nor under the Ikhshīdids, does one notice great works of literature, let alone works on Islamic economics. Praise as well as ridicule comedy did exist however, as it was rewarded extravagantly, and as it was, amazingly and amusingly, directed to the same ruler. The confrontation between the Ikhshīd ruler the Abyssinian eunuch Abū-al-Misk Kafur and the renowned propagandist poet al-Mutanabbi is a well known example. Having fallen out of favour with Kafur, al-Mutanabbi praise turned into a bitter attack, which enriched books of Arab literture.

Poets seemed to have replaced jurists in the royal entourage of these states as they were more pleasing and generally praising. Moreover, the power of the media, by the standard of the day, was needed to boast the ruler's image and provide him with political propaganda.

But the Turks were destined to play a major part in the Islamic history for many years to come. It began in around 956 when a chieftain called Saljuq had settled with his nomad clan in the region of Bukhara. They embraced Islam zealously and became a major political force in its history. By 1055 they entered Baghdad where they were received and honoured by the Caliph who was pleased to receive their protection. The history of the Saljuqs, who extended their conquests in all directions, until Western Asia was, once more, united, is regarded as a brilliant period in Islamic history (Hitti,

1963). This marked the influence of the Turkish Saljuqs, which was the beginning of the sweeping Turkish influence in Islamic history for centuries to come.

The Collapse and Restoration of the Caliphate

The final blow to the weak Islamic caliphate came at the hands of the Mongols, whose destructive waves created havoc in the Islamic world. History books are full of examples of their brutality, destruction and devastation of any sign of culture. In 1258 the caliph with his few hundred officials met the Mongol commander Hulagu in an unconditional surrender, but they were all put to the sword. In Syria, Hulagu's progress was eventually halted. His army was destroyed in 1260 by Baybars, the Mamlūk Egyptian commander.

But it was the Ottoman Turks, kinsmen of the Mongols, who were to restore the past military glory of Islam and reinstate the Islamic caliphate. In 1516 the Ottoman Turk leader Salim revived the caliphate to a person who, supposedly, was the last in line of the Abbasīd caliphs (ibid.). Under the name of al-Mūtawakkil, this previously unnoticed person became the first restored caliph.

Intellectual Diversity

The intellectual environment that surrounded the writing on Islamic economics during that period had three distinctive influential factors: the spread of Islamic religio-political philosophy, the increasing interest in the critique of the Greek philosophy, the development of the Islamic juridical philosophy, and the separate movements in the Islamic state. While the first three factors have been highlighted above, the effect of the last factor needs a further examination.

Had the separate political movements in the Abbasīd caliphate affected the intellectual development in the Islamic land? And if it had, was the effect favourable or unfavourable?

Although it is difficult to generalize, it can be said that, with very few exceptions, the intellectual development, surprisingly, witnessed further progress under the separate dynastic movements that led to the dismemberment of the caliphate. This, of what seems to be an interesting result, is in contrast to what could be expected.

The progress in intellectual development, or otherwise, seemed to have been based on, and conditioned by, the cultural character and background of the founder of the dynasty. We find for example that the separate movements that did not have a particular ideology but were based instead on merely the military powers of their founders who lacked intellectual backgrounds were very poor in their intellectual achievements. The most notable examples of these were the Saffarīd dynasty whose founder was the head of a gang of outlaws and who ruled all of Persia to the Indian frontiers from 867 to 908. There was no intellectual progress during that dynasty. A similar example could be taken from the Ikhshīds of Egypt who were, yet again, a Turkish slave dynasty governing Egypt from 935 until 969. That dynasty, short as it was, left no intellectual achievements either.

However, apart from the Saffarīds and Ikhshīds, we find the dynasty normally surrounding itself with patronage of poets, scientists, and Ulama'. The example of the Samanīds whose founder was a Zoroastrian aristocrat, taking away Khurasān from the Saffarīds in 900, was a worthy one. The Samanīds paid considerable attention to learning and surrounding themselves with patronage of Arab and non-Arab intellectuals. The dynasty, as we saw earlier, took particular pride and interest in promoting education, building schools, madrasah, and was keen on, or at least keen to be seen as being interested in, protecting the religion of Islam. For the dynasties that did not have the Holy Shrines of Makkah and al-Medīnah within their geographical domain, protecting Islam would take the alternative form of protecting and preserving the Sharī'ah. The protection and perseverance of the Sharī'ah would be demonstrated, at least in the eyes of the populace, by surrounding the court with a patronage of Sharī'ah scholars, Ulama'. The inclusion of the Ulama' in the dynasty's royal court aimed to provide the rulers with the most needed guidance and direction on Sharī'ah matters and to help derive religious opinions, fatwa, if the need had arisen. Moreover, keeping the Ulama' in the royal court would be perceived by the public as the Ulama' being in support of the ruling dynasty which would add to their religious legitimacy and reinforce public support. Establishing educational centres was a demonstrable example of the rulers' support of education and learning centres in the dynasty, and a demonstration of their intention of improving the state of the people. The Fatimid is another good example of a dynasty that paid considerable attention to the support of leaning and education. For example, Al-Azhar, the oldest surviving university was built by the Fatimids in 972, and Dar al-Hikmah, hall of wisdom or of science, which was established by them in 1005, are both still, in addition to being a visiting tourist attraction, operating for the purpose for which they were built as centres of learning in the heart of Cairo.

It could be argued, even with caution, that the political decline of the state, the religio-political uncertainty in the Islamic world, and the division of the central government did not provide the ideal environment for the development of the Islamic economic literature and this may have slowed down the writing on Islamic economics during that period. The political decline could be said to have restricted the potential support provided by the state to scholars in the field. Nevertheless, such a suggestion may have to be taken with caution, as it cannot be proved empirically since there is no pattern to compare it with. What is left for us is perhaps to hypothesize. It could be said further that the attention given to the Greek philosophy could have lead to a further diversion of the interest of writers who could have been potential writers on economics. Moreover, the intellectual preoccupation by religion-political issues may have also lead to the dispersion of the attention of scholars and may have limited their contribution to the development of economics. Furthermore, all these factors together could be said to have influenced writing on the subject.

The fact remains that the writing continued, despite frequent interruptions, reflecting the political instability of the Islamic world. During the raids of the first Crusade campaign in 1099, for example, Imam al-Ghazāli (1058–1111) wrote his master piece al-Ihya'a, and under the Mongols' destruction Imam Ibn-Taymīya (1263–1328) wrote his al-Ĥisbah in Islam. Their work will be explored in the next chapter.

To sum up, it might fair to say that Muslim writers on Islamic economics, who were the Ulama' of the day, mostly judges and jurists, were too preoccupied by several factors to give the Islamic economic literature a further impetus during that period. These factors were mainly the consolidation of coherent schools of religious sects and the need to respond to them, the novelty of the Greek philosophy and the curious desire to explore it and react to it Islamically, and the exogenous military aggression of the neighbouring forces. These factors were perhaps more influential than the breakdown of the central government of the caliphate.

Despite these limiting factors, some scholars managed to leave for us a fine legacy of writing on the subject. This has enriched the literature of Islamic economics, some of which are discussed below.

Abū al-Hasan al-Māwardī (364–450 A.H., 972–1058 A.C.) *al-Aĥkām al-Sūltāniyyah, Book of State Ordinance*

The Author

Abū al-Ĥassan Ali Ibn Muĥammad Ibn Habīb al-Māwardī was a Shafī'i, born in Baŝrah in 972 A.C. Like many scholars of his time, he studied the Qur'ān and Sunnah and then proceeded to learn *Fiqh*, Islamic jurisprudence. His proficiency in jurisprudence, ethics, political science and literature proved useful in securing him a respectable career in Baghdad where, after an initial appointment as a judge, he became the Chief Justice (Rahim, 1993). During the time of the Abbasīd Caliph al-Qaīm bi Amr Allah (1031–1075) he was appointed, perhaps with the ratification of the Būwayhīds, as a traveling ambassador and was sent to a number of countries as the head of special missions, (Zahoor, 1997) That was the period when the Būwayhīds ruled the caliphate until they eventually fell under the power of the Turkish Saljuqs who put an end to their rule in 1055. In this capacity al-Māwardī seemed to have played a key role in establishing harmonious relations between the declining Abbasīd Caliphate and the rising powers of Būwayhīds and Saljukes. He was still in Baghdad when it was taken over from the Būwayhīds by the Saljuq Turks.

Al-Māwardī's contribution to political science and sociology comprises a number of monumental books, the most famous of which are *Kitāb al-Aĥkām al-Sūltāniyyah*, *Qanūn al-Wazarah*, and *Kitāb Nasihat al-Mūlk*. The books discuss the principles of political science, with special reference to the functions and duties of the caliphs, the prime minister, other ministers, and the relationships between the public and government. Two of these books, *al-Aĥkām al-Sūltāniyyah* and *Qanūn al-Wazarah* have been published and also translated into various languages. One of al-Māwardī's works is *al-Hāwi al-Kabīr*, the All-Encompassing Book, which is one of the most comprehensive books on *fiqh*, jurisprudence, in general and the Shafī'i *fiqh* in particular. He was a supporter of the 'Doctrine of Necessity' in political science.

As such, he was in favour of a strong caliphate and was against delegating unlimited powers to the governors, which, in his view, tended to create chaos. Also, he has laid down clear principles for the election of the caliph and the quality of the voters, among which the attainment of a degree of intellectual level and the purity of character are particularly important.

Al-Māwardī is considered as one of the most famous thinkers in political science in the Middle Ages. His original work influenced the development of this science, together with the science of sociology, which was further developed later on by Ibn-Khaldūn.

Al-Māwardī died in 1058 A.C.

The Book

What concerns us of al-Māwardī's works is his *al-Aĥkām al-Sūltāniyyah wa al-Wilayāt al-Dīniyyah*, State Ordinance and Religious Governance. The first general observation about *al-Aĥkām* is that, as indicated previously, the title of the book relates to the new political culture within which al-Māwardī wrote his work. It refers to a political title that had not been used by Muslims before, until the growing influence of the Turkish element in the Abbasīd caliphate. Whether al-Māwardī wrote his *al-Aĥkām* to the Būwayhīd ruler, in parallel to Abū-Yūsuf's writing of al-Kharāj to his caliph al-Rashīd, is something that cannot be ascertained with certainty. But judging by his choice of title and his reference to his book by al-Sūltāniyyah, it might be inferred that he was indicating where the centre of power was and, indirectly, paying homage to the effective ruler of the state, the Ŝulṭān.

The main purpose of the book

The purpose of writing *al-Aĥkām* seemed to be threefold: first, to help those implementing the law to understand it well, so that justice could be achieved, second, to help those who make the law understand the rules of the Sharī'ah so that laws might be derived within its rules with no deviation from the established religious rules, and third, to help jurists and scholars understand the bases upon which these Sūltanate rules were based and invite them to make a contribution to the establishment of future rules if necessary. All this was for the purpose of achieving justice.

In al-Māwardī's words, these objectives, as explained in his *al-Aĥkām*, are as follows (Al-Māwardī, 1985):

The rationale for writing the book is,

> Sūltanate rules are needed more for those who execute them than for other (users).

But the problem is that,

> As Sūltanate rules become mixed with other orders and as the officials who execute them become overburdened with political and administrative matters, it may become difficult to follow and scrutinise these orders.

Therefore,

> I have written this specialised book to focus on these orders in accordance with the orders of those whose obedience is required.

So that,

> Judicial jurists may know what needs to be filled and fulfilled

For the ultimate objective of:

> Achieving justice in judgment and implementation and realising ultimate fairness

There was a need, therefore, at least as al-Māwardī saw it, to write a book on the state orders and to explain the Sharī'ah bases of these orders to those involved in implementing them. It was meant to be of assistance to the general ruler, the Ŝulṭān, who issued the rules, province governors as government officials, who exercised the rules, and judges and jurists who passed the judgment and expressed views while reaching a judgment. The need for these rules, particularly during that period of political turmoil, would not be surprising.

Despite the growing influence of the Būwayhīd over the caliphs, Al-Māwardī, to his credit, did not put the ruler above the caliph. We find him in his introduction stating that the caliphate is God's arrangement in which the caliph is the Prophet's successor. We also find him putting the caliphate, perhaps in its symbolic spiritual role, above the Ŝulṭān (al-Māwardī, 1985).

Al-Aĥkām is divided into twenty chapters covering a wide range of topics of state and religious ordinance, of which nine chapters are on the administration of the state finance. In line with the prevailing political culture that witnessed the dispute over the caliphate and the contention, perhaps resentment, among Muslims, over the legitimacy of political leadership, a contention that was fueled by the growing power of non-Arab rulers, al-Māwardī must have found it necessary to begin his book with the discussion of the *imamah*, religio-political leadership. In line with his support of the jurisprudence of necessity he seemed to have been in support of the idea that a strong ruler, who is able to protect Islam and maintain the religion, ought to be obeyed even if there was another who might have had a more rightful claim to the political leadership—a compromise that must have pleased the Būwayhīd Ŝulṭān. He went even further to ascertain that an unjust ruler who is able to protect religion is preferred to a just one who is not able to do so, until such time when a ruler who is both just and powerful can be found. The alternative of "the theory of the second best" perhaps.

Al-Aĥkām, its structure, and the circumstances in which it was written brings to mind Abū-Yūsuf 's *Kitāb al-Kharāj*. There seems to be a similarity between the two books. Both books had been written at the instructions of the rulers, both were meant to provide just rules in matters related to the administration of the state's affairs, both were meant to provide guidance to those managing the state, and both were written by chief judges who were close to the rulers. But there are five major differences:

While Abū-Yūsuf wrote his book for a powerful caliph, al-Māwardī wrote his to a strong ruling commander, who ruled from within the caliph.

While the instructions for writing the book are shown explicitly in Abū-Yūsuf's *al-Kharāj*, these instructions are inferred in al-Māwardī's *al-Aĥkām*. In addition while Abū-Yūsuf's was a Sunni Ĥanafī, al-Māwardī was a Sunni Shafī'i, which reflected the variation in their thinking.

The structure of *al-Aĥkām* seems to be clearer with some expansion on the topics covered, which is a conceivable development bearing in mind the effect of learning through the passage of time and the development of the further political complications. Examples of the expansion can be seen from the discussion of the administrative side of the state in separate chapters, beginning with the *Imamah*, or caliphate, followed by *Wazarah*, or the office of prime minister, province governorship, and deputation of general and/or specific tasks and missions.

The book contains an important chapter that was not particularly specified before him in previous works. It is a chapter on *Ĥisbah*, or public duties. Interestingly, the work on *Ĥisbah* was subsequently developed further after him, where we find specialized books, like that of ibn-Taymīya, devoted entirely to *Ĥisbah*.

In his jurisprudence approach we find al-Māwardī, in dealing with an issue, examining the opinions of Abū-Hanīfah and Abū-Yūsuf (who was a Ĥanafī as shown previously), and he may agree or, invariably, disagree with them. In his disagreement he would look at the views of Mālik and al-Shafi', provide evidence from the Qur'ān and Sunnah and express his views which, as a Shafī'i, coincide with the Shafī'i school of thought.

By the standards of the day, *al-Aĥkām al-Sūltāniyyah* was a major addition to literature. Even with what might be viewed as a parallel similarity with Abū-Yūsuf 's *Kitāb al-Kharāj*, al-Māwardī wrote his book almost four and half centuries after Abū-Yūsuf completed his. The book was also written during a period of political instability in the Islamic state in contrast to the stability of the early Abbasīd caliphate. In such chaotic circumstances the need for a book of this nature must have been imperative to achieve justice and observe the Sharī'ah. Al-Māwardī's work could be viewed as a major contribution to maintaining the rules of the Sharī'ah in relation to public finance and achieving justice in matters related to raising state funds through taxation and otherwise. The inclusion of a special chapter on *Ĥisbah*, public duties, is an early recognition by al-Māwardī of the importance of the subject as a separate topic of study.

Al-Māwardī and his *al-Aĥkām* was a major landmark that positively interrupted a period of silence that spread over the Islamic economic literature for several centuries. His *al-Aĥkām* is a major reference work for scholars in the field.

Now we turn our attention to microeconomics once more. Al-Māwardī was a writer who was not concerned with how the state manages its finance as much as he was with how the individual and the community manage their economies. He is al-Rāghib al-Aŝfahānī.

Al-Rāghib al-Aŝfahānī (d. 502 A.H./1108 A.C.)
al-Ẕarī'ah fi Makārim al-Sharī'ah, Means of Glorious Sharī'ah

The Author

Abū-al-Qasim al-Ĥusayn ibn Muĥammad ibn al-Mufdal al-Rāghib al-Aŝfahānī, a different Aŝfahānī from the scholar renowned for his famous book, al-Aghanī, seemed to have acquired his name from the city of Aŝfahān, as he lived between Aŝfahān and Baghdad during the first part of the eleventh century. His date of birth does not seem to be known, though it is said that he died in 502 A.H./1108 A.C. (Al-Agami, 1985). He is said to be of the Sunni-Shafī'i school of thought, though some have included him among the Shi'iah as his writings show a considerable admiration to the house of Caliph Ali. As for himself, he never declared a political inclination to either the Sunni or Shi'ī. He did not show a particular interest in the prevailing political dispute among Muslims at that time. As for being among a particular sect of intellectual thinkers of the day, some suggested that he was a Mu'tazili as he devoted a significant part of his thinking to the importance of mind and mental reasoning, while others related him to other sects such as the Ash'ari who adopted an opposite view in their interpretation of religious texts. This perhaps symbolises the state of contradiction, and even confusion, among the several religio-political sects of the day.

Further, the works of al-Rāghib al-Aŝfahānī may be classified under moral philosophy, as he mixed his ideas, economic or otherwise, with moral and ethical issues—an early history of moral economics if we use the terms of today. Even though, the emphasis on ethical issues should not be inferred as being particularly related to moral philosophy as we can hardly see Qur'ānic texts separating secular issues from ethical values. But the interest in classifying al-Aŝfahānī's works, and those of others, as such, could have been a product of the influence of the Greek philosophy which began to have a significant impact on the thinking of Muslim philosophers at that time.

The Book

The book, which has some relevance for Islamic economics, is "al-Zarī'ah fi Makārīm al-Sharī'ah", or 'Means of Glorious Sharī'ah'. Although the book's title is not on Islamic economics exclusively, the script includes important issues relating to the subject. Of the seven chapters of which the book consists, two are on economic issues exclusively, while other chapters are not entirely void of discussion of issues related to economics such as consumer behavior. In total, the issues covered in the book could be categorised as follows (Donia, 1984):

1. Man: his importance, functions and needs
2. Production activities: importance of production, cooperation and specialisation, means of production, employment and unemployment, and the scope of economic activities.
3. Wealth and its sources: the relationship between man and wealth, riches and poverty, and money.
4. Spending: balance and imbalance in spending, and consumption.

The main points in al-Aŝfahānī's al-Zarī'ah are discussed as follows:

Al-Aŝfahānī's Zarī'ah begins with a first chapter on man. This is not particularly surprising as man is regarded in Islam as the centre of the universe for whom God has made every thing possible. Starting his book with a first chapter on man, his/her nature, creation, duties, needs, and motivation is an intelligent realisation by al-Aŝfahānī of the position of human beings in the universe as manifested in the Muslims' sacred book. In terms of a logical classification of the contents of a book on economics, a first chapter on human beings, needs and behaviour, could be a reasonable start as he/she is the consumer, producer, distributor, investor, wealth seeker, entrepreneur, decision maker, and so on, and as such, man is the pivot upon which economic decisions revolve. One cannot ignore this simple fact even in books on positive economics that are not related to Islamic economics in particular.

Human Needs: Consumption

Bringing the issues close to home, al-Aŝfahānī looked into the needs of man as a consumer and divided human needs into categories depending upon the purpose of satisfying these needs. In his view, human needs are divided into two main categories: physiological needs and spiritual needs which are related to satisfying ethical and moral values. In his classification of physiological needs, we find al-Aŝfahānī in addition to mentioning food, clothing and shelter, he specified marriage as one of these needs. By including marriage, the list represents a full recognition of human needs, and, by being stated by a religious Muslim scholar, is a reflection of the view of Islam of the basic human needs. The needs are fulfilled, or ought to be fulfilled, as al-Aŝfahānī stressed, in accordance with God's rules and commands, or Sharī'ah. When Sharī'ah rules are fulfilled the first type of spiritual needs is fulfilled. Worship and meeting other religious duties would contribute towards satisfying spiritual needs further. Included in the spiritual needs, in terms of non-physiological needs, is the need to learn and acquire knowledge in religious and secular matters. The levels of consumption are divided further by al-Aŝfahānī into severe, minimum, desire, abundance, and extravagance. A higher level of consumption is an expansion of the previous level in quantity and quality. The level of extravagance is regarded by him as a wasteful use of resources, and, not surprisingly, is forbidden by God.

In brief, al-Aŝfahānī emphasised two further needs in addition to food, clothing and shelter: (a) in contrast to any religiously puritan call from an Islamic or non-Islamic court, he specified marriage as among the basic human needs, and (b) with the academic acknowledgment of mental curiosity he stressed learning and the pursuit of knowledge as part of these basic human needs. Al-Aŝfahānī's classification of human needs would have various implications when determining the role of individual, community, religious groups, and above all the state in relation to meeting these needs. For example, if the state is assuming the responsibility of making the necessary arrangement for satisfying these needs, the role will not stop at the level of feeding, clothing and providing shelter, it will go beyond that to ensure the provision for marriage, or family building, and the pursuit of learning. By including these as needs, the satisfaction of them occupies a priority it would not have otherwise occupied.

Human Role: Production

Turning his attention to the function of human beings in the universe, we find al-Aŝfahānī highlighting this as being of three types: first; working towards the development of the universe, or economic development, second; worship of God, and third; acting on earth as the vicegerent of God. He provides the evidence from the Qur'ān of the validity of his classification. Economic development is the first of these functions because it ensures provision for human beings' needs. Having civilized the earth and provided for basic needs, the worship of God in thanks for His help and in seeking His support would follow. The worship ought to be manifested in following God's rules and commands in the management of development, maintaining it, and distributing its outcomes in a manner that pleases God. As such, human beings would be acting on earth as vicegerents of God, which cannot be achieved unless the development in earth is managed in accordance with God's rules and commands through the guidance of the Sharī'ah. Interestingly, al-Aŝfahānī's definition of economic development does not stop at the level of providing for physiological needs, it goes beyond that to "facilitate life and make things accessible". It is to increase the utility of what is available to improve the quality of life, physically and spiritually.

Al-Aŝfahānī's views on the functions of man in the universe and his emphasis on economic development as a starting point of these functions, before worship, could be viewed as a reply to the Ŝūfī prevailing thinking at the time. The Ŝūfīs, as indicated previously (Chapter 5), focused on worship as the most important function of man, superior to any other, including working to meet the basic human needs. Al-Aŝfahānī, as al-Shaibānī before him, disagreed with that; he opposed the idea of neglecting working in favour of worshiping, or abandoning the pursuit of means of living for the sake of solely God's worship. It looked as if al-Aŝfahānī, in opposing the extreme Ŝūfī's view, had taken the extreme opinion himself of putting striving for a living, emphasised in developing the earth, marginally prior to worship. Conceivably, if a person died from starvation, there will be nothing left of him/her to worship God with, he argues. Sustaining life is therefore important to practice worship, a logical reasoning, even if we assume that working for a living is a form of worship.

Further, al-Aŝfahānī's views on production can be outlined as follows (Donia, 1984):

He emphasised the importance of labour to the production function and in affecting the value of goods and services.

On a global perspective, he stressed the importance that the individual should contribute to production by at least as much as the equivalent of his needs for consumption. Any surplus that may be consumed by the individual of production beyond the equivalent of his contribution to production is regarded as an injustice to his fellow citizens.

He outlined the damaging effect of unemployment and highlighted the relationship between unemployment and inflation, reduction of economic activities, and the standard of living, indicating the effect of unemployment not only on the unemployed but also as a general socio-economic problem.

He criticised severely the Ŝūfīs who advocated the superiority of worship to work for production, providing evidence against their views from the Sharī'ah.

He stated that if voluntary unemployment, as advocated by the Ŝūfīs, is regarded as an injustice to society, the state should endeavour to avoid compulsory unemployment.

Man in Society: Cooperation

In an opening statement, al-Aŝfahānī in introducing his chapter on industry, earnings, and spending, stated that co-operation between individuals is imperative to fulfill their needs. He used the analogy of producing a loaf of bread that requires the co-operation of groups of individuals of different means and ability, and reiterated the Prophet's saying, "Believers to each other are like a building in which parts strengthen each other". In stressing the importance of cooperation further he emphasised, "if every one aims to be self-sufficient, this may lead to the global malfunction" (Al-Aŝfahānī).

Man in Economic Efficiency: Specialisation

From co-operation, he turned to specialisation. He emphasised the need for specialisation and stressed that it leads to a better and more efficient performance. People are different in their ability, readiness, and desire to take different occupational tasks, and with that they are able to excel otherwise, if forced into other occupations they will grow bored and become less efficient. By implication, training should therefore be tailored so as to suit the trainees' ability, traits, and aspirations. In a religious connotation, he indicated that variety of abilities and willingness is a bounty from God, with which best, production performance may be achieved.

Man in Economic Activities: Economic integration

Economic integration was, however, emphasised by al-Aŝfahānī while discussing specialisation and co-operation. He highlighted how every industry is in need of another and how each is either a producer of goods needed by another and/or a user of the products generated by the industry. Though he did not touch on input/output economic tables, he provided an insight into how industries, voluntarily or obligatorily, are integrated.

It is interesting to notice that al-Aŝfahānī, in contrast to al-Shaibānī whose work, *Earnings*, was examined earlier (Chapter 5), did not put agriculture above all types of economic activities. In his views all activities, agricultural and industrial, are of equal importance with no specific priority given to any. He differentiated between economic activities, however, on three grounds: (a) the nature of toil and effort needed for the activity and whether that of purely physical, intellectual, or a mixture of both, in parallel perhaps to the need for innovation, (b) the nature of the return from the economic activity and whether that is of use to a particular group of individuals, or to society, as a whole, the wider the beneficial base the better the activity's, and, (c) the recognition of society to the work needed in the activity and whether the skill required is regarded as a distinctive attribute or not.

Al-Aŝfahānī's recognition of all economic activities, agricultural, trading and industrial, of being of equal importance could have been shaped by the effect of his surrounding economic environment. The city of Aŝfahan, where he lived, was a centre for many types of economic activities. Asfahan was one of the great cities in the Islamic world (Lambton, 1981). It was surrounded by an intensely cultivated area, had rich pasture in the neighbouring districts, served as a distributing center for the villages in the neighborhood and many of the smaller towns, and was favourably situated with regards to communications. It not only had an important long-distance trade, but was also a center of many local industries, especially textiles, which, together with luxury articles, were carried to all parts of the world (Bahar, 1939). Having been brought up and living in such a city, it is not surprising therefore to see al-Aŝfahānī recognising the importance of all economic activities and putting them on an equal footing.

Man and Psychology: Motivation for work

In an indirect recognition of the relationship between demand for goods and their constrained availability, al-Aŝfahānī suggested that the drive for work and production is the fear of the lack of goods despite the need for them. The concept of economic goods could perhaps be detected from this reference. "Poverty and the fear from it is the drive for striving hard to generate what is beneficial to others, either voluntarily or compulsory" (Al-Aŝfahānī).

Man and Money

It is interesting to note that, although his discussion of money was brief, al-Aŝfahānī raised some pertinent points (Donia, op. cit).

First, in the recognition of the vital role of money in the economy he stated, "Money is one of the ways upon which worldly (economic) life is established".

Second, he acknowledged the relationship between money and availability of goods in saying, "If money has increased in value it becomes difficult to acquire what is necessary to facilitate people's living".

Third, he pointed out the functional role of money as a means of exchange in stating, "Serving the process of economic co-operation was made possible by the use of money. Money is given by a person to another from whom a benefit is sought, of which some is given once again by that person to a third in exchange for a benefit requested, so that their economic affairs are smoothed out".

Fourth, he detected the relationship between money supply and price increases in saying, "Hoarding money from being used by people in their transactions is like hoarding the interests of people, as with money their (economic) life is facilitated. Further, this is why, quoting the Tradition, the use of gold and silver as utensils is forbidden as this leads to restricting the availability of these metals in using them as money in facilitating their transactions, which may lead to hardship in people's livelihood", (Al-Aŝfahānī, p. 388).

Fifth, he finally stated that money is not needed per se but for the purpose it serves, "Money has been made by God to be used for the purposes for which it was created and should not be wanted for itself" (ibid.)

Al-Aŝfahānī has been credited with influencing the writing of distinguished authors after him such as al-Ghazālī. It has been suggested that such an eminent writer, like al-Ghazālī, had a high regard for al-Aŝfahānī's al-Zarī'ah (Al-Agamy, 1985). "Ihya'a Ulūm al-Dīn", by al-Ghazālī is our next book.

Abū-Hamid al-Ghazālī (450–505 A.H./1058–1111 A.C.)
Iĥya' Ulūm al-Dīn, The Revival of the Science of Religion

As a Ŝūfī al-Ghazālī looks at economic issues, as well as other issues, from a particular angle: religious devotion. The behaviour of human beings should not only be for the purpose of avoiding God's dissatisfaction but, more important, also with the aim of worshiping Him in a complete piety. In classifying levels of consumption, for example, we find him differentiating not only between what is lawful and unlawful, but also between what is lawful and what is pious. For him, all economic activities of the individual, consumption, production, accumulation of wealth, etc., should be within the purpose of, and with a view to, bringing the individual to the level of piety—a level that goes beyond what is merely lawful and acceptable, to what is pious and puritan. In that sense, al-Ghazālī represents a distinctive characteristic of Muslim writers whose aim is to take the believer to a highly refined level of religious piety.

Despite being a Ŝūfī, al-Ghazālī's views, however, are distinguished from those of the extreme Ŝūfīs who advocated an entire abstinence from materialistic life. Even further, we find him criticising these views severely and condemning those who prefer to live on charity for the sake of devoting their entire life to worship God.

Al-Ghazālī's writing on economics is different from that of Abū-Yūsuf whose main concern was with public finance, and al-Shaibānī who focused on earnings. He comes nearer to al-Aŝfahānī in his collective views on man and his role in the universe, though what distinguishes him from al-Aŝfahānī is his emphasis on, not what is lawful and unlawful but, what is pious and not pious. It is the approach of piety rather than lawfulness that is the basic approach of al-Ghazālī's analysis of man's behaviour, economic or otherwise. And he never diverted from this main theme throughout his work.

In the following section we will look into the main views of al-Ghazālī as depicted in his well-known four-volume book, "Iĥya' Ulūm al-Dīn", "the revival of sciences of religion".

The Author

Abū-Hamid Muĥammad al-Ghazālī, usually referred to as Imam al-Ghazālī, was born in 450 A.H.–1058 A.C., in the village of Taberan, the district of Taus, in Kurasan, Persia. There, he also died in 505 A.H.–1111 A.C. On the day of his death, it is said that he got up from his bed, performed his morning prayer, sent for his coffin cloth which he lifted up to his eyes and said, "God's command is to be obeyed". In saying that, he extended his legs and then immediately breathed his last breath.

At an early age, he was appointed lecturer at the Nizamiah School in Baghdad by the Turkish ruler, where he mixed with people of different religions and sects, including Christians and Jews. He discarded his early Shafī'i views after his appointment, and turned to Ŝūfīsm. He gave up his lucrative post in Baghdad, wore Ŝūfī dress and moved between Damascus, Jerusalem, Makkah and al-Medīnah. His mixing with people of other religions seemed to have affected his writing. In the Iĥya' we find him quoting sayings from Jesus Christ, alongside the sayings of the Prophet and of course quotations from the Qur'ān. "A wise man is reported to have said", is also invariably repeated in his writing.

His legacy of books is enormous. This covers mainly theology, jurisprudence, logic, philosophy, scholastic theology and interpretation of the Qur'ān. Iĥya' Ulūm al-Dīn, our main focus, is regarded as the master piece of al-Ghazālī.

The book

The Iĥya' Ulūm al-Dīn covers a wide range of topics in which economic issues are mentioned in relation to other matters, and, in some cases in special chapters. The book is divided into four volumes, outlined as follows:

The book of worship. It comprises of ten chapters: acquisition of knowledge, articles of faith, secrets of purity, secrets of prayers, secrets of Zakāh and alms giving, secrets of fasting, secrets of pilgrimage, Qur'ān recitation and interpretation, rules of invocations and supplications, and observance of daily duties according to fixed times. The approximate size of this volume is about 110,000 words (English version).

The book of worldly usage. This includes ten chapters: rules of eating and drinking, rules of marriage, rules of earnings, trade and commerce, lawful and unlawful issues, rules of companionship and brotherhood, rules of habitation and solitude, rules of journey, music and ecstasy, rules of enjoining good and forbidding evil, rules of living as exemplified by the character and conduct of the Prophet. The size of this volume is over 90,000 words.

The book of destructive evils. This volume is composed of, yet again, ten chapters: wonders of soul, discipline of the soul, harms of greed and sexual passion, harms of tongue, harms of anger, hatred and envy, evils of the world, evils of wealth and miserliness, evils of show and power, evils of self conceit and pride, and evils of vanity. The size of this volume is also large, over 120,000 words.

The book of constructive virtues. Ten chapters, again, compose this book: repentance, patience and gratefulness, fear and hope, poverty and asceticism, Tawhīd (unity of God) and Tawakkul (full reliance on God), love and contentment, intention, truthfulness and sincerity, self examination and self accounting, meditation, and death and power over death. The fourth volume is over 178,000 words.

In total, the four volumes of al-Iĥya' consist of over 1500 pages containing over half a million words!

The Importance of Learning

In the early part of his first chapter al-Ghazālī emphasised that seeking knowledge is compulsory for every Muslim, male and female. Interestingly, he seems to have taken the importance of learning almost to the extreme when he said, "To be present in an assembly of a learned man is better than praying one thousand rak'a", (Volume 1 page 20). But that reflects how important learning was to him.

Learning would be sought for itself and also as a means to an end. As learning helps improve the results of the task performed it also gives the feeling of self-satisfaction, which contributes to the ultimate feeling of happiness. Furthermore, acquisitions of knowledge, and its teaching, are excellent actions for seeking rewards in this life and the hereafter.

Learning to al-Ghazālī is not only the process of acquiring knowledge in religious matters, but also of acquiring the necessary skill and expertise to run worldly affairs. Linking learning to production activities is therefore important. With this emphasis, al-Ghazālī stressed the importance of labour in production activity. We find him, after stating that acquisition of knowledge is important to "this world", proceeding to explain, "The affairs of this world do not become orderly except through activities. . . . without which the world cannot go in order". He then continued to discuss these activities such as agriculture, weaving, architecture, government, iron-crafts, eating, drinking, and tailoring and so on. Learning and acquisition of knowledge and expertise for economic activities are regarded by al-Ghazālī as compulsory religious duties on the community (*Fardh Kifayah*). We find him stating strongly, "The sciences that are necessary for progressing the world are praiseworthy, such as medicine, and mathematics are *Fardh Kifayah* . . . and the sciences which should be learnt for agriculture, administration, industry, horticulture, weaving, etc., are *Fardh Ayn*", (Vol. 1, p. 31). *Fardh Kifyah* is a binding duty on the community as a whole, while *Fardh Ayn* is a compulsory duty on the individual himself.

Money

All precious things fall into one of three groups: (a) what is sought for its own intrinsic value, (b) what is sought as a means to an end, and (c) what is sought for both. What is sought as a means to an end is gold and silver which are pieces of metal having no value of their own. If God had not made them instruments of purchasing things, their values would have been equal to other stones. (Vol. 1, p. 26). In volume IV, al-Ghazālī expands on the function of money. He perceives the function of money as a means of exchange and as a store of value. Emphasising the function of money as a means of exchange, which facilitates transactions, al-Ghazālī states, "Gold and silver are gifts from God and with their help all worldly acts are smoothly done. These are nothing but metals and have got no value of their own. People want to have them, as by their exchange commodities of the world can be purchased", (Vol. IV, p. 95). He proceeded to explain the idea by referring to a man who has got food but has got no camel and another who has got a camel but no food. Between them, therefore, "there is the necessity of exchange of these two things and fixation of their value". But, "value of these things is not equal. Therefore, gold and silver work as judges for all things, for the fixation of value, and for getting the things through their medium". As a measure of value he states, "Then it is said that a camel's price is 100 dinars, and that the price of 100 fowls is the same. So by the help of gold and silver their values are adjusted, though gold and silver have no value of their own. God appointed them as judges for ascertainment of values and prices of all things and for their exchange". As a store of value, he clarifies, "Gold and silver are dear to men. He who has got them possesses them as if it were all things". In the educational manner of a lecturer, he elucidated this concept by giving an interesting analogy of a mirror that has no great value of its own but it derives its value of being able to reflect images and pictures, "a mirror has got no value of its own, but its value lies in the fact that it assumes pictures of all things" (Vol. IV, p. 96).

He outlined the effect of money supply and price levels by stating that hoarding gold and silver is a misuse of the purpose for which they were made. Emphatically, the person who hoards gold and silver "does oppress and makes inoperative the purpose for which God had made them". They are not meant to be for individuals per se but for being as a medium of exchange of goods. Also, affecting the supply of these precious metals by using them for utensils, cups and the like, is sinful and the person in this case, "acts contrary to the object for which these are created", and, "is ungrateful to God and commits sins", p. 96.

Trading in gold, by selling gold for gold, or in silver, by selling silver for silver, for the purpose of making profit is condemned by al-Ghazālī. It is a transaction that, "has got no meaning", as it restricts the function of these metals as a medium of exchange. Selling gold for silver, or vice versa is permissible, however. He explained this by stating that there are goods, the value of which is so small and can only be priced in pieces of silver, which have a lower value than that of gold. Exchanging gold for silver makes it possible therefore to conclude these transactions of small value; the opposite is also true, (Vol. IV, p. 97).

Industrial integration

The affairs of this world do not become orderly except through activity. Human activities are divided into three categories:

(a) The first category includes four fundamental activities without which the world cannot go without, and these are agriculture, weaving for manufacturing clothes, architecture for building houses, and government for regulation of human relations to facilitate living in peace and harmony.
(b) The second category includes such activities as are helpful to the above mentioned activities, such as iron-crafts, or ploughs for cultivation, machinery for spinning and weaving clothes and other implements.
(c) The third category includes such activities as are supplementary to the principal industries previously mentioned such as eating, drinking, making dresses, and sewing clothes, (Vol. 1, p. 27).

Al-Ghazālī emphasised further, "if the various kinds of trade and industry are given up, it will be difficult for the people to manage their livelihood and the majority of the people would be destroyed", (Vol. II, p. 71). On another occasion we find him referring to economic activities as causes of engagement in the world, which are five main industries: cultivation, grazing, hunting, weaving and construction, (Vol. III, p. 209). For smooth living, administrative works, judicial works, and military works are necessary. Mankind therefore is divided into three main classes from the point of view of these activities: cultivators and industrialists, soldiers, and officers of government. The religious men, who are of different classes, according to their piety and perception of life and life-after, are added to the above classes. (Vol. III, p. 209).

The above activities are necessary for human habitation just as the various organs of the body are necessary for the maintenance of life. In an interesting analogy, al-Ghazālī relates the principal industries to the heart of the body, other subsidiary industries and economic activities to different parts of the body in the order of what is fundamental, what is helpful, and what is supplementary. The government occupied an important role in al-Ghazālī's thinking. It is the most noble of activities, he said. His reasons are straightforward: with government, peace is maintained and peaceful habitation becomes possible. This is not a surprising thought, bearing in mind the state of political instability that prevailed in the Islamic state during that period. (Vol. 1, p. 27).

Consumption and Consumer Behaviour

In parallel to al-Aŝfahānī, al-Ghazālī divided the level of consumption into various levels ranging from necessity to extravagance. Necessity ought to be fulfilled by the consumer and the fulfillment of these is a religious duty. In that al-Ghazālī is in opposition to the extreme Ŝūfī view of neglecting the self for the sake of the divine force. In that al-Ghazālī advocates, "The object of the wise is the vision of the Lord in the hereafter and the only way to gain it is learning an action . . . but it is not possible to stand constantly on them without having a healthy body which is also not possible without food and drink which are absolutely necessary and which are taken according to prescribed rules", (Vol. 2, p. 1). The level of extravagance, as we know by now, is forbidden. What distinguishes al-Ghazālī from the others in this respect is that he provided a quantitative measurement of the levels of consumption specifying the quantity one should consume of wheat and the like in each level. (Vol. III, p. 94). The quantification of these levels, however, are determined from his point of view as a Ŝūfī who would be content with very little in comparison with non-Ŝūfīs who might be aiming to achieve a greater quantity to meet their full satisfaction. Furthermore, the consumer in his view should refrain from consumption if the object consumed is surrounded with doubt as its lawfulness, even if the jurists may permit it. The level of pure piety should be the ultimate objective, which may lie in its religious requirement and adherence to the rules above, which might be regarded as a moderate level. For example, Ŝūfīs who are renowned for wearing rough clothing, eating less than others, and not aiming for realising great satisfaction from worldly physiological needs, may not be regarded as the norm in the eyes of other Muslims. Like those before him, basic needs are defined to include clothing, housing, as well as food and drink. Al-Ghazālī distinguished between four levels of piety. The first is the piety which is required for attestation of the truth. The second level of piety is that of a pious man; he saves himself even from doubt whether a certain thing is lawful or unlawful. The third level of piety is that of the God-fearing man who gives up even a lawful thing for fear of falling into an unlawful one. The fourth level is the level of piety of the extremely religious man who gives up everything for the sake of God. (Vol. 1, p. 35). Marriage is important, but it does not seem to be as clearly specified in the basic needs as with al-Aŝfahānī.

On Earnings, Trade and Commerce

At the outset, and driven by his Ŝūfī convictions, al-Ghazālī started his chapter on earnings, trade and commerce by stating, "Earning is not the aim of human life but it is a means to an end", (Vol. II, p. 53). This signals two distinct messages: moderation in spending time and effort on earning a livelihood, and wealth is not to be accumulated or accumulated for itself. Proper human motivation should not be geared purely towards seeking wealth. "There are three kinds of men", al-Ghazālī states, "(a) one kind forgets the return and makes the earnings of livelihood as the sole object of his life, he is one of those who will be destroyed, (b) another kind is the one who makes the return to the life-after his sole object of life and remains busy in earning his livelihood, and (c) the third kind of men is near the middle path who keeps his goal of returning to the next world as fixed and takes to trade and commerce for a livelihood". By implication, the second type is most favoured. Also, in what al-Ghazālī said was a criticism of the Ŝūfī who went to the extreme by refraining from work, devoting all of their time to worship and relying on charity for living. Earning a livelihood is therefore a duty.

In his chapter on earnings, trade and commerce al-Ghazālī elucidated various points covering lawful earnings, justice, kindness and fear of religion. He divided these topics further and examined each in detail. For example, the lawful earnings section is divided into bargaining in buying and selling, trade through credit, taking advance payment, to work for wages and to accept rentals, to do business with others by advancing capital, and joint business in fixing shares. It is compulsory in his view that the Sharī'ah rules in these matters are learned. Moreover, he divided the above topics further and discussed them in more detail. For example, on bargaining in buying and selling, he looked into the position of the parties in the contract, the buyer and seller, the commodities for sale, and the contract.

Linking the conditions of the market with the concept of justice, al-Ghazālī condemned bad market practice and regarded that as violating the concept of fair trade. Bad market practice leads to two types of loss: loss to the public at large, and loss to a group of individuals. Hoarding foodstuffs with the aim of artificially enhancing prices causes harm to the public at large and therefore is condemned. The Sharī'ah condemns hoarding. Al-Ghazālī however took the issue further and argued that while hoarding foodstuffs is condemned, and indeed cursed in the Sharī'ah, hoarding articles that are not principal foodstuff, such as Za'afran, etc., is not prohibited. Delaying making the articles available for sale in the market may also be regarded as prohibited if this leads to suffering by the public. The legality or illegality of hoarding, therefore, depended in the mind of al-Ghazālī upon the harm caused to the public. This seems to be a compromising view coming from a Ŝūfī, however. But al-Ghazālī was perhaps more concerned with the concept of justice in the market conditions, which, to him, should be extended to both the buyer and the seller. Other conditions of fair trade were also discussed by al-Ghazālī, such as accurate measurement and weight, not concealing information from the public and not giving wrong information about the subject of sale. The ultimate purpose of the al-Ghazālī's discussion of market conditions was to bring it to, or very near to, the condition of the perfect competitive market.

Al-Ghazālī did not advocate the maximisation of profit, though he did not condemn it. "To take less profit is *Iĥsan*, doing good deeds", but, "to take greater profit is not unlawful". This is because, "Sale is for profit in a business and there is no profit unless a thing is charged more than the price by which it is bought", (Vol. II p. 67). Also, consideration may be given to a poor seller even if it may lead to the buyer carrying some losses. "If a buyer buys from a poor man, there is no harm to buy at a higher price to show kindness to him", p. 67, and "Don't be greedy in markets and business", (Vol. II, p. 73). So, although he advocated free market conditions, his market was not a market that was void of consideration for the poor or less affluent and his profit objective tended to be more concerned with profit satisfaction than a profit maximisation. It is a free market with a conscience.

In connection with just market conditions, al-Ghazālī looked at the counterfeit coins. It is oppression on the public to use counterfeit coins and, "the first man who uses such coins will be liable for the sins of those who subsequently transfer them to other persons", (Vol. II, p. 63).

Turning his attention to wealth, al-Ghazālī neither condemns nor praises wealth, "Wealth is good from one point and bad from another" (Vol. III, p. 243). If the intention of acquiring wealth is good, wealth is good, and if the intention is bad wealth is bad. Also, wealth should not be sought in excess, as one should seek to obtain only what one and his dependents need, "Earning of excess wealth should be avoided. Only what is necessary should be earned. What is necessary for food, cloth, and habituation should be earned. There are three stages of each of these three objects- low, middle, and high stages. So long as you remain near the low stage and near the necessary limit you have got the right therein. When you cross that limit, you will fall in the lowest Hell" (Vol. III, 244). This is a view that is different from that of al-Shaibānī, as we saw earlier, whose view was that there was no need to put an artificial restriction on the pursuit of wealth, providing that other duties are not neglected. But al-Shaibānī was born rich, while al-Ghazālī was a Ŝūfī. Once again, wealth satisfaction will replace wealth maximisation in the consumer's utility function according to al-Ghazālī.

The next author is a scholar and a merchant who devoted his work to wealth, trade and management of business. He is Ja'afer al-Dīmashqī.

Ja'afer al-Dīmashqī (late 12th century)
al-Isharah fi Mahāsin al-Tijarah, Book of Good Trading

It is not certain when al-Dīmashqī was born or when he died, though it has been suggested that he had lived during the latter half of the twelfth century. This can be inferred from the date when al-Dīmashqī said he had finished writing his book, "al-Isharah fi Mahāsin al-Tijarah", a date which had been stated by him as being 570 A.H., corresponding to 1175 A.C. He must have lived part of his life in Damascus, Syria, before he moved somewhere else as we see him nicknamed "al-Dīmashqī" or the "Damascusan", the man from Damascus. The period in which al-Dīmashqī lived witnessed the end of the rising power of the Fatimid caliphate in Cairo, under which Syria was also governed, and the rising influence of the Mamlūk Ŝulṭān Ŝalaadin (or Ŝalah-al-Dīn).

The Book

"Al-Isharah fi Mahāsin al-Tijara", "Indicators, or summary, of Good Trading", has various distinctive features, as we can see below.

Wealth

Al-Dīmashqī did not start his book with man, his necessities, and needs or spending, as the writers before him had. Instead he started with the definition of wealth, "*Māl*"—a reflection of him being a business man or an entrepreneur, as well as a scholar. He equated "*Māl*" with "possessions", regardless of that being great or small. Interestingly, he provided a taxonomy of wealth that is based on the nature of the item of wealth of being able to generate wealth or otherwise. To use modern terms, al-Dīmashqī's classification of wealth could be looked at in terms of whether the item is a fixed asset, in an accounting sense, or a current asset. In other words, an asset that may be used in producing another asset, or an asset that is ready, per se, for final use.

He classified wealth into four categories:

First, what is not subject to trade, though it could be important to the business, such as money,

Second, what could be subject to trade, such as stock, moveable goods, metal and the products made from it,

Third, estate properties which are divided into two main types, the first was what he called roofed, such as houses, hotels, shops, public baths, mills, bakeries, and the second is the cultivated, such as orchards, vineyards, pastures, woods, and the right to the use of rivers, and

Fourth, which he seemed to have viewed as living beings, such as animals and, in accordance with the practice at the time, slaves.

His classification of wealth seemed to have been a managerial type of classification, that focused on the role of the possessions, or assets, and their functions in generating extra wealth, rather on their uses otherwise. Al-Dīmashqī's classification could be arranged as mobile, current or short-term, items, which are used mainly in trading, and fixed, or long-term items, which are kept basically for the purpose of generating trade. Either in accounting terms or economic terminology, al-Dīmashqī's classification pre-empted, to a considerable extent, our modern accounting and economic classification that has emerged centuries after him. Coming from as early as the twelfth century, this can but reflect how far sighted his views were in perceiving the interrelationships in the process of wealth creation and how aware he was of the importance of a proper understanding of the structure of business assets to the entrepreneur. It is a noteworthy classification of wealth, or assets if we use modern terms, that is of a paramount importance to managers in the process of decision making.

Sources of Wealth

In an interesting presentation, al-Dīmashqī explained the various sources of acquiring wealth, with some sources more acceptable than others. These are two main sources, with the second further subdivided into three subsources. The first source is accidental, which is mainly related to reasons of inheritance and the like, while the second source is particularly articulate in that it requires an endeavour and intent to work towards it. The second source is divided into three further types, the first is authoritative, the second is entrepreneurial, and the third is a mixture of both. The authoritative source is divided further into governmental, Sūltāniyyah, and non-governmental. The Sūltāniyyah source could be either through the power of the government of raising funds, such as taxes, and/or the government ownership of businesses, and the non-governmental source such as theft and forced robbery, which is illegitimate. The entrepreneurial source is divided into three types: trade, commerce and industry, and a combination of both trade and industry. Turning his attention to the mixed source between entrepreneurial and authoritative, al-Dīmashqī explained that it was represented in the commercial business of the Ŝulṭān, in which, "transactions are beyond the full control of the market as no one can out-price the Ŝulṭān or limit his market monopoly", (p. 61). The Ŝulṭān's business as such was a monopolistic form of business, which seemed to have thrived during this period. Another form of monopoly was also pointed out by al-Dīmashqī at the same time: the monopoly of the few rich merchants who were able to control the market and, "limit the ability of the public to buy, and sell, what they needed". The reference to these types of monopolistic controlling powers in the market by (a) a major seller, and (b) a group of buyers, and (c) a group of sellers, in al-Dīmashqī's classification and reference to market forms, are in parallel with modern classification of conditions of the market, which reflects his great awareness and a delicate understanding of market forces. This could be regarded as highly creditable particularly from a writer who wrote about the subject some eight centuries ago.

Labour

In line with those before him he looked into the division of labour, specialisation and economic integration. He related division of labour and specialisation to the ability of the individual to acquire knowledge, which is controlled by the restriction of time, the individual's life span, and his readiness and willingness to learn. The multi faceted needs of the individual, with the limited ability to acquire knowledge, would require specialisation, and with the variety in human needs, specialisation in its turn would necessitate variety of economic activities, which dictates economic integration. In explaining the idea al-Dīmashqī, like al-Aŝfahānī and al-Ghazālī before him, resorted to the example of making bread, and added to that another example from cloth manufacturing.

Money

He elucidated the reasons for the use of money as a means of exchange. "The timing of the need of the individual from the services and goods provided by other individuals is not the same, the amount of goods and services needed to be exchanged are not equal, the value of each good in terms of units of another good is not known, and the relative value of the remaining un-exchanged part of the good in terms of other goods cannot be determined for certain, is not known", he explained, "therefore there is a need for something that can be used to ascertain a value to all goods and articles and by which the relative value of articles to each other can be measured", he added. The thing that is used to assign values to goods would need to be a precious metal and the best of that is gold, and silver. The merits of gold are "it is not perishable, it is not subject to rust like iron and copper, it does not change in colour such as lead, it is not too soft like lead, it is controllable and can be shaped and reshaped without a loss of value, it has no smell and has pleasant appearance, it can be buried without a loss of value or appearance, it maintains the imprinted marks during minting for control purposes". For these reasons people had agreed to use gold and silver as the chosen precious metal from which they made money. As a store of value, al-Dīmashqī states, "Whoever has obtained this metal has obtained the ability to acquire all goods, services and possessions for which the metal can be exchanged, and whenever the person wishes to do so", (p. 21).

Cost of Production and Value

With the mentality and awareness of a businessman, al-Dīmashqī outlined that the value of the good depended upon three main factors: the cost of the product, the amount of labour involved, and the demand for the product. For the amount of labour involved we find him giving an example of the Emerald and how its value changed dramatically depending upon the amount of work added to it and the level of skill the work requires. "The value of the emerald increases dramatically for the craftsmanship involved", he states (p. 36). Being aware of the cost, and indeed the level of accuracy, al-Dīmashqī took into account transportation costs and custom dues in addition to other costs when the price of the product is determined—the mind of a cost accountant (p. 74). His awareness of the effect of the state of demand on the price of the good could be seen when he advised his fellow merchants not to buy the goods for which the demand had declined (p. 81). And more precisely, "Prices do not increase because of abundance of goods but because of the shortage of the goods in relation to the demand for it" (p. 70).

Demand, supply and price

The relationship between demand, supply and prices seemed to have been clear in al-Dīmashqī's mind. We find him stating this relationship in pointing out that prices of a good might increase as a result of, "blockage of the transportation road, delay in delivery, increase in demand, or shortage in the quantity available due to natural, heavenly or worldly reasons" (pp. 28–29).

Furthermore, it is interesting to note that al-Dīmashqī classified the increase in prices into different categories and described them with different terms. In his view, the starting point is what may be regarded by experts as the average price, in accordance with the type of goods, the conditions of the market, the region and the custom of the trade in the region. "An increase above this average price would be referred to by different terms depending upon the size of the increase", he clarified. He scaled the increase into five progressing stages: a move, a sell out, an uplift, an expensive increase, and an exorbitant rise. A change in the opposite direction is also classified into stages, which are six ranging from "calm" to "slump". The classification of price movement as such reflects the highly advanced degree of thinking of al-Dīmashqī and his entrepreneurial awareness of the economy and business environment.

Price disparity

Price disparity of goods had been pointed out by al-Dīmashqī when he referred to different prices of goods in different regions and countries. To him, "Pricing goods and the level of what could be regarded by experts as the average price varies from one place to another, and what can be priced in India at a certain price might have a different price in Morocco, which could also be different from that in al-Yemen. And this is because of the closeness to the source of the material and the craftsmanship in making the product". Price disparities, despite the theory of the "law of one price", have been acknowledged in Western literature as one of the limiting factors to the theory of price parity. Was al-Dīmashqī preempting modern thinking? Probably.

When investigating the market's demand for goods, we find al-Dīmashqī recognising the state where the demand for goods increases when their prices increase. Luxury, or prestigious, goods, which are acquired by a class of consumer for purposes other than physiological or intellectual benefits can be highly demanded by the affluent, and the higher the price of these goods the higher the demand for them. Social pride, or showing off, is usually the main drive for buying these products, and the demand for these goods in relation to their prices is an exception to general rule. The opposite is also true; the quantity demanded may come down as a result of a reduction in their prices. In that al-Dīmashqī emphasised, "Precious stones may be demanded by kings and Ŝulṭāns for their exorbitant prices and may be demanded by others for showing off".

Profit satisfaction and business objectives

The concept of profit satisfaction rather than profit maximisation seemed to have been what al-Dīmashqī advocated as an objective of the business. Tolerance and benevolence should be the basis upon which business transactions are conducted. Tolerance and benevolence are major factors for earning a livelihood and the promotion of business in al-Dīmashqī's views, "do not say 'I should have tried harder to charge the customer more as he seemed to have accepted the price easily', because this would lead to the buyers going elsewhere". The effect of tolerance on business was particularly emphasised in al-Dīmashqī when he said, "a profit of one dinar could be viewed as one half of it being generated from tolerance and benevolence in weighing, charging the price, gratis, or a discount if the customer asked for a discount as the customer may be thinking of all that". Moreover, honesty and fairness to the customer, and the business, are fundamental principles in conducting the business. In a nutshell, "going to the extreme in seeking financial benefits may lead to a shortage of goods and the excessive efforts in maximising profit resulting in the loss of profit" (p. 66).

In contrast to al-Ghazālī, therefore, al-Dīmashqī was in favour of riches. In a complete diversion from the Ŝūfī thinking, he suggested that being rich is better than being poor. This was argued on two grounds: first, if the rich was rich because of inheritance, this would indicate the creditworthiness of his family, which adds to the credability of the person's family line, and, second, if he was rich because of his hard work during his life time this would add to the person's credability as being a hard worker, highly motivated and strongly driven to better himself and his family. Furthermore, the rich who became rich as a result of their hard work and good management of business reflected a high quality of mind. The Ŝūfīs are in disagreement concerning these ideas. To them it suffices that the person works to earn only enough to meet his needs and those of his dependents, and the rest of the time should be spent in worship.

The next writer is a highly distinguished writer in an area that was beginning to take an independent form in the writing on Islamic economics. He is Ibn-al-Ukhūwwah, and the area is the Institution of *Ĥisbah*. But before looking into the work of Ibn-al-Ukhūwwah, it is proper to look into the institution of *Ĥisbah* first with a view to examining its meaning and the circumstances surrounding the development of the writing on the subject.

The Institution of Ĥisbah and Business Sector Governance

The *Ĥisbah*, as Ibn al-Ukhūwwah said in his "Ma'alim al-Qūrbah", is one of the spiritual orders of Islam, that aims at enforcing what is Islamically ordained, *ma'ruf*, and preventing what is religiously unlawful, *mūnkar*, (Ibn al-Ukhūwwah). The range of duties is very wide. In particular, it includes matters related to two main aspects, *ibadat*, which focuses on the essence and forms of worship, and *mu'amalat*, which concentrates on the core and forms of the financial behaviour of the individual. Securing the obedience to the two aspects of the religion is essential in order for the Muslim society, that is based on the Sharī'ah, to be regarded as complete. Further, while *ibadat* disciplinary matters are imposed on Muslims, *mu'amalat* regulatory issues are ordained for both Muslims and non-Muslims.

In the early days of Islam the task of the *Ĥisbah* was vested with the Prophet and the caliphs after him. The Prophet is reported to have rebuked some merchants in the market for misleading the buyers over the quality and quantity of the goods displayed. "Whoever cheats us is not one of us", the Prophet is reported to have said after discovering some market irregularities during a round of inspection. Matters related to disclosure of information, pricing, price bidding, speculation, and so on are discussed in detail in the Sharī'ah. After the Prophet, the caliphs, particularly during the rightly-guided caliphate, are reported to have exercised the *Ĥisbah*.

With the growth in the complexity of the state, the spread of its geographical location and the decline in the piety of individuals in general and business ethos in particular, it became necessary that the task of *Ĥisbah* was to be assigned to a specialised agency the duties of which would cover the securing of the adherence to the rules of the Sharī'ah. The first of these specialised agencies is reported to have been established during the reign of the Umayyad caliph Hishām ibn Abd al-Mālik (105–125 A.H./724–743 A.C.), (Al-Ťabarī). That seems to be an innovation that Hishām introduced to the state administration as explained in chapter four. Arabicisation, monetary reforms, agrarian reforms and the establishment of just markets were some examples of what had been innovated at the time. The institution of *Ĥisbah* seemed to have had considerable authority and prestige, and the appointment of the head of the agency, al-Muĥtasib, was later surrounded with a distinct ceremonial procession. The analogy to the agency in modern time could be that of the two important departments in modern governments: Department of Trade and Industry and Central Auditing Office. Indeed, one more agency could be added, the British RSPCA, Royal Society for the Prevention of Cruelty to Animals, as one of the duties of the Muĥtasib was to make sure that animals were not overloaded with excessive loads beyond what they could normally carry, or they were badly treated. The religious function would be added to this modern analogy, as al-Muĥtasib was also responsible for the adherence to the rules of worship and the proper practice of the religion.

Writing on Ĥisbah

The first of what we could see reported of writing on *Ĥisbah* was a chapter in al-Māwardī's *al-Aĥkām al-Sūltāniyyah*, chapter twenty. Even as a chapter in a book, and not a separate book on the subject, al-Māwardī's chapter on *Ĥisbah* was the first specialised work on the subject. In a more specialised work al-Māwardī wrote a book on *Ĥisbah*, "*al-Rūtbah fi Ťalab al-Ĥisbah*". Contemporary to al-Māwardī was the chief judge Abū Ya'ala al-Fara', who was born some fifteen years after al-Māwardī, (988–1066). He also wrote a book that, surprisingly, carried a similar title to that of al-Māwardī, "*al-Aĥkām al-Sūltāniyyah*", (Abū -Zayd, 1986). The difference between al-Māwardī and al-Fara' however, was that while the former was a Shafi'i the later was a Ĥanbalī. Apart from this difference, which was reflected in the treatment of topics, the arrangement of the book and the topics covered were very similar. By writing his *al-Aĥkām*, al-Fara' wanted perhaps to respond to al-Māwardī's coverage of the subjects from a Ĥanbalī point of view. The subject attracted other writers of considerable importance. The following are some examples:

Al-Ghazālī (1058–1111) in his *Iĥya' Ulūm al-Dīn*,
Ibn-Taymīya (1263/1328) in *al-Ĥisbah fi al-Islam*,
Al-Shayzari in a forty chapter work on *Nihayat al-Rutbah fi Ťalab al-Ĥisbah*,
Ibn-Bassam in another, *Nihayat al-Rutbah fi Ťalab al-Ĥisbah*, a work of 118 chapters, which seems to be based on the work of al-Shayzari,
Ibn al-Ukhūwwah (d. 1329), *Ma'alim al-Qūrbah fi Aĥkām al-Ĥisbah*, a work in seventy chapters.

Interestingly enough, prior to al-Māwardī's specialised chapter in his *al-Aĥkām* there was no special writing on the subject, and if there was any indirect writing, such as Abū-Yūsuf's on policing, it was not referred to as a piece of work exclusively on *al-Ĥisbah*. If an interpretation was to be found for the appearance of an exclusive work on the subject it would be because of the possible increasing level of corruption in the society and state administration, that would have instigated the jurists and judges of the day to write on the subject. On a more favourable note, the complexity in the everyday life of the community and state organisation could have provoked the writing. The two reasons, the increasing level of corruption and the growing degree of complexity, could have worked together to encourage such specialist writing.

Of the specialised writing on *Ĥisbah*, we will look into the work of Ibn ul-Ukhūwwah and Ibn-Taymīya. The reason for the choice is that while Ibn-Taymīya looked into the theoretical foundation of *Ĥisbah*, Ibn-al-Ukhūwwah provided a more detailed examination of the practical problems facing the Muĥtasib in exercising his duties. That served as a manual to the officers involved in implementing the assigned tasks. The two writers, however, have lived during the same period, the first died in 1329 and the second in 1328.

Ibn-al-Ukhūwwah (d. 1329)
Ma'alim al-Qūrbah fi Aĥkām al-Ĥisbah
Rules of Accountability and Public Duties

The Author

Diya' al-Dīn Muĥammad ibn Muĥammad ibn Ahmad al-Qurashi al-Shafi'i is the full name of this author whose nickname was Ibn al-Ukhūwwah. The date of his birth is not known but he died in 729 A.H./1329 A.C. Little is known of Ibn al-Ukhūwwah except that he was an Egyptian. His work was renowned in Syria and elsewhere (Levy, 1938).

The Book

Ma'alim al-Qūrbah consists of seventy chapters covering a wide range of topics. A number of chapters, particularly the first ten cover general issues on the conduct of *Ĥisbah* and the governance of the market and business activities, while the rest address each type of business and industry in detail. The general issues deal with the following topics:

The qualifications required for the *Ĥisbah* and the duties of the Muĥtasib
Enforcement of the law and prevention of what is unlawful
Wine and unlawful trade
Prohibited transactions
Practices forbidden and practices permitted
Unlawful conduct in public markets
Weights and how they should be controlled
Scales and measurements of capacity and lengths
Preachers,
Judges and witnesses,
Military commanders and civil governors and the activities of the population that concern them,

The chapters that cover the types of trade and industry deal with an exhaustive range of industries and businesses. For example the range covers the following: flour merchants and millers, bakers and bread makers, seller of roast-meat, sausage makers, butchers, sellers of liver and appetisers, vendors of cooked heads, cooked meat sellers, pickled meat sellers, fish fryers, sellers of desserts, seller of milk, druggists, drapers, weavers, tailors, shoe makers, vets, physicians, oculists, surgeons, sieve makers, sellers of straw, timber merchants and sellers of palm-logs, and so on. Even further, in case a topic was not discussed, Ibn al-Ukhūwwah devoted a final chapter on, "Details concerning the *Ĥisbah* not elsewhere discussed".

Ma'alim al-Qūrbah is a manual on *Ĥisbah* that has provided in detail, practical methods of governing the market and business sector but without entirely ignoring the theoretical side of the subject. Ibn al-Ukhūwwah's book is especially useful to five particular groups of users:

(1) The Muĥtasib, in exercising his duties,
(2) The ruler whether that was the caliph, his prime minister, the Ŝulṭān, or the province governor in explaining the duties expected from the Muĥtasib,
(3) The other forms of authority namely the police, and courts and judges in distinguishing between the authority and duties of the Muĥtasib and those of their own,
(4) Businesses in knowing what is prohibited and what is permitted so that potential ambiguity could be removed, and
(5) The public, in being made aware of their rights within the rules of fair trade.

For the above, Ma'alim al-Qūrbah provided a clear and concise guide to business deals that may serve as a market and business charter. It laid down the rules of Sharī'ah regarding the conduct of business, the amount of information that should be made available to the public in business deals, the clarity of rules to all parties concerned, particularly the customer and the entrepreneur, and the attitude of other government authorities in relation to market rules. Today, this could be referred to as the market or business governance.

Should the Muĥtasib be strictly concerned with implementing the rules or should he also be allowed to interpret them and derive subrules from them, is a question that concerned ibn al-Ukhūwwah and al-Māwardī before him. The importance of the question lies in that whether the Muĥtasib be allowed to exercise discretion in jurisprudence, *ijtihād*, and if he is, would that include rules related to revealed law, *sharia*', rules connected with customary law, *'urf*, or both? He explained that there were different opinions on this matter. Some believed that al-Muĥtasib has the right to give effect to a decision on the authority of his own *ijtihād* in matters of revealed law, *sharia*', as well as in customary law, *ʿurf*. Others were of the opinion that he must be able to give opinion on matters related to customary law, *ʿurf*, but not on those of the revealed law, *sharia*ʾ. Ibn al-Ukhūwwah explained further that the difference is based on the fact that the principle in revealed law, *sharia*ʾ, rests upon the body of Sharīʾah whereas in customary law, *ʿurf*, the dominant factor is usage and practice.

In drawing the lines between the domain of different government authorities in observing market conditions Ibn al-Ukhūwwah differentiated between the authority and responsibilities of the Muĥtasib and those of the judge (court). He states, "The Muĥtasib authority is greater than that of the judge in that he may proceed independently of any complaint to investigate cases where he suspects illegality, whereas the judge can proceed only where there is a complaint. Further, he has a measure of secular authority and has the right to use force in pursuance of his duty and to inflict punishment. In these respects the *Ĥisbah* resembles the work of some courts, court of *mazalim*, but it differs from it in being incompetent to hear cases beyond the jurisdiction of the judge", (Ibn al-Ukhūwwah, Levy, 1938). Concerning the level of authority of the Muĥtasib, as a market controller, Ibn al-Ukhūwwah emphasised that it ought to be limited to the specific authority delegated to him by the sovereign. Also, in exercising his duties, the Muĥtasib should not over involve himself in people's affairs beyond what his office would require.

Turning his attention to commercial transactions Ibn al-Ukhūwwah, in chapter six of his Maʾalim, clarified what may be regarded as legal and acceptable and what may be considered invalid and forbidden. In determining what is legal or otherwise an examination should involve three basic factors: the contractor, the subject of contract, and the form of contract. The general purpose of invalidating the transaction is the protection of the parties to the contract. Businesses should not be contracted with persons under age, lunatics, or people with physical disability in as much as the physical disability may have a bearing on the condition of the transaction. Blindness is an example of the last case. Interestingly, this is in line with modern statutory laws. For example, in modern law we may find that some transactions are invalid if the contractor is under eighteen years of age. Six conditions are laid down by Ibn al-Ukhūwwah to validate the subject of contract. These are: (a) the subject of contract may not be ritually unclean either by essence or by association such as in the case of contamination, (b) the subject of contract should be of beneficial use, (c) the subject must be in the actual ownership of the original selling party, (d) articles must be capablc of delivery, (e) the quantity of the good subject to sale must be specified, and (f) the articles for sale must be within the possession of the original selling party in that sale and delivery should be taken place simultaneously. The last condition in particular raises a question about the validity of transactions in the stock market when a sale is concluded with a view to delivering the shares within a specified period in the near future (for further discussions of this point see El-Ashker, 1995). It is within the duties, and authority of the Muĥtasib, as Ibn al-Ukhūwwah emphasised, to observe these issues when inspecting the work of the market. But as far as pricing is concerned, "The Muĥtasib is not permitted to fix the prices of commodities in opposition to the owners", which is in line with the practice of the Prophet. To complete the factors of the validity of contracts with regard to the form of contract, Ibn al-Ukhūwwah clarified that there must be a formal offer by the seller and acceptance by the buyer for the deal to be concluded.

In implementing the governance rules of the market, ibn al-Ukhūwwah has provided various recommendations to the Muĥtasib. The following are some examples, (Levy, 1938, Ibn al-Ukhūwwah):

(1) The Muĥtasib must remain close to the markets, observing them at all times and going amongst the traders.
(2) He must investigate shops and streets and test weights and measures and see what is adulterated.
(3) He must make his visits unannounced and at any time of day or night.
(4) He must seal up for the night any shop which he has not been able to search during the day and make his investigation early the next morning.

And about his assistant:

(5) He must have reliable assistants but must depend upon his own examination when taking a decision.
(6) He must always have assistants by his side whether he is seated at home or riding abroad.
(7) The assistants must be people of chaste honourable life, strong and courageous.
(8) He must hold them in check and train them in their duties.

(9) When they summon a party to a dispute they must never inform him of the charge lest he should think out an argument by which he may release himself.

(10) If an offender is summoned to be present with all his stock and equipment he must be brought as the Muĥtasib assistants found him and must not be allowed to leave any of his weights in his shop or let them fall on the way.

(11) No messenger should go out before consulting the Muĥtasib and when he does go out he must do so with determination and courage and seek the offender swiftly, for this is what terrifies and deters from evil-doing.

(12) If an offender is to be punished the punishment should be in the manner that is bearable by the offender and in line with the offence. The Tradition is that when the offence is against God there is pardon, but not where it is against man.

It is interesting to note that the duties of the Muĥtasib cover a particularly wide range. Basically these duties are divided into two main divisions: the enforcement of the law, *al-amr bil maʾruf*, and the prevention of illegality, *al-nahy un al-Munkar*. Each includes three main parts: what is due to God, what is due to man, and what is due to both jointly. Enforcement of the law regarding what is due to God involves duties binding on the whole community, mainly Friday prayers, Eid prayers, and the call for prayers. As public prayers concerns the ritual principles of Islam, it falls within the duties of the Muĥtasib to ensure the adherence to these features of public worship.

The second category of enforcement of law, which addresses matters related to man, is divided into two groups: those related to the community and others connected with individuals. With regard to the former the Muĥtasib should ensure that facilities provided to the community are met, and if the public treasury cannot provide for these needs the Muĥtasib may call upon the rich to provide for these needs. Where the rights concerned are those of individuals, such as the payment of debt, the Muĥtasib should order the debtor to discharge the debt as long as the debtor is able to do so. It is his function to compel the debtor to appear before the judge on application by the creditor. In matters related to the community, the Muĥtasib should see that the community needs are satisfied. Ibn al-Ukhūwwah points out that if an individual wilfully neglects worship beyond the proper time he may be warned but if the whole population of a town decide to celebrate public worship at a latter hour than the Muĥtasib thinks proper, providing that this is within the permissible time, it is a question whether or not he may submit to the common law (Levy, op. cit.) This is a degree of flexibility given to the population of the town providing that the ritual rules of the religion are not breached.

Now, in the same vein of writing on Ĥisbah, we turn our attention to a great writer of his time, Ahmad ibn-Taymīya.

Ibn Taymīya (661–728 A.H./1263–1328 A.C.) *al-Ĥisbah fi al Islam, Public Duties in Islam*

The Author

Taqi al-Dīn Ahmad ibn Taymīya was born in Harran in 661 A.H./1263 A.C., and died in Damascus in 728 A.H./1328 A.C. A Hanbalī, he is regarded as one of the most influential thinkers in Islamic history.

At an early age he became a professor of Ĥanbalī law and a teacher of Qur'ānic studies. What distinguishes Ibn Taymīya is that he had an innovative mind and was able to reconstruct Islamic thought on the pure foundation of the Qur'ānic teachings and the Sunnah. He suffered for his independence of thought and action. He spent many years in prison. Ibn Taymīya wrote a large number of books related to different aspects of Islamic thought and practice. His *al-Ĥisbah fi al Islam* remains a major contribution in the field of Islamic social studies, in which he expounded its theoretical foundation and its socio-economic functions. In this book his main theme is "commanding what is *ma'ruf* (good; fair; right; and proper) and prohibiting what is *munkar* (evil; unfair; wrong; and improper). As Holland says, excessive zeal in this area may horrify some, and be a temptation to others, but if this work has any influence it should be to reassure the alarmist and restrain the potential fanatic, since ibn Taymīya calls for a moderate and realistic approach, with great stress on the importance of knowledge, gentleness, patience, forbearance, and generosity of spirit (Holland, 1983).

The book

Ibn Taymīya's book on *Ĥisbah* comprises ten chapters. These cover the following topics (ibid.):

Basic principle of *Ĥisbah*
Ethical guidelines for regulating business and economic life
Collective good and the state's responsibility
Price controls: some controversial aspects
Crime and punishment
Commanding good and forbidding evil
Strategy for reform
Men and movements
Society and leadership
Summing up on knowledge, justice, and the duties of the rulers and the ruled

The first concern of Ibn Taymīya in his *Ĥisbah* was, like those writing on *Ĥisbah* in general, the ethical issues in business. Like others before and after him, he reiterated the Qur'ānic and Sunnah teachings regarding the right weights and measurements and the role of the Muĥtasib in supervising these aspects of the market.

Emphasis was also given to the amount and quality of information provided regarding both the product and the market. The purpose is to prevent market imperfections caused by the intentional concealment of information that may affect the parties' decisions or the deliberate provision of misinformation that would conceivable affect the judgment of contractors. Contracts concluded on the basis of the concealment of information that could have been provided, or the injection of misinformation to affect the decision of either the buyer or the seller, are regarded as invalid. The Muĥtasib was to endeavour to stop this side of market imperfections and to investigate the claim made by either party to that effect. Included in these market imperfections, for example, is the interception of goods before reaching the market and the conclusion of a deal with the seller before the latter knows the prevailing prices in the market. In this example, the right of "option on reaching the market" has generally been established by the Prophet with a view to protecting the harmed party, with minor conditions specified by jurists of different schools of thought. Newcomers to the market are also protected and should not be hurried to a bargain before they knew what the market conditions were likely to be.

Emanating from the same principle of preventing market imperfections, hoarding, particularly hoarding of necessities, should be checked. Ibn Taymīya went as far as stating that the authorities, the Muĥtasib, are entitled to force the sellers of necessities to sell their stock for fair value when the goods are urgently needed even if the sellers were unwilling to sell at that price in preference for a future higher price when the goods experience further shortage. This view establishes the need to protect the economy from arbitrary manipulation of the market with a view to protecting the consumer and producer against economic injustice (Holland, 1983). Ibn Taymīya's opinion may seem in contradiction of the free market conditions advocated in Islamic economics, but what Ibn Taymīya was advocating was the importance of the state intervention when the conditions of the free market fail to function as a result of being distorted by monopolistic actions. It is noted, however, that the intervention in market forces by the state is only required when the goods subject to monopoly are of a vital importance to the community. The criterion of whether the goods are vitally important to the community or otherwise is echoed elsewhere in Ibn Taymīya's views about price control as seen below.

Price control

Ibn Taymīya's views on pricing are an important input into Islamic market forces. To him the general condition of a free market that is based on market forces including, in particular, pricing, as established by the Prophet, is not without restrictions. The restrictions are mainly that whether pricing through market forces is leading to injury to people or otherwise. Price fixation by the authority, therefore, may be "an impermissible wrong", or may be "just and permissible". Ibn Taymīya proceeded to say, "If it, *price fixation*, (italics ours) involves injury to people *the sellers* and forcing them without justification to sell at a price not agreeable to them, then it is illegal. But if it involves just dealing between people, as when they are compelled to do their duty by exchanging for a fair price, and preventing them from doing what is unlawful for them in taking more than a fair consideration, then it is not merely permissible but indeed obligatory". Intervention in market forces through price fixation by the state is therefore mandatory on the state, though it is still conditional. Ibn

Taymīya explained that further in stating that if the sellers are selling their goods in a proper manner, without artificial manipulation of prices, and the current price happens to rise either through the scarcity of an article or an increase in the demand, then these are market conditions. In these circumstances compelling the sellers to sell at a particular price would be unjustified and wrong. But if the sellers refrained from selling in anticipation of a price more than the reasonable price at a time when there is an urgent need for the goods, they would be doing wrong as they would be manipulating market forces in order to sell for more than the fair value. "Price control has no meaning other than compulsion to sell at a fair value".

Turning his attention to monopoly, Ibn Taymīya condemned all forms of monopoly including, interestingly enough, oligopoly, and regarded them as a serious form of market manipulation. "A more serious matter is where people have a monopoly of a particular commodity that are sold only to them and then retailed by them", which leads to "any would-be competitor being restrained either harshly, by imposition, or by some gentler means less open to abuse". In this situation price fixation is a must, "prices must be controlled so that monopolists sell only for fair value and buy people's goods only for fair value", (ibid.) This is because, "If the monopolists were licensed to set their own prices the public would be injured on two sides: the sellers wishing to sell their goods to them on the one hand, and those purchasing goods from them on the other", (ibid.)

The removal of economic injustice through the manipulation of market forces was the main concerned of Ibn Taymīya in justifying the intervention by the state in market conditions. To him price control by the state is not only an undisputed right but also a compelling duty. Three conditions seemed to have been put however by Ibn Taymīya to organise the intervention of the state and, seemingly, curb its power. First, the commodity subject to market imperfection ought to be of a particular necessity to the consumers at large. By implication, he did not seem to be particularly concerned about goods of a luxury nature; these could be afforded by the well-off consumers. Second, there ought to be a manipulation of the market conditions through the sellers refraining from sale in anticipation of a future shortage of supply that would lead to a price increase. This is a manipulation of supply forces. Third, manipulation of market forces through monopolistic activities, which would jeopardise the choice of both consumer and producer when the commodity is for manufacture. Fourth, the manipulation of the market is for the purpose of achieving a price higher than the fair value of goods. Fifth, the fixation of prices should be fairly exercised with the aim of achieving a fair value for the buyer and the seller, the consumer and the producer. Any fixation of price below or above the fair value is impermissible. Sixth, the ultimate objective of price fixation is to remove injustice to the community. Without these conditions and with no such purpose, intervention in market forces is not permissible.

Provision of Essential Supplies

On the production side, another form of state intervention in market forces, in ibn Taymīya's opinion, is the case of the provision of essential goods. Market forces should not be left to operate freely in the production section if they fail to provide the community with the type of goods that may be regarded essential to the community. In that he explained, "It may be that people are in need of the industry of certain individuals, e.g. the public need for farming, weaving and building, unless the citizens import sufficient for their needs they will require someone to weave their cloths for them." (ibid.) Using the educational approach, he stated that initiating and operating these industries is a collective obligation, *fardh kifayah*, on the capable individuals in the community, since the public welfare is incomplete unless these industries are provided. The nature of these obligations is that when one man performs those tasks, which are collective duties, they become the personal responsibility of this individual, *fardh ayn*, especially if there is no one else is capable of performing them. In a formal approach, he regarded the state as responsible for ensuring that these industries are provided when there is no individual is willing to do so. In his words, "If people are in need for farming or weaving or building, the task becomes a binding duty on those capable of performing them, and the authority may exert compulsion if they refuse, setting a fair rate of remuneration", (ibid.) The role of the state is therefore twofold: (a) to encourage those who are able to meet these essential needs of the society to set up these industries voluntarily with all possible help from the government motivated by the pursuit of a reasonable profit, and (b) when this fails, to use enough force to see that the able individuals are engaged in the provision of these needs providing that this is done without the exploitation of individuals through paying them fair wages, (Holland, 1983).

A condition was well established by Ibn Taymīya, if the state takes such a role: the individuals providing the service should not be authorised to demand more than a fair value from the public, nor the public should wrong them by giving them less than their fair value or the government paying them less than a fair wage. The state intervention should be seen within the general condition that market forces failed to provide the society with these collective goods.

Now we come to perhaps the most renowned study in the Islamic social history, Ibn-Khaldūn's Mūqaddimah.

Ibn-Khaldūn (1332–1406) *al-Mūqaddimah, An Introduction to History*

The Author

Abd-al-Rahman Abū Zayd ibn Muĥammad ibn Muĥammad ibn Khaldūn, was born in Tunis in 1332 A.C. Ibn-Khaldūn's life was extremely colourful: a descendant of an aristocratic family, a jurist, a statesman, a prime minister, a chief judge, a courtier, a prisoner, an exile, and a scholar. This experience added to the quality of his thinking and made him the scholar we know. In this Rosenthal says, "The love of learning and intellectual pursuits for which his father and grandfather were noted, coupled with the political aspirations that fired a long line of his Moorish forebears, produced the rare combination of philosopher and statesman that we find in ibn-Khaldūn", (Rozenthal, 1967). Like the scholars of his time, his education began with studying the Qur'ān, the Sunnah, jurisprudence, and later, the study of the Arab mysticism and the philosophy of the Moorish Aristotelians. He was appointed in a government position, to be thrown in prison on suspicion of his loyalty to the Ŝulṭān, to be released after a year or so, to be appointed again in the service of the successor Ŝulṭān. In his life, he moved between Tunis, Fez, Cordoba, and Cairo where he was made the Grand Judge of the Mālikī for Cairo, Damascus and Makkah for pilgrimage. After a rich life of learning, political and social experience, including a personal tragedy when all his family drowned in a wrecked ship when they were sailing from North Africa to join him in Egypt, he died in 1406. He was buried in the Ŝūfī cemetery outside Cairo.

The Book

Ibn-Khaldūn's treatise, which is called the Mūqaddimah (introduction) to history, was completed in 1377. It includes his preface and Book I which has been described as "the earliest attempt made by any historian to discover a pattern in the changes that occur in man's political and social organisation", (Rosenthal, 1967). Rosenthal adds, "Rational in its approach, analytical in its method, encyclopedic in detail, it represents an almost complete departure from traditional historiography, discarding conventional concepts and clichés and seeking, beyond the mere chronicle of events, an explanation-and hence a philosophy of history", (ibid.).

His approach to writing his Mūqaddimah

The analytical approach of Ibn Khaldūn is clear in his writing, as stated himself and verified in his writing. "The writing of history is an art", he states, "that requires an investigative mind and thorough examination which leads the historian to the truth . . . as the mere transmission from the others may lead to slips and error". To avoid error, historians, to him, should relate events to the principles of custom, the essential facts of politics, the nature of development of civilisation and the growth of society. With a scientific mind, he stated that various reasons could be attributed, in his opinion, to abusing historical information. These are (ibid.):

Partisanship for opinions and schools
Reliance, without investigation, upon disseminction of information
Unawareness of the purpose of an event
Unfounded assumptions as to the truth of an occurrance
Ignorance of how conditions conform to reality
Treating high-ranking persons with excessive deterence
Ignorance of the nature and various conditions arising in civilizations

As for the purpose of writing his book, Ibn-Khaldūn ascertained, "The purpose of this first book of our work, (which) is an independent science with its own peculiar object, is human civilisation and social organisation. It has its own peculiar problems which are explaining in turn the conditions that attach themselves to the essence of civilisation". Civilisation is the focal point of his attention, as in his understanding, "all sciences, laws, rules and principles, including the divine rules and religious doctrines that aim at the perseverance of civilisation".

Interestingly enough, Ibn-Khaldūn provided an explanation of the concept of civilization which he adopted in his writing. To him it means, "That human beings have to dwell in common and settle together in cities and hamlets for the comforts of companionship and for the satisfaction of human needs, as a result of the natural disposition of human beings towards co-operation in order to be able to make a living". This concept of civilisation, to him, is not necessarily exclusive to sedentary conditions as found in "cities, villages, towns, and small communities that serve the purpose of protection and fortification by means of walls". It can also include Bedouin civilisation such as, "what can be found in outlying regions and mountains, in hamlets near pasture in far away regions at the fringe of desert land".

The focal point of Ibn-Khaldūn's attention was therefore the existence of communities, regardless of whether they were inside towns and cities, or situated at the fringe of deserts in oasis or at the bottom of mountains. To him, seemingly, living in community is the basis for establishing a civilisation. Living in communities requires communication and cooperation, which lead to economic integration that results in its turn in human comfort and companionship and the satisfaction of human needs. He, consequently, presented his discussion in his book in six different chapters:

Human civilisation in general, it's various kinds, and the portion of the earth that is civilized
Bedouin civilization including untamed tribes and nations
Ruling dynasties, the caliphate, royal authority, and ranks of Ŝulṭāns
Sedentary civilization, countries and cities
Crafts, ways of making a living, means of earnings
Sciences, their acquisition and learning

Ibn-Khaldūn's Economic Thoughts

Economic integration

At the outset Ibn-Khaldūn confirmed the need for economic integration as a basic ingredient for a societal living. He gave an example, once more like those before him, from making bread—a process that requires the cooperation of many. Human beings are social by instinct, he states, and if they are to live in a society they will have to cooperate in their economic activities. This cooperation, particularly when further complicated production activities are required, such as producing what is needed for self defense, leads to, and necessarily requires, economic integration.

Commercial activities by the ruler (government)

In Ibn-Khaldūn's view commercial activity on the part of the ruler is harmful to his subjects and ruinous to the tax system. It is harmful to the subjects in many ways. First, farmers and merchants will find it difficult to buy livestock and merchandise and to procure cheaply the things that relate to farming and commerce. As the ruler is much more able financially to buy than the subjects whose wealth is restricted principles of competition are harmed. The ruler will be able to buy what they cannot buy. Second, the ruler can distribute much of the agricultural produce and available merchandise at will. He can do this by force or by buying items at the cheapest possible price. No one will be able to bid against him, and he can also force the seller to reduce his price. Third, the ruler may force the buying merchants to buy from him, and this may be at the highest price. This may lead to exhausting the liquid cash of the merchants and lead to liquidity problems and hardship in making a living. In their need for cash, they may have to sell the goods they purchased from the ruler dearly at a low price. This may lead to the merchants being forced out of the market.

State competition with the public may lead to work disincentive and the ruin of the fiscal structure. As most of the revenue from taxes, and custom duties, come from farmers and merchants, and with farmers giving up farming and merchants going out of business, the revenue will be dangerously reduced. If the ruler compared the revenue from taxes with the small profits he achieved from his commercial activity, he would realise that the latter is much smaller than the former. The finances of the ruler can be increased and the resources of the state improved only through the revenue from taxes, with no royal commercial activity. The tax revenue can be increased through the equitable treatment of the people with property and regard for them. This raises their aspiration and incentive to work, make their capital grow. In turn, this increases tax revenue.

Furthermore, the misuse of the commercial activity by the ruler may lead to the destruction of the economy and the disintegration of the ruling class. When the farmer and merchants cannot make their capital grow through agriculture and commerce, as a result of shrinking profits, the capital will decrease and eventually disappear as a result of using it in covering expenditure. This will ruin the economy.

Another form of the abuse of power for economic benefits, which is damaging to the economy, is when the ruler buys the goods from farmers and merchants at a price determined by the rules in order to sell to the public at a higher price. This is even more damaging and ruinous to the interest of the public. Furthermore, another form of misuse of power for commercial purposes is when the ruler shares business interest with merchants. Merchants, who are professional by the virtue of their occupation, pay the ruler a share of their profit. They work with him but for their own benefits as they may sell at increased prices to achieve high profits. They may also manage to gain exemption from taxes and custom duties for the share of the profit given to the ruler.

Prosperity to consumption, labour and economic development

From his observation, Ibn-Khaldūn reached an interesting conclusion in relation to propensity to consumption. Consumption may have a positive effect on economic development and the growth of towns and cities as trading centres. By inference, lack of consumption may lead to the opposite effect, the paradox of saving, so to speak. Taking labour as a starting point in creating wealth and economic development, he clarified his view by stating that as the combined labour available in a town or a city produced more than the needs and necessities of the workers, the surplus labour may be directed towards providing two things: (a) the conditions and customs of luxury in the city, and (b) the satisfaction of the needs of the inhabitants of other cities. As the demand for these luxury products increased, and the demand for exported goods to other cities increased, and as the profit was the realized value of labour, this would lead to the increase of wealth in the city with the surplus labour. A demand for skillful workers was therefore created which would be reflected in the price of their labour. Consequently, industry and crafts thrive, and "the income and expenditure of this city increases and affluence comes to those who work and produce these goods by their labour".

The above cycle would be repeated further when population increased. The available labour increased, demand for luxury increased in its turn in line with the increasing profit, crafts would be created to obtain luxury products, the value realized from them would increase, and as a result profits would again be multiplied in the city. Production in the city would thrive even more than before.

In a nutshell, this sounds as if Ibn-Khaldūn was saying that the increase in population does not impose per se a problem for economic development. On the contrary, it may lead to further economic prosperity. One would say in reply to Ibn-Khaldūn's view, production opportunities must exist for his theory to materialise otherwise the increase of population may lead to unemployment. In other words, this will depend upon whether the economy is in a state of full employment and upon the procedures taken by the state in creating employment opportunities. Keynes's theory of the effect of public expenditure on the creation of employment opportunities, and the effect of propensity to consumption on income may be mentioned here in comparison with Ibn-Khaldūn's opinion. Interestingly enough, we find Ibn-Khaldūn, in clarifying his observation further, stating, "Income and expenditure balance each other in every city; if the income is large the expenditure is large, and vice versa. And if both income and expenditure are large, the inhabitants become more favourably situated, and the city grows".

Prices

In a striking awareness of the effect of the power of markets on prices, we find Ibn-Khaldūn's stating that prices were affected by two main factors: demand and supply. The effect of cost of production on the state of supply was similarly ascertained. All depended upon the state of prosperity, as he stated, with varying degrees of effects on basic as compared with luxury goods. If a community was prosperous, prices of necessities would be low, while prices of luxury goods would be high. The opposite is true in the state of lack of prosperity. In this case, the demand and supply of necessities would play an influential role in determining the price of these goods. He continued to clarify that in the state of affluence enough labour and suitable natural resources would be devoted to the satisfaction of the needs of the affluent society. And while the demand for these basic goods in this society was steady, by virtue of the state of saturation and the absence of natural disasters, the supply of goods would be able to meet the demand and the price would become low. Conceivably, in case of natural calamity or high production costs, the supply would not meet the demand and the prices of these basic goods would rise. Elasticity of demand could be inferred here, although Ibn-Khaldūn did not use the term explicitly. In case of luxurious goods in these affluent societies, the situation would be different: if the supply was in a state of normality, without interrupting disasters, prices would be high, but if the supply was interrupted by any state of abnormality the prices would come down. The elasticity of demand, once more—for basic goods the elasticity is low, but it is high for luxurious goods. But the inferred state of elasticity of demand was not to be constant as it was changeable with the state of economic prosperity, as Ibn-Khaldūn clarified. In his words, "when a city has a highly developed, abundant civilisation and is full of luxuries, there is a very large demand for conveniences and for having as many of them as a person can expect in view of his situation. This results in a very large shortage of such things. Many will bid for them, but they will be in short supply. They will be needed for many purposes, and prosperous people used to luxuries will pay exorbitant prices for them, because they need them more than others. Thus as one can see, prices will come to be high". One can detect from this explanation a state of backward demand. Demand increases even when the price is rising.

Price of labour

Turning his attention to price of labour, Ibn-Khaldūn clarified that labour cost may increase with the increase in the level economic development. "Crafts and labour are expensive in cities with abundant civilisation", he stated. In his view, this was for three reasons. First, their skill was much needed because of the need for luxury goods. Second, industrial labourers would price their services highly as they did not have to work as long hours as they might have done in case of a less affluent society. Third, the existence of a great number of people with "money to waste" on these luxury goods, who would be motivated by the desire to have an exclusive access to these goods and consequently their readiness to pay for the service more than it was inherently worth.

Earnings, income, capital and value

From a religious perspective Ibn-Khaldūn differentiated between *rizq* and *kasb*. *Rizq* is what is provided by God, even if man has not strived to obtain it, such as the rain used in irrigation. *Kasb* is what man acquires through his effort and work in combination of what God has provided. *Kasb*, Ibn-Khaldūn continued, constituted two things: first, livelihood, when this corresponded to necessities and basic needs, and second, luxuries and capital accumulation when *kasb* generated a surplus above the basic needs. *Kasb*, therefore, could be referred to as earnings, which could be spent on sustenance and luxuries and saving, or in other words, earnings equal consumption and saving. The line between earnings and income seems to be fine, and if the two words can be used interchangeably, Ibn-Khaldūn's equation would become, in modern economic terms, income equals consumption and saving—the Keynesian equation.

Furthermore, Ibn-Khaldūn's analysis differentiates between what is earned by the person himself through his work and effort and what is acquired through the transfer of earnings. While the first is referred to as earnings, the second, though is regarded as earnings to the transferor, is not so considered to the transferee, instead, it is a transfer of wealth. Inherited wealth is an example. While the inherited legacy was of the deceased's earnings during his life, and regarded as such, it is not considered as such to heirs to whom the legacy is a transfer of wealth. This is a fine differentiation that has two implications: first, the emphasis on the ethical value of work and effort in acquiring earnings, and second, the differentiation between earnings, or income, and capital. In emphasising the last point, Ibn-Khaldūn clarified that when the legacy was used by heirs, the benefits generated from it would be referred to as income.

Turning his attention to the concept of value, Ibn-Khaldūn, without ignoring other factors, relied on labour as a main determinant factor of value. "A portion of value whether large or small, comes form labour", he stated. But he conditioned the application of that concept by two main factors: first, the type of article to which the value was measured and the relative importance of the component of labour in the production of the article, and second, the level of skill and expertise required in production. About the first, using an example from the farming industry, he ascertained, "The share of labour may be concealed in regions where farming requires little care and few implements". In relation to the second, the skilled labour and high expertise, he verified, "It should be further known that the capital a person earns and acquires, if resulting from a craft, is the value realised from his labour. There is nothing here except the labour, as it is not desired by itself as acquired". To expand on Ibn-Khaldūn's example, ornaments, work of art, beautification of materials, embroidery of fabrics, etc., are valuable because of the level of skill, artistic ability and expertise required in their production. Or as Ibn-Khaldūn explained further, "Some crafts are associated with others. Carpentry and weaving, for instance, are associated with wood and yarn, but in these two crafts, the labour (that is put into it) is more important, and its value is greater".

One should realise however that at the time of Ibn-Khaldūn mass production was not yet known and the artistic input of work in production was based mainly on human expertise. Labour may take a second place in these circumstances. In mass production when the input of labour is not particularly dominant, the portion of value assigned to labour would be small, giving way to others portions of value that may be associated with, and more dominant than, other factors of production such as capital and entrepreneurship. However, and in anticipation of our thinking, Ibn-Khaldūn already stated that a portion of value, "whether large or small" came from labour.

Trade

Ibn-Khaldūn provided some interesting discussions on trade and its associated financial risk. He, first, defined trade, which, to him, meant, "increasing one's capital by buying merchandise and attempting to sell it for a price higher than its purchase price, either by waiting for market fluctuations or by transporting the merchandise to a country where that particular merchandise is more in demand and brings higher prices, or by selling for a high price to be paid in a future date". From the definition, the following points could be highlighted:

Trade is a means by which the capital grows, "increasing one's capital", and this done by,

selling at a higher price than the purchase price, a difference in prices to which Ibn-Khaldūn referred as 'profit', through

waiting for market fluctuation, or

transporting the merchandise to another country where prices are higher, or

selling now for payment to be made in a future date.

The definition fits in adequately with economic concepts that became known from the nineteenth onward. The Physiocrat Turgot's concept of value-exchange, valeur appreciative, the concept of profit, the concept of the comparative advantage in international trade, and credit sale and time value of money are some examples.

Furthermore, Ibn-Khaldūn provided an interesting concept in business, and perhaps in determining the profit margin by the entrepreneur in cost-plus pricing. He explained that although, "the profit is small in relation to capital, when the capital is large, the profit becomes large, because many times a little is much". If this argument is to be expanded further, it could be applied to the difference between the internal rate of return on capital employed and the net present methods in investment appraisal. In large projects in particular, the present value method is advocated as being superior to the internal rate of return. True, Ibn-Khaldūn did not talk about the net present value as such, but the analogy in relation to the conceptual principle does exist.

Financial risk

Ibn-Khaldūn identified a number of business and financial risks that may face a business, or the trader. These are mentioned as follows:

Physical risk, "tampering with the merchandise which may ruin it"

Bad debts, "delay of payment which may ruin the profit, since such delay while it lasts prevents any activity that could bring profit"

Moral hazard, "There will also be non-acknowledgment or denial of obligations, which may prove destructive of one's capital unless the obligations have been stated in writing and properly witnessed. The judiciary is of little use in this connection, since the law requires clear evidence.

Loss of profit or capital, "All this could cause the merchant a great deal of trouble. He may make a small profit, but only with great trouble and difficulty, or he may make no profit at all, or his capital may be lost".

Amazingly, and amusingly, Ibn-Khaldūn suggested that as a result of these surrounding risks, not everybody could be suitable to be a merchant. He should be a person who is willing to accept the risk and has some "qualities" of being a merchant. He should not be afraid of quarrels, knows how to settle an account, and is always willing to enter into dispute and go to court, as in this way he stands a better chance of being fairly treated in his trade. More amazingly, he stated, "the person who is afraid or unassertive, and who, in addition, lacks the influence of rank with judiciary, must avoid trade". This is because, "he will become the prey of traders, and he may not get his rights from them. People, as a rule, desire the possession of other people. Without the restraining influence of laws, nobody's property would be safe. This applies especially to traders and the low-class mob". Ibn-Khaldūn's strong statement highlights the importance of a good financial control system and adequate legal services for the success of business. Dishonest traders do not escape Ibn-Khaldūn criticism, however.

Turning his attention to the importance of skilled labour in the process of production Ibn-Khaldūn emphasised the importance of occupational training and acquiring knowledge. He spoke about the effect of training in one occupation on the level of skill and expertise, advocating that change of occupation during one's life time may not lead to mastering the skill needed in the craft, in an indirect reference perhaps to the advantage of division of labour. He also devotes a substantial chapter to sciences and knowledge discussing the various kinds of sciences, the methods of instruction and the conditions that obtain in these connections. He covered a comprehensive list of sciences, though, unfortunately, economics as a science was not specifically included. But economics was not known to be a science until recently!

Having looked at the development of Islamic economic thought during a difficult period of Muslim life, we turn our attention in the next chapter to studying yet another important period in the Islamic history. It is a period that preceded a stage in Islamic history when Muslims decided to return to the principles of their religion in their attempts to find answers to their social, economic and political problems.

We move in the next section of this work to a new phase in Islamic history. Re-emerging from the ashes of its decline, the Islamic world has experienced what could be rightly described as a renaissance. It is a phase that is normally referred to by historians as Islam returning triumphant. And surprisingly, those who burned its civilization to ashes were those who later carried its banner to glory.

CHAPTER SEVEN

THE THREE EMPIRES AND THE ISLAMIC PHOENIX (1400 A.C.–1800 A.C.)

Introduction

The Phoenix is said to be a bird of an Arabian Desert, which lived for several centuries, burned itself to death, and then was reborn from its ashes—a legend the analogy of which is not very dissimilar to that of the legacy of Islam. The two centuries from the mid-thirteen to the mid-fifteen centuries seem to tell the tale.

As mentioned in the previous chapter, Baghdad, the capital of the caliphate, was destroyed by the Mongols (1220–1500), and the Euphrates, as historians tell us, were swamped with corps and skulls. Even the lives of the Abbasīd caliph and his delegates who hurried to receive the Mongol Chieftain Hulagu in a welcoming surrender were not to be spared. Until they were finally checked by the Egyptian Mamlūk Baybars in the decisive battle of Ain Jalut, north Palestine, in 1260, they turned the Islamic land into ashes. Ain Jalut was not a strategic battle that had to be won to balance the score, but it was a battle for survival; survival of Muslims and survival of Islam itself. The Mamlūks of Egypt were the last remaining stronghold facing the Mongols in their unstoppable destructive march to the west and had the Mongols had the upper hand over the Mamlūks the road to the Islamic sacred shrines in Makkah and al-Medīnah would have been wide open for further destruction. Seeing the Islamic ritual shrines at risk of destruction must have prompted the populace to rally behind the Mamlūks, who were Sunni Muslims, and to turn the confrontation into a Holly War, *jihād*. In the hearts of Muslims, it was not a battle for land or even the caliphate; it was a battle for God. Nevertheless, by the end of the century, the fate of the Muslim world was to take an unexpected turn.

By the end of the thirteenth and the beginning of the fourteenth centuries the Islamic ashes in the aftermath of the Mongol's destruction burst into flames and those who turned the Islamic world into ashes were those who ignited the flames. The four Mongols empires had converted to Islam and had become staunch Muslim supporters in the central Islamic land. These were the Il-Khans in the Tigris-Euphrates valley and the mountainous regions of Iran, the Chaghaytay in Syr-Oxus basin, the White Horde in the Irtysh region, and the Golden Horde around the river Volga. From these four, two powerful Islamic empires emerged: the Shī'ah Ŝafawīd Empire which became the foundation of what Iran is today, and the Sunni Moghul, or Mongol Empire in the Indian subcontinent which constitutes the present Pakistan and some parts of India. Moreover, to the west of the Mongols, came another, and long lasting, source of support to Islam, the Ottoman Turks.

These three empires dominated the political scene in the Islamic world: the Ottoman, the Ŝafawīd and the Mongol. Each had different socio-economic conditions, features of intellectual development and influence over the development of Islamic economics as shown below.

The Ottoman Empire

The Ottoman Turks, the Mongols' kinship, grew in power in Anatolia and developed into a force that shaped the Islamic world for centuries to come. Established in 1299 by its founder Uthmān, who reigned from 1299 to 1326, the Ottoman Turkish state, which began as a principality of march-warriors, was one of several states that appeared in Anatolia after the break-up of the Seljuq Sūltanate. It lasted until 1922. Their predecessors the Seljuq Turks, are said to be devoted Muslims who had never been conquered by Muslims but by Islam itself (Lewis, 1979). The Ottomans grew in power and despite a temporary setback in the early fifteenth century when the last Mongol Emperor Timur Lane (Timur the Lame) defeated them in Angora in 1402, they managed to recover after Timur's death in 1404, and to emerge as an influential player in the political scene.

The conquest of Constantinople that held steadfast for many centuries against all previous Muslims' endeavours, by the Ottoman Ŝulṭān Muĥammad the Conqueror in 1453, hailed the Turkish Ŝulṭān as a great Muslim hero, nicknamed him the "Conqueror" and enhanced the standing of the Ottomans amongst Muslims. Further victories in Europe, the Indian Ocean, North Africa, Egypt and al-Hijaz, and the overthrown of the Mamlūks in Egypt assured the Ottomans of their military hegemony and made them the custodians and defenders of the faith.

By 1550, the Ottoman Empire extended from the Persian Gulf to the south of the Caspian Sea and Georgia in the east, Moldavia and Hungary up to the Adriatic Sea in the north, the African Coast including Algeria in the west and Egypt and al-Hijaz in the Arabian Peninsula in the south. Soon, the Ottomans transferred the caliphate capital to Constantinople, which had become Istanbūl. Baghdad was no longer the centre of power and Cairo was not seen as Baghdad's replacement as it once was during the Fatimids and the Mamlūks. In their zeal to make Constantinople the centre of power, the Ottoman caliph-Ŝulṭāns ensured that the new capital was enriched with talents from different nations and races. Some of the best talent of the conquered lands were mobilised and channelled to the capital; there they were to be utilised for the glory and advancement of the imperial state (Hitti, 1964).

The Ottomanisation of the Caliphate

As mentioned in the previous chapter, the Islamic state is observed to have moved into a state of political decay beginning from the reign of the Abbasīd caliph al-Must'asim (833–842) who was overpowered by his Turkish bodyguard. The culmination of the political decay became more distinct, however, with the murder of the al-Mūtawakkil (847–861) by his bodyguards, and from that time onward caliphs were appointed and removed at the will of the state's military rulers—the Ŝulṭāns. This marked the introduction of the dualistic formula of the caliphate whereby the Abbasīd caliph's function was confined to spiritually religious ceremonial matters, while the actual governing of the state rested in the hands of the Ŝulṭāns. The religion was for the caliph while the government was for the Ŝulṭāns. In practice the caliph ceased to be a source of any effective power.

The Mamlūks of Egypt did the same with the Abbasīd caliph. The last of the Abbasīd caliphs, al-Mūtawakkil (another Mūtawakkil, died in 1543) only played a symbolic role in Cairo under the patronage of the Mamlūk Ŝulṭān in Egypt. That practice continued until the Ottoman Ŝulṭān Salīm, on crushing the Egyptian Mamlūk Sūltanate in 1517, took al-Mūtawakkil to Constantinople and reinstated him as the caliph. Nevertheless, al-Mūtawakkil was later to be accused of the misuse of trust funds, and was held prisoner until the death of Ŝulṭān Salim. When Salim's son became the new Ŝultan, he released him from prison and finally allowed him to retire to Egypt. There, al-Mūtawakkil died in 1543, and by his death the Abbasīd caliphate, figurative as it had become, came to a final end. Subsequently, the Ottoman Turkish Ŝulṭāns assumed the caliphate to themselves, arguably on the premise that the last legitimate caliph volunteered a delegation of his position to the Ottoman Ŝulṭān. The newly invented dualistic concept of the caliphate, one for religion and another for government, came to an end when the Ottoman Ŝulṭān claimed both the spiritual and political functions of the caliph and declared himself a full-fledged caliph. The titular caliphate was to remain with the Ottoman Turks for almost four centuries, until 1924 when it was repealed, sixteen months after the foundation of the new Turkish Republic.

By claiming the caliphate to himself, the Ottoman Ŝulṭān put an end to the political struggle between the Sunnis and the Shi'is over the caliphate. The argument over whether the caliphate should rest with the Abbasids, the descendants of the Prophet's uncle, or the Alids, the descendants of his cousin, came to an end, at least within the Ottoman Empire. We recall that the issue of the kinship to the Prophet was a main religious device that the Abbasīd movement introduced in order to entice support and rally the masses particularly when the Abbasīd movement was first launched. Similarly, it was the same issue upon which the Alids based their argument for the legitimacy to the caliphate as advocated by Shī'ah clerics and manifested mainly in the establishment of the Fatimid caliphate in Cairo. But the Ottoman Turks were Sunnis, with no particular inclination, much to their convenience, to overemphasise the factor of the Prophet's kinship in matters related to the effectiveness of government in the Islamic state. On both accounts, first, the delegation of the caliphate by the last Abbasīd caliph to the Turkish Sultan, the authenticity of which was not clear, and second, the premise that the caliphate did not have to rest exclusively with the Prophet's descendents, as in the view of the Sunnis, the Ottoman Sultan claimed the caliphate for himself.

The separation of religion and government was a distinctive diversion from the political features embedded in Islam as a doctrine that does not admit a separation between Church and state. Such diversion seemed to have opened the door for a wide application in different parts of the Islamic world particularly during the decay of the Ottoman Empire. Muslim rulers found in the separation a practical, if not convenient, solution to the problem of the involvement of the clerics, Ulama' in the affairs of government. The supporters of the separation of religion and politics had become stronger, and the application grew wider. During the wave of secularization that engulfed the Islamic world in the late nineteenth and early twentieth centuries when secularization was deemed as a twin of modernisation the argument for the separation of religion and politics became crucial. It was only in the late twentieth century, and particularly during and after the Iranian revolution of 1978–79, when the world had come to notice that the heads of state in Iran appeared in turbans and black robes, mixing politics with religion, that the world had realised that the demarcation line between Islam and politics had become less visible. Encouraged by the Iranian example, the support for uniting Islam and government re-emerged and grew stronger in different parts of the Muslim world.

Intellectual and Socio-Economic Impediments

Although the Ottomans have left a considerable legacy in arts, architecture, and military endeavour, their legacy of Islamic economics literature is rather limited. This is shown below

Islamic Economics Literature under the Ottomans

Compared with other aspects of development in architecture, work of arts and military organisation, the attention paid to economic thinking under the Ottomans was of a marginal nature. We could hardly witness any particular socio-economic work or cultural activity comparable to that of Muslim thinkers in the few preceding centuries. The work of Ibn-Khaldūn, (1332–1404) and to a far lesser degree that of al-Maqrizi after him (1364–1441), seemed to have stamped a seal on the last of the great socio-economic works of Muslim thinkers. The Ottoman Empire, it seems, had left very little legacy of a specifically socio-economic nature. This is not to say that there were not notable achievements by the writers of the period, there were, but these mainly involved bibliographical works, biographies, compilation and commentary works, as shown in the following examples (Hitti, 1963).

Hajji Khalifah (d. 1657), nicknamed by the Turks, Katib Chelebi (the young scriber), who started his career as an army clerk, produced a major bibliographic work on names and titles, *Kashf al-Zunūn in al-Asāmi w-al-Funūn* (removing the doubts related to names, titles, and terms of science). In this bibliography Hajj Khalifah arranged alphabetically all the Arabic, Persian and Turkish names of books that were known to him. Although Hajji Khalifah was Turk, he excelled as an Arabic writer, a rare example, and probably an exception that was not to be repeated among his Turkish contemporaries.

From Egypt came Abd-al-Wahhāb al-Sha'rānī (d. 1565), a Ŝūfī tried by the Orthodox Ulama' for claiming to have been speaking to angels and prophets. Al-Sha'rānī compiled the lives and history of all renowned Ŝūfīs in his "*al-Tabaqāt al-Kubra*" (the great classes or great layers).

Al-Zabidi was another example from Egypt. Al-Sayyid Murtada al-Zabidi (1737–1791), an Indian by birth, produced in Cairo a voluminous commentary on Al-Ghazālī's Iĥya' Ulūm al-Dīn.

Al-Jabarti, Abd-al-Rahman ibn Ĥassan al-Jabarti (d. 1822), who was appointed by Napoleon Bonaparte as a member of the Grand Council and held a chair of astronomy in al-Azhar produced a master piece entitled *Aja'ib al-Athār fi al-Tarājim w-al-Akhbār* (the wonders of relics in biographies and events).

In Lebanon the major writers were Maronite Christians the most renowned of whom was Yūsuf Sim'an al-Sim'ani (1687–1768) whose masterpiece Bibliotheca Orientalis embraced researches on a large number of Oriental manuscripts in Arabic, Hebrew and other oriental languages.

From Syria came Muĥammad al-Muhibbi (d. 1699) whose chief work was a collection of twelve hundred and ninety biographies of renowned Muslims who died in the century between 1591 and 1688, and Abd-al-Ghani al-Nabulsī (d. 1731) whose work focused mainly on the holy shrines and the legends surrounding them.

The above writings, though substantial and impressive, were more informative and instructive than innovative or creative. There were very little original thoughts or new ideas. The closure of the gate of jurisprudence was perhaps showing its effect.

A number of factors, stretching over a century or so, could be said to have contributed to the absence of an Ottoman Islamic legacy of literary achievements, particularly in Islamic economics. Some of these could be: the decline in the formal use of Arabic language, the closure of the gate of jurisprudence, the Western intellectual penetration, the alienation of religion in pursuit of secularization and the lack of encouragement of judicial work. These factors are briefly discussed below.

The Decline in the Formal Use of Arabic Language

The shift of the pendulum of political power to the Ottoman Turks could be said to have led to the decreasing role of Arabic language as the formal language of the Islamic state. Neither were the rulers of the state of Arab origin nor was Arabic their means of communication with their peoples. It may be true to say that the signs of separation between the masses and Arabic language could be witnessed earlier when the Persian language began to push its rival out of the scene, which was particularly the case after the increasing domain of the Persians prior to the fall of Baghdad to the Mongols in 1258. Nevertheless, it might be equally true to infer that, in contrast to the Abbasids who were Arabs and surrounded their court with an Arab entourage, the new caliphs were not Arab nor was their language Arabic. As such, the Arabic language would lose the opportunity of being the language of the masters of the land, and as a consequence of not being acknowledged as the formal language of communication in the caliphate court, it would be driven out of practice by court officials and be shun by the public at large in their formal communication with state officials. This was different from the case of the Abbasīd caliphs who, even if under the Persian influence they became figurative, they were still seen as Arabs and the Arabic language was still perceived as the formal language of the caliphate.

There were signs, however, indicating that the ruling Turks made sincere endeavours to project themselves as the preservers of the Islamic traditions including that of the language of the Qur'ān. They adopted the Arabic alphabets to their Turkish writing, which lasted until 1928. However, it may be argued that while the Persian genius had expressed itself in a splendid national literature (Nicholson, 1993) the Turkish rivalry did not seem to be a plausible Persian contestant. The Ottomans could not however be accused of a lack of enthusiasm for Islam, as they embraced the religion with tremendous zeal. Indeed, the Ottoman Empire had given Islam a driving force and unmistaken momentum for two centuries or so from the mid-fifteenth century onward.

The Western influence added a further reason for the eclipsed role of the Arabic language. Educationally, the medium of communication with the imported expertise from France, Italy and England was to be their own foreign languages, not Arabic, and Muslims in the Turkish and Turkish Egyptian army had to learn the language of their teachers. Missionary and other Western established schools had French and English as the linguistic medium of learning in Syria, Lebanon and Egypt. The attraction of Western modernization in as far as the language was concerned had driven intellectuals further into believing that to be included in the intellectual elite was to be seen as able to speak a Western language. Politically, with the increasing political dominance of western powers in the Muslim world, and the subjugation of the Arab Muslim regions, foreign forces ensured that school curricula included learning a Western language, and, even further, official government documentation was to be presented in both Arabic and Western languages. Many Syrians and Lebanese were able to speak French, Egyptians to speak English, Libyans to communicate in Italian, and Moroccans, Algerians and Tunisians to converse at ease in French. This continued to be the case until the mid twentieth century. This left an unfavourable legacy for the occupied countries after their liberation. For example, the Algerian government after liberation from the French occupation in the early 1960s had to embark on a serious programme of Arabicisation aimed at educating Algerians in the Arabic language. But the Ottoman Arabia, the cradle of Islam, remained pre-dominantly Arabic and from there and al-Azhar University in Cairo came notable Muslim scholars who continued to be intellectuals in their native Arabic tongues.

The Closure of the Gate of Jurisprudence

When the gate of jurisprudence was actually declared closed and what details surrounded the closure does not seem to be very clear. Some modern scholars even argue the contrary, maintaining that such a metaphoric gate was never declared shut. But historical texts refer to closure as being recommended by the jurists, Ulama', of the eleventh century or so in an attempt to curb intruders from injecting illegitimate juristic opinion under the claim of *ijtihād*. The closure was urged for several reasons:

By the eleventh century there appeared to be a fair mixture of scholars of different affiliation that may not be exactly Islamic. That did not meet the qualifications for *ijtihād*.

To begin with, for a jurist to claim *ijtihād*, he ought to fulfill strict conditions, of which the command of the language of the Qur'ān, Arabic, the full understanding of the Holy Text and the Sunnah of the Prophet, the complete knowledge of the General Consensus of the Prophet's Companions, are but some examples. There did not appear to Muslim jurists then that these conditions were entirely met in those newly comers to Islam who claimed the ability to engage in jurisprudence.

Second, it was feared that some new comers to the science of jurisprudence may have been under the influence of newly secular Muslim rulers who may have had a desire for a religious ruling, *fatwa*, to legitimise an unworthy secular inclination of their own.

Third, with the spread of several religious sects and subsets whose religious practice were not always generally accepted but sometimes doubted and very often frowned upon, there was a fear that the opinion and practice of these sects may be perceived, or misperceived, as in conformity to the genuine practices of the early devout Muslims. To put a halt to any process of legitimising these practices and to confine them, instead, to their sources which are the initiating sect leaders, there was a need, seemingly, to declare that no further process of general legitimisation through jurisprudence was to be exercised.

Fourth, which summarises the whole purpose of stopping any further work of jurisprudence, there was a need to stop false non-religious innovation, *bida'h*, under the false proclamation of religious modernisation, *tajdid*. To confirm the refusal of newness in the religion, the jurists declared that any false innovation is, *bida'h*, every *bid'ah* is misleading infidelity, *dhalalah*, and every misleading infidelity (and its innovator) is in Hell. Until the present day, accusing a person of introducing a *bida'h* can be a serious religious condemnation. Although the accusation does not necessarily imply the intention of taking a person to a religious court, it does cut deeply into the person's own religious pride and belief.

Western Intellectual Penetration

The Western influence during the Ottomans was not confined to commercial agencies. Encouraged by the success of commercial agencies, Christian missionaries looked to the east, as in the old days of the Crusades. The liberal policies adopted by some Muslim leaders added further encouragement. For example, the Lebanese Prince Fakhr-al-Dīn II (1590–1635) not only imported scientists and engineers from Italy, but also welcomed Christian missionaries mainly from the French Catholic church (Hitti, 1963). Before long, the French Catholics established centres in major cities and villages in the Lebanese and Syrian soil. During the Egyptian occupation of Syria (1831–40), the commander-in-chief Ibrahem, son of Muahmmad Ali of Egypt, declared, and forced, the right of non-Muslims to hold office in the local government, and proclaimed, and put into effect, the equality of all members of religions before the law. Resistance to his liberal policies was forcibly silenced. This, in addition to the general state of security, encouraged other churches from other denominations to follow the French catholic example. By the seventeenth and eighteenth centuries Christian missionary activities led to the establishment of churches in Syria and Lebanon. British and American Protestant missionaries established a strong presence in Lebanon, and in 1838 the Native Protestant Church of Syria was established. In 1857, during the reign of Khedive Sai'd (1854–63) the American United Presbyterian Mission began their activities in Egypt (ibid.).

Further signs of Western intellectual penetration that took place at the invitation or the welcoming gesture of the rulers could be also seen elsewhere in the decaying Ottoman Empire. In Syria and Lebanon, in addition to the Christian missionary activities, as we saw earlier, educational missionaries became significant. In 1830, the American School for Girls was founded in Beirut. In 1866, the Syrian Protestant College, later to be the American University of Beirut, was established, and in 1881, the Jesuit educational mission established the University of Saint Joseph in Beirut. Most of these schools are still providing educational services until today, and still regarded as exemplary models of education. With English being used as the medium of teaching and with curricula designed by American educationalists, the Islamic input in the educational programmes was well controlled and carefully measured. There was very little room, if at all, therefore, for a substantial existence of Islamic education. That seems to have remained the case until the latter part of the Twentieth century when the Islamic world witnessed what became known as Islamic revivalism that more of Islamic themes were seen to be included in the curricula.

The Alienation of Religion and Islamic Culture in Pursuit of Secularisation

Not all Western influence was forced upon Muslim states, however. Some was imported at the will of their rulers in pursuit of modernisation. The first of these rulers was Muĥammad Ali (1769–1848) who was appointed Egypt's governor, *pasha*, by the Porte in 1805 and who is frequently referred to in history books as the founder of modern Egypt. Prior to Ali, the Napoleonic expedition brought with it features of Western development that was not known to Muslims before. The Arabic press was an obvious example. Brought by Bonaparte, the Arabic press was not to be used for the development of the learning process of the Egyptians as much as it was for the publishing of leaflets in Arabic in the 1798 French propaganda campaign that aimed at questioning the populace and winning their support. Later, after Bonaparte, the press served as the corner stone in establishing a full fledged press house in the Cairo quarter of Bulaq, Maktabat Bulaq (ibid.). The press was the first of its kind as it was a novelty to Muslims in Egypt and elsewhere, and as such it was a demonstrable example of Western modernization. Furthermore, the French army brought with it scientists and interpreters who with the discovery of Stone of Rashīd, were able to unravel the Hieroglyphic alphabets. The seemingly French preparation for a long stay in the Egyptian soil signaled an abrupt end after the destruction of the French fleet by the British navy and the French defeat in the battle of Alexandria in 1801. In eighty years or so the British army was to land at the Egyptian Mediterranean ports, to remain there for almost eighty five years.

Impressed by the French example of modernization, Muĥammad Ali embarked on a programme of reform that, though it was harsh, brought the country out of the backwardness of the Mamlūks. In his zeal for modernisation he established schools of engineering, in 1817, and another of medicine, in 1827, with teachers imported mainly from France. Military and educational missions were brought from France and Italy, and missions from the Egyptians were sent to study in France, Italy, Austria and England at the cost of the state. Politically, he rid himself from the Mamlūks once and for all by arranging what is known until today in the schools' history books as the Slaughter of the Citadel. Ostensibly invited for a party in the Cairo's well-fortified Citadel, the Mamlūks were directed to a narrow passage where they were slain and slaughtered by his guards. With the exception of the very few, the lives of all the Mamlūks of Egypt were put to an end. In his economic policies, Muĥammad Ali was equally harsh. He confiscated all the land of Egypt and declared himself the sole proprietor of the land, and by creating a monopolistic ownership of land and products he was the only producer, manufacturer and contractor. The conditions of work for the conscription labour for irrigation and water-canal projects and state enterprises were so sever that many thousands lost their lives and others had to amputate part of their hands to render themselves unfit to work (Armstrong, 2000). Western penetration in science and engineering developed into a western intellectual penetration in Egypt. During the reign of Muahmmad Ali's grandson Ismāīl (1863–79), who was more inclined towards the Americans than the Europeans, an American college was established in Upper Egypt in 1865, and the American College for Girls in Cairo was founded in 1865.

Lack of Encouragement of Judicial Work

The lack of enthusiasm towards the work of jurists, as opposed to architectural and artistry achievements, under the Ottoman Turks may be mentioned as a further reason for the notable absence of judicial work, including that on economics. True the Ottomans showed a particular zeal towards compiling some of the best talents of the conquered lands in the empire's capital, with the intention of utilising them for the glory of the imperial state, but it is also true to notice that these were not of the juristic type. The talents needed to glorify the empire were mainly of the vocationally artistic type in architecture and industry. Artistry was what was needed in the new military Empire not the Sharī'ah, and artistry was what the Ottoman administration seemed to have aimed to achieve in art and architecture, not jurisprudence. In addition as the state was mainly a military state, with an inherent tendency towards militarisation, as was depicted in their inherited system of the Turks Seljuqs, the Ottomans had very little to offer contemporary jurists to develop their work. Further, the Ottomans who were keen on the development of their military state may have found the views of jurists, the most of whom looked suspiciously at any attempt of "modernisation", too rigid and too slow to keep up with the empire's pace of needed innovation. Moreover, the Jurists on their part, seeing the economic hardships of the population, may have come to realise that the ultimate objective of the state, as it was, was not geared towards the realization of welfare to the society as much as it was to achieve the welfare to the state and the Ŝulṭān. Sharī'ah therefore was left lagging behind.

The role of the Ulama' under the Ottomans was of a mixed nature. At the early start of the Ottoman rule, the Rightly Guided theologians, the Ulama', and the Sharī'ah, enjoyed a privileged treatment by the new masters of the land. In their desire to be seen as devout Muslims with sincere intentions to promote Sharī'ah in the empire, or merely their wish to control the masses particularly the Arabs through the device of religion, the promotion of Sharī'ah by the Ottomans was given an official shape. They set up the Ulama' in offices and establishments and established Sharī'ah courts, probably for the first time, headed by judges, *qadhis*, who were assisted by a religious consultant, *mufti*, to provide interpretation of the law and derive a religious opinion on the case in hand. These courts with their *qadhis* and *muftis* were part of the official establishment where positions were assigned by Ottoman officials, and income and subsidies paid by the Treasury (Armstrong, 2000). Furthermore, religious schools, *madrasah*, were also organized with teachers appointed, like *qadhis* and *muftis*, as part of the government office. Sharī'ah courts served their purpose for very long and were still operating in Egypt until the mid 1950's when they were abolished by the secularized government of Egypt of 1952.

When Istanbūl's government was strong the relationship between the Ulama' and government was a relationship of cooperation. But when the decay began to show its effect on the central government, whenever the Ulama' had grounds for expressing an objection, or an unfavourable opinion about the conditions of the people, they were curbed and had their properties confiscated (ibid.). With their livelihood under the control of government, they had too much to lose, and, consequently, very little to say. In Muĥammad Ali's Egypt, for example, the Ulama' were harshly treated. Of the properties Muĥammad Ali confiscated, there were religious endowments, *waqf*, which were properties donated by devout Muslims for the purpose of supporting the poor, religious causes, students of Sharī'ah and Ulama' (Armstrong, 2000). That was a loss of a source of sustenance which aimed to silence the Ulama'. But sporadic resentment mainly from non-official Ulama' had arisen. Abd-al-Wahhāb al-Sha'rānī (d.1565) was a particular example. Despite his weaknesses, belief in superstition and his claim that he could communicate with angels and prophets, he was concerned about the state of misery and poverty, which the Egyptian peasants suffered under the dual control of the Turkish *pasha* and Mamlūk *bey*. Seeing the harshness of tax collectors in levying and collecting the taxes from the peasants, the cultivators of the land, and how the peasants had to sell the whole produce and sometimes their working ox to avoid imprisonment for not being able to pay the tax, and how every lucrative business was crushed with confiscation, al-Sha'rānī was highly critical. In his bitterness he contrasted the miserable lot of the peasantry under the Turkish regime with their comparative prosperity under the Mamlūks (Nicholson 1993). But al-Sha'rānī was not a regular paid *qadhi* nor was he a member of the government corp. He was a simple mystic Ŝūfī who lived on very little and did not give serious attention to materialistic matters. But this resentment was not to be let continue. By conspiracy or otherwise, al-Sha'rānī was to be tried by the official Ulama' for claiming to have spoken to God and angels.

As the Ulama' were curbed and religious studies were marginalized in preference of secularization, it was not surprising that the Ulama' felt alienated, grew resentful to the changes that were brought under the band of modernisation.

How much each factor of the above had contributed to the negligence of work on literature activities in general and socio-economic issues in particular, is difficult to tell. But it would not be exaggerated to say that, on the whole, these factors did not help provide the right environment for a work of this nature. After three centuries or so the intellectual life burst into flames again in what became known as reform movements as we will see later. On the bright side, it could be said, in reconciliation, that the Ottomans, as military rulers, paid considerable attention to law and order. This could have helped the growth of the spirit of capitalism had the socio-economic conditions been favourable.

The Fall of the Ottoman Empire

After a few centuries of military success, the Ottoman Empire began to undergo some decay. This could be related to several factors: economic decay resulting from the decentralization of government to province rulers who later exploited the weakening of the government, the discovery of the Cape of Good Hope, and the Western commercial and political penetration. These are highlighted below.

The Economic Decline

The economic decay in the Ottoman Empire could be attributed to two main factors: the maladministration of the Turkish provinces and the shift of trade route from land to sea after the discovery of the Cape of Good Hope.

Maladministration

The provincial maladministration could be clearly witnessed in Egypt and Syria. With an average tenure in office of only two years or less, the turnover of the appointed Turkish viceroys, *pashas*, in these two countries reached a phenomenal figure. In the first hundred and eighty years (1517–1697) there were one hundred and thirty three *pashas* in succession in Damascus and in the two hundred and eighty years of Turkish rule in Egypt there were no less than a hundred Turkish *pashas* changing office (Hitti, 1963). While the intention for the short tenure of office was to block the way against any attempt by *pashas* to grow in power enough to break away from the central government in Istanbūl, the policy led to adverse economic effect with devastating results. Knowing the short tenure of their office, and bearing in mind the hefty cost they bore in getting the provincial seats, which were effectively purchased from the Porte, the *pashas* had a short pay-back-period in which they could recover their capital and make a profit. With heavy taxes, relentless treatment from rulers, both the Turkish *pashas* and the local Mamlūk *beys* in Egypt or *walis* in Syria, and with no economic reform, the natives fell in a deep misery and poverty. By the middle of the eighteenth century, what was once the Fertile Crescent, stretching from east Syria to the Euphrates, turned into desert and has remained so until the present time (Bonne, 1945). By the end of that century the entire Syrian population had decreased to about a million and a half and the Egyptian population dropped to one-third of its size (ibid.). Iraq had similar poor administration to that of Egypt and Syria. With similar *pashas* from the Porte and local lords and Mamlūks struggling for power and influence in the province, the misery of the populace continued. What distinguished Iraq from other countries, however, was that by embracing the Holy Shrines of the Shī'ah, the tomb of Imam Ali in Najaf, and his grandson's al-Ĥusayn in Karbal'a, and of the seventh and ninth imams' in al-Kazimayn, the country was a stronghold of Shi'ism and as such Iraq had a strong link with the Shī'ah Ŝafawīd Empire to the east (Armstrong, 2000). It was not unusual for Shi'ī inhabitants to cross the borders between the Ottoman's Iraq and the Ŝafawīd land, and back, to seek help and assistance which was invariably given. Conceivably the Shī'ah Ŝafawids developed interest in the Shī'ah holy land in Iraq and their concern grew over their fellow Shi'īs in the neighbouring country. The interest, and the concern, developed into attempts made by the Ŝafawids Shahs to take over Iraq and although some succeeded in occupying Baghdad for a decade or so, Iraq returned as a province of the Ottomans (ibid.). The strong link between the Shī'ah regime in the Ŝafawīd Empire, now Iran, and the Shī'ah holy shrines and population in Iraq has always presented a dilemma in war and peace until today. The strategic importance of Iraq never ceased. Lying on the trade route between West and East, Iraq was of a particular interest to the English East India Company in the early seventeenth century, and having the second largest oil reserve in the world, after Saudi Arabia, Iraq has recently become of particular interest to the world at large.

The Discovery of the Cape of Good Hope

The discovery of the Cape of Good Hope added a further reason for the economic decay of the Ottoman Empire. Although the discovery of the Cape (1498) and the advance of the Portuguese and other European nations into the Indian Ocean was beneficial to Europeans, it had its negative effect on the trade route that was running through the Arab eastern states. It diverted part of the European trade that had for centuries pursued its routes through land in the north and the Red Sea in the south, to another route outside the Islamic world. The Muslims' spice trade, for example, was severely damaged by European competition, which had the opportunity to channel these valuable products from the very source of production without having to pass through the Islamic world (Raymond, 1981). The new route had substituted the Portuguese for Muslims in the international trade. Other provinces in the Empire suffered similar effect, as Islamic lands were commercially avoided. Furthermore, the discovery of America in 1492 shifted the centre of the universe westward. All had led to undesirable economic effect on the Islamic world. It was three and half centuries later that the route of the Cape of Good Hope was to face sever competition when the Suez Canal was opened in 1869. Only then, the Red Sea, which was once the centre of trade, came back to life.

The Western Commercial and Political Influence

The Western influence in the Ottoman Empire began with marked commercial, cultural and intellectual penetration of the Islamic world, which was the inherited consequences of the Crusades. Although the Crusades led to unfavourable political and military results, they helped increase the interaction between Muslims in the East and Non-Muslims, mainly Christians, in the West. On the commercial side, one of the effects of the Crusades was the establishment of new organised commercial communities in the ports of the Levant. Italian merchants, for example, formed organised communities subject to their chiefs and governed by their own laws (Lewis, op. cit.) Notably, the recapture of these ports by Muslim did not seem to have revoked these foreign communities or put an end to their commercial activities. On the contrary, Muslim rulers were careful not to discourage this trade, which was advantageous to them as well as to those involved in trade (ibid.) This encouraged the appearance of other European communities in other parts of the Mediterranean ports such as Alexandria in Egypt.

Their residence was organised through bilateral treaties between governments. Numerous agreements, that became known later as capitulations, were concluded between European states and Turkey, Egypt and other Muslim Mediterranean countries authorising the citizens of the state to trade and reside in the other country without being subject to the disabilities imposed on non-trading subjects (Lewis, op. cit.). The first of these agreements was concluded in 1521 between Sulyman the Magnificent and the Venetians. In 1535 the French were granted their capitulations and the English followed suit in 1580. This encouraged trade and helped European commerce to flourish and expand. The side effect of these capitulations, however, became obvious when European communities grew significantly in influence and power, while the political power of the host state was in decline. When commercial disputes arose between European and local traders, European traders demanded, and were granted, exemptions from the rulings of local laws, in preference to their own laws. The application of foreign laws in their homeland was no doubt confusing to local traders who did not know the foreign law, which put them at a disadvantage in relation to their foreign counterparts. The legal complications led eventually to the establishment of what became known as Mixed-Courts; with yet further complications added to the judicial system. Interestingly, some of these courts still functioned until the late twentieth century when it was only abolished as part of the growing concern with national independence and some court buildings in Alexandria Egypt are still displaying the engraved stone, "The Mixed Court".

The lesson was later to be learned. When the host country is strong, privileges to foreign investments could be beneficial to the country and could spur economic development but when the host state is economically weak and politically feeble, privileges could lead to the concentration of power, first economic, and second political, in the hands of foreign agencies.

By the last quarter of the nineteenth century the political penetration of Western power became obvious. The opening of the Suez Canal in 1869 increased the political interest of the Great Powers, England and France, in Egypt even further. In 1879, almost a century after Napoleon's unsuccessful campaign to occupy the Egyptian soil, England and France put the country under their dual control, and Khedive Ismāīl, in whose reign the Canal was opened, was deposed. The defeat of the Egyptian army by the British in 1882 provided England with the right opportunity to occupy the country and send Ahmad Orabi, the Egyptian officer who led the campaign against the British, to exile. The country was later to be declared a British protectorate after World War I, and to remain under the British occupation, though with a quasi-independent government, until 1952. In 1936, however, and as a result of the Egyptians struggle against the British occupation, an Anglo-Egyptian treaty was concluded that confined the British army to the Canal Zone, over one hundred kilometers from the capital Cairo. The country, however, with its king and people, remained under the British command, and it was only in 1954 that the British soldiers departed from Port Said.

The countries of the Arab Crescent were under the British and French mandates, Palestine and Iraq were under the British and Syria and Lebanon were under the French. That remained the case until, as a result of the intensive struggle of the people under occupation, the last French soldier leaving Syria in 1945 gave the country its independence, and in 1927 Iraq, which was governed under a twenty-five treaty with Britain, was declared independent.

The Ŝafawīd Empire

The Ŝafawīd dynasty (1502–1736) was named after the great grand father of its founder, Sheikh Ŝafi-al-Dīn (the highly refined man of the faith), whose family was said to be descendants from the seventh Shīʾah Imam Musa al-Kazim. The founder, Ismāīl, the sixth descendant of the Sheikh, conquered Tabriz in 1501 and subjugated the rest of Iran in the following few years. Ismāīl, who turned Twelver, declared that the Shī'ah was the official religion of the new Persian state, a religion which remained in Iran until the present day. Ismāīl, or carrying the Persian title, Shah Ismāīl, embarked on a mission to eliminate the Sunni opposition in Iran. His enthusiasm for opposing the Sunnis took him across his borders. In 1510 he drove the Sunni Uzbecks out of Khurasān forcing them north to the Oxus and collided with the Ottomans in 1514, but to be defeated by Ŝulṭān Salim I (1512–20) and as a result he had his capital Tibriz, Mesopotamia, and Armenia occupied by the Turks. Soon the Ŝafawids realized that extremism in opposing the Sunnis was futile. They, instead, embarked on a programme of intellectual reforms where Arab Shī'ah Ulama' were imported for the purpose of teaching the people a more traditional form of Twelver Shi'ism (Armstrong, 2000). In his programmes of reform, Shah Abbās I (1588–1629), built schools, *madrasah*, as centres of teaching and learning, where the Ulama' would teach and reside, and he provided financial support to both the teaching Ulama' and the learning candidates. Shah Abbās's capital in Isfahan enjoyed a cultural renaissance, like that of the Italian renaissance in Europe, drawing inspiration from Persian culture, and with parks, palaces, and huge squares, imposing mosques and *madrasah*, Isfahan was a magnificent city (ibid.). The Ŝafawīd *madrasah* had generated several scholars and Ulama' whose views have shaped the Iranian's way of thinking until the present day. This was in sharp contrast to the Ottomans who looked mainly towards Western culture for modernization.

Role of Ulama' under the Ŝafawids

Compared with their Sunni counterpart under the Ottomans, the Shī'ah Ulama' under the Ŝafawids had relatively more operational autonomy. Although, they enjoyed the state's financial support, like their Sunni neighbours under the Ottomans, they managed somehow to maintain their intellectual independence. As they were Arab Shī'ah who were brought to shoulder the educational and legal responsibilities of Shi'ism, they were inclined to confine themselves to these responsibilities avoiding, at least for most of them, official government positions. Whether they as immigrants were particularly concerned about taking up a rank that would unfavourably elevate them above the native subjects, or they were genuinely keen on promoting the Shī'ah faith among the populace, is difficult to tell. But there was a particular distinction between them and the Sunnis, which had helped reinforce their position among the population. While the Sunnis would acknowledge a secular ruler who was not a descendant of the Prophet as head of state, or caliph, the Shīʾah, as we know by now, would insist that the caliphate ought to be resting within the Prophet's line of heirs particularly that of Caliph Ali. And as the last heir to the caliphate was hidden, the Hidden Imam, the Twelver Shiʾī Ulamaʾ regarded themselves the only legitimate representatives of the Imam. The Shahs were accepted as heads of state until the Hidden Imam would return, but the shah was not a replacement to the Imam. The Imam rules with the knowledge passed on to him from one imam to the next, as bestowed on them by God. And it was only the Ulama', not the shah, who would be the vessel of this knowledge until the return of the most taught human: the Hidden Imam (Armstrong, 2000). Conceivably, that gave the Shiʾī Ulamaʾ a great power that was not to be enjoyed by their Sunni counterparts.

A further distinction between the Shiʾī Ulamaʾ and the Sunni need to mentioned. In contrast to the Sunni, the Shiʾī Ulamaʾ were, and are, in support of innovation so much so that the innovative a'alim (Plural Ulamaʾ) is described as *mujtahid* (from *ijtihād*, exertion of self to reach a religious opinion through reasoning). Further, they never agreed to "close the gate" of jurisprudence. This is in sharp contrast to the Sunni who regarded, and some still regard, an innovation as *bida'h* which would merit Hell Fire. This has provided the Shīʾah with a continuous stream of innovation in judicial religious thinking.

Intellectual Development under the Ŝafawids

Literary intellectual activities under the Ŝafawids seemed to have been more active than that in the Ottoman Empire. Three factors could be said to have provided a suitable environment for literary intellectual activities: firstly, the relatively political and economic stability of the state, secondly, the support of the state, and thirdly the distinguished position of the Ulamaʾ.

First, by being smaller than the Ottoman Empire, the Ŝafawīd Empire was more politically manageable, hence more politically stable than its Turkish neighbours. It was only during the ideological and expansionist attempts of Shah Ismāīl, when he tried to rid the empire from the Sunnis and to enlarge his boundaries against the Turks, that the empire experienced lack of political stability. Although he had some success with the Sunni Uzbecks pushing them from Khurasān to the north of the Oxus, he was less successful with the Sunni Ottomans who defeated him in 1514 and had his empire truncated. But internally there was more political stability as Shah Ismāīl was successful in keeping the empire overwhelmingly Shī'ah. That minimized, if not eradicated, the political disturbances arising from a possible internal schism between the Shi'is and the Sunnis. From the seventeenth centuries onward the country has been Shī'ah until modern times.

Second, the state's support for intellectual development that was most noticeable during the reign of Shah Abbās I (1588–1629). In his zeal to enhancing the understanding of the Shī'ah religion, Shah Abbās I (1588–1629), embarked on a religio-educational reform by importing Arab Shī'ah from abroad, built schools, *madaris*, (sing. *madrasah*) as centres of teaching and learning, and provided the most needed financial support to both the teaching Ulama' and the learning candidates.

Third, the position of the Ulama' under the Ŝafawids was not as marginalised as it was under the Ottomans. Though they were supported by the state, the Ulama' were deemed as the teachers of the Twelverism to the masses. Their financial support came mainly in lump sums and generous gifts instead of small regular amounts. This made them more independent. Furthermore, by refraining from undertaking government posts they were not under the administrative control of government as the Sunni Ulama' were under the Ottomans. And if there were a government pressure on them they would leave for the most sacred Shī'ah shrine, the tomb of Imam Ali, in the neighbouring Najaf, in Iraq (ibid.).

Of the Shi'ī Ulama' the names of Mir Dimad, Mulla Sadra, and Muĥammad Bāqir Majlisi occupy the top of the list. Mir Dimad (d. 1631) and Mulla Sadra (d. 1640) were in support of mysticism and falsafah and founded a school of mystical philosophy at Iŝfahan. They advocated that the Ulama' should not dismiss science and philosophy as a way of thinking while holding to their intuitiveness and spirituality in seeking the truth. Mulla Sadra did not see a separation between political preparation and spiritual training.

But the name of Muĥammad Bāqir Majlisi (d. 1700) stands out as one of the most renowned Ulama' of the Shī'ah. He was against mysticism, *irfan*, and religious philosophy, *falsafah*, and advocated strongly the need to focus on jurisprudence, *fiqh*, in learning and teaching Islam. His influence can still be detected until the present day (ibid.). Majlisi resistance of the teaching of mysticism was directed to the earlier school of Shi'ism that was founded by Mir Dimad and Mulla Sadra a few decades before him. To link spiritual enlightenment with the world of politics, he advocated, as elucidated in his al-Afsan al-Arbaah (the fourfold journey), that the political leader should undergo a form of spiritual training before embarking on a career in politics.

There does not seem to be a notable work on Islamic economics under the Ŝafawids, however. The Shī'ah jurists' preoccupation with teaching the public the Shī'ah's doctrine seemed to have left little room for literature on Islamic economics. However, from the Shī'ah, a notable piece in Islamic economic thinking emerged. "Iqtisāduna", Our Economics, is a major piece of work on Islamic economics by an eminent Shi'ī scholar, Muĥammad Bāqir al-Sadr. The book was written in the late nineteen sixties. The book will be examined in chapter nine.

The Mongol Empire

The persecution of the Sunnis in the Ŝafawīd Empire and the hostility the Ŝafawīd emperor Shah Ismāīl against the Uzbecks, was in effect a reason d'être for the establishment of the Moghul Empire. The initial founder of the Moghul, or Mongol, empire was Babūr (d. 1530), whose memory came back to life in December 1992 when members of the Hindu fundamentalist party, Bharatiya Janarta Party (BJP), dismantled his mosque in ten minutes, under the rolling cameras of the press and a watching army, claming that the mosque was built by Muslims on a destroyed Indian temple (Armstrong, 2000). Babūr was a Sunni fugitive who fled to the Afghan Kabūl during Ismāīl's war with the Uzbecks then managed to establish his control over the remains of the Mongol empire that was left by Timur Lane in north India. But his initial success was to be hindered by the factional power struggle among the Afghan amirs, which lasted until 1555. In 1560, Akbar (1542–1605), a descendant of Babūr began to establish his authority over the amirs until he was finally acknowledged as the undisputed ruler of the Empire. Retaining the old Mongol system of a military government under the direct premiership of the Ŝulṭān, Akbar pushed the frontiers further and the Mongol Empire began to expand to include Hindustan, the Punjab, Malva, and the Deccan. For his novelty of thinking, his desire for innovation, and wish to build the Empire on a perfect model of society, Ŝulṭān Akbar was indeed the king who turned philosopher. He merits be included among Muslim reformers and Islamic intellectuals and thinkers.

The Intellectual Development in the Indian Subcontinent

In the Sunni Indian subcontinent, the wind of intellectual development, and of reform, seemed to have blown much earlier than it did in the neighbouring empires. The early development came from the highest in the hierarchy, the shah of the empire himself. Realizing the religious and ethnic diversity of the Indian community in his empire, Shah Akbar adopted a policy of the equality of all religions, and, in addition, castes and races, *mhabat-al-kull.*

From India came a welcomed, and a long waited for, change in the writing of Muslim thinkers; Shah Wali-allah came with his *hujjah Allah al-baligha*, a master piece in socio-economic and government governance, which is also discussed below.

Shah Akbar and maĥabbat—el-kull: the King Philosopher

Shah Akbar seemed to have been a pantheist who believed in the equality of all religions. More important, he practiced what he preached and adopted a policy in ruling his Mongolian empire in India on this basis. To understand his policy it might be worthwhile to link his ideas with that of Ibn-al-Arabi who was a Ŝūfī Muslim theo-philosopher and who introduced the idea of the equality of all religions.

Muĥammad ibn-Ali Muhyi-al-Dīn ibn al-Arabi, was a mystic thinker who left his fingerprints on the work of some Muslim thinkers for centuries to come. He was a Hispano-Arab who was born in Mursiyah in 1165 and after growing in popularity in Seville until 1201–2 he settled in the East until he died in Damascus in 1240. What concerns us in his teachings is his conclusion that God and the universe is one, and there is no real difference between God and His creation as His creation is part of His will. In conclusion, Ibn-al-Arabi formulated his theory of the unity of the universe stating that God would be found in all religions. As a consequence, to him, all religions were equal and should be treated on an equal footing. Ibn-al-Arabi's philosophy flourished after him and was developed by subsequent scholars into various derived concepts such as universal peace, '*sulĥ-el-kull*', and universal love, '*maĥabbat-el-kull*' (Mahmoud, 1986).

Shah Akbar's approach to religion seemed to have been diverting away from the strict rules of the Sharīʾah with distinct inclination towards Ŝūfīsm and Religious Philosophy, *falsafah*. Either for practical reasons, of running an Empire with a wide diversity of religions, or for personal reasons motivated by his self inner belief, Akbar seemed to be wanting to develop a model society in which all are equal despite of their race or religion. His policies worked to the advantage of the people and he was successful in managing the peace in a well diversified empire of religions and culture until his death.

Shah Akbar did not attempt to force the populace to convert to his Sunni doctrine. The Muslims were the ruling minority, and had he tried a forcible conversion, religious fractions would perhaps have torn the Empire apart. Every Hindu caste had its own religious practices, and Buddhists, Jacobites, Jews, Jains, Christians, Zoroastrians, Sunni Muslims and Ismāīlis, had all been allowed to worship without hindrance (Armstrong, 2000). During the fourteenth and fifteenth centuries, Hindus of all castes and even a few Muslims had joined forces in establishing a spiritualized, contemplative, form of monotheism, which led to sectarian intolerance. The Sikh religion, founded by Guru Nanak (d. 1539) had grown from these circles, insisting on the unity and compatibility of Hinduism and Islam. Akbar went even one mile further; he abolished the Jizyah tax. Furthermore, to woo the Hindus he became vegetarian and gave up hunting which was frowned upon by other religions as blood sports. Moreover, he built temples for Hindus, and in 1575 set up a "house of worship" where scholars of all religions could meet for discussion, and founded his own Ŝūfī order, dedicated to "divine monotheism", *Tawhīd-e ilahi*, based on the premise that the one God could reveal Himself in any rightly guided religion (ibid.). He was exemplary of religious tolerance, reflecting in his policies on the central theme of ibn-al-Arabi.

For his novelty of thinking, adaptation of the Islamic doctrine to serve the community best, Shah Akbar is suited to be included among Muslim reformers, even if he was a king. Rightly, Shah Akbar was a king who turned into a philosopher and reformer.

Shah Wali-allah

Born in Delhi in the Indian subcontinent in 1702, where he lived until he died in 1763, Qutb al-Dīn (the pivot of Islam) Abd al-Rahman, known as Shah Wali-Allah, had been a prominent figure in the intellectual history of Indian Muslims from the nineteen into the twentieth century.

From Shah Akbar's ideas of the unification of religions to the social and economic ideas of the Ŝūfī reformer Shah Walli-Allah there was a considerable development that was not always favourable. The opposition to the idea of religious universality began to be heard and made itself distinctly obvious by the teachings of yet another Ŝūfī, Ahmad Sirhindī (d. 1625). Sirhindī called for the return to the Sharī'ah and in addressing the core of Ibn-al-Arabi's philosophy, the inspiration to Shah Akbar's policies, he advocated that the unity with God can only be achieved through observing His rules through the application of the Sharī'ah. He called for the return to the basic teachings of Islam as clarified in the Sharī'ah and to the purge of Islam from the intruding philosophical ideas particularly those of mystic Ŝūfīsm and Shi'ī rituals. Sirhindī's views found support in the policies of Shah Aurengzebe (1658–1707) who reversed his grandfather's policies of religious pluralism with strict severity. Shi'ī rituals were curbed, Hindu festivals were met with less enthusiasm from the emperor, the Jizyah tax was re-instated, and a wave of hatred erupted and sectarianism spread in the Indian empire (Armstrong, 2000). Although the intention of Aurengzebe in returning to the Sharī'ah may be understood, his application of the rules seemed to have been taken to an unjustifiable extreme. The results were devastating. By the death of Aurengzebe, the empire was in a state of disintegration with Hindus and Sikhs beginning to look for a state of their own.

Muslims who were the ruling minority were put under pressure internally and externally. Indigenously, the pressure came from the Hindu and Sikh uprising, while exogenously, it came from the increasing political influence of the well established British trade in the region. Faced with a possibility of being controlled by non-Islamic forces, Hindus and Sikhs from within and, or, the British from outside, and with the consequence of being reduced to a minority caste, Muslims began to question their roles and identity. How Muslims, and Islam, could be returned to its glory and restore its fading influence, was a question that was more often than not asked by many Muslim thinkers during the ebb and tide of the politics of Islam. The answer has very often become the same: the return to Islamic values. An important figure who contributed to answering this question in the Indian subcontinent was the Ŝūfī thinker Shah Walli-Allah.

In his religio-political vision, Qutb al-Dīn Abd al-Rahman, known as Shah Wali-Allah, of Delhi continued the vision of Ahmad Sirhindī (d. 1625) before him, and indeed those before Sirhindī such as ibn-Taymīya (1263–1328). Like his predecessors, Shah Wali-Allah emphasized that the reason for the weakness in Muslims was the diversion from the path of the Sharī'ah, and the way to restore Islamic identity and dignity was to return to the Sharī'ah. But Shah Wali-Allah did not hesitate to divert from the thoughts of Sirhindī when he found it necessary to do so. He saw that the political situation in India had radically changed since the time of Sirhindī and he propounded a system that would be congenial to the spiritual environment of the Indian subcontinent, and at the same time calculated to regenerate Islamic forces (Fazlur Rahman, 1970). For example, he went a step further by emphasizing that the Sharī'ah should be "adapted" to suit the prevailing conditions of life in the subcontinent. Adaptation would imply innovation in *ijtihād*, the self exertion in reaching a religious rule based on reasoning, to accommodate new socio-economic and religio-political situations. This view would certainly be in contrast with the views of another reformer Muĥammad ibn-Abdel-Wahhāb who appeared in al-Hijaz in the late eighteen century calling for the return to the Sharī'ah but condemning any innovation in it through *ijtihād* as being anti-religious, *'bida'h'*. Furthermore, in his endeavour to consolidate all religious forces, Shah Wali-Allah was in favour of accepting Ŝūfīs and their rituals in the new movement for reform rather than rejecting them.

The socio-economic issues were of a particular concern to Wali-Allah as we will see in his writing shortly. He attacked the social and economic injustice in society, criticized the heavy taxes to which the peasantry was subjected, and called upon the Muslims to build a territorial state which might be integrated into an international Muslim super-state (ibid.). He emphasized other factors such as the need for Muslims to unite in facing their enemies, both from within and outside, and to mend their sectarian differences. Muslims should aim in his view to have the upper hand politically and military and this can be achieved through return and unity; return to Islamic rules as in the Sharī'ah and unity with one another despite sectarian differences. Shah Wali-Allah seemed to have been more of an innovator than a follower, and of revolutionary than evolutionary. His views continued to be popular among the Muslims of India well into the twentieth century.

The Economic Thought of Shah Wali-Allah

The political environment of Shah Wal-Allah, as was depicted above, was a case of Muslim's disorientation, disillusion, loss of power over what used to be a Muslim empire, and almost a loss of identity. His major work *Hujjat Allah al-Bālighah* (Allah's Overwhelming Proof) is still studied by Muslims until today as an exemplary treatise that blends the Holy Text with the power of reasoning in searching for Islamic ideals. Even with the norms of today, the anthropological analysis of Shah Wali-Allah seems remarkable. For that, his views deserve to be given special attention in a book of this kind.

The central theme of his work is social justice, conceivably in reflection to the prevailing injustice in his time, and state governance. This is based not only on the fundamental concept of social justice in Islam but also on "*irtifāq*". The emphasis on "*irtifāq*" is an emphasis on the need of individuals for one another, as *irtifāq* connotes the meaning of co-operation and the collective effort necessitated to accomplish a mission economic or otherwise (Jalboni, 1992, Baljon, 1992).

While *irtifāq* may not be so required in a primitive form of living, or what might be called loosely a primitive society, it becomes a necessity in a more developed form of community living together, and the more the community life develops the more becomes the needs for *irtifāq*. In an advanced complicated society where excel in skill and specialization in expertise are the main features, co-operation and collectivity of task performance, *irtifāq*, becomes inevitable. By the mere reasoning, as collectivity is necessary for the development, particularly economic development, collectivity in sharing the benefits of work becomes of equal necessity.

In a logically progressive manner, Shah Wali-Allah proceeded to look into the various phases of life, which he enumerated as four phases, beginning from the purely individualistic form, or the primitive or jungle life, to the final form of life which is the internationalization phase. It was as if he anticipated the globalization as we know it today. In this last phase, he devoted considerable attention to the problems of an advanced society: duties of the ruler, or government using modern terms, agreement of people on the forms of co-operation, *irtifaqats* (plural of irtifaqah), causes of corruption, and the need for the proper distribution of labour. Conceivably, as in line with his thinking, Islamic rules, Sharīʾah must be observed and Islam must prevail. It is remarkable to observe in Shah Wali-Allah's teachings that if injustice prevails, people may rise in revolution if the circumstances were compelling.

The fourth and final phase in the development of society, in Shah's deliberation is particularly interesting. It comes when the state becomes large and the boundaries extend too far for a central government to be in full control. Decentralization seems to be what Shah Wali-Allah advocates as he suggested that the state would be divided into provinces with a ruler, governor, heading each province. The province should be managed on a self-sufficient basis where it would have its army, income resources, and administration, all under the rulership of the central ruler who should be powerful enough to hold the province accountable to him and have exemplary ideal for others to follow. The emphasis in Shah's view seems to be on the powerful ruler who governs not only by force and assertiveness but also, which is equally important, by giving his subjects a good example of himself.

On governance, Shah Wali-Allah explains that the need for ruler, or government, is necessitated by the fact that although, ideally, people should have mutual care for each other, this may not be the case and by the virtue of the great number of population in the society a conflict of interest may arise. A political order would therefore be required. The order needs to be headed by a ruler, and the ruler should fulfill certain qualifications. From here Shah Wali-Allah proceeded to examine the qualifications that ought to be fulfilled in a ruler and good government. To begin with, the ruler should be elected. But the election, interestingly enough, is not, in Shah's mind, to be exercised by the masses, instead it is to be undertaken by the wise and headmen of the community. Is this a reflection of the state of the low level of educational awareness in India at the time, which would render the populace incapable of choosing their ruler, or is a continuation of a late practice of the Islamic norm of paying allegiance to the potential ruler, baiʾah? It is difficult to tell. Nevertheless, it is a sound approach to safeguard the community from the mishaps of a rigged election.

To counter any possibility of a misuse of power or influence of the electing party over the elected ruler, Shah Wali-Allah hastens to confirm important points which can be outlined as follows (Jalboni, 1992, Baljon, 1992):

(1) The ruler, head of government, should be powerful enough to compel all, including the heads of the community, to obey the law and preempt insecurity and disorder. One would infer then there is a process of setting up a set of regulations and orders that constitute the law.
(2) The ruler should be a man of good character, brave and bold-hearted; otherwise he would gain no respect from either his own people or his enemies.
(3) Tolerance and leniency are further required characteristics.
(4) Skill in running the state administration efficiently is a must.
(5) He should be able to demonstrate nobility and readiness to help his subjects and eagerness to work for the improvement of their welfare.
(6) He should be able to win the love and respectability of his subjects through his sincerity and hard work.
(7) Rewarding the subjects generously, but punishing offenders, is expected from the ruler.
(8) He should not punish an accused until the offence is proven.
(9) He should be using positive incentives in encouraging good work and irreproachable deeds of his assistants (government administration).
(10) Psychologically, the ruler should be able to understand the psychology of his people and be able to foresee events before they occur.
(11) The powerful ruler should be able to take up arms and fight disruptive elements in society. These elements should be wiped out of the society, as they as cancerous to the body of the community.
(12) With greed and ambition for accumulated materialistic possessions conflict of interest arises among individuals and if this is not overcome it will lead to chaos in society. It is the duty of government to suppress the tendency towards the use of illegal means to achieve these objectives and to exercise justice in settling the disputes among members of society in a just and fair manner. To be able to establish justice, the government ought

to be powerful and to have the means to lay down the laws and to force their implementation.

(13) Immoral economic behaviour, when it occurs, ought to be suppressed and the government should be on the watch for such conduct and endeavour to eliminate it. One would infer that this would require setting up a system of control to ensure the adherence to rules and regulations. But Shah Wali-Allah did not seem to have elucidated on this.

(14) Government should have no hesitation in facing those powerful individuals in society who may grow in power and influence and wish to force their own way against the law, to fight them even to the extent of waging a war against them in order to protect the general interest of society.

(15) Government should have a council of wise men and advisors and should pay heed to their views with regard to the maintenance of country and society. One would assume that these wise men and advisors would be from the Ulamaʾ and religious circles as they more aware than others of the rules of Sharīʾah and its applications.

(16) Negligence of religion and spread of immoral behaviour among individuals should be overcome by the government through providing individuals with the right advice and council.

(17) In terms of government finance, Shah Wali-Allah emphasised the importance of having a Treasury that is always full. This would ensure the ability of the government to provide for necessary provisions in war and peace. The Treasury, through government, may resort to various kinds of taxes that should be levied without overburdening the tax payers beyond what their income can bear. Taxes can be imposed on those of high wealth and income, such as property owners whose possessions are continuously increasing, traders and the owners of industries. However, Shah Wali-Allah seemed to have advocated a tax threshold, as he emphasised that taxes should be imposed on only the extra income beyond what is needed to cover necessities.

(18) In dealing with enemies, the government should endeavour to have as much information as possible about potential enemies, weaken their position, and set up, interestingly enough, an espionage system to provide information and assistance.

The above points seem to serve as a constitution for the government, which lay down the foundation for its general policies. Further details would be necessary to outline the detailed policies that a government should follow to exercise these guidelines.

Furthermore, in addressing the issue of government, Shah Wali-Allah referred to various issues related to the unfortunate appointment of a bad administrator, the corrupt government, the duties of the powerful ruler, the proper distribution of labour.

If all did not work, Shah believed it was inevitable that a revolution would take place. And he seemed to be in favour of it. In justifying his views, he states that sacrifices, even with one's own life, is sometimes necessary as a final resort towards rectifying the wrong done. But it should be seen only as a final course of action after all other course are sincerely pursued and fully exhausted.

Shah Wali-Allah seems to have leaned more towards a radical form of reform than a moderate approach to change. He calls for a powerful government of law and order, of war and peace, and of justice and fairness—all in one. He is particularly concerned about security, stability and fairness: security of individuals in society against maladministration, safety of a country against political disturbances from inside and outside enemies, and fairness in dealing with the subjects. These basic principles of societal security seem to be echoed throughout his writings. This is not surprising given the circumstances that prevailed before and during his time. Indeed, with some reservation about his call for a revolution if the need arise, his views can serve even in a society that may come after him of peace and tranquility if potential political and economic mishaps are to be avoided. It is not surprising, therefore, to see the views of Shah Wali-Allah popular in the subcontinent even after a few centuries following his death.

In the next chapter we turn our attention to the reform and revival in the period that preceded the renaissance in Islamic economics in the twentieth century.

CHAPTER EIGHT

THE CRISIS OF MODERNISATION AND ISLAMICISATION: FROM REFORM TO REVIVAL (1800 A.C.–20TH CENTURY)

Introduction

Whenever Muslims are in a state of despair they turn to their religion for help and assistance. Throughout the history of Islam, religious leaders emerge, invariably identifying the problems of Muslims as being the result of their desertion of the correct path of their religion. To improve their conditions, the argument always goes, Muslims have to return to the purity of Islam and apply its fundamental teachings to their daily life. This has always been the case throughout history from the time of the first schism in Islam over the caliphate, *Fitnah*, to the time of the crushing defeat of the Egyptian, Syrian and Jordanian armies by the Israelis in the 1967 six-day war. Calls for religious reform did not go unopposed. The call for secularisation was equally strong though it was a call for a move in the opposite direction. The effect these movements may have had on the environment of the development of Islamic economic literature in the twentieth century are outlined below.

Conveniently, our starting point is the late eighteenth century and the movements are divided into three main categories: Traditional movements, reconciling movements and secularised movements. For the purpose of this classification, the traditional movement refers to the call for the return to the Qur'ān and Sunnah in a strict manner. Modernization ought not be imported at the sacrifice of Islamic norms and ideals. Innovation in religious rules, in both sides of Sharī'ah, ritual and societal, is not permissible and is regarded as *bid'ah*, and every *bid'ah* is *dhalalah*, and every *dhalalah* is in Hell Fire. The second movement is the reconciling movement which while confirming the need for a return to the Islamic prime sources in the Qur'ān and Sunnah, sees no harm in importing Western culture and knowledge if it were for the general benefits of the community. The third group argues that secularization is the way forward as it is imperative for the modernization of society that is necessary for Muslim counties to become competitive. The movement contends that while Islamic norms and ideals are of great religious value, they should be: (a) confined to the individuals' in shaping their personal and social pattern of behavioural with no effect on the politics of government or the affairs of the state, and (b) Islamic Sharī'ah rules need to be re-examined to avoid what has become, in their view, redundant and unsuitable to the community of today, such as polygamy and divorce rules. Some representative examples of these movements are highlighted below.

First: Traditional Reform Movements

The Wahhābiyyah Movement

The Wahhābiyyah movement which is named after its founder emerged from the heart of the Arabian Peninsula. Calling upon Muslims to return to the fundamental teachings of Islam as in the Qur'ān and Sunnah to re-shaping their life and society, Muhammad ibn Abd al-Wahhāb (d. 1792) embarked on an uncompromising radical reform that called for the purification of Islam from what he saw as un-Islamic cults inherited from the practice of Ŝūfīsm and other sects. In that it may be argued that he followed the footsteps of the earlier reformer Ibn Taymīya (1263–1328) who, among others, called for the return to the basic teachings of the Qur'ān and Sunnah when the Islamic land was under the occupation of the Mongols. Like Ibn-Taymīya, Ibn-Abdel-Wahhāb did not reject *ijtihād*, the exertion of self to reach an Islamic opinion that would provide an answer to a situation that did not exist at the time of the Prophet, but unlike Ibn-Taimiya, he was strict in basing *ijtihād* on the basic source of the religion, the Qur'ān and Sunnah. He rejected all forms of Islamic medieval schools of thought, and was in essence entirely Hanbalī (Fazlur Urahman, 1970). Though the Wahhābiyyah movement managed to purge Islam from intruding customs which may be described as not entirely in conformity with the practice of the Prophet, the Wahhābis deprived the Sharī'ah from the basic tools of innovation that may be available in jurisprudence. They, however, had been successful in bringing into relief the principles of Islamic egalitarianism and co-operation, and had thrived to establish co-operative farm villages (ibid.).

The Wahhābis had the political aim of achieving independence from the Ottoman Empire. Muĥammad ibn Abdel Wahhāb broke away from the Ottomans and established an independent state in central Arabia and the Persian Gulf. But that was not to be tolerated by the Turks. To curb the movement, the Porte called upon the Turkish viceroy in Egypt, Muĥammad Ali, with an assignment to reclaim Arabia. In a war that lasted from 1811 to 1818, Muĥammad Ali's army defeated the Wahhābis and brought Central Arabia back to the Ottoman's rule. Despite the military defeat, the Wahhābiyyah movement awakened the nostalgic feeling of many Muslims to the early days of the puritan Islam and to the possibility of establishing a state based on Islamic norms.

The Wahhābiyyah came back to life and served as the theological foundation on which the Kingdom of Saudi Arabia was founded in 1932. In the first quarter of the twentieth century the founder of the al-Saud dynasty, Abdel-Azīz ibn-Saud, rose to power, brought to an end the reign of the al-Rashīd family in Ha'il in the north of Arabia in 1921, captured Makkah, the seat of the self-declared "king of Arabia" Sharif Hussayn in 1924 and proceeded to occupy al-Medīnah and nearby Jeddah in 1925. In 1932 he declared himself the new king of Arabia under the title Kingdom of Saudi Arabia, a name and a dynasty that has remained until today. He introduced radical reforms to the new kingdom. It was, however, the discovery of oil, beginning with concessions given to the Arabian American Oil Company in 1932, which has changed the economic, social and political map of the Kingdom until the present time. The teachings of the Wahhabism are still practiced in Saudi Arabia by the populace, and declared the official line of religion by the royal dynasty.

The Idrīsī Movement

The Wahhābiyyah movement inspired further similar movements in North Africa. They all had a similar message and purpose, the awakening of the people through the restoration of Islam. In Morocco, Ahmad ibn-Idrīs (1760–1836), emerged as a Ŝūfī reformer who called for the necessity to educate people and enlighten them about the rules of their religion. Travelling extensively in North Africa and Yemen, teaching and preaching, he came to the conclusion that Muslim Ulama' were too busy with *fiqh*, jurisprudence and Sharī'ah to teach people the basic rituals of their own religion. This, to him, was a failure on the part of the Ulama'. Different from Muĥammad Abdel-Wahhāb before him, Ahmad ibn Idrīs had no political ambitions.

The Sanusiyyah Movement

The Sanusiayyah movement rose in Eastern Libya under Muĥammad ibn Ali al-Sanusi (1787–1859) whose aim was to re-shape the Muslim society and mold it in the form of the early Muslim society of the Prophet's time. As a Ŝūfī, al-Sanusi rejected extravagance and called for a return to the simplistic, almost desert life style, of the early Muslim community. Politically, al-Sanusi and his followers achieved remarkable success in integrating the surrounding tribes into his religious movement and establishing a network of a brother's society and trading posts stretching from north Libya to the Sudan (Cleveland, 1994). The Sanusiayyah movement resisted the Italian invasion of Tripoli in 1911 and the French expansion in north and central Africa. At the end of the Second World War the victorious Allied powers found in a grand son of al-Sanusi a suitable king for Libya in 1950. That remained the case until 1st September 1969 when a military revolution led by Colonel Mu'ammar al-Qażafī ousted the Sanusi family from power and, later, declared that the Libyan kingdom was to be a Republic.

The Mahdiyyah Movement

Another movement emerged in the North of Sudan headed by Muĥammad Ahmed al-Mahdī (1844–1885) who proclaimed himself the awaited Mahdī. His aim was to revive the religion and bring Islam back to the puritan practice of the Prophet. It had the same purpose and message of the previous movements. But al-Mahdi had a strong political agenda of resisting the British-Egyptian occupation of the Sudan and to free the country from foreign occupation (ibid.). By declaring a *jihād*, al-Mahdī embedded a religious call into his religious teachings that proved useful in achieving military success. Soon, the Mahdis conquered most of north Sudan, capturing the capital Khartoum itself in 1885. The Mahdists remained in power until 1898 when Khartoum was re-captured by the Anglo-Egyptian army under the command of Kitchener. Although the Mahdiyyah movement was short lived, only twenty years, the Mahdī's remarkable success in challenging the Anglo-Egyptian armies and establishing an indigenous Islamic state has been inspirational to Muslims everywhere in proving that Islamic revival is a viable alternative to Westernisation.

Second: Reconciling Reform Movements

When the Islamic world came under the full occupation of the English, French and Italian forces beginning from the mid nineteenth century, it discovered how lagging it was behind the Western world in science and technology, socio-political science, and educational systems. On the one hand, Muslim reformers, without exception, resented and resisted the occupation of their land by Western Christian forces, while, on the other, realized that these forces had a more advanced scientific, technological, and political culture than their own. The dilemma was to find a way to lessen the gap between their standards and Western standards and to bring their countries to the stage of modernism. Two main streams of reforms came from two different parts of the Islamic land: one from Egypt and the second from the Indian Subcontinent. The teachings of the two streams were interwoven in one another.

Reformers from Egypt

Until Napoleon Bonaparte landed with his naval army in Alexandria in 1798, the Ottomans, and the world at large, did not realize the strategic importance of a country that played a major part in history a few centuries before when defeating the Mongols. On conquering the Mamlūks of Egypt, the Ottomans paid little attention to the country leaving its administration to her ex-masters, the Mamlūks, contented with appointing a viceroy, *pasha*, from the High Porte and leaving the country under the occupation of an army from the Turkish Janissaries. The country was divided into twelve provinces with each province headed by a Mamlūk given the title *bey*. With the payment of annual tribute to the Porte, the Mamlūk *beys* had a free hand in administering the land, imposing taxes and building up their own armies. With a policy of not leaving a viceroy in office for more than two to three years, lest they should break away from the central government in Istanbūl, the viceroys focused on their own personal benefits and soon lost interest in the affairs of the country. Before long, the viceroy from Istanbūl ceased to have any real control over the land or the army, leaving that entirely in the hands of the Mamlūks.

Under the dual form of control, the *pasha* from Istanbūl and the *beys* from the Mamlūks, native Egyptians became progressively poorer. With heavy taxes, no proper irrigation systems, no reclamation of land or proper cultivation drainage schemes, and with relentless treatment from rulers, both the Turkish *pashas* and the local Mamlūk *beys*, who were only interested in collecting the tax quota, the peasants fell into a state of deprivation. The tax quota system, *nizam al-iltizam*, was introduced with a view to delegating the administration of the land to the overseer who provided the highest bid of tax revenue to the *bey*, the province governor, in the contest for the post. In his turn, the *bey* would provided the highest tax quota to the *pasha* and the latter, in his turn, pledged the highest tax quota to the Porte. In the end, the tax burden fell heavily upon the cultivators of the land. Worse still, to maximize the net tax revenue the overseer had to ensure that his expenses on the land were kept to minimum. Corruption and bribery prevailed, and insecurity, famine, and pestilence added to the natives' state of misery the population of the land, which under the Romans reached some eight millions, had by the end of eighteenth century decreased to one-third of its former size (Hitti, 1970).

In the middle of the quarrel of the Mamlūks over the governorship of Egypt and their attempt to breakaway from the Porte, France, which was in a continuous rivalry with Britain, developed a sudden interest in Egypt ostensibly under the pretence of punishing the Mamlūks for trying to breakaway from the High Porte and restoring the values of Islam which, in Bonaparte Arabic written war propaganda words, the Mamlūks neglected. When Bonaparte landed in Alexandria in 1798, only then, the misery of the native Egyptian was put to a temporary rest, but not for very long. Britain became aware of the real intention of the French expedition, which was to control the British dominated trade route between Asia and the West (ibid.). Almost a century later, Egypt ended up occupied by the British forces and at the outbreak of World War I the country was declared a British Protectorate.

In the middle of that political turmoil, an Egyptian reformer appeared, the liberal reformer Muĥammad Abdou (1849–1905). With his teacher Jamal-al-Dīn al-Afghānī (1839–97) they were the chief leaders of modernism in Islam in Egypt.

Abdou and al-Afghānī

As political Islam was seen humiliated by Western occupation, people developed two ideas in their minds: first, a strong feeling of resentment to the Western power and to all that came with it, and second, expectation from the Ulama', as the protectors of the faith, to lead the way forward and to take them into an appropriate course of action. The Ulama' responded, but they, or at least some of them, had a dilemma. The Western forces were aggressors and ought to be forced to free the land, but the West had developed so much in science, technology, and socio-political concepts and ideas that Muslim countries, as soon they found out, were lagging behind. Muslim countries would have to adopt these Western technologies and may have to accept Western socio-political ideals, if they are to advance and develop. However, if this is to be done, Muslim countries should not be seen as being amenable to Western occupying forces. That was the dilemma to Mohammad Abdou (1849–1905) and his teacher, and fellow struggler, Jamal al-Dīn al-Afghānī (1839–97).

Both, al-Afghānī and Abdou were anti British, and they associated themselves with the unsuccessful revolt of the Egyptian army under Ahmad Orabi, for which Abdou, in consequence, was exiled to Syria. Both were Sunni and were highly respected in religious circles. In addition, by being the *mufti* of Egypt, Mohammad Abdou was in the highest religious position in the country. Both had been exposed to the Western culture, traveling and lecturing in France, and together edited an Arabic paper in Paris. But they differed in their approaches to solving the problem of the undermined Islam and the occupied land. Although al-Afghānī and Abdou agreed on the need to revive Islam as a way of life and the desire to liberate the Muslim world from the foreign occupation, they departed on the issue of the importation of western science and socio-political ideas.

Gamal al-Dīn al-Afghānī was of the view that the remedy to Muslims' problem should emerge from the religion itself: Islam. No importation of Western culture, in his views, would serve as a panacea to Muslims' problems or to improving their conditions, and any attempt at modernisation by importation would be fatal instead of useful. The answer to the problem, he emphasized, should come from within, the Sharī'ah. But he advocated that in order for the

Sharī'ah to keep pace with the changes in the world it has to renew itself. The closure of the gate of jurisprudence, *ijtihād*, should be re-nounced, and the Ulama' should encourage the use of rational thinking and reasoning in formulating religious opinions that would fit in with the contemporary needs of Muslims. In that he was in line with the Shi'ī Ulama', who were in favour of *ijtihād* and *tajdid*, innovation. Politically, al-Afghānī was in favour of political revolution to achieve reform, an issue on which Muĥammad Abdou was in disagreement.

Being the *mufti* of Egypt gave Abdou not only the highest religious position of a cleric in the country but also made his religious opinion, *fatwa*, highly influential. As a patriotic Egyptian, Abdou resented the country being under the subjugation of the foreign great powers. But as a Muslim leader, as he saw himself part of the Islamic community, *ummah*, as a whole, beyond the political borders of Egypt, he has to bear the interest of all Muslims in mind in addressing their problems and concerns. Though an Egyptian and an Arab, he was of the view that it was Pan-Islamism, not Arab Nationalism, which would lead Muslims to political salvation. In his call for reform he reflected a deep sense of history and vision. He saw it as inevitable that the West would continue to advance in science and technical knowledge, and the Muslim East would continue to have the gap in these fields widening by the passage of time. He argued that not all of which comes from the West was evil, which conceivably should be avoided, but from the West comes also science, technology, educational development, and new forms of political cultural and application of democracy, that would all suit the Islamic East. There was no conflict between Islam and Western science, as he emphasized, and as such Muslims should endeavour to learn the science of the West and adopt, and adapt, it to the land of Islam (Esposito, 2001). Abdou's formula for reform was a conscientious compromise between the ideals of Islam with its inherent values and principles, and the scientific advance of the West with its practical use and advantages. Without undermining the Islamic values and ideals, Western pragmatic approaches to knowledge and education could be introduced to Islamic education and political systems. The sphere of knowledge in Islam, he advocated, should be widened to include other worldly branches of knowledge, and religious schools, *madaris*, should include in their curriculum the study of modern sciences (Armstrong, 2000). Notably, al-Azhar until the late nineteen fifties and early nineteen sixties was limiting its curriculum to religious studies, but from the nineteen sixties onward further subjects were added under the government of the 1952 revolution such as medicine, science, law, economics and business studies. Turning his attention to the Sharīʾah, Muĥammad Abdou, like al-Afghānī, emphasised that the Sharīʾah would have to keep pace with the fast advances in society and be ready to derive legal concepts and provide rules, particularly concerning social legislation, that while still in conformity with Islam would not hinder modernisation.

Muĥammad Abdou paved the way for many others who came after him such as Muhammad Rashīd Rida (1865–1935) who was also the first to have advocated the establishment of an Islamic state that is fully modernized and but also fully based on the Sharīʾah.

Ĥassan al-Banna and Muslim Brothers Society

The Muslim Brothers Society was founded in Egypt in 1928 by the school teacher Ĥassan al-Banna (1906–49). Al-Banna believed that Western societal elements of modernisation were alien to Islamic societies, corrupting and weakening these societies and were per se bringing decline and decay (Bari, 1995). In 1928, al-Banna founded the Muslim Brothers Society (*Jamaat al-Ikhwan al-Muslimūn*) that aimed at awakening the religious feeling and Islamic ideals at the grass roots of the Egyptian masses. The Society had other aims in mind namely to revitalize Islamic beliefs, provide social caring and charitable services to those in need through the institution of Zakāh and charitable donation, and, as a long term strategic aim, to establish a government based on Islamic principles (ibid.). To him, these objectives would not be feasible without first purifying the masses and bringing them back to the values of Islam.

The Society gained an initial support as a mass movement aiming at improving the educational and religious status of its members and, in addition, by resisting the British occupation of the Egyptian soil it gained the nationalists' support. The Muslim Brothers Society, however, fell out of favour with the ruling government of the 1952 revolution and when a charge of an assassination attempt on the country's leader was brought against one of its members, the Society was banned and legally dissolved in 1954. Yet in the recent general election of Egypt in 2005, while the ban on the Muslim Brothers Society was still in effect, there were as many as twenty per cent of total seats, won by Islamists contesting the election as Independents (of political parties). They fought the election under the slogan: Islam is the Answer.

Reformers from the Indian Subcontinent

Muĥammad Iqbal

An Indian by upbringing, Muĥammad Iqbal (1876–1938) is an example of a reformer who was educated in the West but still identified himself with Islam and Islamic traditions. He studied in Germany, where he earned a doctorate degree in philosophy, and in England where he got a degree in law from London (Armstrong, 2000). Like al-Afghānī and Abdou before him, he was keen on modernism but still believed that modernism should be achieved not at the expense of casting out Islam and Islamic heritage. In linking modernism with religion, he advocated that Islam was the most suitable of all religions to accommodate movements of modernism as it is the religion that always urges Muslims to observe God's creation, think and reflect deeply, learn from observation and thinking, and transfer what is learned through teaching, which leads to increasing the stock of knowledge. Islam, Iqbal asserted, is the most rational of all religions, which encourages scientific thinking through God's commands of thinking and learning. There is no contradiction, in Iqbal's mind, between Islam, as a religion and culture, and scientific and socio-political development. The advancement of the West, Iqbal ascertained, was not because of the superiority of Christianity over Islam, rather, it was because Muslims did not utilize fully the potential of their religion, a reassuring thought which would help, perhaps, restore Muslims self-confidence and reaffirm further their belief in their faith and past. Ŝūfīsm and mystical rituals had no place in Iqbal's agenda for reform. Moreover, they are in conflict with the basic ingredient of scientific development that reaches conclusion through observation and reflection, not superstitious beliefs or mystical rituals. Iqbal criticized individualism, which was to him a side product of the European modernism, and was instead in favour of a benevolent society. Not that Iqbal was unfamiliar with the social aspects of life in the European society, he lived in Germany and England to earn his degrees, but he must have come to this conclusion, through his most advocated approach to learning: observation and reflection. Iqbal tried to bring the best of the West, science, Western philosophy and social-political ideals, and the best of the East, Islamic heritage and ideals, together. And, once more, like modernist reformers before him, he asserted that Sharī'ah would need to adopt an innovative approach to religio-political issues if it was to keep pace with modernism. In that he asserts in The Reconstruction of Religious Thoughts in Islam, "No wonder then that the young generation . . . demand a fresh orientation of their faith. With the reawakening of Islam, therefore, it is necessary to examine, in an independent spirit, what Europe has thought and how far the conclusions reached by her can help us in the revision, and if necessary, reconstruction of theological thought in Islam", (Iqbal, 1968).

Abū A'la Maudūdī and Jamaat-i-Islami

Abū A'la Maudūdī (1903–1979) carried the banner of re-Islamisation in Pakistan in trying to mobilise the masses to return to the Islamic values and ideals. To help achieve this objective, Maudūdī founded *jama'at-i-Islami* (Society of Islam) in 1941 as a centralised, strictly hierarchical organisation, similar to the Muslim Brothers in Egypt (Sagiv, 1995). Like the Muslim Brothers Society in Egypt, the Pakistani Jama'at had a similar long term objective of establishing an Islamic state which Maudūdī called a "Theo-democracy", (Sivan, 1990).

Although, like Abdou, al-Afghānī and al-Banna in Egypt before him, Maudūdī acknowledged that there might be a necessity of importing Western science and technology he maintained that technology could be applied without Islamic values being sacrificed as there was no contradiction between the two.

He stressed a theory of "new Jahiliyyah", referring to Jahiliyyah in pre-Islamic Arabia that meant ignorance and misguidance. He ascertained that the state of Muslims in the twentieth century was a state of ignorance of their religion and Islamic ideals and as such they were living in a new Jahiliyyah. He went further to state that the majority of Muslims had become alienated from the original intention of Islam and were therefore apostate, and as such they usurped the divine authority by designing their own law (Davidson, 2003). Maudūdī went as far as characterizing governments in Muslim countries that did not implement strict Sharī'ah as apostate, obligating the true believer to wage *jihād* against them (Esposito, 2002). He invited his followers in Jamaat-i-Islami to remain outside government until such time when society had been Islamized (Sagiv, 1995). Consequently, as a parliamentary party the Jamaat deliberately stayed out of government until 1948, after which time when it accepted the idea of a gradual reform within government.

Third: Secularisation Reform Movements

Secularization was seen by some Muslim leading intellectuals and policy makers as essential for modernization. To speed up modernization in countries that were occupied for years ranging from short of a century to more than a century, political and intellectual leaders looked at the West and its way of life as the shortest way to catch up with what had been missing in order to narrow the gap between the Islamic East and the Christian West.

This is not to say that political leaders were distancing themselves from Islam as a religion per se, quite the opposite. Political leaders appealed to the masses through Islam; they were keen to be seen attending Friday prayers, taking part in religious ceremonies, sending delegates to international Islamic gatherings, and declaring Islam as the formal religion of the state in the countries' constitutions. President Anwar el-Sadat of Egypt, for example, was eager to be nicknamed the "Faithful President". Nevertheless, in running the affairs of the state, Islamic governments, supported by leading intellectuals, were willing to drop Islamic ideas in favour of Western alternatives for the sake of what was perceived as modernism. Sources of laws were cited as primarily the French Law, leaving Islamic Sharī'ah tailing behind at the end of a list of sources. The intention of governments was not insincere as all political leaders of Muslim countries wanted to strengthen their economies, improve education, and reinforce armies, but to them the way to do that was primarily to adopt Western ideas.

Of the early advocates of secularization in Egypt two names come to mind: Qasim Amin (d. 1908) who was the first Muslim to have criticized polygamy, divorce, and the veiling of women, and Ťaha Ĥusayn.

Ťaha Ĥusayn and the call for Secularisation

Ťaha Ĥusayn, an intellectual emerging from the Egyptian village, took an entirely secular approach to modernism. He argued for the separation of religion and politics. To him, that would best serve the needs for the modernization of society, not the pursuit of an Islamic path. The urge for modernisation, and probably the influence by the Western culture where he lived while getting his doctorate from the Sorbonne, seemed to have influenced Ĥusayn's thinking. In his "Future of Culture in Egypt" he foresaw that in the years to come, the roots of Egypt, and those of Islam, would be bound to the West, a prophecy that seems to be materializing in the early years of the new millennium. His admiration of the Western culture and his zeal for the modernisation of Egypt, took him even further when he stressed that Egypt shared common grounds with the West, the Mediterranean countries and the monotheist religion, and apart from Islam and the Arabic language, Egypt had no common grounds with the Arabs. This would make Egypt more of a Western than an Eastern country, or as he puts it, "there are no intellectual or cultural differences to be found among the peoples who grew up around the Mediterranean and were influenced by it" (Ĥusayn, 1982). In stressing that secularism had always been part of Egypt, we find him asserting, "From earliest times Muslims have been well aware of the now universally acknowledged principle that a political system and a religion are different things, which a constitution and a state rest, above everything else, on practical foundations". Therefore, in his conclusion, it was only natural that the Egyptians should adopt European customs and institutions from table manners to railroads and political, legal, and educational systems. When these thoughts are those of the Egyptian Minister of Education, as Ťaha Ĥusayn was from 1950 to 1952, his views are not to be taken lightly. Ťaha Ĥusayn, a renowned Egyptian writer and highly respected personality, represented the mixed feeling, and probably frustration, that spread among Muslim modernist intellectuals who in their endeavour, and zeal, to modernize the Muslim society found the Ulama' unwilling, or perhaps, unable, to look at innovation favourably. Surprisingly enough, Ťaha Ĥusayn as he is telling us in his novel-autobiography "*al-Ayyam*", the days, he, as a blind child, was brought up in a religious environment where he was taught, and was able, to recite the whole Qur'ān in an early age of his life.

Islam Triumphant: the Revival

The effect of the above Islamic reform movements seemed to have been fundamental to the resurgence of Islam in the twentieth century. Muslims became more convinced than ever that their religion could still provide practical solutions to their problems: spiritually, politically and economically. In the wave of Islamic revivalism that characterized the mid to the late twentieth century two main developments occurred as far as economics was concerned: the emergence of an extensive body of literature on Islamic economic and the establishment of Islamic banks.

Until the early years of the new millennium, if a single event was to be singled out as a political landmark of the twentieth century Islam, this would be the liberation of the Islamic world from Western foreign occupation. By the mid twentieth century Western forces were seen, first, as less involved in the domestic politics of the occupied land and, later as more willing than before to accommodate the wishes of national struggles for independence. This paved the way for the emergence of what has become to be known as Islamic resurgence or revivalism.

The liberation of the Islamic world was not entirely free from an aftermath. Nor did it lead directly to the resurgence of Islam as a re-born socio-political force. True, the Indian subcontinent was divided by religion into the two states, but the division was more of a political necessity, than an Islamic prerequisite. It took Islam two more decades or so to emerge after a long battle with another rival: secularization. There was already a gap between what secularisation has achieved and what Islamists promised Islam could achieve. In the absence of practical alternatives such as Islamic banks, economic policies or educational programmes, and with the growing nationalist movements which were mainly local, Islamic socio-economic and political ideas were wrestling hard with other forces to present solutions and suggest practical ideas. It was only after a few political setbacks, which engulfed Middle Eastern Islam in particular, that secularization started to lose ground and Islamic movements were beginning to gain support. The premise was that secularization did not work because it lacked the depth and motivation that Islam could provide. The most notable example of these setbacks was the Arab-Islamic defeat and the Israeli triumph in what has become known as the six-day war. To Muslims the shock was very great: in six days, the whole Egyptian Sinai, the Syrian Golan Heights, and the Jordanian West-Bank including Jerusalem, were lost to the Israelis—a dramatic humiliation to the Arab Muslims. There was a deep feeling among Muslims that the humiliation of the six-day war was a result of not observing the faith of Islam in full. With despair, once more, the shock seemed to have awakened the religious feeling of all and at all levels. The huge support among the masses at all levels for religious teachings marked the beginning of the emergence of what has become known as Islamic revivalism.

Main Features of Revivalism

A number of features could be said to have marked the stage of Islamic revivalism. The adoption of Islamic practice by the masses as a way of living, the establishment and re-emergence of Islamic religio-social organizations, the establishment of the Organization Islamic Conference and in what concerns us in pursuit of the history of Islamic economic thought, the establishment of the Islamic Development Bank, the increasing popularity of Islamic socio-economic literature that led to the convening the First International Conference on Islamic Economics, the establishment of specialized institutes on Islamic economics and Islamic thought, the tendency towards the Islamisation of economic systems in some Muslim countries, the establishment of Islamic financial institutions, and the establishment of Islamic business enterprises are of the main landmarks of the Islamic revivalism.

Religious Features: Revival of Islamic Practice

The adoption of Islam by the masses could be noticed in the way individuals were beginning to behave and, more noticeably, to appear. By mid nineteen seventies beards began to appear on young faces, white robes, quftans, replaced western costume among male youth, veils for women including young school and university girls descended on their hair and faces, Qur'ān was more spoken of and Qur'ānic verses more quoted, and mosques were filled more, prayers times observed and religious study circles more attended. At the initiative of their heads, mosques, it was observed, arranged free evening tuitions to help school and university students pass their exams; the free voluntary help came from school teachers and university professors. There was a developed sweeping feeling among the masses that they wanted to adhere more than ever to the faith that had been, among some at least, almost forgotten.

Socio-political organisations

The reemergence of the Islamic socio-political organizations could be noticed in Egypt by the revival activities of the Muslim Brothers society, after being re-admitted to operate during Sadat's presidency. Further religious societies and groups were established, all proclaiming the call for the teaching and increasing the awareness of Islam among the populace, though some were to be discredited later and be stopped from operation. Of these organisations the OIC is particularly prominent.

The Organization of the Islamic Conference (OIC)

The OIC is an inter-governmental organization that by 2006 incorporated fifty-seven states which have decided to pool their resources together and combine their efforts to safeguard the interest and ensure the progress and well-being of their peoples and those of other Muslims in the world over (OIC Website). When the First meeting of the leaders of Islamic states was held in September 1969, in the wake of the arson offence committed by an Israeli on the Muslims' sacred Aqsa Mosque in Jerusalem in August 1969, the heads of states decided to establish a permanent organization of Islamic conference to unite Muslim states in their action with the aim of "liberating Jerusalem and Al-Aqsa from Zionist occupation". At that meeting, and with that mission in mind, the OIC was established. Six months later, the First Islamic Conference of Foreign Affairs Ministers, held in Jeddah, set up a permanent General Secretariat, and Headquarters in Jeddah. Two years later, in 1972, the Charter of the Organization was adopted, which aims at strengthening solidarity and cooperation among Islamic states in political, economic, cultural, scientific and social fields.

Under the Charter, the OIC has the following main objectives:

1. To strengthen: (a) Islamic solidarity among member states, (b) cooperation in the political, economic, social, cultural and scientific fields, and (c) the struggle of all Muslim people to safeguard their dignity, independence and national rights.
2. To coordinate action to: (a) safeguard the Holy places, and (b) support the struggle of the Palestinian people and assist them in recovering their rights and liberating their occupied territories.
3. To work to: (a) eliminate racial discrimination and all forms of colonialism, (b) create a favourable atmosphere for promotion of cooperation and understanding between Members States and other countries.

To be able to exercise its duties and responsibilities, the OIC has constituted various committees, affiliated institutions, and set up subsidiaries, which are established by resolutions adopted by heads of states and or Foreign Ministers of member states. A quick glance at these bodies, of which some are headed by heads of states and others by officials at ministerial levels, reveals the type of activities the OIC has been undertaking. A comprehensive list of these is provided in the publications of the OIC, but it suffices for our purposes to highlight the main bodies related to our subject. Following the OIC classification, these may be pointed our as follows:

Subsidiary Organs: the Statistical, Social Research and Training Center for Islamic Countries, Turkey, the Research Center for Islamic History, Art and Culture, Turkey, the Islamic Institute for Technology, Bangladesh, the Executive Bureau of the Islamic Solidarity Fund and its Waqf, Saudi Arabia, the Islamic University of Niger, and the Islamic University of Uganda

Specialized Institutions and Organs: the Islamic Development Bank, Saudi Arabia, the Islamic Educational, Scientific and Cultural Organization, Morocco, and the Islamic States Broadcasting Organization, Saudi Arabia

Affiliated Institutions: Islamic Chamber of Commerce and Industry, Pakistan, Organization of Islamic Capital and Cities, Saudi Arabia, Islamic Committee of International Crescent, Libya, Islamic Shipowners Association, Saudi Arabia, World Federation of International Arabo-Islamic Schools, Saudi Arabia, and International Association of Islamic Banks, Saudi Arabia

Standing Committees: Al-Quds (Jerusalem) Committee, Standing Committee for Information and Cultural Affairs, Standing Committee for Economic and Trade Cooperation, and Standing Committee for Scientific and Technological Affairs

Economic Features

The Establishment of the Islamic Development Bank (IDB)

In implementation of the OIC recommendation, the Conference of Finance Ministers of Muslim Countries, held in December 1973, passed a Declaration of Intent of establishing an Islamic development bank to serve the Muslim communities. In July 1975 the Islamic Development Bank was formally established and in October 1975 it was officially opened. The purpose of the Bank is to foster the economic development and social progress of member countries and Muslim communities individually and jointly in accordance with the principles of Sharī'ah.

The functions of the IDB are to participate in equity capital and grant loans for productive projects and enterprises besides providing financial assistance to member countries in other forms for economic and social development. Moreover, IDB is required to establish and operate special funds for specific purposes including a fund for assistance to Muslim communities in non-member countries. IDB, which is authorized to accept deposits and to mobilize financial resources through Sharī'ah compatible modes, is charged with the responsibility of assisting in the promotion of foreign trade among member countries; providing technical assistance to member countries, and extending training facilities for personnel engaged in development activities in these countries (IDB website).

The shareholders of IDB are governments of Muslim countries, some 57 countries which are members in the Organization of Islamic Conference (OIC), represented on the Board by the members' Ministers of Finance (the Treasurers). The authorized capital of the Bank increased from two billion Islamic Dinars in 1975, to six billion ID in 1992, and to fifteen billion ID in 2001, with a par value per share of 10,000 ID, and a subscribed capital of slightly over eight billion ID. Starting with a Head Office in Jeddah, Kingdom of Saudi Arabia, at the time of, and for a few years after, its establishment, IDB widened its scope of representation to include regional offices in Rabat, Morocco, Kula Lumpur, Malaysia, Almaty, Kazkhastan, and field representatives in another eleven member countries in the Middle-East, Central Asia, South-East Asia, and Africa. Interestingly enough, to facilitate communication, IDB has three official languages: Arabic, English and French.

IDB operations cover a wide range. They are mainly: project financing, trade financing, private sector promotion, special assistance and scholarships, technical cooperation, young researchers support programme, Islamic banks' portfolio, unit trust investment fund and infrastructure fund.

In line with the Sharī'ah, modes of finance in IDB are mainly as follows (IDB website):

Loans. These are interest free but with an administrative charge ranging between 0.75% and 2.5% per annum, with a grace period that may extend to ten years for loans of 30 years maturity. The main purpose of these loans is to provide a long-term finance for projects that are expected to have a significant socio-economic impact and which are not of the revenue generating type. They are most suitable for infrastructure projects.

Leasing. This is used to finance capital equipment and other fixed assets in income generating projects. As in leasing in general, the ownership of the assets is transferred to the leasee (the beneficiary) at the end of the lease period. With a gestation period that may ranges between six and 48 months, the lease period may extend to 15 years. The lease payment (rental) is set so as to provide an average rate of return to the Bank of about 6% per annum. To safeguard the interest of the Bank, the lease is provided subject to government or bank guarantee.

Installment Sale. In this mode of finance the Bank buys the equipment, which is mainly capital assets, and sells and delivers them to the beneficiary in installments. The overall installment period can reach 15 years, and the average rate of return to the Bank from installment sale is about 6% per annum.

Istisna'a. Istisna'a involves a contract whereby the Bank undertakes to have specific equipment manufactured at the specifications required by the beneficiary and to sell these to the beneficiary at a price to be paid over an agreed period. The period may not exceed 15 years. The return to the Bank is about 6%.

Equity participation. The maximum participation of the Bank is one third of the business' capital. Needless to say, the business has to be run in accordance with the Sharī'ah.

Profit sharing. It is a form of partnership between the Bank and entrepreneurs where the profit is divided in agreed upon proportions between the Bank and the partners.

Lines of finance. These are standard lines of finance to the national development financing institutions (NDFI) and Islamic banks for the financing of small to medium-size enterprises. The period of financing is normally shorter than the period in the above modes of finance. The rate of return remains at about 6%.

Technical assistance. This, which is for financing pre-investment expenditure, such as research and development, takes the form of grants or an interest-free loan for a maximum period of 16 years, including four years grace period, with a service fee of about 1.5%.

The IDB role in financing projects and trade, as well as other services, has been of considerable help to Muslim communities. The policies of the Bank have been compassionate, but not slack, prudent, but not severe. The interest of both beneficiaries and providers of finance has been under careful examination by the IDB management. Or to conclude with the words of the IDB vice-president, "It is important to note that IDB does not have any policy conditionalities attached to its financing, be it for project or trade operations. The Bank is definitely not a "fair weather" friend. We are friends for all seasons to all member countries. We are always there for them, in good times and bad times. Our financing activities are based solely on the good intention to assist the development efforts of the Ummah in member countries" (Aznan, 2003) There is a strong evidence to suggest that the assertion made by the Bank carries conviction.

The Islamisation of Economic Systems in Some Muslim Countries

The declaration of the Pakistani government in 1979, under the presidency of General Ziaul Haq, of transferring the whole economic system to an Islamic economy was the first serious attempt by an Islamic government to put Islamic economic principles into real application. Various steps were taken by the government towards the Islamisation, which were mainly: the application of an Islamic taxation system, the establishment of the Zakāh institution and the elimination of interest from the financial system and replacing it with a system of profit and loss sharing (PLS).

The first phase of substituting interest by a profit and loss sharing system came in 1979 when the government changed the basis of operation of the National Investment Trust (NIT), a Trust that was established in 1962 under the patronage of government to mobilize savings for investment in the corporate sector, on an interest free basis with effect from July 1979. The reaction of savers to the change was positive; the NIT achieved a substantial increase in net sales, and dividends and capital gains following the conversion (Shahab, 1982). Similar changes of the basis of operation had also been applied to the Investment Corporation of Pakistan (ICP). The ICP was established in 1966 to operate as an investment bank with a view to developing the capital market and broadening equity investment. The conversion of the basis of operation to an interest free system, which was exercised in phases, converted debenture financing into the Participating Term Certificate (PTC) financing. Once more, the conversion led to successful results with above average declared dividends (ibid.). Furthermore, a new investment institution was established in 1979 under the name of Bankers Equity Ltd., which aimed to provide PLS finance to private sector investment in large and medium size industrial enterprises. Further major changes were introduced in 1980: the promulgation of the Mudharabah Companies and the Mudharabah (Floatation and Control) Ordinance, and the amendment of the banking laws to allow for the opening of profit and loss sharing accounts instead of interest based accounts.

The Establishment of Islamic Financial Institutions

The first surviving endeavor of establishing Islamic financial institutions was the establishing of Mit-Ghamr Savings Bank in Upper Egypt in 1963. The pioneer of setting up the Mit-Ghamr bank was Ahmed al-Naggar, an Egyptian academic with practical experience in local savings banks in (West) Germany, who wanted to bring a German experiment to the land of Nile. The Bank's operations were based on the Islamic principle of the profit and loss sharing with no-interest from borrowers or depositors. The bank, however, was not referred to as "Islamic", in the 1960's Nasser's Egypt was swiftly moving to socialism, or Arabic Socialism as President Nasser called it, with sweeping decrees of nationalization of both foreign and major national investments. It was difficult in these circumstances; it seems, to have referred to the bank as being "Islamic". Names to al-Naggar, as he tells us, did not matter much as long as the Bank was seen to be run on the Islamic no-interest basis (al-Naggar 1973). The philosophy of the Bank was to mobilize local savings for the purpose of financing small businesses and entrepreneurs; an ideology which seemed acceptable to the ruling authority. Similar to all banks in Egypt at the time, the Mit-Ghamr Saving bank was owned by the government, hence regarded as a public sector institution, and was accountable to the Ministry of Finance. But the Bank was given a degree of operational autonomy, which was unusual by the standard of the day. The Bank's operations were mainly: deposit accounts, loan accounts, equity participation, direct investment, and social services (for further details of operation see al-Naggar, 1973 and 1976, and el-Ashker 1987).

Further Islamic banks and corporations were established in the Islamic world in the 1970's and 1980's. In chronological order these were the Dubai Islamic Bank in 1975, Kuwait Finance House in 1977, al-Rajhi Co. for Currency Exchange and Commerce in Saudi Arabia in 1978, Jordan Islamic Bank for Finance and Investment in 1978, Bahrain Islamic Bank in 1979, the Iran Islamic Bank in 1979, the Islamic Exchange and Investment Corporation in Qatar in 1979, the International Bank for Investment and Development in Egypt in 1980, International Islamic Bank in Bangladesh in 1983, Tadamon Islamic Bank in the Sudan in 1983, Bank Islam Malaysia in 1983, Beit Ettamouil Saudi Tounsi in 1984, and West Sudan Islamic Bank in the Sudan in 1984. A group of Faisal Islamic Banks, named after the late King Faisal of Saudi Arabia, emerged in 1970's and 1980's: in Egypt in 1977, in the Sudan in 1977, and in Turkey in 1985. The al-Barakah group emerged in the early 1980's: al-Barakah Bank in Sudan in 1982, al-Barakah Investment and Development Co., in Saudi Arabia in 1982, al-Barakah Islamic Investment Bank in Bahrain in 1984, and al-Barakah Turkish Finance House in 1984.

Even further, Islamic banks were carried to the heart of Europe: Islamic Investment Company, the Bahamas, in 1977, Islamic Banking System in Luxembourg in 1978, al-Rajhi Co. for Islamic Investment, UK, 1980, Dar-al-Māl al-Islami, Switzerland, in 1981, Islamic Bank International, Denmark, in 1983, and al-Barakah International PLC., UK, in 1983.

One cannot conclude without making a welcoming gesture on the arrival of a new addition to Islamic banks and financial institutions in South East Asia. This is the establishment of an Islamic bank in Thailand. In a country where Muslims are a minority, probably not more than ten percent of the population, the establishment of an Islamic bank in the capital of Thailand, Bangkok, with branches spreading in the north and south of the country. The Islamic Bank of Thailand is by all standards a major event. One hastens to emphasize that prior to the establishment of the Islamic Bank, Islamic "windows" were also opened in non-Islamic banks in the country such in Krung Thai Bank; which is a further welcomed move. Even further, financial societies, such as Othman-ibn-Affan Financial Society have been operating successfully in the south of Thailand for almost a decade. The Society caters particularly for the south provinces of Thailand where Muslims represent the majority of the population. The operational success of the Society, represented in increasing capital, income, contribution and a diversification of its operational activities suggest a similar success to the new Islamic bank in Thailand.

Several factors could be said to have contributed to the establishment of the above Islamic banks and financial institutions in the Islamic world: first, the increasing Islamic awareness among the masses at the grass root level, second, the financial support of wealthy Muslims, and the support of government.

First, the establishment of Islamic banks would not have been possible without willing clients, depositors and users of funds who believe in the Islamic mission and ideals. These would, indeed, make the Islamic financial markets. Without depositors and users of funds who are willing to apply the Sharī'ah to their way of savings and investments, Islamic financial institutions, though they may be successfully launched, may not have the ingredients for continuity, progress and survival. To put another way, though the establishment of Islamic financial institutions is a major move towards the application of Islamic principles to the financial sector, the growth, continuity and survival of these institutions is equally important. The willingness of using the facilities provided by these institutions, by the participants in the financial markets, i.e. depositors and users of funds, would create the width and depth of the market and, substantially, contribute to the growth, or survival, of the institutions providing the services. Competition among non-Islamic and Islamic financial institutions, when both types of institutions are allowed to operate in the same market, cannot be ignored on the premise that the customer is religiously motivated in pursuit of his financial transactions. Clients, both depositors and users of funds, will certainly make a comparison between the two systems if not for anything else it is for making sure that the system in which he believes is working. Management of Islamic financial institutions bear a heavy managerial role, greater than that of western-based-banks management to ensure the efficiency of their operations.

Second, the availability of the initial funds required to establish the banks. In establishing the above banks and financial institutions, funds came mainly from three sources: first, wealthy Muslims, particularly Arabs, who believed in the viability of an Islamic banking system as a substitute to the interest based system, such as in the financing of Dar-al-Māl-al-Islami and the al-Barakah group. Second, government financial support has also been important, as in the case of the Kuwait Finance House or Bank Islam Malaysia. Third, the contribution of the public at large has also been significant, as in the case of the Jordan Islamic Bank. It is (a) domestically owned, (b) 98.7 percent of its capital is owned by private individuals (1.3 percent financed by the Housing Bank of Jordan), (c) none of its shareholders is a major shareholder, and (d) it is not established in a typically wealthy oil country. The bank is a good example of the possibility of establishing an Islamic bank with very little support from government or wealthy initiators.

The establishment of Islamic financial institutions has directly and indirectly encouraged the establishment of Islamic business enterprises. Directly, as these institutions provided Islamic finance to enterprises willing to be run on Islamic basis, and indirectly as some of these enterprises relied on the financial resources to the extent that some attracted capital from Muslim participants who wished to invest their savings in these enterprises. Islamic business enterprises were involved in a variety of commercial and industrial activities covering a wide range of products: textile, furniture, electronic equipment, building and construction, housing, medical equipment, plastics and building materials.

Intellectual Developments

The First International Conference on Islamic Economics

The First International Conference on Islamic Economics was held in Makkah, Saudi Arabia, under the auspices of King Abdul-Azīz University, Jeddah. For almost a week, from 21 February to 26 February, 1976 (1396H), some two hundred Muslim economists and Ulama" had the opportunity to present papers, hold seminars, have discussions and exchange views on a subject that had always been close to their hearts. "It was a dream that came true", as the president of the conference said. The presented papers covered a wide spectrum including:

1. The concept and methodology of Islamic economics,
2. Production and consumption in an Islamic economy,
3. The role of the state in an Islamic economy,

4. Insurance within the frame work of the Sharī'ah,
5. Interest-free banking,
6. Zakāh, taxes, and fiscal policy,
7. Economic development in an Islamic framework,
8. Economic co-operation among Muslim countries,
9. Public interest and the just price,
10. Two surveys of contemporary Islamic economic literature, one on "Muslim economic thinking", and the other on, "Contemporary Turkish literature on Islamic economics"; these proved very useful for researchers in the field.
11. Teaching Islamic economics with a view to examining the possibility of introducing Islamic economics to university degree curriculums, problems surrounding research on the subject and possible solutions and remedies.

A particular observation could be made about the First Conference on Islamic Economics. In addition to academics and practioners, the participants included the Ulama'. By including the Ulama', the conference provided the opportunity for clerics and non-clerics to meet and exchange views, spontaneously, on a crucial issue of Islamic economics. This would help narrow the gap between the Islamists who are keen on modernization, *or tajdid*, and the clerics who perceive themselves as the preservers of the faith. A further observation is that in their research papers Muslim economists were determined to be seen applying Western analysis and technique, such as marginal analysis, to Islamic economics. But Sardar does not seem to like it. In his, "Islamic Futures, 1985", he argues that Muslim economists are too busy applying Western economic techniques to Islamic economics, which, to him, would lead to a problem of defocus rather than a desired depth of treatment, (Sardar, 1985). However, regardless of whatever camp to which one would feel inclined, one would not fail to recognize the importance and the volume of work that the First Conference, and other contribution of Muslim economists that has enriched the subject of Islamic economics. The languages of the conference, interestingly, were both Arabic and English with papers presented in both languages. The papers have been revised in the light of the discussions that followed the presentation and published in two volumes, one in English, incorporating English papers and the other in Arabic embracing Arabic papers (see bibliography, Ahmad K, and Sakr M for English and Arabic collections respectively).

The two volumes are valuable resources for readers in Islamic economics, banking and finance.

In addition to other recommendations, the Conference recommended the establishment of an international centre for research in Islamic economics at the King Abdul-Azīz University, Jeddah. A few months later the Centre was opened.

The International Centre for Research in Islamic Economics (ICRIE)

As mentioned above, the Centre (ICRIE) was conceived at the First International Conference in Islamic Economics. In 1977 it was established with the following objectives in mind (ICRIE publications and website):

1. The establishment of a specialized library that would collect scholarly works in the field of Islamic economics in various languages and issue catalogues to research scholars everywhere.
2. Conduct and support theoretical and applied research in various fields of Islamic economics, publish text-books in the field for the use of Muslim universities and organize training courses needed by Muslim economic establishments.
3. Provide research facilities and scholarships for visiting Muslim scholars to undertake research in their fields of interest.
4. Promote co-operation in the field of Islamic economic research among various universities and institutions.
5. Publish research papers and periodicals in Islamic economics.
6. Help establish chairs for teaching of Islamic economics, provide scholarships for research in this field and promote lectures, conferences and regional symposia in this field.

The ICRIE has been active in various activities such as:

1. Conducting pure and applied research in various areas of specialization in Islamic economics
2. Producing, distributing and translating teaching materials in Islamic economics
3. Organizing guest lectures and workshops
4. Publication of its own professional journal
5. Publication of occasional papers and monograph series
6. Organizing and conducting seminars and conferences nationally and internationally

7. Organizing scholars exchange programs
8. Offering in-house training facilities
9. Awarding fellowships for doctoral and post-doctoral studies to young Muslim economists

Reinforced by professors of Islamic economics of a particularly high caliber, drawn from both national and international resources, and with generous financial support from the Dallah-al-Baraka Banking group and King Abdel-Azīz University, the ICRIE is a major academic centre for research and education in Islamic economics.

The Islamic Research and Training Institute (IRTI)

Emanating from the Islamic Development Bank, IRTI was established in Jeddah, Kingdom of Saudi Arabia, in 1981. One of the stipulated Articles for the establishment of the Islamic Development Bank (IDB) states that the IDB is required to, "extending training facilities for personnel engaged in development activities (in member countries) and undertaking research for enabling the economic, financial and banking activities in Muslim countries to conform to Sharī'ah". In implementation of this Article, the IDB Board of Governors passed a resolution in 1979 for the establishment of an institute to undertake research and provide training for the benefit of member countries. As a result the Islamic Research and Training Institute was established in 1981 and became operational in 1983.

The functions of IRTI are as follows (IRTI website):

1. To organize and conduct basic and applied research with a view to developing models and methods for the application of Sharī'ah in the field of economics, finance and banking,
2. To provide for the training and development of professional personnel in Islamic economics to meet the needs of research and Sharī'ah-observing agencies,
3. To train personnel engaged in development activities in the Bank's (IDB's) members countries,
4. To establish an information center to collect, systematize and disseminate information in field related to its activities, and
5. To undertake any other activities that may advance its purpose.

Similar to ICRIE, the Institute has its own publication activities and an academic journal, which cover a wide range of research in Islamic economic banking and finance. Its training programmes reach Muslim member countries and countrics with Muslim majorities, in Africa, Asia and the Middle-East. It also incorporates researchers of high caliber. But unlike ICRIE, IRTI is not a teaching institute generating academic degrees; rather it focuses on research, professional training and, with its Information Centre, it provides valuable information to members countries in various industrial, banking and financial fields. In addition to these activities, IRTI organizes seminars and international conferences, guest lectures, visiting researchers programmes for senior researchers and academic professors, translation of major works, and provides a vital linkage with other research centers and universities in the field, and financial support to Islamic research projects in both Islamic universities and Western universities with a curriculum in Islamic economic, banking and finance. Once more, IRTI is a major achievement in the field of Islamic research and training.

The International Institute of Islamic Thought (IIIT)

The IIIT was established in 1981 with a view to polarizing the efforts of Muslim scholars and intellectuals to work towards re-modeling the contemporary Islamic thought and knowledge in the field of social science and humanity studies so as to help revitalize the role of Islam in present society. The idea of establishing the Institute emerged at an international seminar held in Switzerland in 1977 that incorporated some 30 leading Muslim intellectuals to discuss the crisis of Islamic community, the Ummah, and the means to take Islam forward to next century. The members came to believe that there was a need to establish an international institute of Islamic thinking that would contribute to providing Muslims with an in-depth examination of the rich heritage of their religion and suggesting means of solving their Islamic intellectual problems. The first major work undertaken by the Institute a year after its establishment was the organization of an international conference on the "Islamicisation of knowledge", which was held at the International Islamic University in Islamabad, Pakistan. Operating from its headquarters in Hendon, Virginia, USA, the IIIT organizes seminars, symposia and conferences, publishes valuable research, academic theses and textbooks, and provide support and scholarships to researchers in the field. The publications of the IIIT, in English and Arabic, cover a wide range of series the main examples of which are as follows (IIT website):

1. The Islamicisation of knowledge
2. The Islamicisation of culture
3. Contemporary issues in Islamic thought
4. Islamic methodology
5. Academic researches and theses
6. Public and guest speakers' lectures
7. Technical dictionaries, terminology and research synthesis
8. Islamic heritage and Islamic history
9. Reform movements

The IIIT provides a valuable source of knowledge about Islam to both Muslims and non-Muslims, and by operating on an international spectrum it represents a most needed link between the Muslim East and the Christian West.

The Islamic Foundation (United Kingdom)

Established in 1973 in the city of Leicester, England, the Islamic Foundation aimed to be a major centre for education, training research and publications. Moreover, the Foundation aims to seek bridges between Muslims and non-Muslims in the world in general and the United Kingdom in particular, (the Islamic Foundation website).

With its three main inputs: a rich library, a valuable research unit and a validated teaching and training programme, the Islamic Foundation is a major Muslim landmark in the heart of the United Kingdom.

The International Islamic Universities (Malaysia)

Not surprisingly, IIUM is today one of the best known educational institutions in the Islamic world. In the University's own words, right from its inception, IIUM has spared no effort to ensure that it provides the best tertiary education possible in all branches of knowledge. Its state-of-the-art facilities—physical and otherwise—are the envy of other institutions in the Islamic world (the University's website).

The establishment of IIUM in 1983 was the fulfillment of one of the major aspirations of the contemporary global Muslim community to regain the Ummah's leadership in the quest for knowledge. This yearning of the Ummah is a key element in IIUM's vision statement:

> To be an international centre of educational excellence which integrates Islamic revealed knowledge and values in all disciplines and which aspires to the restoration of the Ummah's leading role in all branches of knowledge. (ibid.)

IIUM operates under the direction of a Board of Governors with representatives from the eight sponsoring governments and the Organisation of Islamic Conference (OIC). It maintains links with governments and institutions all over the world, such as the League of Islamic Universities, the International Association of Universities and the Association of Commonwealth Universities. It is also affiliated with several Malaysian-based businesses that provide opportunities for students to gain practical work experience.

Currently, in 2006, IIUM is home to 15,000 students and 3,000 teaching and administrative staff members. Many of the students and members of the academic staff are expatriates. In all, about 100 countries are represented. This is a far cry from its humble beginnings in 1983 when it operated from temporary quarters with 153 students and a handful of lecturers and administrators (ibid.).

Most importantly, IIUM is committed to: "To revive and revitalise the Islamic concepts and traditions of learning, which regard the quest for knowledge as an act of worship and the spirit of science as emanating from the holy Qur'ān. The university endeavours to introduce a unified teaching and learning process along with the inculcation of moral and spiritual values through Integration, Islamisation, Internationalisation and Comprehensive Excellence (IIICE).", (ibid.)

IIUM offers a wide range of academic programmes geared towards both skill-building and scholastic attainments and designed in accordance with IIUM's philosophy, which is built upon the belief that knowledge must be pursued and propagated in the spirit of Tawhīd, as an act of worship, in full recognition that it is a trust which Allah has placed upon mankind, (ibid.).

It might be interesting to look into the University's philosophy as it emphasises the Islamic input of knowledge, as shown below:

1. Knowledge shall be propagated in the spirit of Tawhīd, leading towards the recognition of Allah as the Absolute Creator and Master of mankind.
2. The recognition of Allah as the Absolute Creator and Master of mankind represents the apex in the hierarchy of knowledge.
3. Knowledge is a trust (amanah) from Allah and its development

shall be in conformity with the purposes behind Allah's creation of the universe.
4. Knowledge should be utilised by man, as the servant (abd) of Allah and vicegerent (khalifa) on earth, in accordance with the will of Allah.
5. The quest for knowledge is regarded as an act of worship (ibadah).

Notably, the religious input in the above philosophy is particularly distinct.

The International Islamic University (Islamabad)

The foundation stone of the Islamic University, Islamabad was laid on the first day of the fifteenth century Hijrah i.e. Muharram 1, 1401 (November 11, 1980). This landmark of the beginning of the new Century symbolizes the aspirations and hopes of the Muslim Ummah for an Islamic renaissance. The desire to produce scholar and practitioners, imbued with Islamic Learning, character and personality, and capable to meet the economic, social, political, technological and intellectual needs of the Muslim Ummah was the reason for the establishment of this University (IIU website, January 2006).

The University was reconstituted as 'International Islamic University' with the promulgation of an ordinance in 1985.

The University is located around the domineering Faisal Mosque, a symbol of international Islamic brotherhood and unity. It is designed by a famous Turkish architect and is donated to the University by late Shaheed Kind Faisal bin Abdul Azīz. The Mosque is spread over an area of 189,705 sq. meters and can accommodate about 200,000 Muslims.

The broad aims and objectives of the International Islamic University are:

1. To offer all-around and harmonious development of individuals and society
2. To reconstruct human thought in all its forms on the foundation of Islam
3. To develop an Islamic character and personality among the students, teachers and the supporting staff in the University
4. To encourage and promote education, training and research in Islamic learning, social, natural, applied and communication sciences, and other branches of knowledge.

5. To take practical steps for ideological, moral, intellectual economic and technological developments, ideas and principles in accordance with the norms of Islam and to take necessary steps for developing practical solutions of contemporary problems.

Like IIUM, IIU is not confined to a narrow curriculum of Islamic studies. It has a wide range of faculties covering the following main areas: applied sciences, management sciences, usuluddin/Islamic studies, Arabic language, Sharī'ah and law, social sciences and language and literature. In addition, the university has two main specialised institutes: Islamic Research Institute and International Institute of Islamic Economics that were established in 1987, two years after the establishment of the University. The research objectives and functions of institutes can be shown as follows as stated in the publications of the Islamic Research Institute (IRI, IIU, 1987):

1. Act as the research arm of the University and conduct research in the field,
2. Develop and disseminate methodology for research in various fields of Islamic learning,
3. Study/interpret the teaching of Islam in the context of the intellectual and scientific progress of the modern world,
4. Publish monographs, books, research reports, research journals and such other research material as may be considered necessary for the promotion of knowledge of Islam,
5. Serve as a clearing house of knowledge of various aspects of Islam,
6. Appoint study groups for identifying issues facing Muslim society,
7. Organise seminars, conferences, symposia, and workshops to promote harmonious understanding amongst various schools of thought in Muslim societies,
8. Perform such other functions as may be necessary for realization of objectives.

The Islamic environment has become ripe for a renaissance in the Islamic economic literature. This is our main concern in the following chapter. Having explored aspects of revivalism in the Islamic world, academic and otherwise, we are now in a position to look into the development of Islamic economics in the twentieth century. This is our next, and last, chapter.

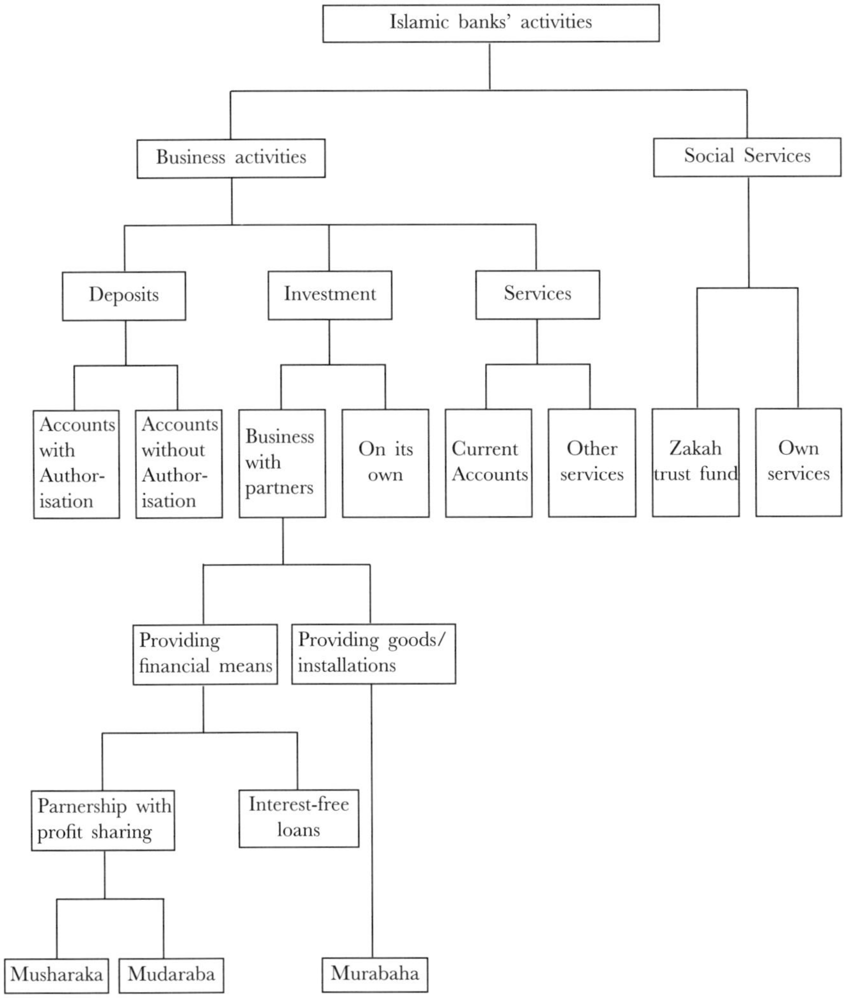

Figure: 8.1: Islamic Banking Operations (From El-Ashker, 1987)

CHAPTER NINE

ISLAMIC ECONOMIC RENAISSANCE: ISLAMIC ECONOMICS IN THE TWENTIETH CENTURY

Introduction

From the second half of the twentieth century the substantial amount of work on Islamic economics was beginning to have an impact on economic thinking, especially amongst Muslims. Siddiqi cited some 700 titles of original and commentary works on Islamic economics; most were written in the period from the early 1950's to the late 1970's (Siddiqi, 1980). The titles cover a wide range of topics: economic philosophy of Islam, (80 citations), economic system of Islam, (418 titles), Islamic critique of contemporary economics, (over 100 citations), economic analysis in an Islamic framework, (about 50 citations), history of economic thought in Islam, (40 citations), and bibliographies. Earlier surveys were also published such as; "A Guide to Researcher in Islamic Economics" by Attiyah, (a pioneer in Islamic banking who took Islamic banks to Europe), in 1974, and an, "Annotated Bibliography of Contemporary Economics Thought in Islam and a Glossary of Economic Terms in Islam" by Khan in 1973, followed by "Islamic Economics: Annotated Sources in English and Urdu," vol. 1, 1983 and vol. 2 in 1991.

The volume of work is impressive, including Turkish literature on Islamic economics that also came to prominence. In his "Contemporary Turkish Literature on Islamic Economics", Zaim cited over 200 pieces of work by Turkish authors on Islamic economics during the same two decades or so from 1950's to late 1970's. The Turkish authors seemed to have been determined to make their contribution felt. The tremendous amount of work in the area has generated a problem of riches for those wishing to write on the contemporary development of Islamic economics. It has become rather difficult to single out a name, or a group of names, as the author, or authors, of the century, as we were able to do so in previous chapters. But a problem of riches of writing in Islamic economics is much more preferred to a problem of shortage. The former is much more welcomed.

The twentieth century, therefore, is marked with an abundance of writings on Islamic economics. In the eighth century there was only one Abū-Yūsūf and we were able to highlight his work, but in the late twentieth century there were so many like Abū-Yūsūf that it would be difficult to single one writer out. As an alternative it might be conceivable to approach the subject by looking into the main trends in the literature guided by the main areas of interest in the writing on the subject. Different emphasis will be given depending on the continuity of the subject and the prominence of the subject area. No doubt some names will be overlooked in this harsh process, but it is an unfortunate inevitability. This does not mean, however, that the missing inputs lack importance or suffer weaknesses. Rather, it is the regrettable outcome of the conditions of constraints in a book of this nature. A reference to annotated bibliographies, for direction or recommendation, will, however, be made in due course to fill in the gap and to help the reader. One more factor will be borne in mind in the process of selection is that; lengthy research papers, monographs, books and papers presented at major Islamic economic conferences will be given some priority.

Influencing Factors

It was not until 1976 when the First International Conference on Islamic Economics was held that the subject of Islamic Economics gained recognition nationally and internationally. Apart from lengthy research papers, monographs, and specialised books, articles were mainly published in journals and magazines of religious or general social science nature that were geared towards Islamic studies as a whole rather than a particular discipline, economics or otherwise. Or as Khan states in his Annotated Sources in Islamic Economics, ". . . most of the literature on Islamic economics is scattered in journals and periodicals of a diverse nature. It may be found in religious magazines, periodicals of general interest and purely academic journals . . . books on Islamic economics are not classified under any single specified heading", (Khan, 1983). With very few exceptions, mentioned below, there were hardly any comprehensive books on Islamic economics of a rigorously analytical nature or primary sourced documents. Consequently, in the shadow of economics and indeed of that of Sharīʾah studies, Islamic economics grew, referred to sometimes as "an Islamic Approach", other times as "an Islamic economic system", or very often as an economic issue "from an Islamic perspective", rather than an independent subject of its own merits. It would take two decades or so for Islamic economics to be legitimized as an independent area of study.

In the absence of an organized institution that would coordinate the work on Islamic economics literature, several factors served as instigators to the development of the work on the subject. Five main factors could be said to have helped boost the development of Islamic economic literature at that stage: (a) the personal motivation of the writers themselves who were driven by their own religious zeal to promote Islamic economics, or the Islamic approach to economics, as a means of promoting the religious cause, (b) sponsoring academic and non-academic institutions and organisations that had the pro-motion of Islam within their set of missions, (c) religious societies, (d) Muslim students associations, and (e) dedicated publishing houses. Below is a brief evaluation of the influencing role of these factors.

The Personal Factor

Prior to 1976, particularly up to the late sixties, a great deal of writing on Islamic economics was mainly the outcome of individual efforts that were motivated chiefly by a personal and religious impetus. The personal and academic traits of the early writer on Islamic economics were of almost a unified nature. Up to the first half of the twentieth century, and well into the nineteen sixties, early writers on the subject were mainly: (a) educated in Islamic religious studies, (b) either religious scholars, such as Sharīʾah jurists, or (c) economists by education and profession, (d) economists with mostly Western economics education either in their home countries or abroad, (e) all religiously motivated, driven by their zeal to defend Islam first, in addition to their inborn academic curiosity, and (f) all with a persisting urge to prove to the doubting Muslims and non-Muslims that Islam can still work in the modern twentieth century, that it has the ingredients to accommodate new changes in modern society and that it has the ability to serve as a vehicle to foster economic development, run governments and re-establish nations. Above all, these scholars had one aim in mind: to rid Muslims society from what they saw as the perils of secularization and to bring it back to the purity, and practicality, of Islam—a major objective of Islamic revivalism.

Various factors seemed to have ignited the religious feeling among these writers to develop the work on Islamic economics by the turn of the second half of the twentieth century. First, the intensive activities of religious groups that aimed at mobilizing Muslims towards a return to the values of Islam and to the belief in it as a way of life in the contemporary Muslim society with a view to providing an opposition to the adopted secular model. When Islamic economics was among the challenging areas, the call for the revival of Islam helped prompt a call for a revival in the Islamic economics literature. The Muslim Brothers, *jamaʾat al-ikhwan al-Muslimūn*, which was founded in Egypt in 1928 by Ĥassan al-Banna (1906–1949) and Society of Islam, *jamaʾat-i-Islami*, founded in Pakistan in 1941 by Abūʾl aʾala Maudūdi (1903–1979) who carried the banner of re-Islamisation in Pakistan in his endeavour to mobilise the masses, are two distinct examples of these societies. Whether the writers of the mid twentieth century were affiliated to these organized religious societies or not is difficult to establish, nor is it the concern of this book, but it can be said that the strong call of these societies for the return to Islam as a source of values and strength to Muslims and a way of life to Islamic society in modern time had helped create the urge to write, the expectation to read, and the willingness to change. Furthermore, it must be noted that Al-Azhar University of Cairo has helped a great deal in generating graduates of high caliber in both Sharīʾah studies and other scientific subjects of which economics is one. Notably, Al-Azhar scholars, professors and graduates have made a number of contributions in Islamic economics in Arabic.

Sponsoring Institutions and Organisations

Of the academic institutions that fostered research on Islamic economics in the early part of the twentieth century, Al-Azhar University of Cairo stands out, as not only the oldest Islamic and one of the oldest universities in the world but also as an academic institution that paid particular attention to Islamic research and researchers. The University has established the Academy of Islamic Research as an affiliated academic body within the University to set up conferences and conduct research. The first of these annual conferences of the

Academy was held in 1964. Research, however, embraced research on Islamic topics of different nature, including, but not exclusively, Islamic economics. Research on Islamic economics was welcomed if not encouraged. Furthermore, the Academy would shoulder the responsibility of publishing the proceedings of the conferences and of the individual researches to make the benefits of the work widely available. It was only a decade or so later, when the Islamic economics grew further and expanded wider that a need for a specialised conference on the subject became obvious. It was then that the first International Conference on Islamic Economics of 1976 was convened.

To demonstrate the degree of influence that Al-Azhar Academy has had on the literature of Islamic economics at that phase of development, the following, which are published by the Academy, and are all in Arabic, are given as some examples of what Siddiqi has shown us in his survey of contemporary Islamic economics literature (Siddiqi, 1980):

> Al-Khafif, Shaikh Ali, "Individual Property and its Limit in Islam", 128 p., First Conference, 1964; Ĥasan, Abdel Raĥmān, "Financial resources in Islam", 64 p., First Conference, 1964; Hussaini, Ishaq Musa, "Hīsbah in Islam", 255–277 p., First Conference, 1964; Al-Araby, Muĥammad Abdūllah, "Islamic View Point Regarding the Ways of Productive Employment of Property", 124–136, Second Conference, 1965; Al-Araby, Muĥammad Abdullah, "Contemporary Bank Transactions and Islam's View", 79–122, Second Conference, 1965; Abū Zuhra, Shaikh Muĥammad, "Zakāh", 137–201, Second Conference, 1965; Proceeds of the Seventh Conference, Sept. 1972, "Economic and Legal Discourses", 410 p., Seventh Conference, 1973; Al-Shahawi, Ibrāhīm Dasuqi, "Hīsbah: a Social Function", 64 p., Seventh Conference, 1973; and Al-Tahawi, Ibrāhīm, "Islamic Economics: a School of Thought and a System, a Comparative Study", 2v, 616 and 400 p., 1974.

Still in Egypt, as another example of institutional involvement, we find the High Institute for Arabic Studies (a post-graduate study institute) producing an interesting treatise in Arabic on "Inheritance and Legacy in Islam with an Introduction to Inheritance amongst Arabs and the Romans", 400 p., 1960, by Muĥammad Yūsūf Mūsa. As this institute is within the government establishment and under its educational supervision, the contribution of government to encouraging research in Islamic studies and Islamic economics cannot be ignored. Another example of the role of government in Egypt can be taken from the High Council for Fostering Art and Literature, which is a government agency. As an example, the High Council held an international seminar on Islamic insurance the proceedings of which were published in Arabic in a substantial piece of work titled, "Islamic Jurisprudence Week and Ibn Taimiyah Celebrations", 1963, 925 p. (ibid.). This is yet another example of the contribution of government to promoting Islamic economics thinking at that early phase of the subject's development.

Last but not least, the World Muslim League may be added to the list of sponsors of Islamic economics. "Economics of Social Structure of Islam", by Muĥammad Abdūllah al-Araby, Singapore in 1966, and, "Social Justice in Islam", by Ahmad Zaki Yamani, both in Singapore, 1966, and "Characteristics of Islamic Economics", by Mahmūd Muĥammad Babulli, in Makkah, 1969, (ibid.) are some examples of the researches presented to, and supported by, the League.

These were the key institutions that pioneered research on Islamic economics. But from the late seventies onward, more sponsoring institutions came to the scene with substantial financial resources and expertise. Examples of these are mentioned in the previous chapter on Islamic revivalism in which it was mentioned that the effect of these institutions on the development of Islamic economics has been tremendous.

Religious Societies

The effect of these societies has been of twofold: the effect of religious teachings on the writers on Islamic economics that has contributed to enhancing their initiatives, and the public call for Islamic revivalism in Muslims' life with a return to the basic ideals of Islam. Religious societies represented by those mentioned earlier, extended their influence among the public through lectures, mosque schools and the weekly regular Friday congregational prayers. The military disaster that bewildered the Muslim world after the defeat in what became known as the six-day war, or mildly referred to in the Muslim world as the setback, made the message of religious bodies for the return to Islamic ideals more persuasive. Many concluded that the religious reason for the defeat was that Muslims were not fully commited to their religion and if they were to achieve any future victory in battlefield or factory they ought to return to the pure rules of their religion.

Muslim Students Associations

Despite what could be thought of as minor bodies with no distinctive academic arms, Muslim Student Associations have proved to be effective in the publication of Islamic writing on Islamic economics. Either nationally or internationally some associations have been notably productive. For example, we find the Cultural and Religious Committee of the Students Muslim Association, Faculty of Engineering of the University of Cairo producing an interesting research on the "Property and Ownership in Islam", 1972, under the Committee's name (Siddiqi, 1980). For a student association of a faculty of engineering to produce an Islamic economics research paper, this must indicate a high religious motivation, as the topic is beyond the curricula of study. In another association within the same university, though nearer to the subject of study, we see the Society of Islamic Studies, Faculty of Commerce, University of Fouad I (the old name of Cairo University before it was changed after the 1952 Revolution), producing research on "Economics in the Light of Islam", 114 p., in 1951, under the patronage of the Society (ibid.). Producing a monograph on economics in Islam, in as early as 1951, reflects an early interest in Islamic economics in Cairo university circles.

The Muslim Students Association (MSA) of US and Canada, the name of which was changed later to the Association of Muslim Social Scientists, was active in encouraging research and publication on the subject. A list of the MSA publications includes: Kahf, Monzer, "A Model of the Household Decision in Islamic Economy", 19–28 p., 1974; Cotemporary Aspects of Economic and Social Thinking in Islam", 1973 which is a proceedings that included high caliber researches such as Abdul Hamid Ahmad Abū Sulaiman's, "the Theory of Economics of Islam: the Economics of Tawheed and Brotherhood; Philosophy, Concepts, and Suggestions", (ibid.).

Dedicated Publishing Houses

In modern times, without publishing houses it would be difficult, if not almost impossible, for academic work to grow and flourish. Differentiated from preachers in houses of religions, writers and academics rely on publishing houses for seeing their work spread, their ideas travel, their message reaching far, and their mission continued. Publications provide an effective means to achieve these goals, and without publishers publications would not be. For Islamic studies in general, and Islamic economics in particular, there had been in the Islamic world dedicated Muslim publishers who carried the task of publishing papers and researches, motivated mainly by the religious drive; not ignoring however whatever gain that may bring with it. Dar-al-Fikre al-Arabi, House of Arabic Thought (Cairo), al-Dar al-Arabiyah, Arabic House, (Cairo), Dar al-Nahdah al-Arabiyah, Arabic Renaissance House, (Cairo), Dar al-Kitab al-Lubnani, the Lebanese Book House, (Beirut) and Sh Muhammad Ashraf (Lahore), are some examples of the many publishing houses that helped promote the writing on Islamic economics.

The help of Islamic journals, even with their lack of speciality in Islamic economics, was also notable and very encouraging. Islamic Review (London), Islamic Literature (Lahore), Islamic Thought (Aligarh), Islamic Quarterly (London), Al-Azhar (Cairo), al-Manar (Cairo), Criterion (Karachi), al-Nadwah (Makkah), Islamic Culture (Hyderabad), Islamic Studies (Islamabad), Islam and the Modern Age (New Delhi) and Voice of Islam (Karachi) are examples of these religious journals that devoted pages and issues to Islamic economics, among other Islamic studies, and helped the subject develop.

The Topics

The early topics covered were, by implication, of religious-social-economic nature, but not, by necessity, political. There was a conscious intention to avoid any clash with governments, the majority of which were in favour of secularisation as a way forward to economic development. The topics were revolving around social justice and Islamic social solidarity, two firmly embedded values in Islam. Zakāh and Ribā, the charge and earning of interest, were a plausible start and they appeared more than others in the mid twentieth century writing, as they represent the two basic sacred values in Islam of justice and solidarity. That remained to be the case at least up the third quarter of the twentieth century, beyond which the Islamic economics writing began to spread to topics of a highly technical nature. Now, the topics are on par with almost all technical issues in Western economics.

The following topics will be explored below as pioneering and major examples of writing on Islamic economists in the twentieth century:

Zakāh and taxation
Abolition of ribā
  Interest-free banking
  Monetary policies, fiscal policy and resource allocation
Islamic economics theory, ethics and economics
Consumer behaviour
Insurance
Economic cooperation among Muslim countries
Indexation
Economic development

Zakāh and Taxation

Whenever Zakāh is mentioned in a bibliographical list, or sought as an entry in the literature, a reference book comes always to mind, that is "fiqh al-Zakāh" (jurisprudence of Zakāh) by the jurist Yūsūf al-Qardawi. The book, which has been translated from Arabic, its original language, to many other languages including English, has been republished several times, and is still universally demanded. In two volumes the book provides an encyclopedia of the third pillar of Islam. Al-Qardawi seems to have exhausted the coverage of the subject by looking into it from the perspective of the four main schools of Islamic thought, concluding with his own opinion. The purpose of the book was threefold: first, to educate Muslims on their religious obligations as far as Zakāh is concerned, second, to adapt the application of Zakāh to the twentieth century's society given the complexities of estimating the Zakāh tax base, and third, to stress the merit of Zakāh as a societal caring tax on the one hand and an investment incentive levy on the other.

The reasons for writing on Zakāh in the twentieth century are several, as al-Qardawi is telling us in his preface to the first 1969 edition of his *fiqh* book, which is repeated in the edition of 1981, (Al-Qardawi, 1981):

(1) The importance of the subject per se as the third pillar of the five pillars of Islam, on the one hand, and the corner stone of an Islamic economics approach on the other, and the need to rewrite the subject in a manner that suits modern times as compared with the works of classical jurists. The rewriting is particularly needed given the difference of opinions between the

classical jurists in the four main schools of thought. Muslims in modern times are searching for a unified view on the subject not a variety of opinions, and that is what the author tries to provide. This point draws the attention at the outset to the intention of al-Qardawi of bringing Islamic writing to the attention of the Muslims in a modern society: not a debate on the issue but a unified and precise work.

(2) There are new issues in Zakāh that did not exist at the time of the early classical jurists or, if they existed, were not on the same scale as today, and these issues require explanation and thorough discussion so that the Zakāh treatment would be clearer in peoples' mind. Some examples of these issues are the revenue generated from commercial activities that have become present in modern societies such as property rental, particularly when it is on a large commercial scale, profits from manufacturing in the modern industrial sector, fixed or mobile assets that result in substantial income generation such as ships, commercial vehicles, and aircrafts, as well as, different types of companies with various capital structures and forms of ownership. Other examples can be seen in the income generated in the non-industrial service sector, and income generated from employment in the form of wages and salaries. In all these cases and others it may not be straightforward to calculate the Zakatable base, the threshold or the rates with reference to the classical books of fiqh. The quantification of quantifiable elements of Zakāh in terms of modern financial reporting will add to the problem. This may lead some to believe that the old rules of Zakāh, and Islamic economics with it, are not applicable to modern society. Al-Qardawi, therefore, finds it necessary to write on the subject in the language of the society of today in a serious attempt to bridge the gap between the ruling of the classical jurisprudence and realities of today. The change of economies from being mainly based on barter to being based on monetary transactions, as al-Qardawi tells us, adds to the necessity of rewriting on the subject in the economic language of today.

(3) The relationship between taxes in the modern Islamic state provides a further necessary reason for rewriting on the subject. The question of whether the Islamic state may or may not have the right to impose other levies besides Zakāh, or what may be referred to as taxes, is vitally important not only in the mind of

> lay Muslims, but also in the debating corridor of Islamic public finance. The views on this issue are divided: some believe that the state may have the right to impose further levies besides Zakāh if the revenue from Zakāh is insufficient to cover the society's needs, some restrict the right of the state to situations where there is a call for jihād and a need to finance military operations, and others rule out entirely the right of the state to impose any levies besides Zakāh.

The methodology of fiqh al-Zakāh is that of an academic researcher. In his fiqh, al-Qardawi first, collects all Qur'ānic verses and authenticated Hadiths that deal with the subject, second, divides the contents in a sequentially coherent manner that makes it easy for the reader to follow, and third, provides a thorough comparison between the ruling of the early Rightly-Guided Caliphs as well as the jurists of the main schools of thought, on the one hand, and a comparison between Islam and other divinely revealed religions on the issue of Zakah on the other, fourth, provides an analytical explanation of the ruling to highlight the reasons for it and the intention behind it, and fifth, concludes with his own opinion on the debatable issue supported with reasons and explanation provided with considerable clarity. Al-Qardawi examines all these issues and comes up at the end with a recommended view that reflects, by his own statement, his effort in reaching an opinion within the rules of *ijtihād* (see chapter two of this book for further discussion of *ijtihād*).

Al-Qardawi's *Fiqh al-Zakāh* is a crucial contribution to the Islamic economics literature. In the twentieth century of Islamic economics, it stands in parallel to the Abū-Yūsūf's eighth century *Kitab al-Kharāj*.

Islamic social security is added to the list of topics that were of interest to Islamic writers in the late nineteen seventies to early nineteen eighties. Al-Fangari introduced to us his "Islam and Social Security: a Comprehensively Concise Study of the Application of Zakāh as a Tool to Achieving Islamic Social Solidarity" in its first edition in the late nineteen seventies and continued to the third edition in the early nineteen nineties, (Al-Fangari, 1990). With his high position as a government official in the Egyptian legislative council, and as an academic in al-Azhar University, al-Fangari views reflects his status as a senior government administrator and a distinguished researcher in the oldest Islamic university in the world.

Al-Fangari's main concern in his book is the role of Zakāh as an institution and a policy tool for the achievement of Islamic social security. Having referred to what Islam has guaranteed individuals of levels of satisfaction that are beyond the level of sustenance, al-Fangari starts by differentiating between social insurance, social solidarity and social security. To emphasize the role of the state he clarified that social insurance is a system that although organized by the state involves the payment of a regular insurance premium by the individual, while social solidarity is a voluntary arrangement by individuals to help one another even if that may take a collectively organized form. The role of the state in the latter is much less than that of the former. In contrast, social security involves the financial obligations of the state towards its citizens, by providing the necessary help to the needy and old without necessary expected payments from them towards these provisions. Al-Fangari argues that this obligation on the state is clearly stated in the Qur'ān and Sunnah in the stipulation of the institution of Zakāh. This is a strong emphasis that may, by implication, render a government as non-Islamic if it is not providing a system of social security. Islam, the author ascertains further, has provided for both systems: a system of social solidarity through ordaining individuals to pay out of their own wealth to those in need and a system of social security by obliging the state to establish the institution of Zakāh in the manner described in the primary sources of the religion: the Qur'ān and Sunnah. Social security, the author reiterates, is part and parcel of Islam and the right of individuals to it is above all rights as it is part of the blessing of God for His subjects.

Al-Fangari concludes his study by salient recommendations. Two of these are particularly prominent, first, the need to establish a Ministry, Secretary, of Zakah in the cabinet of Islamic governments, and the need to hold international conferences on Zakāh. Interestingly enough, perhaps because his voice has been heard, it is not unusual to see now ministries of Zakāh in the cabinets of some Islamic governments, and also to observe the organization of international conferences on Zakāh, the first of which was initiated by the Kuwait Zakāh House in 1984 (El-Ashker and Haq, 1995).

The reason why we feel that one more book can be added to the list of our discussion of books on Zakāh is that Abū-Saud's Contemporary Zakāh has unique coverage. The book was published in both Arabic and English almost simultaneously, it was published by a specialised publisher in the field, the Zakat Research Foundation, and it was published in the United States. The reason for publishing the book in both languages is that the English speaking audience is very large, or as the author tells us in his foreword, "the non-Arabic speaking Muslims are almost ten times greater than the Arabic speaking Muslims" (Abū-Saud, 1988), and there is a need that the message in the book is to reach them promptly.

What prompted Abū-Saud to write his book, was, he explained, (a) "the thick obscurity enveloping the rulings of this corner stone of Islam", (b) "the contradictory rules of the various Islamic schools", and, (c) "the lack of vision regarding the modern patterns of transactions with their new concepts and models of income and investment", (ibid.). Even though one might find these reasons already stated in al-Qardawi's fiqh some two decades earlier, the significance of Abū-Saud's contemporary Zakāh is that, by his own assertion, although "the work of al-Qardawi has been of great value to this author" the author "has his own reservations" and points of view that do not coincide with those of al-Qardawi. In a nutshell, although the intention of both authors, al-Qardawi and Abū-Saud, is the same, which is to deal with contemporary issues that either did not exist at the time of early or Medieval Islam, or existed but were not on the same scale or of the same relevance, they differ on their recommendations, opinions, or *fatwa*, given on how best these new issues can be treated.

In effect, the traditional debate that led to the appearance of the various schools of thought does not seem to have come to a halt. In more than one place in his book, we read Abū-Saud's disagreement with both the classical and the contemporary jurists, "we do not agree with the tradition set up by ancient jurists and adopted by al-Qardawi and many contemporary jurists" (ibid.). Throughout the book we invariably find Abū-Saud, after explaining the ruling of the Rightly Guided Caliphs, the opinions of the classical jurists, and the views of the contemporary jurists, stating, "we may not adhere to that", "we have strong reservations", or "we strongly object", before proceeding to give his own point of view.

The zeal of Abū-Saud is undoubted, his self-exertion in reaching an opinion is sincere and Contemporary Zakah is a valuable addition to fiqh books on the subject. The difference of opinions is a difference of application that aims at achieving the most plausible methods and principles of calculating the levy in modern times. It is a difference on technicality to achieve the utmost fairness. But the recognition of Zakāh as a social, economic and religious institution is unanimous.

Zakāh continued to occupy the attention of Muslims for the rest of the twentieth century until today. Conferences on Zakāh were held, training sessions were arranged by leading institutions, such as the Islamic Research and Training Institute (IRTI) of the Islamic Development Bank (IDB), and governments from the late nineteen seventies onward became active in enacting Zakāh laws and directives in introducing Zakāh formally to their financial systems.

The first international Zakāh conference was held in 1984 in Kuwait, initiated by the Kuwait Zakāh House as already indicated. Two years later, the second conference was held in 1986 in Riyadh, Saudi Arabia, sponsored by the Zakāh and Income Tax Department of the Ministry of Finance and National Economy of Saudi Arabia. As a follow-up action on the recommendation of the second conference, a third international conference was held in Kuala Lumpur, Malaysia, in 1990 sponsored by the Islamic Centre of Malaysia, the Zakāh and Income Tax Department of Saudi Arabia, the Zakāh House of Kuwait, the International Sharī'ah Board of Zakāh of Kuwait, and IRTI.

The third conference was particularly pragmatic in its approach to dealing with Zakāh as it focused on the administrative arrangements for the implementation of Zakāh in the economies of Muslim states that wish to, conform to Sharī'ah. Because of the particular significance of these issues and their implication for the application of Islamic economics and its development in dealing with complex administrative problems, the third conference is given due space below.

The third conference had one main focus: the administrative aspects of Zakāh. From that perspective, the conference aimed to achieve three main objectives: (a) disseminate information, knowledge and experience among member countries of the OIC, the Organisation of Islamic Conference, in connection with the administrative side of Zakāh, (b) help member countries wishing to introduce Zakāh into their financial systems to overcome the initial administrative difficulties of implementation, and (c) further an understanding of the economic significance of the various institutional frameworks for Zakāh (El-Ashker and Haq, 1995). Two particular factors could be said to have contributed to the elimination of Zakāh from government financial systems in Muslims countries: first, the long-standing absence of Sharī'ah application from governments' systems, which became more pronounced with the military subjugation of the Muslim world to Western forces, and second, the belief that Islamic systems, economic and otherwise, should give way to secularized systems if Muslim countries were to reap the benefits of modernization. Therefore, the third conference on Zakāh was particularly important as it focused on issues related to these two points; explicitly to the first and implicitly to the second. The papers presented at the conference portrayed that theme, with reference to the application of Zakāh to Bahrain, Egypt, Iraq, Jordan, Kuwait, Libya, Saudi Arabia, the Sudan, Yemen, Iran, Bangladesh, Pakistan and Malaysia. The countries that intend to enact Zakāh laws within their legislation will find the comparative study particularly useful as they may benefit from the experience of these countries.

The conferences papers could be divided into three main sets. The first deals with financial control systems of Zakāh, the second looks into the effect of obligatory as compared with non-obligatory systems of collecting Zakāh on government revenue and tax payers, and the third investigates the experimental practice of several countries in managing Zakāh collection and distribution.

The control system focuses on three main kinds of control: Sharī'ah control, to ensure that the collection and disbursement of Zakāh is in accordance with the Sharī'ah rules, financial control, to make sure that the collection and payment of Zakāh is within the basic governmental accounting and financial rules without any financial irregularities, and economic control to examine whether the application of Zakāh has lead to the purposes for which Zakah was introduced and if that is at the minimum cost of administration.

In his case studies of the countries under examination, Fouad al-Omar stresses a few points with respect to the control of Zakah. Two points are most prominent: first, the implementation of Zakāh still poses a great challenge to Zakah administration with regard to the collection and distribution of Zakāh. Second, Zakāh systems need to be implemented in such a way as to keep administration costs to a minimum. He suggests that serious efforts are still needed to create new distribution channels for the Zakāh revenue so as to alleviate poverty and discourage beggary, (Al-Omar, 1995). These points are shared with Muĥammad Akram Khan in his study of Zakāh in Pakistan. Of the several views he mentions in his study, Khan is concerned with the problem of control over idle funds that might reach as much as a few billion Rupees that could have been distributed among the targeted population (Khan, 1995). Khan provides an interesting comparison of the administration of Zakāh in Pakistan and Kuwait. Given the different sizes of wealth and land between the two countries, the comparison is quite intriguing. The two countries share some similarities but have a few distinct differences. The similarity is mainly that the two countries introduced Zakāh to their systems around the same time, 1980 and 1982, for Pakistan and Kuwait respectively, and the differences are in that the economic and socio-political set-up of the two countries is vastly different. It is a case of comparing the implementation of Zakāh in a rich petroleum country like Kuwait and a less fortunate country where poverty is more desperate such as Pakistan. Conceivably, the level of geographical dispersion in the country is expected to influence the size and shape of the administrative structure and the level of wealth is anticipated to influence the choice of the method for collection. Khan found that the organizational structure of the administrative body of Zakah in Pakistan comprised of five hierarchal layers (central, provincial, district, tahsil, and local) while that of Kuwait was largely centralized. Also, while the collection of Zakāh in Pakistan was found to be obligatory, that in Kuwaiti was voluntary (ibid.).

The Sudan provides an interesting case study. It was the domicile of the Islamic Mahdi reform movement in the late nineteenth century that was founded by Mohammad Ahmed al-Mahdi (1844–1885) who proclaimed himself the awaited Mahdi and who aimed to establish an Islamic state in the Sudan. During the time of the Mahdi state, Zakāh was implemented within the process of the Islamisation of state administration. In the late twentieth century, Sudan took five years to finalise the organizational structure of its Zakāh system. Zakāh was reintroduced in two phases: (a) a voluntary phase in 1980 by the enactment of the Zakah Fund, and (b) compulsory in 1984 when the Zakāh and Taxation Act was passed. As al-Sawory explains, the Zakāh control system in the Sudan is exercised at three different levels: Sharīʾah control, financial control and administrative control. He emphasises the need to provide Zakāh staff with proper training and ensure their adequate recruitment.

The importance of publicity on the distributing of Zakāh revenue is stressed by Abdūllah in his study of Sudan. Abdullah believes that Zakāh departments should disburse Zakāh in accordance with Sharīʾah openly so that Zakah payers are reassured of the way in which Zakāh revenue is used, otherwise a gap will always exist between the assessment of Zakāh on available wealth and what is actually collected by Zakāh departments (Abdullah, 1995).

The second main issue in the administration of Zakāh is the question whether it should be obligatory, where Zakāh is regarded as a right of the state, or non-obligatory, where Zakāh is left to individuals to pay to beneficiaries voluntarily. The economic implications of these two systems occupied the attention of Abdin Salama who looked into the effect of changing the system from non-obligatory to obligatory in the Sudan on the level of Zakah revenue. Compared with Zakāh proceeds before the introduction of the compulsory system, the proceeds after the change of the system to obligatory increased substantially. But administrative costs, particularly with regard to the distribution of Zakah revenue, seemed to be particularly high. The low revenue before the introduction of the obligatory system in 1984 does not seem to be caused by lack of religious motivation among the Sudanese, but rather it was due to lack of confidence by Zakāh payers that the government administration would use the Zakāh proceeds solely for purposes stipulated in the Sharī'ah. There seems to be suspicion that government administration did not separate Zakāh revenue from that of other taxes and used Zakāh for financing general purposes that are not related to the needs of Zakāh beneficiaries. Hence Abdullah's emphasis on the need to publicise the distribution of Zakāh (op. cit.) and Salama's stress on the necessity of separating the Zakāh department from other tax departments in the same ministry (op. cit.).

How and to what degree does the application of a compulsory Zakāh system affect the voluntary payment of Zakāh to beneficiaries directly, is a question that has occupied the attention of Islamic macroeconomic researchers. The existence of the ritual aspect of Zakāh implies that there is not necessarily a causal negative relationship as Zakāh is paid to please God. In an empirical study applied to Pakistan, Faiz Muĥammad arrived at some important conclusions: (a) the needy, the poor and charitable organizations depends more on unofficial Zakāh payments than on official payments from government Zakāh agents, (b) people's drive for voluntary Zakāh payment has not subsided after the introduction of the compulsory system, and (c) voluntary Zakāh payment depends on a number of socio-economic and religious factors prominent in the community (Muĥammad, 1995).

The above studies and many others can provide the country that wishes to introduce Zakāh to its financial system with the choice of models that should help public administrators decide how to deal with one of the most important aspects of economics in a Muslim country. Needless to say, the above section does not intend to provide an exhaustive list of what has been written on the subject. The interested reader may wish to refer to bibliographical sources in Siddiqi (1980), Khan (1991) and Kahf (1994).

Writing on Zakāh continued until the end of the twentieth century. The treatment of the topic, however, was broadened to examine the issue within the framework of fiscal policy and a just allocation of resources. To take but one example, Zakāh, by necessity, was an important subject for the attention of participants in seminars on "Monetary and Fiscal Economics of Islam", held in Makkah in 1978 and Islamabad in 1981. The Makkah Seminar addressed some of the major theoretical issues, while the Islamabad Seminar focused on the examination of some of the experiments in Islamic banking. Zakāh can be seen clearly discussed by researchers on fiscal policy in Islamic state as presented in the Seminar Proceeds (see, Ahmed, Iqbal and Khan, 1983). It is not surprising to see Zakāh mentioned under a variety of headings. Zakāh is a multi dimension subject and by necessity or implication it is appropriate both to examine Zakāh per se and to look into its effects on other issues. The importance of the topic rests on two main dimensions: Zakāh as a worshiping practice being the third pillar of Islam, and Zakāh as an economic activity for its economic and financial implications. For the latter, Zakāh has a significant impact on various issues such as: fiscal policy of the state, (b) taxation policies, (c) economic development, (d) social justice, (e) distributive justice and need fulfillment, (f) saving and investment decisions, (g) financial policies of the business enterprise, (h) consumer behaviour. It is not surprising, therefore, to find Zakāh one of the most researched topics in Islamic economics.

Having given Zakāh the due respect in space and time, we turn our attention now to the second area of interest that has preoccupied the thinking of Muslim economists both before and after the First International Conference on Islamic economics: Ribā.

Abolition of Ribā

What is new about the writing on Ribā-free, or interest-free, Islamic economics in the twentieth century, particularly in the later half of the century, is that Islamic economists treated the subject in relation to major contemporary financial issues: (a) the operation of banks and financial institutions, and (b) monetary and fiscal policy. The objective was very clear: on the one hand it was to address the question of modernity once more with a view to proving that Islam is still relevant to contemporary life, but indeed it required innovation in financial instruments and banking systems in order to ensure that banks can be successfully run on an interest-free Islamic basis.

Interest-free banking

Interest-free banking was a new concept that was not taken seriously until the middle of the twentieth century. Indeed commercial banking itself is a nineteenth century invention and the early writing on the subject only attracted the attention of Islamic economists during the mid twentieth century. In his "Banking without Interest", first published in Urdu in 1969 and in English in 1973, Siddiqui (later to be changed to Siddiqi) discusses the banking operation from an Islamic perspective and furnishes us with valuable information about the contribution of those who wrote on the subject of interest-free banking before him (Siddiqui, 1973). The subject had attracted contributions in Urdu, English and Arabic. In Urdu we find two major contributions from Syed Abul A'la al-Maududi's "Ribā", in 1961 and Sh. Ahmad Irshad's "Banking Without Interest", in 1964. In English, Anwar Iqbal Qureshi's, "Islam and the Theory of Interest", published as early as 1946, Mohammad Uzair's "An Outline of Interestless Banking", in 1955, and Afzalur Rahman's "Banking and Insurance in Islam" in 1979 are distinguished contributions. Mahmoud Abū Saud's "Is it Possible to Establish Islamic Banks?", Mohammad Abdūllah al-Arabi's "Contemporary Banking", in 1965, and Isaa Abdou's "Banks without Interest" in 1974, are distinct pieces of work in Arabic. The common factor among the writers is that they maintained that despite the foreseen difficulties, Islamic banking could be operated on the basis of profit-and-loss-sharing, providing that the countries' banking laws permit. The bank as an independent party enters into a partnership contract with the depositors who wish to invest their deposits. Depositors unwilling to invest would keep their deposits on demand. Further analysis and more technical discussion and clarification of these general principles were examined in Siddiqui's "Banks Without Interest". Realizing the size of the task ahead, Siddiqi in 1973 invited Islamic economists for further discussion of the subject (Siddiqui 1973). And these discussions continued well into the nineteen nineties.

Another important stream of writing at that early stage came from banking academics and practitioners. Reflecting on his experience in establishing and running the first Islamic bank in Egypt in 1963, al-

Naggar tells us about the Mit-Ghamre Bank in the upper Egypt's village of Mit-Ghamre where he introduced the idea of Islamic banking wrapped, as he is telling us, in a not particularly Islamic slogan. Savings Banks were a successful endeavour for a decade or so until the government moved in and put the bank under government supervision and regulations (Al-Naggar, 1973, 1976). The Nasser Social Bank, the state institution that took over the Mit-Ghamre Bank, is still operating in Egypt. It has a particular social function: collecting and distributing Zakāh and providing social loans to those in needs.

The two decades or so after the beginning of writing on, and indeed the establishment of, Islamic banks, witnessed distinct focuses in the literature on Islamic banking. Ariff provides us with an interesting survey of these studies from the early stage during the mid nineteen sixties to the late nineteen eighties when contributions to the subject attracted much attention (Ariff, 1988). Even with different emphasis and various degrees of elaboration, there was unanimous agreement among Islamic economists that Islamic banking operations should be based on the PLS (profit and loss sharing) principle instead of on the basis of interest. Despite the abundant theoretical work on Islamic banking up to the end of the twentieth century, empirical work on the operation of Islamic banks seemed to be very limited. Some case studies have been conducted in Bangladesh, Egypt, Malaysia, Pakistan and Sudan (ibid.) but the number of studies is still small. From field studies it is evident that there are similarities and differences in the application of the PLS principle to Islamic banks in these different countries. For example, the Islamic bank of Bangladesh has been offering PLS Deposit Accounts, PLS Special Notice Deposit Accounts, and PLS Term Deposit Accounts, while Bank Islam Malaysia has been operating two kinds of investment deposits, one for the general public and the other for institutional clients (ibid.). The studies also show that the profit sharing ratios and methods of payment vary from place to place and from time to time. For example, profits are provisionally declared on a monthly basis in Malaysia, on a quarterly basis in Egypt, on a half-yearly basis in Bangladesh and Pakistan, and on an annual basis in the Sudan (ibid.).

Furthermore, to add to the problem of operational technicality, Islamic banks do not have a yardstick against which profit ratios are measured in Murabaha operations or otherwise except for LIBOR, or similar. It is well known that LIBOR is based on interest rates and when Murabaha operations are based on such a yardstick they are based in effect on the rate of interest. Also, in Islamic banking operations other than Murabaha, the same basis of comparison is used: profit rate compared with LIBOR. To help Islamic banks solve this problem a profit-index may need to be established which can be used in Murabaha and other investment operations. A theoretical framework for the establishment of such an index has been initiated by El-Ashker, (El-Ashker, 1995), though additional work is still needed to examine further the suggested models of the index and to test their plausibility.

Despite the valuable work on Islamic banking up to the last quarter of the twentieth century, the literature had two particular limitations: first, writers based their analysis on the premise that Ribā would be absent from the economy, and second, they did not discuss, or at least not thoroughly, issues concerning monetary and fiscal policy. This was to come a decade or so later within the writing on an interest-free economy and the Islamic banking system, that continued to the end of the century.

Monetary and Fiscal Policies and Islamic Resource Allocation

The monetary policy became of interest to Islamic economists shortly after the early waves of the establishment of Islamic banks. In 1978, the first seminar on the monetary and fiscal economics of Islam was held in Makkah followed by a second in Islamabad in 1981. The proceedings of the two seminars, which were co-published by the Institute of Policy Studies, of Islamabad, and International Centre for Research in Islamic Economics, of Jeddah, included well focused research papers. The general theme of the papers was whether a fiscal policy is possible in an Islamic state and if it is, how it will be different from other non-Islamic fiscal policies. The common answer to the first part of the question among the writers is a positive reply in the sense that, yes, a fiscal policy is possible. Writers, however, have slight differences in expressing their views on the second part of the question as to how and what policies could be followed to achieve these Islamic policies. To begin with there is a general consensus that fiscal policy in an Islamic state should be Islamic ideological oriented and in contrast to other policies of non-Islamic policies it cannot be value-neutral (Ahmed et al., 1983). The functions of the Islamic state would be more or less like those of secular states except that in addition to these functions the Islamic state has the duties and the responsibility to not only promote the Islamic ideology, but also to defend it.

The difference between the researchers into the Islamic fiscal policy came when taxation was the subject of discussion. Kahf, basing his views on the premise that the responsibilities of the state do not go beyond ensuring that the socially determined subsistence standard of living to the poor is fulfilled, argues that with the exception of taxes required for the purpose of defense, the Islamic state has no financial rights beyond Zakāh (Kahf, 1983). Quoting the views of the consensus of earlier jurists, Kahf is of the view of limiting the authority of the state either in imposing taxes or in other policies of fiscal management. Consequently, Kahf is against using taxes as a tool for income redistribution (ibid.). Kahf's views are not however shared by other writers who argue that the Islamic state should have a more effective role in using taxation, including imposing taxes beyond Zakāh, and other policies to achieve the desired objectives of an Islamic society, such as promotion of a more egalitarian socioeconomic order, acceleration of economic growth, and maintenance of monetary stability (Ahmed et al., 1983).

In assigning a high priority to the Islamic fiscal policy, Metwally has a novel idea. In his emphasis on the importance of fiscal policy to achieve stabilization and equilibrium in the money market, and with the absence of interest that may help achieve this objective, the Islamic state may impose "economic dues" on "income and idle assets whose rates may vary depending upon the stabilization conditions, which by making idle cash costly, may provide an incentive to investment (Metwally, 1983). The idea might look theoretically sound, but practically it may lead to side effects such as increasing consumption instead of savings. In addition this may amount to imposing a levy on the cash twice, once by Zakāh and another by Metwally's economic dues, which is not permissible in the Sharī'ah.

In outlining the major objectives of the monetary policy in an Islamic state, three main objectives have been identified (Ahmed et al., 1983). These are: stability in the value of money, economic well being with full employment and an optimum rate of economic growth, and promotion of distributive justice. Al-Jarhi stresses that it is almost obligatory on the central bank of an Islamic economy to maintain the value of money and suggests that the central bank should allow expansion of money supply only to the extent that it is justified by a potential contribution to growth in real balances (Al-Jarhi, 1981). Stability of the value of money ought to be given high priority in the Islamic monetary policy, in the view of Chapra, for the implications this may have on the concept of Ribā in Islam as in the absence of interest the real value of loan when returned would not have been compensated by any means if the value of money has depreciated (Chapra, 1985). This would entail unfairness to the lender who is lending at zero interest rate. This is in addition to the adverse effect inflation may have on the socio-economic justice and general welfare in the Islamic community.

In as far as the achievement of economic growth and full employment, is a goal of the Islamic monetary policy, Chapra stresses that while he is in full agreement with this objective, he warns against seeking the maximization of economic growth per se as an overall objective for Islamic fiscal policy. Unnecessary and morally questionable goods ought not to be produced just to maximize production, as this, in the views of Chapra, implies the misuse of divinely bestowed natural resources. Also, a balance should be maintained between the production of goods for present consumption and those for future consumption (Chapra, 1985).

Turning their attention to the use of monetary policy for achieving distributive justice, most Muslim economists are of the view that monetary policy should be used to actively promote the goal of distributive justice in an Islamic economy (Ahmed, et al., 1983). Ariff, however, is of the view that too much concern of distributive justice in formulating and implementing monetary policy may unfavourably affect its overall efficiency and effectiveness in attaining other goals in monetary policy (ibid.). In laying down his argument Ariff does not imply that achieving distributive justice is not important, but quite the opposite. He agrees with others in that reduction in income inequalities should be an important policy objective of the Islamic state, but he is of the view that this objective can be implemented by other economic policies rather than overburdening monetary policy with too many objectives to achieve (Ahmed et al., 1983).

As a policy tool, Islamic monetarists are of the view that in the absence of the use of interest as a tool in the non-Islamic monetary system, the central bank can concentrate on controlling the money supply instead. Adequate control can be exercised on money supply in an Islamic economy by regulating high powered money, defined as currency in circulation and reserve assets of banks. Moreover, a variation in the cash reserve ratio, the liquidity ratio, and credit ceilings may be used to bring about desired changes in money supply. Moreover, in addition to controlling money supply, monetary policy may be used to influence the allocation of resources. Profit-Loss-Sharing ratios in the Islamic system can replace interest rates in a non-Islamic system (Ahmed et al., 1983). These views are among that Chapra has elucidated competently in his "Towards a Just Monetary System", as this work provides a through explanation of the technical and operational mechanisms of fiscal and monetary policy in an Islamic economy (Chapra, 1985). Of the many contributions on the subject Chapra's Towards a Just Monetary System is a distinguished addition to the Islamic economics literature: it is comprehensive, well integrated, conceptually analytical, and operationally pragmatic.

Islamic Economics Theory, Ethics and Economics

The first international conference on Islamic economics demonstrated a variety of interest among researchers and participants. The first was an interest in laying down the conceptual and theoretical framework of Islamic economics—a conceivable start in a first conference of its kind. With different emphasis on the economic activities of the individual and the state, Islamic economists are, as expected, unanimous that their subject draws its concepts and principles from the Sharīʾah, the Divine Law. Consequently, ethics as emanating from Islam, are the paramount foundation of Islamic economics. In theorizing on Islamic economics, the issues of Zakāh and banking without interest are, inevitably, in a prominent position.

Having started by defining economics as a science, Sakr proceeded to look into Western economics theories with a view to providing what seems to be a common ground between Islamic and Western economics. The conclusions appear to be: as there are already embedded ethical values in Western economics, manifested in normative economics and advocated by altruist economists, there are also ethical values in Islamic economics that is based on Islamic norms and religious ideals, which would, or should, make Islamic economics per se more readily acceptable to Western economists as an independent branch of economics, (Sakr, 1981). On the role of the state in the economy, he proceeded further, outlining the role of the Islamic state in managing the economy. This should be based on: optimum employment of economic resources, directing public expenditures for public benefits, state surveillance of market operations, controlling prices if necessary, fighting monopoly and promoting competition, interference in the labour market with a view to protecting workers and ensuring justice and equal opportunity to all (ibid.).

In contributing to the theorization of Islamic economics, al-Fangari, whom we have cited before in the writing on Zakāh, expresses his concern over what he sees as: a lack of understanding of Sharīʾah subjects by Muslim economists, and lack of understanding of economics by Sharīʾah scholars. The result is that, "Many of those who write on Islamic economics confine their writing to specific topics revolving in particular around Zakāh and the prohibition of Ribā, as if Islamic economics were only concerned with Zakāh and Ribā", (Al-Fangari, 1981). He recommends that Muslim economists, in addition to being technically competent in contemporary economics, should be thoroughly educated in Sharīʾah. In reconciling Islamic economics with its fourteenth century history with contemporary economics, al-Fangary ascertains two important points:, first, concepts and principles of Islamic economics are to be taken from the primary sources of the religion, the Qurʾān and Sunnah that are not subject to change, and second, the application of these concepts and principles may vary from time to time and from one situation to another as the contemporary circumstances may demand (ibid.). Consequently, Islamic economics according to al-Fangary can be divided into two main dimensions: first, "the Islamic Economic Approach", which cannot be changed as it is based on Qurʾān and Sunnah, and the "Islamic Economic System(s)", which can be adaptable to changes in society. What is particularly interesting in al-Fangari's thinking is that he is in favour of "*ijtihād*", which is the exertion of self to reach a rule in a situation that either did not exist in the past or existed but not at the same dimension and regards "the closure of the gate of *ijtihād*" as harmful to Islam (ibid.). This is in contrast to fundamental jurists who advocate that *ijtihād* in religion is an invention, and every religious invention is misguiding, and every misguidance is in Hell fire. When the call for *ijtihād* comes from a professor of economics at al-Azhar University, and a member of a legislative body, the State Council, in Egypt, al-Fangari's call for the application of *ijtihād* carries particular conviction.

The need for a comprehensive book on Islamic economics was anticipated and fulfilled by Mannan's "Islamic Economics: Theory and Practice", 1970. Mannan's book came at a time when providing a text-book on Islamic economics was still in its infancy. The book is instructive and educational to those wanting to learn about the subject in a comprehensive and integrated manner. Mannan helped the reader to avoid distraction in having to consult fragmented topics in different sources, and, instead, provided him/her with a comprehensive book of learning. Written in the form of a textbook, Mannan's Islamic Economics, which is a valuable early addition to the literature, covers almost all aspects of the economics of Islam including some comparison with capitalist economics (Khan, 1983).

Turning our attention to the ethical values in Islamic economics, we find that Islamic economists stress that in contrast to other economic systems, ethical values are embedded in Islamic economics. These values are rooted in Islamic philosophy on which Islamic economics is based, in such a way that makes it impossible to build an Islamic economic model, or to envisage Islamic economics, on a value-neutral premise. Islamic economists and Sharī'ah scholars agree on this with no exception.

Naqvi is among those Islamic economists who took the point further with a focused deliberation. In his "Ethics and Economics: an Islamic Synthesis", having stated that the key to a thorough understanding of the originality of Islamic economics lies in its ethical value system, he elaborates on the issue by reiterating that Islamic ethical philosophy is based on four main axioms: Unity, Equilibrium, Free Will and Responsibility (Naqvi, 1981). Unity, which in an absolute concept refers to the unity of God, reflects that man's life on earth is, or is perceived to be, well integrated in its entirety in a complete coordination between the universe, life on earth and man as being amalgamated in one unit. Equilibrium, which is inferred as justice or al'Adl, requires that within its homogenous whole which life is in an Islamic perspective, its various elements must be equilibrated to produce the best social order. But the Islamic equilibrium, or social harmony, is not so much a static property in the sense of a plea for the status quo, as a dynamic quality releasing powerful forces against evil (ibid.). Also, equilibrium, we are told to note, carries with it definite normative underpinnings since on the plane of social existence, it denotes a binding moral commitment of the individuals in any society to uphold a delicate balance in all aspects of their lives. Furthermore, Islam not only emphasises the fact of equilibrium, but also insists on the quality of equilibrium that "represents a first-best conglomeration of natural and social forces to reproduce in human life that harmony which already exists in nature" (ibid.).

Free will gives man the freedom of choice. But Naqvi wishes to emphasise that the human freedom applies to both the "individual man" and the "collective man" as a member of society, with an adequate balance between the two (ibid.). It follows that, the Islamic concept of freedom differs from the Western concept that gives the individual an almost unlimited right to private property with a full reliance on the individual to achieve the maximum contribution to social good. Islam, Naqvi reiterates what Islamic economists unanimously agree on, does not grant unqualified sanction to an individual's right to private ownership as all properties belong to God and man's ownership is ownership by trusteeship.

Turning our attention to the fourth ethical axiom of Islamic economics, responsibility, Naqvi emphasises that it sets the limits to what man can do through his free will. Indeed free will and responsibility can be viewed as the two sides of one coin. As free will gives the individual the freedom of choice, the responsibility axiom restricts his freedom so as to exercise this freedom in a responsible manner. In other words, freedom must be counter balanced by responsibility, if only to satisfy the dictates of nature's equilibrium (ibid.).

But Naqvi extends the point of private property further and takes it to an unusual position. We find him advocating that when there is a state of wealth inequality in society a transfer of private property ought to be made to "collective ownership" through a process he refers to as a process of "collectivization". In developing his argument, we find him stating, "since the existence of private property rights is a major barrier to any move towards equalization, private wealth beyond a certain point will *have to be* (italics ours) collectivized and redistributed" (ibid.). Other means do not seem to be sufficient for him to rectify the situation as he continues, "this point is reinforced by the fact that fiscal devices have been singularly unsuccessful in equalizing the distribution of income" (ibid.). Whether "collectivization" means "nationalization", is a question that may come to mind. Naqvi promptly answers the question negatively; the transfer of property is not to go to the state. As he mistrusts the state and asserts that civil servants may "feather their nests at the expense of the society" (ibid.), the ideal situation to him would be the "collective control of private wealth by the community (Ummah), as a whole, and not State control", (ibid.).

In an Islamic society therefore, explicit laws must be enacted with a view to: (a) limiting the ownership of private property to socially acceptable levels, and (b) having a broad-based ownership of total wealth. Collectivization or nationalization, whatever the term might be, boils down to limiting private ownership at the discretion of the state and transferring designated parts to state ownership. Whether this process is acceptable to Islam or not is another question. An affirmative answer to the question is difficult to find in the Islamic literature. Jurists on the whole agree on the desirability of markets, and in that private ownership may be implied. Arguments for this are based on evidence from *Aĥadīth* in the Sunnah (see Chapter 2). Even the jurists who stressed the Islamic legitimacy of the intervention by the state in the market, qualified their opinion with the proviso that (a) the market conditions are interfered with, (b) traders have misused their power to manipulate the market by deviating from the rules of the Sharī'ah, by for example exercising monopoly and hoarding goods to influence prices, and that (c) this has lead to a state of abnormality in the operational conditions of the market. All are external circumstances that have affected the market environment. Only then, the state may interfere, and its interference would be in so far as these manipulative conditions exist, beyond which the intervention would cease with the return of the market to normality, (see for example, Ibn-Taymīya, Public Duties in Islam, in bibliography). Modern Muslim economists also express their concern. In his foreword to Naqvi's treatise we find Khurshid Ahmad, having admired the author and welcomed the work, expressing his concern that, "There is very little evidence, logical or canonical, to suggest that "collective ownership" is or has ever been the Islamic norm. More careful and rigorous differentiation between private ownership based on the concept of amanah (trusteeship) and the unrestricted private property and enterprise of capitalism as well as the collectivization of property in different brands of socialism deserves to be made. Similarly, a clear distinction between equity and equality, not to say of "absolute equality", would have to be made by Muslim economists", (Ahmad, in Naqvi 1981). Naqvi's discussion provides valuable insights into the conceptual basis of Islamic economics. His fresh ideas, and sometimes controversial views, merit further extension and further discussion.

Consumer Behaviour

The behaviour of consumers had been of concern to early jurists, as indeed had been many other issues in the Sharī'ah, even if they were not economists as such a discipline did not exist in the twelfth or thirteenth century. The jurists al-Shaibānī (750–804), and Abū-Hamid al-Ghazāli (1058–1111 A.D.), whom we cited earlier in chapter 5 when discussing their works on Earnings and Iĥya' Ulūm al-Dīn, The Revival of the Science of Religion, respectively and the jurist al-Shātibī after them (d. 1396), discussed the theory of consumption and the behaviour of consumers in a competent economic manner, (Al-Shaibāni, Al-Ghazāli, 1937, Al-Shātibī, and Al-Raysoony, 1995). The missing element in their analysis, however, if that is to be considered as missing, is the use of modern marginal analysis. The jurists discussed consumption theory with three aims in mind: (a) to draw for the consumer his map of consumption and the basket of goods that he consumes, as this ought to be in line with God's command, (b) to guide the consumer in his/her manner of consumption to the pattern that is blessed by God to show how and how much to consume, and (c) to outline the responsibility of the state in relation to the consumption of the poor and needy in accordance with the order of God. A consumption function lies in the heart of Islamic teachings as examined earlier in chapter 2 in three important aspects. As shown previously, the stand of Islam in connection with these three main issues is that (a) consumers should consume what is only permissible, abstaining from the forbidden and the frowned upon, (b) they should consume in moderation; no niggardliness but also without extravagance, and (c) the state has an obligation to guarantee the level of necessities to the poor and needy through the use of Zakāh resources. Early jurists elaborated on these levels of consumption as well as the role of the state in some detail, and their deliberations have been utilised by modern Islamic economists with the application of new analytical tools such as marginal analysis.

Benefiting from the available knowledge on the subject al-Zarqa embarked on what he referred to as the social function of consumer behaviour (Zarqa, 1980). The social function of consumption, if observed, will lead to the maximization of God's reward in seeking his satisfaction of goods and services consumed. In doing so, the consumer would observe the three levels of consumption, which are divided into: necessities, convenience and refinement. In line with the definition of early jurists, necessities incorporate all activities that are needed to preserve the five foundations for a good individual and social life in Islam, namely: religion, life, mind, offspring (marriage), and wealth. Conveniences embrace all activities and goods that are not vital to the preservation of the five previous categories of foundations. Refinements include activities and goods that go beyond the limits of convenience and incorporate goods that though they do not remove or relieve difficulties and hardships, they compliment, brighten or adorn life (Zarqa, 1980). Zakāh is also discussed as playing a religious and social role in shaping the consumer's social function.

Kahf focuses on the concept of *falāh*, success, as an objective in consumer behaviour (Kahf, 1980). The concept of *falāh* implies success in life and the life after and this would not be achieved unless consumers maximize utilities in both worlds: the here and the hereafter. Kahf concludes by suggesting that: (a) with the virtue of Zakāh, the Islamic economic system will lead to the Islamic consumer having a higher rate of savings than consumer in other systems, (b) the nature of the Islamic system will make investment an integral part of the savings decision, (c) by the effect of Zakāh, the level of wealth will be maintained in an Islamic system, (d) by increasing the disposable income of the poor through the distribution of Zakāh, the Islamic system provides for an increase in aggregate demand and hence an increase in output, (e) the Islamic system secures larger resources for growth and development than other systems, (f) the Islamic system mobolises non-active resources, and (g) the Islamic system provides the state with an effective information tool through the administration of Zakāh (Kahf, 1980).

In his Islamic perspective of the theory of consumer behaviour, Khan focuses on the concept of *muslaha*, or the welfare of society, in shaping the behaviour of the Muslim consumer (Khan, 1992). He differentiates between "wants" and "needs" and argues that the wants are not the motivating forces for consumer behaviour in Islam. Islam, he argues, negates the assumption that all wants are equally important and that unlimited wants need to be satisfied. Instead Islam recognises that there is a set of needs that should be fulfilled first before the wants may be considered and that even these needs have a scale of preference where some may be more important than others. In deciding whether a good or a service is a want or a need, the concept of *muslaha* can be used to examine if the production of the good and the rendering of the service would increase the welfare of society, *muslaha*, or not. If it does it is a need and may be produced and consumed otherwise it is a want that can wait until all needs are satisfied. Therefore, Muslim consumers should be motivated by their needs more than their wants in shaping their pattern of consumption. Reiterating the views of the fourteenth century writer, al-Shatibi, Khan classifies these needs as: life, property (wealth), faith (religion), intellect (mind) and posterity (marriage). All such goods that have the power to promote these five elements as said to be having *muslaha* for human beings. This, by implication, stresses that *muslaha* is not the same as utility, while the former considers what is good for the welfare of society as a whole first in shaping the pattern of consumption, the latter focuses on what is good for the individual consumer in particular in determining their priorities for consumption. Moreover, while this is all related to what the consumer spends on consumption in this world, he is also expected to spend in the cause of God for the sake of the hereafter and to balance his spending between the two realms (ibid.).

The differences between altruism and socio-economic analysis on the one hand and the Islamic analysis of consumer behaviour on the other have been of concern to other writers on the subject. El-Ashker stresses aspects of similarities between the two theories as well as of differences (El-Ashker, 1983). Conventional economists, to begin with, have been criticised by both Western socio-economists and Islamic economists. They are charged with the neglect of ethical values in their economic analysis in general as well as that of consumer behaviour. Such a criticism is not entirely well founded as the analysis of altruism has been considered by Collard for example, a conventional economist (Collard, 1978). Socio-economists criticism focuses on the degree of emphasis rather than on the complete omission. In general, however, the behavioural assumptions in conventional economics are criticised by Western socio-economists who advocate that more emphasis should be given to the social responsibility of the consumer, with a considerable regard to the interest of the surrounding community. They suggest, instead, a social image where the consumer is regarded as a "homo-economicus-humanus" (Nitsch, 1982). Some went even further to suggest linking economic issues with social ethics from Christian thought or "some equivalent set of teaching such as in Islam" (McKee, 1982). Socio-economists and Islamic economists, it seems, agree on one thing: the inclusion of the social responsibility of the consumer to the surrounding community in the analysis of consumer behaviour. Despite the acknowledgement of this similarity, both groups of economists, Western socio-economists and Islamic economists, differ on the following in particular (El-Ashker, 1983 and 1985):

(1) While the former have a set of ethical values that are not necessarily religious, the latter have a set of religious beliefs emanating from the Islamic doctrine. The importance of this difference is related to the two following points,
(2) While the former do not have a specific methodology for the consumer to follow (individuals are free as to the pattern of consumption in relation to their ethical values), the latter have a specific methodology laid down in Islam,
(3) While the objectives of the consumer in the Western socio-economics are twofold—the satisfaction from goods and services consumption and moral satisfaction, the objectives in Islamic economics are threefold—the satisfaction of goods and services consumption, moral satisfaction and the satisfaction from a divine reward in their lifetime and the thereafter.

Criticism may be directed at the Islamic theory of consumer behaviour on the grounds that it might be too idealistic. How much of Islamic ideals are observed by consumers in their patterns of spending, is a question that requires empirical research, but such work is scarce. In one of the few research papers, El-Ashker tries to investigate the behaviour of Muslim consumers and the effect of environment in a non-Islamic country, Scotland (El-Ashker, 1985). The general findings of the study lend some support to the theory, but reject some of the assertions. The findings were as follows:

a. Social caring spending occupies the second highest priority of the respondents' spending after meeting basic needs. This is in line with what the theoretical analysis maintains.
b. The effect of the environment is clear in the study as buying cars for own transport and electrical appliances occupies a high priority in the scale of preference. This may not be the case in other Muslim countries with lower incomes.
c. The majority of savings however, are invested in Western-run banks. Various explanation are offered for this in the study most of which are related to absence of Islamic banks and none is in denial of the Islamic prohibition of interest.

This is but a preliminary study. Further empirical studies are still required to link the practice with the theory.

Insurance

Insurance has been of interest to Islamic economists and Sharī'ah scholars for two main reasons: its novelty and its role as a tool of risk management in modern history. First, insurance is one of the most obvious examples of activities that were not known in its modern form or dimension in the early centuries of Islam and as such it requires analysis to reach a ruling on its Islamic permissibility. Second, insurance is particularly important in modern society as a loss financing technique in the process of risk management, at both the individual and business levels. With an overlapped area between acceptance and rejection, insurance is not entirely accepted or rejected in Islamic economics; some scholars permit all types of insurance and others permit only some types. But they all agree in principle on the importance of insurance in modern society and its necessity for businesses and individuals.

The disagreement seems to concentrate on the methodology of implementing insurance more than on insurance per se. For example, having classified insurance horizontally into mutual, cooperative and profitable, and vertically into property, liability, and life, al-Zarqa (senior) allows all forms of insurance, and sees no clearly decisive rule in the Sharī'ah not to legitimise it (Zarqa, 1980). He argues that mutual insurance, which was known prior to and during the early period of Islam, cannot be prohibited in modern Muslim society, and similarly cooperative insurance, which is similar to mutual insurance, cannot be denied Sharī'ah acceptance. These are types of insurance where insurance is not meant to be for profit, but for allocating the losses, when it occurs, to the contributors to the insurance fund. If no loss or damage is incurred the fund, unless the participants agree to continue keeping it, can be dissolved and the money paid back to the contributors. The same would be the case if the loss or the damage turned out to be less than anticipated; the balance of the insurance fund could be paid back to the contributors (ibid.). There is no disagreement among Sharī'ah scholars on that, but the disagreement is on the form of insurance that aims at seeking profit by the insurer. In modern times this would be insurance through specialised insurance companies. The companies in this case, through the actuary analysis of potential payments of compensation or the value of damage when the insured event incurs, can calculate the insurance premium so as to give the insuring company an acceptable profit.

While al-Zarqa accepts that it is only normal that companies would be driven by profit motivation in these circumstances (ibid.), other scholars reject that reasoning. Ĥassan is among those who, although they accept mutual and cooperative forms of insurance, reject the form of insurance that is motivated primarily by profit seeking (Ĥassan, 1980). He argues that such insurance contracts suffer ambiguity and uncertainty as to the value of damage and the premium, as the latter should be exclusively for covering risks, not for making profits, and this may bring injustice to the insured. Ĥassan seems to be particularly concerned about the insured being unjustly treated and being subjected to potential exploitation by large insurance companies, more than concerned about the necessity of insurance that is managed by large companies in the contemporary financial environment. Al-Zarqa, on the other hand, though he condemns exploitation of the insured, urges insurance companies to practice fairness and to seek a moderately acceptable profit level that would not entail injustice or a heavy financial burden to the insured (op. cit.). The argument boils down into that while Islamic economists and Sharī'ah scholars accept mutual and cooperative forms of insurance, they are divided on profitable insurance: some accept it with caution, and others admonish it with rebuke. But both groups have one thing in mind: the interest of the insured.

Economic Cooperation among Muslim Countries

The subject of economic cooperation among Muslim countries has received much attention from Islamic economists. As might be expected, there is a general call for cooperation and an emphasis on the need for it to overcome endogenous as well as exogenous problems. There is a variation of methods and differences of emphasis, however. Some two decades ago, Yusri suggested an integrated Islamic cooperative system that aims at the elimination of economic dependence on non-Islamic economic communities, which can be based on the following principles (Yusri, 1985):

(1) Introduction of diversification in production and exports to help Muslim countries rid themselves from the one-product economic phenomenon that characterizes the economies of these countries and their reliance on one or two raw material goods exports to industrially advanced countries,

(2) Promotion of multinational Islamic investment ventures among Muslim countries,
(3) Promotion of Islamic banks and financial institutions and providing the necessary help for their establishment and operation,
(4) The application of an Islamic custom dues system that treats Muslim countries favourably,
(5) Abstention from joining economic organisations with a non-Islamic philosophy,
(6) The establishment of an Islamic Customs Union among Muslim countries where these countries may specialise in their production operation so as to achieve the benefits of low comparative costs and the optimum allocation of resources among themselves,
(7) The establishment of an Islamic Central Planning Committee that helps coordinate economic policies among Muslim countries as well as providing the necessary help to investors and entrepreneurs wishing to invest in an Islamic manner in these countries, and
(8) Muslim countries ought to introduce cooperation among them based on the principle of brotherhood that is commanded in Islam among individuals.

Needless to say, Yusri elaborates on the merits of his suggestions with some useful insights into his recommended programme.

Discussing the same issue, economic cooperation among Muslim countries, Zaki concentrates on the epidemic problems of Muslim countries with an attempt to find plausible solutions (Zaki, 1980). These are:

(1) Misallocation of wealth and income,
(2) The one-product economy,
(3) Scarcity of capital,
(4) Scarcity of skilled labour and expertise,
(5) Low technology,
(6) Lack of application of advanced technology in industry,
(7) Lack of coordinated strategic planning, and
(8) Lack of coordination among Muslim countries.

Zaki proceeded to provide recommendations on how to tackle these problems. Better use of natural, human and financial economic resources, speeding up the process of industrialization and agricultural development are some examples of these recommendations (ibid.).

How much of these problems still exist after more than two decades of the analysis of these writers, is not very difficult to ascertain. Although the Islamic Development Bank is playing a commendable role in providing the much needed finance and capital to the OIC (Organisation of Islamic Conference) countries, much more is still needed. The application of technology is increasing, skilled labour is more available than before, and infra structure has improved tremendously in the last two decades or so, but there are still many shortcomings in the area of strategic planning and coordination among Muslim countries.

Yet intra regional trade among the OIC countries is still very limited. For example while between half and four fifths of the trade of Euro Zone countries is with other members of the Zone, intra trade between the OIC countries in 2001, as shown in Table 9.1 below, was about 11 per cent of exports and 14 per cent of imports.

Moreover, given the substantial disparities in economic development and differing economic structure in the Muslim world, there does not seem to be a possibility for Muslim countries to meet the conditions for aligning their currencies with the ultimate aim of establishing a currency union (Wilson, 2004). The three main conditions suggested by Mundell (1961) and McKinnon (1963) for optimum currency unions to be successful are firstly that resources, notably labour and capital, should be mobile amongst member states; secondly, the economic structures should be similar, and thirdly, there should a willingness to closely co-ordinate monetary, fiscal and other economic policies. Mundell and McKinnon also postulate that free mobility of capital and indeed a degree of financial market integration is also a pre-requisite for a successful monetary union. These conditions do not seem to be met across the OIC countries. There are restrictions on movement of labour between all OIC countries with increasingly restrictive conditions governing work permits in order to encourage the employment of local citizens rather than foreign workers (Wilson, 2004). Also, in reality there are few capital flows between Muslim economies, partly reflecting the limited degree of stock market development and the restricted scope for portfolio investment flows. The exception is only in Saudi Arabia and Malaysia where stock market capitalisations exceed $400 billion and where there is significant trading in government bonds, including Islamic *sukuk* certificates in Malaysia.

Table 9.1: Intra-trade among OIC member states, 2001

	Intra-exports $US billion	Share of intra-exports %	Intra-imports $US billion	Share of intra imports %
Algeria	1.33	6.8	0.91	7.9
Bangladesh	0.22	3.8	0.88	9.8
Egypt	0.76	18.4	1.68	13.2
Indonesia	4.81	7.4	4.74	12.2
Iran	3.68	14.0	2.45	13.3
Iraq	1.04	9.4	1.10	21.2
Jordan	1.19	51.8	1.42	29.1
Kuwait	2.12	11.3	1.71	21.7
Malaysia	4.95	5.6	4.71	6.4
Morocco	0.50	7.0	1.88	17.1
Pakistan	1.98	21.5	4.45	43.6
Saudi Arabia	10.33	14.7	3.39	8.0
Syria	1.31	24.0	0.94	14.8
Tunisia	0.73	11.1	0.92	9.7
Turkey	3.90	12.5	5.27	12.7
UAE	6.06	15.1	9.00	20.8
Yemen	0.49	14.0	1.17	38.5

Source: Islamic Development Bank, *Annual Report*, 1423 H, Jeddah, 2003, p. 63.

Contrary to Yusri's recommendation some twenty five years ago, capital is flowing from Muslim to Western countries. Most of the portfolio investment flows recoded in Table 9.2 refer to outflows of capital from the Muslim World to developed countries rather than inflows. The absence of multinational companies with head offices in the Islamic World limits the scope for foreign direct investment (FDI) flows between Muslim countries. Even movements of FDI between Muslim economies and the entire global economy are miniscule as table 9.2 illustrates.

Financial market integration in the Muslim World is also impeded by the foreign exchange controls that are applied universally to the export of capital, the GCC states being the major exception, although much of the funds originating in these countries are invested in the West rather than the Islamic World (Wilson, 2004).

For Muslim monetary union to be successful this would involve setting and meeting convergence criteria similar to those agreed at Maastricht, and subsequently, apart from the debt criteria, largely

Table 9.2: Capital inflows and outflows for selected Muslim economies

	Private K/GDP % 1990*	Private K/GDP % 2002*	FDI/GDP % 1990**	FDI/GDP % 2002**
Bangladesh	0.9	2.6	0.0	0.1
Egypt	6.8	6.6	1.7	0.8
Indonesia	4.1	5.4	1.0	2.1
Iran	2.6	2.4	0.0	0.0
Jordan	6.3	7.8	1.7	0.9
Kuwait	19.3	18.9	1.3	0.5
Malaysia	10.3	19.9	5.3	5.8
Morocco	5.5	3.3	0.6	1.4
Pakistan	4.2	5.3	0.6	1.4
Saudi Arabia	8.8	13.9	1.6	0.5
Syria	18.0	16.8	0.0	1.5
Tunisia	9.5	10.6	0.6	3.8
Turkey	4.3	7.7	0.5	0.7
Yemen	16.2	3.6	2.7	1.1

Notes: * Sum of FDI and portfolio investment inflows and outflows
** Sum of inflows and outflows of FDI
Source: World Development Indicators, World Bank, Washington, 2004.

implemented by countries adopting the euro. As inflation rates varied from over 40 percent in Turkey to virtually zero in the GCC states (World Bank, 2002), and as interest rate differentials and exchange rates movements reflect these disparities, there is little prospect of convergence (ibid.).

Yet Yusri's prophecy, or recommendation, of establishing a Customs Union among Muslim countries is partially fulfilled. In the GCC free trade was easier to achieve, as all of the countries were in a more favourable trading position because of their oil exports, and there were no restrictions on import payments. Deeper integration came in 2002 when the free trade area was superseded by a customs union, with all GCC states adopting a common tariff of five percent, and internal controls being removed on the movement of goods (Looney, 2003). As the GCC countries had already many of the pre-requisites of a common market, notably no outward restrictions on the movement of capital or local nationals, further moves towards even closer economic integration were relatively easy to agree. As a single currency was seen as essential for an effectively functioning customs union, it was only natural to take this further step

(Al-Zoibidy, 2002). The aim of the GCC states is to achieve monetary union by 2005 and for a single currency, probably designated as a dinar, to replace the six existing currencies by 2010.

There are no simple short-term solutions to these potential problems. In the longer term if more Muslim countries with significant exports of manufactured goods and earnings from services adopted the new currency and it evolved from being a Gulf dinar to a true Islamic dinar, the relationship between the exchange rate and energy prices would weaken. The foreign exchange earnings of the Islamic dinar bloc would then become more diversified and balanced, helping currency stabilisation. There would be real incentives for diversification, both in terms of widening the currency bloc through the admission of new members, and for deepening in terms of building up the export and service sector earning capacity of existing states in the bloc (Wilson, 2004).

Indexation

The concern about indexation is twofold: firstly, to ensure that justice between the lender and borrower is observed, and second, to ensure that business arrangements are still valid. The answer to the second question has been much easier than the first, and this is that the fluctuation in the value of money does not affect the validity of business contracts, which are held to be legal despite such changes. In these arrangements profit-loss-sharing is the basis of the relationship in businesses and the fluctuation in the value of money would affect partners in the manner they agreed upon at the initiation of the business—no harm or injustice applied to any. But the case of lending is a more complicated issue. In the absence of interest rates that may compensate the lender for the reduction in the real value of a loan at the maturity date, in case of inflation, the lender in Islam may be unfairly treated. He is getting his loan back at a less real value of money than that at the time of granting the loan. To treat him fairly, the argument goes; he should be compensated by an amount equal to the reduction in the real value of money. This compensatory amount should be paid to him by the borrower. The amount of compensation would be equal to the reduction in the real value of money between the two dates: the date of receiving the loan and the date of paying it back. If no compensation is given by the borrower, the lender would be penalized for giving an interest-free loan (qard Ĥassan).

But compensating the lender, the counter argument is presented, may result in an injustice to the borrower who was not aware at the time of receiving the loan of the possibility of him paying such an increase in the future at the time of repayment, and who, after all, has suffered, like the lender, from the reduction in the real value of money. Moreover, such a compensatory increase may bear with it the suspicion of Ribā. But the proponents of paying financial compensation argue in return that Ribā should not be used as the basis of the rejection of the compensation principle because if the opposite took place and the money appreciated in value over the period of the loan and the borrower paid the same amount of debt in monetary terms to the lender this would still bear the suspicion of Ribā. It would appear as if the lender had charged Ribā on the loan since he would be getting his money back at a higher real value than that of the value at the time of receiving the loan. But this is not a realistic assumption, the argument of the opponents continues, as what is more observed in history than not, is that the real value of money is reduced through time by the effect of inflation. It is important to stress however that the debate is not related to gold and silver if used as currency, which in this case has to be returned at the same quantity, and quality. The debate is related particularly, and exclusively, to other forms of money that carry the power of the authority of government more than the value of the precious metal in it. Examples of this money is money made of less precious metal than gold and silver, such as copper, and in modern times money made at the authorization of Treasury or Central Bank, such as banknotes.

The subject was of concern to the Medieval Muslim jurists as well as to the Islamic economists of today. And the jurists were not unanimously united on the issue; different schools of thought had different opinions. The agreements and differences between the jurists are summarized by Isaa as follows (Isaa, 1993):

The first opinion: the borrower is to pay back the lender the same amount of money that he borrowed regardless of the changes in the value of money. This is mainly to avoid Ribā.

The second opinion: the borrower is to pay back the "real" value of money as was received at the time of concluding the loan or concluding the sale contract if the loan was a result of credit sale. The reason is mainly to maintain the real value of money as a store of value.

The third opinion differentiates between whether the change in the value of money is superficial or substantial; if superficial the debt is paid at the same amount originally borrowed regardless of the change in the value of money, but if substantial it ought to be paid at an increase to compensate the lender, or the credit provider, for the loss in the real value of money. How much is substantial is an important question the answer to which is left to the custom of the trade according to the prevailing circumstances. This is a middle of the road approach, a compromise between the first and second opinions cited above.

Islamic economists have been contributing to the debate with a view to answering this vexing problem. Having discussed the various views of the Medieval jurists, Hassanuzzaman is in favour of indexation and argues that indexation is not illegitimate under Islamic law (Hassanuzzaman, 1985). Iqbal is in favour of indexation and suggests the use of a general price level to which all loans in a country be linked, with the price level continuously reviewed and announced by the government (Iqbal, 1987). Mannan argues that where the changes in the value of money in modern times have become unavoidable, indexation of loans provides more justice to the lender (Mannan, 1981). Isaa, having discussed the topic at length leans towards the view of compensating the lender for the loss resulting from the reduction in the real value of money and suggests an approach to indexation based on linking the value of money to an accounting unit the value of which is derived from the value of a certain amount, one gramme, of gold (Isaa, 1993). The debate does not seem to be concluded, however, and there are no known cases where Islamic banks have charged financial compensation to cover the decline in the value of money.

Economic Development

Economic development is a central and crucial issue for the majority of Islamic economists. This is for two particular reasons, the abolition of interest from the Islamic economy and the effect of Zakāh. With the abolition of interest there is more focus on the development of resources and production, and the implications for land, capital and labour. Zakāh is concerned with the distribution of output or income and with the consequences for wealth, with a view to achieving a just allocation of resources. Therefore, by necessity and explicitly or by implication, economic development is a topic that is well embedded in Islamic economics. And if we add to that other reasons, such as the distinction of Islamic economics from other economic systems in philosophy, mechanisms and objectives, Islamic economists would feel the urge, because of the nature of the subject, to write on economic development from an Islamic perspective.

To begin with, all Islamic economists, both those who have written on the subject and others who have not, but still express their opinion in a different form, agree that Islamic economics is value based and as such economic development in Islam will be characterised by the same prerequisite. The differences among the writers are differences of opinion on details, differences of the degree of emphasis, and their perspective for the examination of development issues.

Khurshid Ahmad's contribution seems to be among the most quoted and his "Economic Development in an Islamic Framework" is frequently cited and deserves a due attention. Ahmad enthusiastically calls for innovation and a full departure from imported ideas either from the West in the form of Western capitalism or the Eastern bloc in the form of socialism. Neither system can provide the Muslim nations with a model for economic development, nor would either be suitable to adapt to fit in a framework of Islamic economics (Ahmed, 1980). The major thrust of Islamic economic development is, or ought to be, directed at human life with the objective of making it purposeful and value oriented. Islamic economic development as such will be based on two main premises: first, development in an Islamic framework and Islamic development economics as rooted in the value-pattern embodied in the Qur'ān and the Sunnah, and second, this approach rules out imitativeness (ibid.). The philosophical foundations of Islamic economic development are laid down as: (a) Tawhīd, God's unity and sovereignty, (b) God's Rububiyyah, divine arrangements for nourishment, sustenance and directing things towards their perfection, (c) Khilafah, man's role as God's vicegerent on earth, and (d) Tazkiyah, purification plus growth (ibid.). In the light of, and based on, these four philosophical pillars, Ahmad derives the parameters governing the concept of development from an Islamic perspective, which are mainly (ibid.):

(1) The Islamic concept of development has a comprehensive character and includes moral, spiritual, and material aspects,
(2) The focus for development effort and the heart of development process is man, in that development means development of man

and his physical and socio-cultural environment, a view which is also advocated by al-Ghazāli in his "Man is the Basis of the Islamic Strategy for Economic Development" (Al-Ghazāli, 1994).

(3) Islamic economic development is a multi-dimensional activity.
(4) Islamic economic development aims to achieve a balance between quantitative and qualitative elements of economic development.
(5) Among the dynamic principles of social life Islam has particularly emphasised two: first, the optimal utilization of resources that God has endowed to man, and secondly, their equitable use and distribution and promotion of all human relationships on the basis of Right Justice.

Finally, Ahmad draws the goals of Islamic economic development policy as follows (op. cit.):

(1) Human resources development
(2) Expansion of useful production, which entails three priority area:
    a. Abundant production and supply of food and basic items of necessary,
    b. Defense requirements,
    c. Self-sufficiency in the production of basic goods,
(3) Improvement of the quality of life, which would include:
    a. Employment creation,
    b. An effective and broad based social security system,
    c. Equitable distribution of income and wealth,
    d. Balanced development
(4) New technology,
(5) Reduction of national dependency on the outside world and greater integration within the Muslim world.

There can hardly be a disagreement on the philosophical foundations or policy objectives in Islamic economic development. The foundations are a reflection of Muslims belief and are embedded in the core of the teachings of Islam, and the objectives are a manifestation of the general feeling among Muslims in general and Islamic economists in particular for closer cooperation between Muslim economies.

The next piece of work that merits a discussion is Donia's "Islam and Economic Development" (Donia, 1979). In almost 450 pages, Donia traces the problem of poverty with a view to exploring how the Islamic state dealt with it at a time when there was no economic development policy other than that of Islamic economics.

Having looked at the theory of economic development in positive economics, economic development in non-Islamic economic systems, the conceptual framework of Islamic economic development, and the historical application of the Islamic economic development, Donia concludes with a positive answer to the question, "Is it possible for Islam to provide an effective and integrated approach to economic development that would not miss out the benefits of other economic systems and at the same time avoid their pitfalls?" In addition to the assertive positive answer, the evidence of which is provided in the study, the following conclusions are reached (Donia, 1979, authors' translation):

(1) Economic development that is governed by the criteria of justice, equality, goodness, and rightfulness, is a duty stipulated in the doctrine of Islam. The responsibility for the achievement of these duties lies with the state and individuals collectively in a joint partnership accountable to God. Notably, Islamic beliefs and how strong Muslims adhere to them is a vital part in the achievement of these responsibilities as whatever programme that might be, it draws its success from the belief of people involved.
(2) Economic labour (labour to earn a living), is a duty on each Muslim able to work, of which the only acceptable part is that which is in line with Islamic norms in so far as the objectives, manner and effect of the work are within the Islamic ideals. If any part of this work is not acceptable from an Islamic perspective, it becomes prohibited, and an activity from which individuals should refrain. Hence, Islamic economic development is bound not to cause harm to any of those involved whether they are the individuals or the state, consumers or producers.
(3) The only acceptable standard in undertaking responsibilities is the efficiency, which, in Islamic philosophy, is based on two inseparable elements: potency and sincerity.
(4) The provision of knowledge, science and information is a social duty that governments should facilitate, and the state as well as individuals, share joint responsibility. Knowledge that does not lead to benefits to society is not acceptable; hence Islam requires that the relationship between science and application be particularly strong.
(5) The ownership of resources has implications for economic development. Islam allows dual ownership, private ownership and

public ownership, with the latter given a particularly influential role in the Islamic economic development literature.
(6) In as far as the financing of economic development is concerned, Islam allows a variety of sources, public and private, with particular emphasis on the maintenance of economic surpluses.
(7) Rational economic planning is a prerequisite for Islamic economic development.
(8) The just allocation of income and wealth is an essential part of Islamic development, so as to provide a minimum level of necessities, while, simultaneously, acknowledging the inevitable differences among the levels of income and wealth in society.

Two points carry particular significance in the above summary of conclusions: Donia emphasises that, first, on the production side the responsibility for economic development is a joint responsibility between the state and individuals, not on the state alone, and, second, on the distribution side the individual can be as rich as they are able to be with no limitation except for one condition: the poor should be provided for, at least at the minimum level of subsistence. Moreover, labour has to be aimed at what is beneficial to society, production to be directed in a similar fashion and the overall righteousness of the community must prevail.

Now we turn our attention to looking into one of the distinguished pieces of work, of a renowned Sharī'ah scholar whose writing on the subject is widely admired among his contemporary, as well as amongst Islamic economists. This is the work of Bāqir al-Sadr, Iqtisāduna.

Bāqir al-Sadr
Iqtisāduna, Our Economics

The reason for singling out Bāqir al-Sadr's "Our Economics" for special analysis and for giving the work emphasis in this book is clear. First, al-Sadr was a Shi'ī scholar and we have not so far had much opportunity to explore the work of a Shi'ī in Islamic economics. Second, Our Economics has not enjoyed the popularity that other works of Sadr's contemporaries have had, (Wilson, 1998). Third, the work merits admiration and appreciation in thought, approach and scope. Fourth, al-Sadr wrote his work, and lived most of his life, under a repressive regime. Fifth, Our Economics appeared in the late nineteen sixties and early nineteen seventies when Islam is said to have been re-emerging in the state that is known as Islamic revivalism. Sixth, as al-Sadr never had the opportunity that was available to his contemporaries in being exposed to Western economics and education, his thoughts on the subject were reflections of his own thinking as based on purely Islamic teaching with little influence from Western culture, at least not at the same degree as his contemporaries. Furthermore, seventh, the book, which, in parts criticises fervently the communist economy, appeared at a time when leaders and policy makers in the Islamic world were calling for a socialist approach to economic development as the way forward. For these reasons, and probably more, al-Sadr's Iqtisāduna deserves the due space and time.

Iqtisāduna is a follow up, as al-Sadr is telling us in the introduction to the first edition, to Falsafatuna, Our Philosophy. The intention, seemingly, was to develop a series of writing on Islamic social science covering a wide range of issues from an Islamic perspective. But that was not to be, as his life was brought short by the anti-Shī'ah repressive regime of the time.

By al-Sadr's own assertion, Iqtisāduna is meant to provide an objectively analytical study of Marxism, Capitalism, and Islamic economics by looking into the systems, conceptual principles and the details of their application. This has been asserted as a subtitle of "Our Economics". At the outset, it would not be difficult to conceive from the start that the comparison would lead to the demonstration of the superiority of the Islamic economic system to other systems. This is an aim that is hardy surprising as writers of all sorts, the apologist and the less-apologist, Muslims and non-Muslims invariably have that end in mind. What differentiates writers, however, are the depth of analysis, the objectivity of criticism, and their knowledge of the subject. And in that al-Sadr is not demonstrating any deficiency.

We find him spelling out his intention in the book's foreword when he asserts that his aim is to compare and evaluate the viability of the European economy, socialist and capitalist, as compared with Islamic economics in spurring the economic development of the underdeveloped Islamic economies.

Economic development was therefore the main concern of al-Sadr. And this can be seen throughout his Iqtisāduna. The idea, hence the main concern, for him was what economic system is the most suitable for economic development, and that was the basis of his evaluation of, and comparison between Marxism and capitalist on the one hand and Islamic economics on the other. Al-Sadr was under no illusion as to when, and to what extend, an economic system may or may not be workable. Cautiously, and objectively, we find him stating that the comparison between economic systems should not be based only on the conceptual framework of these systems or their theoretical philosophy and principles, but should be based instead on the degree of the suitability of the system to the economy being studied and the society which the system is designed to serve. This is a demonstrable example of objectivity.

Even further, we find al-Sadr providing what could almost be justification for the adoption of capitalism by the European community. He looked into the historical development of the European society, explaining, in a philosophically historical manner, how capitalism was chosen by such a society in their pursuit of economic development. The pursuit of profit and materialistic gains became the main drive of such a society, particularly when the belief in man and his ability was perceived as more visible than the ability of an unseen divine power. In that he comes to the conclusion, that despite the suitability of capitalism to a European community, capitalism is not a suitable economic system to spur economic development in a Muslim society that is based on the belief in God, in the unforeseen and a divine code of conduct.

It is interesting to notice the emphasis of al-Sadr on the role of man in economic development. And in Islamic economics, the Muslim man will have a paramount role in the process of economic development. No successful Islamic system, and in this regard an Islamic economic system generally, can be perceived without a Muslim man. The Islamic society with all its Islamic ingredients and beliefs is a pre-requisite for the application of an Islamic economic system successfully. The Islamic economic system and the sound Islamic, not only Muslim, society are inseparable, and there is no guarantee that the former will be successful without the latter. This emphasizes the need to have a well structured Islamic society in order to have a thriving Islamic economic system.

On the importance of man in economic development, we find al-Sadr confirming from the early pages of Iqtisāduna that the needs of an economic system are not confined to the need for a social structure, which the state may adopt and in which the economic development model may be fitted. Economic development, and the fight against backwardness, goes beyond that to reach out for a framework that includes the entire nation and the people for which the economic programme is to serve. An interaction should be developed in the process of economic development between the chosen model of development and the people, as only with the cooperation of the whole nation can economic development be achieved. The cooperation of people and their full devotion to the system is a prerequisite for the success of an economic development programme, as with cooperation people can give the best of their talents and skill in striving to achieve their economic goals. Therefore, the argument continues, people should be offered a system that matches their beliefs and conviction if the benefits of economic development are to be realised. In a Muslim nation, in order to gain the full cooperation of the people, the economic system ought to be Islamic. By implication, therefore, secularization for the sake of modernization would not lead to the best possible results in the process of economic development in an Islamic community, nor would the adaptation of a socialist economic system be any better.

The Islamic philosophy, doctrine and belief are echoed once more in al-Sadr's writing when he refers to economic concepts and principles. Looking at the concept of value for example we find him attempting to answer questions about the sources of value for goods and services and how the price of goods is determined, and whether labour is the source of value or otherwise. The stress, from his point of view, should be on the exploration of the views of Islam as a religion on the concept of profit (as viewed from the capitalist point of view) and to what extent the concept extends to recognize the profit as a just criterion in providing a basis of value. To explore the degree of the legitimacy of profit it is necessary to be aware of the role that capital, labour and other means of production play in the process of production. The study of the roles of these factors of production should be viewed based on the stand of Islam regarding the rights of factors of production to a share in the distribution of output.

Iqtisāduna was written in Arabic, and the second edition extends to just over 700 pages. It comes to us in just over 200,000 words—a considerable size even by the standard of today. Iqtisāduna could be divided into three main sections: Marxism, 200 pages, capitalism, 40 pages, and the rest, about 460 pages, are devoted to Islamic economics.

This shows how much al-Sadr wanted to say about Marxism compared with capitalism, and of course how devoted he was to the Islamic system. He criticises Marxism fervently and even reaches the conclusion that it contradicts itself in its own philosophy. Capitalism to him is based on insincere freedom as, while it advocates the freedom of the market, it does not per se provide the individuals with the economic means, or reinforces his/her purchasing power, to act in a freely economic manner. Freedom of the market therefore becomes restricted as it does not, per se, lead to economic freedom. Such freedom is, therefore, illusory. Islamic economics, he stresses, is a value-laden system, which caters for the needs of both the rich and the poor. The ethical values emanating from the teachings of Islam are quite distinct. Al-Sadr assertion is consistent with the arguments of other Muslim economists and Sharīʾah scholars in general.

If we concentrate on the third section, Islamic economics, we find that in dealing with the main outlines of the Islamic economics al-Sadr has divided the subject into six main sections, as follows:

1. The general structure of Islamic economics,
2. Islamic economics as part of a whole system,
3. The general framework of Islamic economics,
4. Islamic economics is not a branch of science,
5. Distribution as separate from the form of production,
6. Economic problems from an Islamic point of view and their solutions.

In explaining the general framework of Islamic economics al-Sadr states that it is based on three basic foundations: the principle of dual ownership, the principle of conditional economic freedom, and the principle of social justice.

On ownership, we find al-Sadr advocating that ownership is of three types, private ownership, public ownership, and state ownership. The mixed forms of ownership, he warns, do not imply that an Islamic economic system is a mixed economy which allows both forms of private and public ownership. It cannot be described as such, in his views, as Islamic economics has a different ideology from that of the mixed economic system. The mixed economic system is a capitalist system that allows for public ownership, or a Marxist system that permits private ownership. The Islamic economic system is neither as it has its own values that are neither capitalist not communist. Would al-Sadr allow nationalisation? This is not very clear in his early part of writing on Islamic economics, until page 259 of the second edition where he refers to the capitalist experience of nationalizing private ownership for the sake of public interest in what seems to be an approval of what a capitalist government might be doing (Al-Sadr, 1982).

In discussing the ownership of the means of production, al-Sadr qualifies the ownership and conditions on which it is based. With reference to land and natural resources as means of production, he emphasises that maintaining the productive conditions of these sources is a provision for the continuation of ownership. To this effect, he is of the view that if an owner neglects the property, or is unable to utilise it, the state or, imam, may give it to someone else to make use of it. The statutory owner may be given a due share from the economic outcomes of utilization by the new holder. The new holder, however, is not to be given a statutory ownership; he/she is not allowed to transfer the ownership by sale, inheritance or other means. What the new holder has of rights is the right to utilise, not the right to own. This is a delicate distinction that may help make the principle of ownership-transfer more applicable, hence more acceptable. It is, to use a modern term, a form of quasi-ownership of the neglected source of production rather than a full ownership. It remains to confirm that this form of quasi-ownership stays with the holder as long as he is utilising the property, even if the statutory ownership was transferred by other means such as sale or inheritance.

In addition, in relation to the previous point, is the question of the ownership of *iqta'*, the fiefs. During the Umayyad and Abbasīd caliphate, as we saw previously, the caliph would bestow on some of his subjects ownerless lands that became owned by the state, in reward for their services and loyalty. The lands were given away free and were called *qata'i*. This practice, which continued under the Ottomans, grew in size and varied in shape so much so that we find the governor of Egypt, Muĥammad Ali, confiscating the whole land of Egypt and declaring himself the sole owner of the land (see chapter seven). Al-Sadr addresses the *iqta'*, or *qata'i* land, from two important perspectives. First, he differentiated between the early form of Islamic *iqta'* and Western feudalism with its historical and social backgrounds. Second, which is more important in this study, he provides a fundamental justification for the validity of the Islamic *iqta'*. This is the proviso of labour. Supporting his views with the views of early jurists, he states that the Islamic *iqta'* does not grant a person a statutory ownership to the given land, it simply gives him only the right to utilise. Following the same line of thinking with regard to neglected sources of production, al-Sadr emphatically argues that the right of the holder of *iqta'* is only the right to utilise. Hence he is acting on behalf of the giver i.e. the state. Therefore, the form of Islamic *iqta'* may be permissible and the state may grant a means of production, land or another natural resource such as mines, to people to utilise. But the statutory ownership remains, he argues, with the state, or the *imam*. It follows that, the holder, once more, is a quasi-owner, and this quasi-ownership continues with the provision that (a) the holder is utilising the property, (b) in accordance with the state's regulations, and (c) the state is given its share of the economic outcome. "*Iqta'*, therefore, is not a process of a transfer of ownership, it is, instead, a right given by the *imam* (the state) to an individual giving him the priority to utilise a well-defined property in accordance to his readiness and capability" (al-Sadr, 1982, p. 459). Needless to say, the inference of the al-Sadr argument, suggests that the state's share of output is not a substitute to the tax that may be due on the holder's share, it is over and above what the state may impose through taxes in parallel to other subjects and economic activities.

It is worth noting that al-Sadr's views on the ownership of the land of qata'i were in sharp contrast to those of Abū-Yūsūf. In his book, Kitab al-Kharāj, we saw how Abū-Yūsūf maintained that the transfer of ownership should be regarded as full ownership and should be made final without recourse from the caliph, or the ruler. The full ownership would grant the right to transfer the ownership by sale or inheritance. Abū-Yūsūf went even further in stressing that annulling the ownership by the same caliph or those who would come after him and taking back the land from the holder would be like robbing someone and giving the stolen property to someone else. Abū-Yūsuf probably had in mind the need for the economic stability and constancy of transactions more than a possible concern over the conceptual basis of ownership. This was particularly the case as he provided support to his views from the practice of the Prophet, albeit that the Prophet's practice was on a comparatively minor scale compared with that of the land of *qata'i* during the dynastic caliphates. Al-Sadr, on the other hand, stressed the conceptual, and in his views the rightful, basis of ownership over the practicality of the pragmatic Hanafi judge Abū-Yūsūf.

Turning our attention to economic freedom, we find al-Sadr in line with the main-stream of Islamic jurists in arguing that though economic freedom is permitted in Islam, it is not unconditional. The conditions come from two distinctive sources: self and state. Self conditions emanate from the belief of the individual in the ethical code of conduct provided in the Sharīʾah. This increases with the development of the individual's religious conscience and Islamic beliefs. Emanating from al-Sadr's ethical approach to economics, a considerable weight is given by him to this source of conditioning values. Conditions emerge from the right of the state to apply the Sharīʾah rules in any possible deviation from these rules on the part of the individual that may cause harm to society. Individuals' religious conscientiousness is far more important to al-Sadr than the state's corrective agencies. In the absence of a government that is concerned with the application of Sharīʾah to the society, in favour of a less Islamic application of government, individuals' diligence becomes the substitution.

In discussing the distribution of income, al-Sadr, in emphasizing the importance role of labour in the process of production, stresses the significance of rewarding labour as the most crucial factor. Though this sounds as if he came very near to the Marxist theory, particularly in stressing the role of the suppliers of labour as opposed to that of the providers of capital, he diverted from it in basing his arguments on the Islamic moral ideals. The society, to him, is obliged to provide for not only the able and capable but also for the poor and the needy if their conditions of poverty is more related to weaknesses and inability than to laziness and idleness. With the stipulation of Zakāh in the core of the Islamic doctrine, the Islamic economic system is distinguished from both Marxism and capitalism.

In his Iqtisāduna al-Sadr has demonstrated a depth of knowledge and a profundity of thinking on both economics and Sharīʾah matters. One may speculate how his thinking would have developed had he not been executed in 1980 under the orders of the Iraqi political authority at that time (Wilson, 1998).

The Future of Islamic Economics

Mixing the reality of the present day Islam with the Islam of yesterday with its glory when governments were powerful and set-backs when they were less successful, provides, with the benefit of hindsight, empirical evidence to rely on and lessons to derive conclusions from. Historical evidence should be treated with caution however, as history has inherent distortions when it comes to extracting evidence, as the prevailing conditions of the past differ from those dominant in the present. The political and social structure of society, and to a lesser degree cultural structure introduces biases if culture, as is the case with Islamic based culture, has the same source of feeding and enriching. History contains useful lessons to be learned however, providing that this is received with an examining mind and an inquisitive attitude. Historical development of economics and economic thought is no exception. But the least historical examination can tell us, is that the Islamic system per se has the capability of providing the operational norm and the workable model, providing other things are equal. And these "other things" are: (a) the degree of adherence to Islamic norms and ideals, (b) the politically strong Islamic state, (c) the lack of hostility from the political machinery to Islam internally, through national governments, and externally, through international pressure, and (d) the adaptability of Islam to new changes in society, technologically and otherwise. And as the present is an unbroken chain with the past, the future, in a similar historical fashion, is the ceaseless link with the future. In Islamic economics, as Muslim economists wish for a better future for their economies, and they all do, they have realised that studying the problems of today with a view to solving and resolving, enhances the possibility for a superior Islamic economics for tomorrow.

To link the present with the future, there seems to be three major areas that still require particularly further attention: first, on the conceptual side, a need for extracting economic concepts, and even new terminology if need be, from the pure sources of the Sharīʾah, second, non-apologetic discussions of present application of Islamic economics to, particularly, Islamic banking operations, state finance, and global economic connections, and third, more empirical evidence and field studies as very little has been done in this area. Muslim economists have been engaged in an intensive process to reinforce the foundations of their subject for a healthy take off in the future. Efforts have been made to show that Islamic economics: (a) is able to accommodate economic ideas with an Islamic version comparable to those of Western economics; the writing on economic issues "from an Islamic perspective", is not unusual, and (b) is a realistic alternative for a state public policy at the macro level if a state is wishing to Islamise its economic system.

Nevertheless, more efforts are still needed on the side of "rediscovering" economic concepts and ideas as emanating from the religion of Islam itself. To put it another way, the identity of Islamic economics needs to be extracted and highlighted further from Islamic sources: the Qur'ān and Sunnah, and the jurisprudence of the early caliphs and Sharī'ah jurists. Wilson for example wonders why even in a work related to price control in a recent writing on Islamic economics there is no mention of al-Ĥīsbah in Islam (Wilson, 1998). Sardar is taking this issue seriously in his "Islamic Futures: the Shape of Ideas to Come", when he discusses various issues among which are: rediscovering the epistemology of Islam, the Sharī'ah as a problem solving methodology, Islamic economics from partial to axiomatic approach, Islamic concept of development, and other important issues (Sardar, 1985). Sardar advocates a freedom of inquiry approach to an Islamic search for answers and ideas, that is free from imitation and that is guided by the Qur'ān and Sunnah (ibid.). One would emphasize with Sardar the need to look into economic issues with an Islamic fresh pair of eyes. This is not to say that what has been written on economic issues in the Western literature should be discarded by Islamic economists in their pursuit of fresh Islamic economics concepts, that would be a great loss of a considerable amount of knowledge, but it is to stress that Muslim economists in searching for Islamic economics identity may need to look at Islamic economics as a "born new" science that does not have to be necessarily pegged to concepts from the Western economic literature. For example, if Islamic economics is capable by itself to produce its own original concepts and ideas there may not be a need for the often mentioned statement that the economic treatment is "from an Islamic perspective"; a phrase and a statement that seems to be popular among writers in the late twentieth century writing on Islamic economics. One can understand the difficulty of steering away from the inevitable comparison and the "Islamic perspective" syndrome. After all, most of Muslim economists who have, so far, been pioneering the writing in the field are either Western educated or educationally Western influenced. Hence, the comparison might be inevitable and the "Islamic perspective" treatment and phrase is unavoidable. The task might be difficult but not impossible. The importance of this point is twofold: (a) while imported goods might be highly desirable for a community, imported ideas may not be necessarily workable or applicable to the needs of that community; this is not new, we all know it, but there is a need to (b) emphasize that Islam is able to generate its own ideas, including those of Islamic economics. If Islamic economics cannot produce its own ideas without them, simply reflecting the style of western economics, this provides very little evidence that Islamic economics can be viewed as a subject on its own; it might be a subordinate or a branch of the subject of economics, even with the prefix "normative". And as a quick reminder, if a reminder is needed, when medieval Muslim writers wrote on Islamic economics they wrote on "Earnings", "Wealth", "Earnings and Asceticism", "Good Trading", and "State Ordinance", as well as on "Kharāj" and "Ḥīsbah". They did not feel the need to emphasise their Islamic "perspectives". True, the literature of today is far vaster than that of the past, but to overcome the problem writing on Islamic economics may come under one central catalogue: Islamic economics.

On the application side of the Islamic economic ideal to real life practical situation, one of the most vivid examples is, and has been for sometime, Islamic banking. What started as a small size savings bank in a remote village in Egypt and another in Pakistan in the early nineteen sixties has grown to become a major financial sector of Islamic banking and finance in the late twentieth and early twenty first century. Claiming about 200 banks in the world today with total assets of $300 billion, total capital of $50 billion and total deposits of $170 billion, this is a major achievement by any standard. Nevertheless there are problems and in order to look forward to having a much more coherent base for Islamic finance in the future these problems need to be addressed. This has not been ignored and Islamic economists have been engaged in a critical evaluation of these problems with a view to either answering the criticism or genuinely seeking ways of solving them. Some of these problems are as follows (for a detailed discussion of these problems, see for example the Future of Economics, Chapra 2000).

1. The lack of product standardisation of the services provided by Islamic banks and financial institutions. This is mainly a result of not having a centralised Sharīʾah board to which all Islamic banks should refer to for advice and religious opinions (Chapra, 2000).

This brings to mind a similar situation when there is no standardised accounting system and accounting issues are resolved, within the general concepts, in line with the generally acceptable accounting principles (GAAP). One can compare the advantages and disadvantages of both systems, a standardised accounting system like that of France since the mid forties and non-standardised accounting system like that of the United Kingdom that only became homogenous after the set up of supervisory accounting boards.

Islamic banks therefore had to have their own Sharīʾah supervisory boards, or Sharīʾah advisors if they are too small to have a board, which helps Islamic banks reach decisions in conformity with the Sharīʾah rules and meanwhile to confirm to the shareholders and all who may be concerned that there is no infringement of Sharīʾah in the banks operations.

The problem is that this entails extra costs to the Islamic bank compared with the western based bank that is operating in the same financial environment. As the western bank does not bear similar costs, this puts the Islamic at a disadvantage when it endeavours to compete with western banks in a competitive market. To alleviate the cost to the Islamic bank a centralised body of Sharīʾah may be established to provide the needed help and confirmation. The cost of the central board may be allocated to Islamic banks in general which would be much lower than it would be if each bank bears it individually. Despite that, we see the OIC taking the initiative to provide central advice through Fiqh Academy and the International Association of Islamic Banks (IAIB) establishing a Unified Sharīʾah Commission for the same purpose. Nevertheless, it may be quite a while before the needed consensus is formulated on some crucial issues (ibid.).

2. The second major problem is as Islamic banks are operating in a competitive environment where both types of banking systems, Islamic and Western, are allowed to operate, Islamic banks find themselves having to abide by the regulation of the central bank that is mostly suited to western style banks. The most obvious example is the reserve ratio required by the central bank on banks deposits. While depositors in Islamic banks are aware of the conditions of operation in profit and loss sharing basis and make their deposits with the intention of being fully invested, the Islamic bank has to maintain part of these deposits as central bank's legal reserves, which leads to a possible return on this portion of deposits being foregone. This may render the opportunity cost of operation to the Islamic bank higher than that of the Western based bank if the expected rate

of return on investment is higher than the rate of interest. This may very well be the case as, given the higher level of risk for the Islamic bank; the rate of return on investment is expected to be higher than the rate of interest. The opportunity cost of operation may even increase further if the central bank decided to raise the reserve ratio on Islamic banks deposits to reduce the risk of default further.

3. The third major difficulty of operation facing Islamic banks is that they are of much smaller size than their Western counterparts, either those operating nationally or internationally. A Western multinational bank for example has assets far in excess of those of all Islamic financial institutions put together (Chapra, 2000). This makes the competition much tougher particularly, as is the case, when both types of banking systems are operating freely in the country. And in case of financial difficulty, the small bank will go out of the market first.

But probably Islamic banks, small as they are, need not particularly worry. They can build on establishing a good customary relationship with their customers which would be of great help to small to medium size businesses. If Islamic banks develop in-house expertise, reliable financial and industrial data, and good training programmes for their staff, they may compete well with, if not out perform, larger sized banks in providing specialist services to small and medium size entrepreneurs. Put another way, Islamic banks may wish to focus on providing a niche product and concentrate on the niche market rather than competing with multinational banks. Indeed this one of the important aspects of Islamic banking activities as advocated in Islamic banking theory. But to be able to provide such a service at such a level Islamic banks need to have well trained staff and capability in risk management. This might be a particular feature that will appear in the twentieth first century Islamic banking.

4. There might be a need to depart, at least partially in the transitional stage, from the concentration of mark-up trade operations, Murabaha, and become more involved in other forms of investment financing, Mudharabah and Mushārakah. Furthermore, the reliance on the LIBOR bench-mark in trade financing may be creating a feeling of skepticism regarding the validity of an Islamic mode of finance. It might be practical for the bank to rely on LIBOR, and similar rates, as a price taker in the banking operations. But while this provides a practical answer to a perplexing problem, it does not

help promote the sense of Islamisation in the mind of the users of the banks' services either as depositors or as users of finance.

There may be a need in the twenty first century for Islamic banks to be seen diverting away from rates that are more associated with Western banking systems than with the Islamic spirit of the enterprise in the profit and loss sharing principle. Further studies may be needed to explore the possibility of using indices such as a profit index to be applied flexibly and dynamically with changes in economics conditions and modes of financing.

Will Islamic economics survive the years to come? A variety of answers to a question of this sort may emerge depending upon who is in the discussants panel. No unified answer may be reached, or even expected, as the diversity of views on the subject seems observable and the disparity of opinions appears notable. The answer will depend probably on a number of conditions: (a) the degree of adherence to Islamic norms and ideals, (b) the politically strong Islamic state, (c) the lack of hostility from the political machinery to Islam internally, through national governments, and externally, through international pressure, and (d) the adaptability of Islam to new changes in society technologically and otherwise.

(a) The degree of adherence to Islamic norms and ideals. Economic systems and philosophies, like any other systems and philosophies, thrive on people's belief in them and this is particularly the case when these systems are based on ethical values and founded heavily on moral values and religious norms. The departure from these values would result in less manifestation of the systems relying on them and feeble application of their ideas. For the Islamic economic system to survive, let alone thrive, it would need the Muslims' support taking the form of adhering to Islamic norms in their economic behaviour. In a competitive environment where both banking systems, Islamic and Western, are allowed to operate Islamic banks can only survive, and thrive, if they are given a high position in the customers' scale of preference as both investors and users of funds. The level of priority given in the scale of preference will depend on a range of factors, the adherence to Islamic norms and ideals being the most prominent. To put it briefly, there will be no Islamic banking in particular or Islamic economics in general, without having strong Islamic practice in society, financially and economically. And the wider and deeper the spread of Islamic economic practice, the higher the chance of growth and survival of Islamic economics and banking. This is not to say that Islamic financial institutions need not pay attention to their performance, in reliance of supporting religious factor among the consumers. Poor performance, if persistent, drives customers away; Islam does not encourage laziness even in the name of religion. The above points related to the problems and criticism of the operations of Islamic banking and financial institutions need not be stressed further.

(b) The politically strong Islamic state. A politically strong Islamic state nationally and internationally provides the most needed financial and logistic support to Islamic financial and economic institutions for their establishment and continuity. On the international level, the strength of such a state implies less reliance on outside economies that may not be particularly sympathetic to a neighbouring Islamic economic system or ideology. An Islamic economic system can hardly be envisaged in an economy that is relying heavily on financial donation and economic support from the non-Islamic community. Dependence on such outside help makes the system dependent on external forces and hence vulnerable to non-Islamic influences.

(c) The lack of hostility from the political machinery to Islam internally, through national governments, and externally, through international pressure. Internal hostility of the state to Islamic economic ideas emanates from the concern, or the fear, that Islamic forces wish to Islamise the state and take over governments. In the light of this objective, which is hardly made secret by Muslim religious societies, existing governments that do not apply Islamic policies to their systems, economically and otherwise, and lean instead towards a Western alternative, grow concerned and become inclined to oppose the application of Islamic ideas to the affairs of the state beyond that of the pure practice of worship. International pressure has the same direction, especially when a neighbouring Islamic regime is suspected of having a direct or indirect influence on the political mode of the country. Resistance to the regime, and with it the Islamic economics, becomes the norm rather than the exception.

(d) The adaptability of Islam to new changes in society technologically and otherwise. It adds to the complexity of the question that the world has become globalised and globalization seems to be intensified with no indication of changing direction or slowing down. Muslims will find it inevitable, as they have learned by now, that they should deal with economies, and economic systems, that are based on principles which they themselves refute. And when these economies are particularly strong, such as the Western economies, it becomes almost unthinkable for Muslim countries, trying to apply the ideals of Islamic economics to their systems, to live in economic isolation. The importance of adaptability of the Sharīʾah from within to external economic conditions cannot be overemphasized.

Despite these and similar observations, Islamic economics has, by all standards, achieved tremendous progress and Muslims, joined lately by non-Muslim, scholars in the field are working hard to keep the flow of publications coming. The future of Islamic economics has attracted a variety of contributions from a number of Muslim economists, some more critical than others, though the sincerity of all is not to be doubted. There is room for improvement without doubt, as Chapra has emphasised in his "The Futures of Economics", on policy implementation (Chapra, 2000). But there seems to be a general consensus among Muslim economists, bankers and practitioners that they have come a long way and they are here to stay. One may be tempted to be extra cautious in joining Chapra in concluding that the Islamic financial movement has taken off fairly successfully and it may be impossible for any one to roll it back (ibid.). But hope, as the great Ŝūfī al-Muĥāsibī has told us earlier, is not enough to achieve what God has destined for us to achieve. The, *ĥarakah*, or hard work and sincere endeavour, is still needed in pursuit of success. And Islamic banks seem to be in need of a considerable amount of *ĥarakah* in the near future if they are to compete effectively with Western banks and financial institutions nationally and globally in the far future. And "God knows best".

"OUR LORD CONDEMN US NOT IF WE FORGET OR FALL INTO ERROR"

GLOSSARY

Adl: justice, **adālah ijtima'iyyah:** social justice. The principle of social justice is central to Islam.

Aĥādīth (singular *Ĥadīth*): documented sayings of the teachings of the Prophet Muĥammad transmitted through a chain of informants, a process known as *isnad*, where each informant was reporting the saying as being heard from a previous informant by name until all sayings were traced to the first informant who reported hearing, or seeing, the Prophet said, or did, what was reported.

Ahl-al-Ĥadīth: the People of *Ĥadīth*. A school of religious thought that relied heavily on the Aĥādīth in reaching a religious judgment more so than on juristic preference, *istiĥsān*, or analogical reasoning, *qiyās*. The school of thought of Ahl-al-Ĥadīth flourished in Makkah and al-Medīnah.

Ahl al-Ra'y: the People of the Opinion. A school of religious thought that relied mainly on the opinion of the jurist in reaching a decision in relation to matters that did not exist during the Prophet's time or if existed were not on the same scale, guided by the public interest of the Muslim community. The school widened the concept of juristic preference, *istiĥsān*, and analogical reasoning, *qiyās*, with relatively less reliance on *Hadiths*. The school was influential in Kufa in al-Iraq.

Amānah (theological meaning): free-will and responsibility. The Qur'ān states with reference to human beings, "We offered Our trust, *al-amānah*, to the heavens, to the earth and to the mountains, but they declined to bear it for fear of its burden. But man assumed it", (Qur'ān, 33:72), and "Have We not given him two eyes, a tongue, and two lips, and shown him the two paths?", (Qur'ān, 90:8–10).

Amānah (financial meaning): money or other assets entrusted to someone or the bank for safe-keeping.

Bai' Bithaman Ajil (BBA): credit sale at a price of deferred payment. A contract that refers to the sale, or purchase, transaction for a deferred or on installment payment with a pre-agreed payment period and a pre-determined price which includes a profit margin. It is used for the financing of assets.

Bai' al-Dayn: sale of a debt. A transaction that involves the sale and purchase of loan securities or debt certificates that conforms with Sharī'ah. Loan securities or debt certificates will be issued by a debtor to a creditor as evidence of indebtedness.

Bai' al-Ghrar (plural, **Buyu' al-Gharar**): sale surrounded by ambiguity as a result of lack of information. Future contracts when the quantity is not determined is an example. Thus it is what is called "sale of the uncertain", or "Buyu' al-Gharar", which is condemned by the Prophet.

Bai' al-'Innah (Bai' al-Muĥtaj): sale of the financially distressed. A contract, which involves the sale and buy back transaction of assets by a seller. A seller will sell the asset to a buyer on a cash basis. The seller will later buy back the same asset on a deferred payment basis where the price is higher than the cash price. It can also be applied when a seller sells an asset to a buyer on a deferred basis. A seller will later buy back the same asset on a cash basis at a price, which is lower than the deferred price. There may be a doubt surrounding the Islamic legitimacy of this transaction as it might involve a suspicion that the transaction is purely a finance transaction with no genuine interest in exchanging goods. It may be regarded as a "trick", ĥīlah, to avoid the transaction being usurious.

Bai' al-Istijrar: periodical delivery of goods sold on credit. A contract between the client and the supplier, whereby the supplier agrees to supply a particular product on an on going basis, for example monthly, at an agreed price and on the basis of an agreed mode of payment.

Bai' al-Muzayadah: auction sale. An action by a person to sell assets in the open market, which is accompanied by the process of bidding among potential buyers. The asset for sale will be awarded to the person who has offered the highest price. In other words, it is known as the sale and purchase transaction based on tender.

Bai' al-Salam: immediate payment for future delivery. A contract whereby the payment is made in cash at the point of contract but the delivery of asset purchased will be deferred to a pre-determined date. This is also called Bai'-al-Istisna' (sale of goods to be manufactured) as it suits the transaction whereby the manufacturing of goods is financed in advance.

Bai' al-Wafa': fulfillment of promised sale. A contract with the condition that when the seller pays back the price of the goods sold, the buyer returns the goods to the seller.

Dhaman: surety and security. A contract of guarantee whereby a guarantor shall underwrite any claim and obligation that should be fulfilled by an owner of the asset. This concept is also applicable to a guarantee provided on a debt transaction in the event a debtor fails to fulfill his debt obligation.

Dīwān: bureau, or register. The establishment of state bureau could be attributed to Caliph Umar when he set up the *dīwān al-Jund*, Register of Soldiers, to orgasnise the payment of stipends to the soldiers after conquering Syria and Iraq. The Umayyads and the Abbasids expanded the bureau to include:

Ddīwān-al-barīd: bureau of postal service.

Ddīwān-al-rasa'il: bureau of correspondence.

Dīwān-al-khātim: bureau of seal of stamp.

Dīwān-al-asl: provincial administrative bureau.

Dīwān-al-zimam (singular **zimmah**): provincial financial control bureau.

Dīwān al-Mustaghallat: bureau to run and supervise the activities of the government business sector

Fai' (Anfāl): spoils of war gifted from God. *Fai'* is spoils of war that were gained without the toil of actual combat. This is differentiated from *ghanīmah*, spoils of war, as the latter were gained from the enemy through actual combat (Qur'ān 59:6–8). *Anfāl* also took the same rule of allocation; all to God and His messenger, which makes it identical to *Fai'* in distribution. The difference between *Anfāl* and *Fai'* is that while *Anfāl* resulted from actual combat *Fai'* did not. *Anfāl* was however an infrequent case and that was when Muslims disputed over the spoils of the first battle of Badr in 624 A.C. and as a result, all spoils were put under the disposal of the Prophet who distributed them to all Muslims either took part in the battle or not.

Fatwa: A formal religious opinion or decision of a religious scholar on a matter of Islamic issue socially, politically or economically.

Fiqh: jurisprudence, the study and application of the body of Muslim sacred law. Islamic jurisprudence is based on the Qur'ān, the Sunnah and *ijtihād* which is the process of exerting oneself to reach a ruling in an unparallel situation that either did not exist in the past or existed but not on the same scale. The bases on which *ijtihād* is established are: consensus of opinions, *ijma'*, judicial reasoning or derivation, *qiyās*, preference, *istiĥsān*, public interest, *istislāĥ*, and custom and usage, *'urf.*

Fitnah: the religious schism that led to civil wars among Muslims during the latter part of the Rightly-Guided caliphate and the early Umayyad period.

Ghanīmah: technically differentiated from *Fai'* and *Anfāl*, was the spoils of war that were gained during actual combat in military operations. By contrast to *Fai'*, warriors were entitled to the spoils of war, *ghanīmah*, as they used their skills and effort, and they risked their lives in combat. The state was entitled to one-fifth of the *ghanīmah*.

Gharar: fall into deception as a result of holding known information from the buyer. Gharar is an element of deception either through ignorance of the goods, the price, or through faulty description of the goods, in which one or both parties stand to be deceived through ignorance of an essential element of exchange. Gharar is divided into three types, namely gharar fahish (excessive), which vitiates the transaction, gharar yasir (minor), which is tolerated and gharar mutawassit (moderate), which falls between the other two categories. Any transaction can be classified as forbidden activity because of excessive gharar.

Ghassānīds: the Ghassānīds originated from a tribe that emigrated from South Arabia at the end of the third century after the destruction of the dam of Ma'rib and established itself to the south east of Damascus on the south-to-north trade route. The Ghassānīds who were Christianised and had two languages; Aramaic and Arabic were allies and clients of the Byzantines and served as a buffer area between the Byzantine Empire and the nomads' sporadic attacks on the Empire's borders. At the time of the Islamic conquests the Ghassānīds fought alongside the Byzantines in the battle of Yarmūk in 636 A.C. Later the Ghassānīd king embraced Islam, but renounced it afterwards and fled to Constantinople when the second Caliph wanted to reduce him to a Bedouin status in a dispute that erupted between them.

Ĥadīth: see Aĥādīth.

Ĥadramawt: one of the four kingdoms in the pre-Islamic South Arabia, after Saba', Ma'in and Qatabān. It lasted from about 450 B.C. to the end of the first century A.C. The kingdom though was overshadowed by the Sabaeans and the Minaeans, played an important role in organising spice trade.

Ĥanafī: a follower of Ĥanafī school of thought. The founder of the school was Abū-Ĥanīfah al-Nu'man ibn-Thabit (699–767), who relied mainly on juristic preference, *istiĥsān*, and analogical deduction, *qiyās*, in arriving at juristic rulings.

Ĥanbalī: a follower of the Ĥanbalī school of thought. The founder of the School was Ahmad ibn-Ĥanbal (784–855) who strictly adhered to Sunnah to the letter narrowing the margin of the consensus of opinion, *ijma'*, and analogical deduction, *qiyās*, and rejecting any form of human reasoning. Although he was a student of the moderate al-Shafī'i, he adopted an uncompromising approach to Islamic jurisprudence. His followers are mainly in Saudi Arabia.

Ĥaq Mālī: financial right. Haq Mālī are rights on the financial assets. Examples of such rights are haq dayn (debt rights) if the asset is a collateral of a loan, and haq tamalluk (ownership rights).

Ĥawalah: money transfer. A contract that allows a debtor to transfer his debt obligation to a third party. *Al-ĥawala* was another form of *suftaja*, where the debtor would transfer the debt to his own debtor, or to another person able to pay, to pay the debt to the original creditor. It involved three persons, or more, instead of two, which resembled the modern bill of exchange and from which the French word "aval", endorsement on bill of exchange may have originated. In addition, *ĥawala* was issued "payable to bearer".

Hibah: gift. A gift awarded to a person.

Ĥisbah: accountability, public duties. It is one of the spiritual orders of Islam, that aims at enforcing what is Islamically ordained, *ma'ruf*, and preventing what is religiously unlawful, *mūnkar*, in matters related to both the observance of God's worship as well the regularities of market and government operations.

I'atidāl (wasat): not leaning, *wasat*: middle. It indicates the principle of moderation. The principle of moderation stipulates that human bahaviour, economic and non-economic, should be exercised in moderation with no tendency toward extremism. "Let not your hand be tied to your neck (in not spending) nor let it be stretched fully (in spending extravagantly) so that you may not end in poverty and regret" (Qur'ān, 17:29).

Ibra': waiving a debt. An act by a person to withdraw his rights i.e. his rights to collect payment from a person who has the obligation to repay the amount borrowed from him.

Ijarah: leasing/hiring out. A manfaah (benefit) type of contract whereby a lessor (owner) leases out an asset or equipment to a leasee at an agreed rental fee and pre-determined lease period upon the aqad (contract). The ownership of the leased equipment remains in the hands of a lessor.

Ijarah Thumma Bai': initial leasing leading to full sale. A lease contract but with the intention of transferring the ownership of the leased asset to the leasee with the effect of a sale transaction at the end of a pre-agreed upon lease period and for a pre-agreed upon price.

Ijm'a: general agreement. The consensus of the opinion among leading religious scholars that lends support to a religious ruling reached through formulating own opinion.

Ijtihād: the independent reasoning that is reached through exerting oneself to reach an opinion, based on the Qur'ān, the Sunnah, Consensus of Opinion, *Qiyās*, Istiĥsān, Istislāĥ and 'Urf, in dealing with a contemporary situation that had no previous similarity in the past or if it had it was not on the same scale.

Islam: complete surrender to the One almighty God. As a religion, Islam is based on five pillars: witnessing that there is no God but One and that the Prophet Muĥammad is His messenger, practicing the prescribed prayers, ŝalāh, paying the prescribed charity, Zakāh, fasting the month of Ramadān, sawm, and pilgrimage by whoever can afford it, Hajj.

Isrāf: extensive use of resources through extravagance, which is frowned upon as Muslim are ordained to spend in moderation, see I'atidāl.

Istiĥsān: preference. Departure from analogy in reaching a judgment, or formulating an opinion, in preference of another on grounds of seeking a change for the better.

Istislāĥ: public interest. A form of reaching an unprecedented judgment or formulating an opinion in a new case or a case that may not be very dissimilar to a previous case based on, or deviating from previous ruling in pursuit of, public interest.

Istisna': an order to manufacture. A purchase order contract of assets whereby a buyer places an order to purchase an asset that will be manufactured and delivered in the future. In other words a buyer will require a seller or a contractor to deliver or construct the asset that will be completed in the future according to the specifications given in the sale and purchase contract. Both parties to the contract will decide on the sale and purchase prices as they wish and the settlement can be delayed or arranged based on the schedule of the work completed. See Bai' al-Salam.

Ittifaq Dhimni: an implicit agreement. This is an agreement, which must be reached before the contract can be concluded to allow for the bidding process (Bai' al-Muzayadah) to take place.

Jahiliyyah: the age of ignorance. The pre-Islamic period of the Arabian Peninsula.

Ji'alah: commission. Contract of reward; a unilateral contract promising a reward for a specific act or accomplishment.

Jizyah: the poll tax which non-Muslims were required to pay in return for military protection.

Kafalah: surety. It has the same meaning as Dhaman, security.

al-Khilafah: theologically refers to the concept of vice-regency of human beings on earth, as God's deputies. Politically refers to the succession of the state leadership after the pass away of the Prophet. The Qur'ān states, "When your Lord said to the angels: 'I am placing on the earth one that shall rule as My deputy, *khlīfah*' ", "It is He who has made you vice-gerents on earth, *khulafa*" ', and "Have faith in God and His apostle and give in alms of that on which He has made you vice-gerents", (Qur'ān, 2:30, 35:39 and 57:7 respectively).

Kharāj: land tax. Kharāj tax was introduced by Caliph Umar to replace the system of distributing conquered land among Muslim warriors, and became the first tax to be introduced to the Islamic tax system outside those stipulated in the Qur'ān and the Sunnah. The tax was imposed on land, not individuals, with the tax base being the cultivable land and a proportional tax rate.

Khiyanah: betrayal. Refers to deception by not disclosing the truth or breaching an agreement in a hidden way. This is prohibited according to Sharī'ah.

Kindites: they were of South Arabian origin. The Kindite kingdom lasted from 480 to 529 A.C. At its zenith the Kindite kingdom extended to the Euphrates and after the death of the Persian Emperor the Kindite king stretched his influence to the capital of the Lakhmīds. The end of the Kindites came at the hand of the Lakhmīd king in 529 A.C. when the latter defeated them and put their king to death along with many others from the royal family. After embracing Islam the Kindites showed a great zeal in the Islamic conquests in Syria and Iraq and some of them were rewarded by being appointed provincial governors. Also some of the Kindites became great Islamic thinkers such as Ya'qup ibn-Ishaq al-Kinidi who earned the title "the philosopher of the Arabs".

Lakhmīds: they were the mirror image of the Ghassānīds in the east. They originated from Yemenite tribes, called Tanukh, who emigrated to north Arabia around the beginning of the third century A.C. and settled in the west of Euphrates. The Lakhmīds became allies and clients to the Persian Empire and, similar to the Ghassānīds, served as a buffer area between the Persians and the attacks of the Bedouins on the Empires frontiers. The Lakhmīds who spoke Arabic but used Syriac in writing were mostly pagans, with a Christian minority. The influence of Christianity increased during the reign of the last king, al-Nu'man III (580–602 A.C.), when he became Christian.

Ma'in (biblical Ma'on, Me'un and Me'in): spring-water. The second kingdom after Saba' in the Pre-Islamic South Arabia. The Minean period lasted from about 700 B.C. to 70 B.C.

Madrasah (plural: Madaris): a college of Muslim higher education where religious scholars study religious disciplines.

Maisir: gambling. Any activity that involves betting whereby the winner gains the bets and the loser loses the bet. This is prohibited in the Sharī'ah.

Māl: wealth or a depot of income. Something that has value and can be gainfully used according to Sharī'ah.

Mālikī: a follower of the Mālikī school of thought. The school was founded by Mālik-ibn-Anas (715–795) in al-Medīnah, who paid a particular attention to the Sunnah, and the customs of al-Medīnah during the Prophet's time and the consensus of opinions during the reign of the four Rightly Guided caliphs.

Mudhārabah (Qirād and Muqāradah): profit-and-loss-sharing business partnership. A contract between two parties or more to undertake a business venture whereby the parties are two kinds: (a) the capital providers, investors, or rabb al-Mal, and an entrepreneur(s), a mudarib, who manages the business according to pre-agreed upon conditions, with a view to distributing the business profit on the basis of profit sharing ratios determined in advance, while the loss is to be borne by the capital providers on the basis of capital shares with the entrepreneur not bearing a share in loss having lost his work and effort in a futile pursuit.

Mufāwadah Partnership: unlimited-authority profit-and-loss-sharing business partnership. The relationship between partners in the *mufāwadah* partnership is based on mutual surety and mutual agency. The authority of the partner in the *mufāwadah* partnership is unlimited. Profits are allocated to the partners on the basis of their capital contributions, though a greater portion of profit might be allocated to the partner who manages the business in compensation for his work and effort. Losses are born in proportion to the capital provided. The financial liability of the partners is unlimited.

Inān Partnership: limited-authority profit-and-loss-sharing business partnership. The relationship is based on the principles of mutual agency only, not as well as mutual surety as in the *mufāwadah* partnership. The authority of the partner in the *inān* partnership in conditioned. Profits are allocated to the partners on the basis of their capital contributions, though a greater portion of profit might be allocated to the partner who manages the business in compensation for his work and effort. Losses are born in proportion to the capital provided. The financial liability of the partners is generally limited.

Mujtahid: a jurist who has earned the right to exercise ijtihad, usually in the Shi'ī conception.

Muqāssah: contra-debt clearing. Debt settlement by a contra transaction.

Murābaĥah: trading with a promise of a profit. A contract that refers to the sale and purchase transaction for the financing of an asset whereby the cost and profit margin (mark-up) are made known and agreed upon in advance by all parties involved. The settlement for the purchase can be settled either on a deferred lump sum basis or on an installment basis, and is specified in the agreement.

Muqāsamah: sharing. A land tax system recommended by Abū-Yūsuf (731–798 A.C.), whereby the tax is calculated as a proportional crop-sharing tax rate. To him, the system would benefit the Treasury and at the same time alleviate injustice to the taxpayer.

Mushārakah: equity participation. A partnership arrangement between two parties or more to finance a business venture whereby all parties contribute capital either in the form of cash or in kind for the purpose of financing the business venture. Any profit derived from the venture will be distributed based on a pre-agreed profit sharing ratios, but a loss will be shared on the basis of equity participation.

Nabataeans: they were the first rising Arabian state in the Pre-Islamic North Arabia. They were emigrant nomads who came to the area from Transjordan and the northern part of Central Arabia, in the early sixth century B.C. They occupied important cities such as Petra, Bostra and Gerash, the important caravan cities on the south-to-north trade route, and stretched their territory to Damascus at the time of Christ. The year 105 A.C. witnessed their end when the Emperor Trajan annexed the area and declared it a Roman province, a "Provincia Arabia". The Nabataeans developed a high level of civilization with the help of two major economic factors: agriculture and trade.

Palmyrenes: Palmyra, Arabic Tadmur and Semitic Tadmor, in the Pre-Islamic North Arabia. The Palmyrenes were Arabians some of whom came from al-Yemen before the destruction of the Dam of Ma'rib. The city of Palmyra gained its importance as a trade centre between the Roman and the Persian empires. The location of Palmyra on the West-to-East trade route gave the city a strategic importance particularly after the fall of the Nabataeans. Palmyra reached its zenith between 130 and 270 A.C. when, under the protectorate of the Roman Empire, it enjoyed a high level of prosperity with a wide range of international trade. In 270 A.C. the Palmyrenes succeeded in extending their military influence to as far as Alexandria, in Egypt, and to defy the Roman Empire pushing the Empire's garrison as far back as Ankara in Asia Minor. In 272 A.C. the Palmyrene Queen was defeated and the Romans entered Palmyra bringing it to destruction.

Qabdh: reception of cash or of the object subject of the contract. Qabdh means possession, which refers to a contract of exchange. Generally, qabdh depends on the perception of 'urf or the common practices of the local community in recognising that the possession of a good has taken place.

Qardh Hassan: benevolent loan. A contract of loan between two parties on the basis of social welfare or to fulfill a short-term financial need of the borrower. The loan is interest free as the amount of repayment must be equivalent to the amount borrowed. It is however legitimate for a borrower to pay more than the amount borrowed as long as it is not stated or agreed at the point of contract.

Qata'i (singular **Qatī'a**): land granted in reward for services. During the Umayyad and particularly the Abbasīd caliphate, these lands grew in size and became part of the main features of agricultural activities

Qatabān: one of the four kingdoms, after Saba' and Ma'in in the Pre-Islamic South Arabia. The kingdom lasted from about 400 B.C. to 50 B.C. The kingdom though was overshadowed by the Sabaeans and the Minaeans, played an important role in organising the spice trade.

Qiyās: analogical deduction. Judicial deduction by the process of comparison, whereby a ruling is inferred from a previous ruling in a similar case or a case that was very near in conditions and circumstances to the present case. A deviation from a previous ruling in a similar case may be permitted, however, on the grounds of *istiḥsān* or *istislāḥ*.

Rahn: collateral. An act whereby a valuable asset is used as collateral for a debt. The collateral will be utilised to settle the debt when a debtor is in default.

Rashīdūn: the four Rightly Guided Caliphs, who were the companions and the immediate successors of the Prophet: Abū-Bakr (632–34), Umar ibn al-Khattāb (63444), Uthmān ibn Affān (644–56) and Ali ibn Abi Tālib (656–61).

Al-Khilafah al-Rashīdah: the Rightly Guided Caliphate, the caliphate of the Rashīdūn caliphs, which is the most highly esteemed caliphate in Muslims' mind as the only caliphate associated with righteousness and highly spiritual values. The Rightly Guided Caliphate covered the years from 632 to 661.

Ra'ʾs al-Māl (plural **ru'aūs al-amwāl**): equity capital or the loan principle. The Qur'ān states in addressing the issue of *Ribā*, "if you repent you have the right to your capital sums (principal), *Ru'aūs Amwalikum*," (Qur'ān 2:275). This emphasises that there is no differentiation in the Qur'ān between charging interest and usury.

Ribā: interest. An increase, which in a loan transaction or in exchange of a commodity, accrues to the owner (lender) without giving an equivalent counter value or recompense in return to the other party. It covers interest both on commercial and consumer loans, and is prohibited according to Sharī'ah. See the Qur'ānic verse in **Ra's al-Māl**. The Qur'ān states, "Believers, have fear of God and waive what is still due to you from Ribā, if your faith be true; or be warned of war declared against you by God and His Messenger. If you repent, you have the right to your capital sums (principal), *Ru'aūs Amwalikum*, suffering no loss and causing loss to none" (Qur'ān, 2:275–279).

Ribā al-Qur'ān: *Ribā* which has been stipulated in the Qur'ān. It is referred to in various terms which are used interchangeably. These are:

Loan Ribā, referring to it as being related to monetary loans,

Ribā al-Jahiliyyah: referring to Jahiliyyah as being the period before Islam, the period of ignorance,

Ribā al-Duyūn, also **Ribā al-Qurūd:** duyun and qurūd means loans,

Ribā al-Nasī'a: meaning Ribā associated with the payment period.

Ribā al-Buyū' **(Commodity Ribā):** the Ribā that has been stated in the Sunnah, not in the Qur'ān. It might arise as a result of exchanging commodities: (a) with or (b) without, a delayed period. This Ribā is divided into two types:

(a) **Ribā al-fadle:** Ribā that results from an increase in quantity in the exchange an object, of a commodity, with another object of the same type, of same commodity, with an immediate delivery for an increase in quantity. For example exchanging gold for gold, or wheat for wheat immediate delivery.

(b) **Ribā al-Nasī'a:** Ribā that results from an increase in quantity in the exchange of an object, of a commodity, with another object of the same type or another, same or another commodity, with a delayed delivery, future delivery. For example, exchanging gold for gold or wheat for wheat for future delivery.

Riddah: apostasy. No sooner had the Prophet been declared dead than several tribes revolted and rebelled against the payment of Zakāh. The revolt, which seemed to have been triggered by the death of the Prophet, did not necessarily imply a return to paganism, although some claimed false prophethood, but it aimed essentially to break away from the control of the Medīnah government. The apostasy was brought back under control by Caliph Abū-Bakr in 633 A.C.

Ruq'a: an order of payment.

Saba': biblical Sheba. The most dominant of the four kingdoms in the south of the pre-Islamic Arabia. The Sabaean period extended from about 750 B.C., or 1500 B.C. according to some, to 115 B.C.

Sabre: physical and mental endurance. In addition, in Islam sabre is widened to include endurance on continuously and devotionally obeying God's orders and commands, endurance on staying on the right path without being led astray, endurance in military combat with the enemy, and endurance in calling people to do good and abandon evil.

Sabour: the person who practice sabre.

Sarf: money exchange. A buying and selling of currencies.

Sawāfī land: crown estates or fiefs. The term referred to the land the ownership of which was transferred to the state because of mainly: (a) the desertion of the land by the original owners on the Islamic conquest, (b) the death of non-Muslim landowners in wars against Muslims without leaving heirs, and (c) the death of the landowner, Muslim or non-Muslim, without leaving heirs. Initially the land was regarded as belonging to Muslims in general, represented by the state, but beginning from the Umayyad onward that changed and the ownership of the land was gradually transferred to individuals.

Shafi'ī: a follower of the Shafī'i School of thought. The school was founded by Muĥammad Idrīs al-Shafī'i (767–819) who was born in Ghaza. The school strikes a balance between the Mālikī, the upholders of Sunnah, and the Ĥanafī, the upholders of opinion. Al-Shafī'i who was a disciple of Mālik adopted a balanced approach between the two.

Sharī'ah: the body of the Islamic sacred law as based on the Qur'ān, the Sunnah and Jurisprudence.

Sheikh: elder. A titular head who was chosen by the members of the clan by virtue of his seniority in age, experience, wisdom and other personal qualifications and who represented the clan in relation to other clans but did not have the absolute authority in all matters regarding the clan. In serious judicial matters and in questions of inter-clan conflict he would have to consult with a council consisting of the heads of the families in the clan.

Ŝūfism: (Adj. Ŝūfī)**:** purity of self. The state of the complete renouncement of worldly life for the sake of worshiping God, which included abstention from wearing soft clothing and wearing instead harsh surface wool, *suf*, clothing.

Suftajah: money order. A credit instrument issued to a creditor to enable him to use it or cash it at another predetermined venue and at the future date. Also, suftaja were issued "payable to bearer".

Sukūk: (singular **sakk):** deposit certificate. A document or certificate, which evidences the undivided pro-rata ownership of underlying assets—the Sak (singular of Sukuk) is freely tradable at par, premium or discount.

Sunnah: the prophet's way. The Sunnah, or Traditions, represents what the Prophet is reported to have said, done and agreed to be done during his lifetime. As a source of the Sharī'ah, the Sunnah is divided into three main elements: (a) the Prophet's sayings, (b) his practice and (c) his approval of others' practices. The Prophet's sayings were not God's words, though they were inspired by God, and were said to clarify rules and provide further details of the Qur'ānic verses. To avoid confusion between the Qur'ānic texts and the Prophet's sayings, the Prophet, while arranging for the writing of the Qur'ān, instructed his companions not to write his sayings and directing them to erase whatever had been written, letting his sayings be transmitted only verbally. Muslims, therefore, were able to differentiate between the divine texts, the Qur'ān, and the Prophet Sayings and practice, *Aĥādīth or Aĥādīth.* The first attempt to collect the *Aĥādīth* in writing took place in the reign of the Umayyad caliph Umar ibn Abel-Azīz in the mid eighth century.

Tabżīr: wasteful use of resources, which is forbidden. The Qur'ān states, "Verily resource wasters (Muabżżirīn) are brethren to Satan, and Satan is most unbeliever", (Qur'ān 17:27).

Tadlīs al-ʿaib: fault hiding. Refers to the activity of a seller intentionally hiding the defects of goods. This activity is prohibited according to Sharī'ah principles.

Takāful: mutual insurance. This is a form of Islamic insurance based on the principle of ta'awun or mutual assistance. It provides mutual protection of assets and property and offers joint risk sharing in the event of a loss by one of its members. Takaful is similar to mutual insurance in that members are the insurers as well as the insured.

Tanājush: pretence of buying, particularly in auction sale. This is a conspiracy between a seller and a false buyer wherein the buyer pretends of his willingness to purchase the goods at a higher price to encourage other buyers/bidders to increase their bids. This is not permissible in Islam.

Tawhīd: the divine unity. Believing in One God.

Taʿwīdh: financial compensation. Penalty agreed upon by the contracting parties as compensation that can rightfully be claimed by the creditor when the debtor fails or is late in meeting his obligation to pay back the debt.

Ujrah: wage. Financial payment for the utilisation of services. In the context of today's economy, it can be in the form of salary, wage, allowance, commission and the like.

Ulama' (singular: **Aalim**): learned men in Islamic jurisprudence.

ʿUrbūn: down payment. A deposit or earnest money which forms part payment of the price of goods or services paid in advance, but will be forfeited in the event the transaction is cancelled. The forfeited money is considered as hibah (gift).

ʿUrf: custom. One of the bases used in *ijtihad* and is the process of relying on the custom and usage of a particular society in deriving an unprecedented judgment or formulating an opinion in an unparalleled case.

Ushr land: land of the one-tenth. Land on which Zakah was imposed. This is in contrast to Kharāj land on which Kharāj tax was imposed.

Ushūr Tax: (singular, **Ushr**): custom duties. The tax was initiated by Caliph Umar as a reciprocal tax to that which Muslim merchants paid to foreign states on crossing their borders. The rate of the tax was one tenth, or "Ushr" the plural of which is "Ushūr".

Ummah: the Muslim community.

Wadīah Yad Dhamanah: surety in hand. Goods or deposits, which have been deposited with another person, who is not the owner, for safekeeping. As wadiah is a trust, the depository becomes the guarantor and, therefore guarantees repayment of the whole amount of the deposits, or any part thereof, outstanding in the account of depositors, when demanded. The depositors are not entitled to any share of the profits but the depository may provide returns to the depositors as a token of appreciation.

Wakalah: agency. A contract, which gives the power to a person to nominate another person to act on his behalf as long as he is alive based on the agreed terms and conditions.

Zakāh: a prescribed charity ordained in the Qur'ān, spending of which is specifically determined in the Qur'ān and whose detailed rules as to rates and base of calculation is determined by the Prophet in the Sunnah.

BIBLIOGRAPHY

Publications

The Holy Qur'ān

The Holy Qur'ān, (in Arabic)

Interpretation of the Meaning of the Noble Qur'ān in the English Language, a summarized version of At-Tabari, Al-Qurtubi and Ibn-Kathir, Muĥammad Muhsin Khan and Muĥammad Taq-ud-Dīn-Al-Hilali, Dar-us-Salam Publication, 12th Ed, 1995

The Holy Qur'ān, translated into English with explanatory notes, by Abdūllah Yūsūf Ali, Amana Corporation, Bentwood, Maryland, 1989

The Holy Qur'ān, English transaltion of "The Meaning and Commentary", Ministry of Haj and Endowment, Kingdom of Saudi Arabia, 1410 H/1990.

The Sunnah al-Nabawiyyah

Imam Abū-Dawood, *Sunan Abi-Dawood*, al-*Ĥadīth* House, 1973 (in Arabic)

Imam al-Būkhari, *Ŝaĥīĥ al-Būkhari*, Dar A'alam for Books, 1996, (in Arabic)

Imam Muslim, *Ŝaĥīĥ Muslim, with al-Nawawi's explanation*, Dar al-Bian lil Turath, 1987, (in Arabic)

Imam Muslim, *Ŝaĥīĥ Muslim: Sunnah of the Sayings and Doings of the Prophet Muĥammad*, translated into English with explanatory notes and brief biographical sketches of major narrators, by Abdel Hamid Siddiqi, Sh. Muĥammad Ashraf (Publisher), 1976

Imam al-Tarmazi, *Sunan al-Tarmazi*, Dar al-Fikr, 1994, (in Arabic)

Books of Sirah

Ibn-Hishām, Abū Muĥammad Abdel-Malak Ibn-Hishām Al-Mu'afiri, *Al-Sīrah Al-nabawiyyah, known as Sirat-ibn-Hishām*, edited by Muĥammad Ali Al-Qutb and Muĥammad Al-Dalī Baltah, Al-Maktabah Al-A'Ŝriyyah for Publication and Distribution, 1992 (in Arabic)

Ibn Kathīr, *The Life of Muĥammad, al-Sira Al-nabawaiyyah*, trans. Trevor Le Gassick, reviewed by Moneer Fareeed, Grant Publishing, UK, 1998.

Haykal, M. H., *The Life of Muĥammad*, Hayat Muĥammad, tr. by T. R. al-Faruqui, North-American Trust Publications, 1976

The Bible

Aid to Bible Understanding, Watchtower, 1971

The Holy Bible (Revised Version), Oxford, 1926

Others

Abdou, Isaa, *Economics in the Qur'ān and Sunnah*, Dar al-Ma'arif, 1982.

Abdullah, Ahmad Ali, "Zakatable Funds of the State and Modes of their Collection", in Ahmed A. F. El-Ashker and Muhammad Sirajul Haq, (eds.), *Institutional Framework of* Zakāh*: Dimension and Implications*, Islamic Research and Training Institute, Islamic Development Bank, 1995.

Abdel-Rasūl, A, *Sharī'ah as the Basis of Constitution, al Sahrī'ah ka asas lil dustoor*, Dar al-Ma'arif, 1975 (in Arabic).

Abū-Al'Ala' Al-Maududi, *The Islamic law and constitution*, trns. and ed. Khurshid Ahmad, Islamic Publication, Lahore, 1st ed 1955, 7th ed. 1980.

Abū-Saud, M., "The Economic Order within the General Conception of Islamic Way of Life", *Islamic Review*, Vol. 55, no. 2, February 1967, and no. 3 March 1967.

——, "Money, Interest and Qirad", in K. Ahmad (ed.), *Studies in Islamic Economics*, Islamic Foundation, 1980.

——, *Contemporary Zakat*, Zakat and Research Foundation, USA, 1988.

Abū-Ubaid al-Qasim, *Book of Wealth, Kitāb al-Amwāl*, edited by M. K. Harras, Dar al-Kutub al-Ilmiyyah, Academic Book House, 1986, (in Arabic).

Abū-Yūsūf, *Book of Kharāj, Kitāb al-Kharāj*, trans. Ali, Abid Ahmad & A. H. Siddiqui, Islamic Book Centre, 1979.

——, *Book of Kharāj, Kitāb al-Kharāj*, Dar al-Ma'arif for Publication and Distribution, 1979 ed. (in Arabic).

Abū-Zahrah, M, Zakah, *Second Conference of the Academy of Islamic Research, Al-Azhar University*, Cairo, 1965, pp. 123–65.

Abū-Zayd, S. M., *Al-Ĥisbah in Muslim Egypt: from the Islamic Conquests to the Mamlūk Era, (al-Ĥisbah fi Misr al-Islamiah)*, al-Hai'ah al-Misriyyah al-A'mah lil-Kitab, Book Public Egyptian Organisation, 1986 (in Arabic).

Ahmad, I., "Ibn Taimiyah on Islamic Economics", *Voice of Islam*, Karachi, August 1961.

Ahmad Khurshid (ed.), *Islam: its Meaning and Message*, Islamic Council of Europe, 1975.

Ahmad, Khurshid, and Zafar Ishaq Ansari, (eds.), *Islamic Perspectives: Studies in Hounour of Sayyid Abul A'ala al-Maudoūī*, Islamic Foundation in association with Saudi Publishing House, 1979.

Ahmad, K., "Economic Development in an Islamic Framework", in Ahmad, Khrshid, (ed.), *Studies in Islamic Economics*, Islamic Foundation, 1980.

Ahmad, Khurshid, (ed.), *Studies in Islamic Economics*, A Selection of papers presented to the First International Conference on Islamic Economics held at Makkah under the auspices of King Abdul-Azīz University, Jeddah, (February 21–26, 1976), Islamic Foundation, 1980.

——, "Foreword" to S. N. H. Naqvi, *Ethics and Economics*, The Islamic Foundation, 1981.

Ahmed, Ziauddin, Munawar Iqbal and M. Fahim Khan (eds.), *Fiscal Policy and Resource Allocation in Islam*, Institute of Policy Studies, and International Centre for Research in Islamic Economics, 1983.

Al-Agamy, Abū-al-Yazīd, *Means of Glorous Sharī'ah, Kitāb al-Zarī'ah fi Makarim al-Sharī'ah*, Dar al-Sahwah for Publication and Distribution, and Dar Al-Wafa' for Publication and Distribution, Egypt, 1985 (in Arabic).

Al-Aqqād, Abbās Mahmoud, *The Truth of Islam and the Fallacious Claims of its Opponents, haqai'q al-islam wa abteel khusomehi*, Dar al-Kitāb al-Arabi, 1966 (in Arabic).

Al-Aŝfahānī, Al-Rāghib, *Means of Glorious Sharī'ah, al-Zarī'ah fi Makarim al-Sharī'ah*, edited by Abū-al-Yazīd al-Agamy, Dar al-Ŝahwah for Publication and Distribution, 1985 (in Arabic).

Al-Balażrī, Ahmed ibn Yahya ibn Gabir, *Islamic Conquests, Futuh al-Buldan*, Arabic Book Publication, 1901 (in Arabic).

Al-Dimashqī, Ja'afer ibn Ali, *Good Trading, al-Isharah fi Maĥāsin al-Tijarah*, in Shawqi

Ahmed Donia, *Series on Prominent Scholars in Islamic Economics*, al-Khirrijīn Bookshop, al-Riyadh, Saudi Arabia, 1984 (in Arabic).
Al-Fangari, M. Sh., *Social Security in Islam, al-Islam wa al-Dhaman al-Igtimai*, Egyptian Book Public Organisation, 3rd ed. 1990, (in Arabic).
——, "The Islamic Approach to Economic", in International Centre for Research on Islamic Economics, *Islamic Economics: Selected Researches from the First International Conference on Islamic Economics*, King Abdel-Azīz University, 1980 (in Arabic).
Al-Ghazāli, Abū Hamid, *Revival of science of religion, Iĥya' Ulūm al-Dīn*, trans. Fazul-ul-Karim, Vol. I, Book Lovers Bureau, Lahore, n.d.
——, *Al-Mustarfa' fi ilm al-Usul*, Maktabah Al-Tijariyah Al-Kubra, Cairo, 1937 (in Arabic).
Al-Ghazāli, Abdel-Hamid, *Man is the Basis of the Islamic Strategy for Economic Development*, IRTI, Islamic Development Bank. 1994, p. 64.
Al-Gizīri, A., *Islamic Jurisprudence According to the Four Main Schools of Thought, al-fiqh ala al-mazahib al-arba'ah*, al-Tijariah al-Kubra Publication, Cairo, 1972 (in Arabic).
Al-Jarhi, M. A., "A Monetary and Financial Structure for an Interest-free Economy: Instiutions, Mechanism and Policy", International Seminar on Monetary and Fiscal Economics of Islam, Islamabad, January 1981, 32 pp.
Al-Kalby, Muĥammad ibn Ahmad, *Jurisprudence Laws, al-qwanīn al-fiqhiyyah*, Dar al-Kitāb al-Arabi, 1989 (in Arabic).
Al-Khisht, Muĥammad Uthmān, (ed.), *Earnings and Asceticism, al-Muĥāsibī's al-Makasib, al-Rizq al-Halal wa Haqiqat al-Tawakkul ala Allah*, Maktabat al-Qur'ān for Publication and Distribution, 1983, (in Arabic).
Al-Khun, Mustafa Saīd, *A Historical Study of Jurisprudence and its Principles, dirasah tarikhiyah lil fiqhi was usulihi*, United Distribution Company, 1984, (in Arabic).
Al-Maqrizi, T. A. ibn Ali, *learning lessons from the history of nations, al-Maw'iz wa al-Ii'tibar fi zikre al-Khitat wa al-Aathaar*, Nile Publisher, 1324 H, quoted in Philip Hitti, 1963.
Al-Māwardī, Abū-al-Ĥassan Ali ibn Muĥammad, *State Ordinance and Religious Deputy, Al-Aĥkām al-Sūltāniyyah wal Wilayat al-Diniyyah*, Dar of Academic Books, Beirut, 1985 edition. (in Arabic).
Al-Misri, R., "Suftaja: a Key to Understanding Ribā in Islam", *Journal of Research in Islamic Economics*, vol. 2, no. 1, 1984.
——, "Islamic Banking System: Characteristics and Problems", al-Nizam al-Masrafi fi al-Islam: khasa'isuhu and muskilatuhu, in International Centre of Research in Islamic Economics, *Studies in Islamic Economics: Selected Researches from the Second International Conference on Islamic Economics*, King Abdel-Azīz University, 1985 (in Arabic).
Al-Muĥāsibī, Abdūllah ibn al-Ĥārith, *Earnings and Asceticism, al-Makasib wa al-Wara'*, edited by Muĥammad Uthmān al-Khisht, Maktabat al-Qur'ān for Publishing and Distribution, 1983, (in Arabic).
Al-Nabrawi, F., and M N Mihanna, *Development of Political Islamic Thought, taṭawwur al-fikre al-siyasi fi al-Islam*, two volumes, Dar al-Maarif, 1982 (in Arabic).
Al-Naggar, A., *An Introduction to Economic Theory: the Islamic Approach, Mūqaddimah lil nazariah al-iqtisadiah: manhag al-sahwah al-Islamiah*, Dar-al-Fikr, 1973 (in Arabic).
——, *Banks Without Interest, bunuk bila fawa'id*, King Abdel-Azīz University, 1976 (in Arabic).
Al-Neim, A., *Taxation System in Islam and its Applicapility to Saudi Arabia, al nizam al dharibi fi al Islam wa tatbeeqahu ala al mamlakah alsaudiah al Arabiyah*, Dar el-Irshad, 1969, In Arabic.
Al-Omar, Fouad Abdullah, "General Administrative and Organisational Aspects of Zakāh", in Ahmed A. F. El-Ashker and Muĥammad Sirajul Haq, (eds.), *Institutional Framework of Zakāh: Dimension And Implications*, Islamic Research and Training Institute, Islamic Development Bank, 1995.
Al-Qardawi, Yūsūf, *Jurisprudence of Zakāh, Fiqh al-Zakāh*, 2 vols., Mu'assasat al-Resālah, 1981 (in Arabic).
Al-Qattan, Manna', *Legislation and Islamic Jurisprudence, al-tashrī' wa al-fiqh fi al Islam*, Mu'assasat al-Resālah, 1986 (in Arabic).

Al-Qattan, Manna', *Researches in the Sciences of Qūr'ān, mabahith fi ulum al-Qūr'ān*, Dar al-Ma'arif for Publication and Distribution, 1992, (in Arabic).

Al-Qurashi, M., *Ma'alim al-Qurbah fi Aĥkam al-Ĥisbah*, Arabic text in R. Levi (ed.), "Ma'alim al-Qurba fi Aĥkām al-Ĥisbah", Cambridge University Press, 1938.

Al-Qusi, A.M., *Ribā, Islamic Law and Interest*, PhD hesis, Temple University, 1982.

Al-Rayyis, M.D., *al-Kharāj and the financial system of the Islamic state, al-Kharāj wal nuzum al-maliah fi al Islam*, Dar al-Ansār, 1977 (in Arabic).

Al-Raysoony, Ahmed, *The Theory of Intention in the Jurist al-Shātibi's Thinking, Nazariyat al-Maqasid inda al-Imam al-Shātibi*, the International Institute of Islamic Thinking, 1995

Al-Sawory, Ahmad Ali Muĥammad, Legal, Administrative and Financial Control of Zakāh, in Ahmed A. F. El-Ashker and Muĥammad Sirajul Haq, (eds.), *Institutional Framework of Zakāh: Dimension and Implications*, Islamic Research and Training Institute, Islamic Development Bank, 1995.

Al-Shaibānī, Muĥammad ibn-al-Ĥassan, *Earnings of a Clean Living, al-Iktisāb fi al-Rizk al-Mustatab*, edited by M. Arnnos, al-Baz Publishing and Distribution, Makkah, 1986 (in Arabic).

Al-Sharief al-Radhie, *Imam Ali's Nahg al-Balāghah*, Dar al-Ma'arif Publisher, n.d. (in Arabic).

——, *Nahg al-Balāghah: a selection of what al-Sharīf al-Radhie has chosen of the Speeches of Saiyyidna Amir of the Faithful Ali Ibn Abi Taleb, Peace be upon him, with exaplanatory notes of Imam Muĥammad Abdou, Former Egyptian Mufti*, Dar of Academic Books Publication, 1990 (in Arabic).

Al-Shātibī, Abū Ishaq Ibrāhīm, *Al-Muwafiqat fi Usul al-Sharī'ah*, Maktaba al-Tujariyah al-Kubra, Cairo, n.d., (in Arabic).

Al-Suyūty, Galal-Addīn, *The History of Caliphs, Tarīkh al-Khulafa'*, ed. By Muĥammad M. Abdel-Hamīd, al-Maktbah al-Tujariyyah al Kubra, 1964 (in Arabic).

Al-Ťabarī, Abū Ja'afar Muĥammad ibn Jarīr., *History of Nations and Kinds (Tarikh al-umam wal-shua'oob)*, al-Istiqama Publication, Cairo, 1939, Dar of Academic Books Publication, Beirut, 1991 (in Arabic).

Al-Zarqani, Muĥammad ibn Abdel-Baqi ibn Yūsuf Al-Misri Al-Azhari Al-Maliki (d. 1713), *Commentary of Zarqani on Imam* Mālik*'s Muwatta', sharh Al-Zarqani ala muwatta' Imama* Mālik, Dar of Academic Books Publication, 1990 (in Arabic).

Al-Zoibidy, Omar, "Single Currency' Key to Success' of Custom Union", Arab News, Jeddah, 27th March 2002.

Al-Zuhailī, Wahbah, *Islamic Jurisprudence and its Sourses, (al-fiqh al-Islamic wa adellatahu)*, Dar Al-Fikre, Damasqus, 3rd ed., 1989 (in Arabic).

Ansari, Z., "An Early Discussion on Islamic Jurisprudence", in Khurshid Ahmad and Zafar Ishaq Ansari, (eds.), *Islamic Perspectives: Studies in Hounour of Sayyid Abul A'ala al-Maudoūī*, Islamic Foundation in association with Saudi Publishing House, 1979.

Arberry, A. J., "Mysticism", in P. M. Holt, Ann K. S. Lambton and Bernard Lewis (eds.), *The Cambridge History of Islam*, Volume 2B, Cambridge University Press, 1990.

Ariff, Mohammad. (ed)., "Monetary and Fiscal Economics of Islam", selected papers presented to the International Seminar on the Monetary and Fiscal Economics (held in Makkah, Saudi Arabia in 1978), International Centre for Research in Islamic Economics, King Abdel-Azīz University, 1982.

——, "Islamic Banking", *Asian-Pacific Economic Literature*, Vol. 2, No. 2, September 1988, pp. 46–62.

Armstrong, Karen, *Islam: A Short History*, Phoenix Press, 2000.

Arnnos, M., (ed.) *the book of Muĥammad ibn-al-Ĥassan Al-Shaibānī, Earnings of a Clean Living, al-Iktisāb fi al-Rizk al-Mustatab*, al-Baz Publishing and Distribution, Makkah, 1986 (in Arabic).

Attiyah, Gamal al Dīn, *A Guide to Researcher in Islamic Economics, Dalil al-bahith fi'l-iqtisad al-Islami*, al-Muslim al-Mu'asir (Beirut), Nov. 1974: 142–151 (in Arabic).

Aznan, Syed Jaafar, "The Role of Islamic Development Bank (IDB) in the Promotion of Intra–Regional-Trade Among OIC Countries", paper presented at the OIC Business Forum, organized by the Asian Strategy and Leadership Institute (ASLI)

in conjunction with the 10th OIC Summit, 15–16 October, 2003, Putrajaya, Malaysia.
Bahar, Mālik al-Shu'ara, (ed.), *Mujmal al-Tawarikh*, A Compile of History, Tehran, 1939–1940 (From Udovitch, *The Islamic Middle East, 700–1900*).
Baljon, J. M., "Social and Economic Ideas of Shah Wali-Allah", in Abul Hasan Sadeq and Aidit Ghazāli (eds.), *Readings in Islamic Economic Thought*, Longman, Malaysia, 1992.
Bāqir-al-Sadre, *Islamic Economics, Iqtisāduna*, Dar-al-Fikre, 1968 (in Arabic).
Bari, Zohrul, *Re-Emergence of the Muslim Brothers in Egypt*, Lancers Books, New Delhi, 1995.
Ben-Shemesh, A., *Taxation in Islam*, Vol. I, "Yahya Ben Adam's Kitāb al-Kharāj, Leiden E. J. Brill, 1965.
——, *Taxation in Islam*, Vol. II, "Qudama B. Ja'far's Kitāb al-Kharāj, Leiden E. J. Brill, 1967.
——, *Taxation in Islam*, Vol. III, "Abū-Yūsūf's Kitāb al-Kharāj", Leiden E. J. Brill, 1969.
Bonne, Alfred, *The Economic Development of the Near East*, New York, 1945.
Boulaki, J., "Ibn-Khaldūn: a Fourteenth Century Economist", *Journal of Political Economy*, vol. 79, no. 5, September-October 1971.
Cahen, Claude, "Economy, Society and Institutions", in P. M. Holt (ed.), *The Cambridge History of Islam*, Vol. 2B, Cambridge University Press, 1970.
Chapra, M. Umar, "Objectives of the Islamic Economic Order", in K Ahmad (ed.), *Islam: its Meaning and Message*, Islamic Council of Europe, 1975, (174–195).
——, The Islamic Welfare State and its Role in the Economy, in Khurshid Ahmad and Zafar Ishaq Ansari, (eds.), *Islamic Perspectives: Studies in Hounour of Sayyid Abul A'ala al-Maudoūī*, Islamic Foundation in association with Saudi Publishing House, 1979.
——, *Towards a Just Monetary System*, the Islamic Foundatiuon, 1985.
——, *The Future of Economics: an Islamic Perspective*, Islamic Foundation: England, 2000.
Choudhury, Masudul Alam and Uzir Abū Mālik, *The Foundations of Islamic Political Economy*, St. Martins Press, 1992.
Cleveland, W., *A History of the Modern Middle East*, Westview Press, 1994.
Collard, D., *Atruism and Economy: A Study in Non-Selfish Econoics*, Martin Roberston, 1978
Cook, M. A., (ed.), *Studies in the Economic History of the Middle East from the Rise of Islam to the Present Day*, Oxford University Press, 1970.
Davidson, Lawrence, *Islamic Fundamentalism: An Introduction*, revised and updated edition, Greenwood Press, 2003.
Della Vida, Giorgio Levi, "Pre-Islamic Arabia", in Nabih Amin Faris (ed.), *The Arab Heritage*, Greenwood Press Publishers, 1944.
Dessouki, A. E. H., (ed.), *Islamic Resurgence in the Arab World*, Praeger, 1982.
Donahue, John J., and John L. Esposito (eds.), *Islam in Transition: Muslim Perspective*, New York: Oxford University Press, 1982.
Donia, Shawqy Ahmed, *Islam and Economic Development, (al-Islam wa al Tanmiyah al Iqtisadiyah)*, Dar al-Fikre al-Arabi, 1979 (in Arabic).
——, *Series on Prominent Scholars in Islamic Economics*, al-Khirrijīn Bookshop, al-Riyadh, Saudi Arabia, 1984 (in Arabic).
——, *The Economic Thought of Al-Rāghib Al-Aṣfahānī*, Om-Al-Qra University, Makkah, Saudi Arabia, 1987 (in Arabic).
El-Ashker, Ahmed, "On the Theory of Consumer Behaviour: a Socio-economic Approach with an Islamic Emphasis", *Social Science Working Paper No 57*, Paisley College of Technology, 1983, 17pp
——, "On the Islamic Theory of Consumer Behaviour: an Empirical Inquiry in a Non-Islamic Country", *Economic Research Paper No 14*, Centre for Middle Eastern and Islamic Studies, Univeristy of Durham, 1985, 18pp.
——, *The Islamic Business Enterprise*, Croom Helm, 1987.

——, "Towards an Islamic Stock Exchange in a Transitional Stage", *Islamic Economic Studies*, Islamic Development Bank, Vol. 3, No. 1, December 1995.

——, *Profit Index as a Replacement to LIBOR in Islamic Banking Operations and Investment Decision Making*, Islamic research and Training Institute (IRTI), Islamic Development Bank (IDB), 1995.

El-Ashker, Ahmed, and Muĥammad Sirajul Haq, (eds.), *Institutional Framework of Zakāh: Diemnsions and Implications*, Islamic Research and Training Institute (IRTI), Islamic Development Bank (IDB), 1995.

Esposito, John L., *Islamic Threat: Myth or Reality?*, New York: Oxford University Press, 1999.

——, and John O. Voll, *Makers of Contemporary Islam*, Oxford University Press, 2001.

——, *Unholy War: Terrorin the Name of Islam*, Oxford University Press, 2002.

Euben, Roxanne L., *Enemy in the Mirror: Islamic Fundamentalism, a work of comparative political Theory*, Princeton University Press, Princeton, 1999.

Faridi, F. R., "A Theory of Fiscal Policy", in Ahmed, Ziauddin, Munawar Iqbal and M Fahim Khan (eds.), *Fiscal Policy and Resource Allocation in Islam*, Institute of Policy Studies, and International Centre for Research in Islamic Economics, 1983.

Faris, Nbih Amin, (ed.), *The Arab Heritage*, Geenwood Press Publishers, 1944.

Fazlur Rahman, *Revival and Reform in Islam*, in Cambridge History of Islam, Cambridge University Press, 1970.

Ghazāli, Aidit, "Economic thought of Abd Allah Ĥārith al-Muĥāsibī", in Abdul Hasan M. Sadeq and Aidit Ghazāli (eds), *Readings in Islamic Economic Thought*, Longman Malaysia, 1992.

Goitein, S. D., Letters and Documents on the India Trade in Medieval Times, *Islamic Culture*, 1963, July, pp. 188–205.

——, Commercial and Family Partnership in the Countries of Medieval Islam, *Islamic Studies*, Vol. 3, 1964, pp. 315–337.

——, *Studies in Islamic History and Institutions*, Leiden, 1966.

——, *A Mediterranean Society*, vol. 1, Economic Foundation, Berkeley and Los Angeles, University of California Press and Cambridge University Press, 1967.

Harras, Muĥammad Khalil, (ed.), *Book of Welath, Kitāb al-Amwāl by Abū-Ubaid al-Qasim*, Academic Book House, 1986, (in Arabic).

Ĥassan, Ĥussain Ĥamid, "Sharī'ah rule on Insurance Contracts", International Centre for Research on Islamic Economics, *Islamic Economics: Islamic Economics: Selected Researches from the First International Conference on Islamic Economics"*, King Abdel-Azīz University, 1980 (in Arabic).

Ĥassan, Ĥ. Ibrāhīm., *The History of Islam*, Four Volumes, Egyptian Nahda Bookshop, 1959 (in Arabic).

Ĥassanuzzaman, S. M., "Indexation—An Islamic Evaluation", *Journal of Research in Islamic Economics*, International Centre for Research on Islamic Economics, King Abdel-Azīz University, 1985, pp. 31–54.

Hitti, Philip K., *History of the Arabs: from the Earliest Times to the Present*, 8th Ed., Macmillan & Co., 1963.

Holland, Muhtar (trans.), *Public duties in Islam: the institution of Ĥisbah, by al-Shaykh al-Imam ibn Taymīya*, The Islamic Foundation, 1983.

Humphreys, R. S., "The Contemporary Resurgence in the Context of Modern Islam", in Dessouki, A. E. (ed.), *Islamic Resurgence in the Arab World*, Praeger, 1982.

Ĥusayn, Taha, "The Future of Culture in Egypt," in John J. Donahue and John L. Esposito, (eds.), *Islam in Transition: Muslim Perspectives*, New York: Oxford University Press, 1982.

Ibn-al-Atheer, *Complete Compilation of History, al-Kamel fi al-Tareehk*, no date (in Arabic).

Ibn-al-Ukuwwah, Diya' al-Dīn Muahham al-Qurashi al-Shafī'i, *Ma'alim al-Qūrbah fia aĥkām al-Ĥisbah*, edited and translated by R. Levy, Luzak & Co., 1939.

Ibn Khaldūn, *The Mūqaddimah: An Introduction to History*, Princeton University Press, 1958. Complete three volume English translations by Franz Rosenthal. An abridged English version by N. J. Dawood for Princeton University Press, 1967.

Ibn Taymīya, *Public Duties in Islam: the Institution of Ĥisbah*, Muhtar Holland (trans.), Islamic Foundation, 1983.

International Centre for Research on Islamic Economics, *Islamic Economics: Selected Researches from the First International Conference on Islamic Economics*, King Abdel-Azīz University, 1980 (in Arabic).

——, *Studies in Islamic Economics: Selected Researches from The Second Internaitonal Confernece on Islamic Economics*, King Abdel-Azīz University, 1985, (in Arabic).

Iqbal, Muĥammad, *The Reconstruction of Religion Thought in Islam*, Lahore: Muĥammad Ashraf, 1968.

——, "Islam as a Social and Political Ideal", in S. A. Vahid, (ed.), *Thoughts and Reflections of Iqbal*, Lahore: Muĥammad Ashraf, 1964.

Iqbal, Munawar, "Pros and Cons of Indexation", paper presented to the Workshop on Indexation, Islamic Research and Training Institute, Islamic Development Bank, 1987, p. 35.

Isaa, Musa Adam, *The Effect of the Changes in the Value of Money and how it is Treated in Islamic Economics, a'athar al taghayyur fi qimat al-nuqood wa kaifiyyat mu'alagatuha fi al-Iqtisad al-Islami*, Saleh Kamel Series in Univerity Theses in Islamic Economics, Department of Research and Development, Dallah al-Barkah Group, 1993 (in Arabic).

Islahi, Abdul Azim, *Economic Concepts of Ibn Taimiyah*, Islamic Foundation, Leicester, 1988.

Islamic Development Bank, *Annual Report*, 1423H, Jeddah, 2003.

Islamic Development Bank, Islamic Research and Training Institute, *The Financial Resources in a Modern Society from an Islamic Perspective*, 1989.

Islamic Research Institute, International Islamic University, 1987.

Issawi, Charles, *An Arab Philosopher of History*, John Murray, 1950.

Jalbani, G. N., "The Economic Thought of Shah Wali-Allah", in Abul Hasan Sadeq and Aidit Ghazāli, (eds.), *Readings in Islamic Economic Thought*, Longman, Malaysia, 1992.

James, Simon and Christopher Nobes, *The Economic of Taxation*, Philip Allan, 2nd ed., 1983.

Jomo, K. S. (ed.), *Islamic Economic Alternatives*, Macmillan, London, 1992.

Kahf, Monzer, "Taxation Policy in an Islamic Economy," in Ahmed, Ziauddin, Munawar Iqbal and M. Fahim Khan (eds.), *Fiscal Policy and Resource Allocation in Islam*, Institute of Policy Studies, and International Centre for Research in Islamic Economics, 1983.

——, "A Contribution to the Theory of Consumer Behaviour in an Islamic Society", in Khurshid Ahmad, *Studies in Islamic Economics*, Iinternational Centre for Research in Islamic Economics and Islamic Foundation, 1980.

——, (ed.), *Zakāh Training Package*, Islamic Research and Training Instiute, Islamic Development Bank, 1994.

—— (ed.), *Economics of Zakāh*, Islamic Research and Training Institute, Islamic Development Bank, 1994.

Kettani, M. Ali, "The Muslim Minorities", in Khurshid Ahmad and Zafar Ishaq Ansari, (eds.), *Islamic Perspectives: Studies in Hounour of Sayyid Abul A'ala al-Maudoūī*, Islamic Foundation in association with Saudi Publishing House, 1979.

Keynes, J. M., *The General Theory of Employment, Interest and Money*, Macmillan, London, 1936.

Khallaf, Abdel Wahab, *the Science of Jurisprudence, ilm usul al-fiqh*, Dar al-Qalam Publishing and Distribution, 1942 (in Arabic).

Khan, Muĥammad Akram, *Annotated Bibliography of Contemporary Economic Thought in Islam and Glossary of Economic Terms in Islam*, Islamic Education (Lahore), 1973.

——, Islamic Economics: Annotated Sources in English and Urdu, 2 vols., The Islamic Foundation, 1983 and 1991.

——, Legal, Adminstrative and Financial Control of Zakāh, in Ahmed A. F. El-Ashker and Muhammad Sirajul Haq, (eds.), *Institutional Framework of Zakāh: Dimension and Implications*, Islamic Research and Training Institute, Islamic Development Bank, 1995.

Khan, M. Fahim, "Theory of Consumer Behaviour in Islamic Perspective", in Ausaf Ahmad and Kazim Raza Awan (eds.), *Lectures on Islamic Economics*, Islamic Research and Training Institute, Islamic Development Bank, 1992.

Kuran, Timur, "The Economic System in Contemporary Islamic Thought", in K. S. Jomo, (ed.), *Islamic Economic Alternatives*, Macmillan, London, 1992, pp. 9–47. An earlier version is in *International Journal for Middle Eastern Studies*, vol. 18, no. 2, 1986, pp. 135–164.

Lambton, A. K. S., "Reflections on the role of agriculture in medieval Persia", in A. L. Udovitch (ed.), *The Islamic Middle East, 700–1900: Studies in Economic and Social History*, The Darwin Press, 1981.

Lapidus, I. M., *Muslim Cities in the Latter Middle Ages, Cambridge*, Mass., 1967.

Lapidus, Ira M., "Arab Settlement and Economic Development of Iraq and Iran in the age of the Umayyad and early Abbasīd caliphs", in A. L. Udovitch (ed.), *The Islamic Middle East, 700–1900: Studies in Economic and Social History*, The Darwin Press, 1981.

——, *A History of Islamic Society*, Cambridge University, 2002.

Levy, R., (ed.) *The Ma'alim al-Qūrbah fi Ahkām al-Hisbah of Diya' al-Dīn Muhammad ibn Muhammad al-Qurashi al-Shafi'i, known as ibn al-Ukhuwwa*, printed by Cambridge University Press and published by Luzac & Co., 1939 (edited in English with original text in Arabic).

Lewis, Bernard, "Politics and War", in Schacht, J. and C. E. Bosworth (eds.), *The Legacy of Islam*, Oxford University Press, 1979 (156–209).

Lombard, Maurice, *The Golden Age of Islam*, trans. Joan Spencer, North-Holland Publishing Company, 1975.

Looney, Robert E., "The Gulf Co-opeation Council's Cautious Approach to Economic Integration", *Journal of Economic Coperation Among Islamic Countries*, Vol. 24, No. 2, April 2003, pp. 137–160.

Mahdi, Mushin, *Ibn Khaldūn 's Philosophy of History*, George Allen and Unwin, 1957.

Mahmoud, Abdel-Qader, *the Islamic Thought and the Opposing Philosophies, al-fikre al-Islamī wa al-falsafāt al-mu'aridah*, Egyptian Book Public Organisation, 1986 (in Arabic).

Mallat, Chibli, "Muhammad Baqer al-Sadr", in Ali Rahnema (ed.), *Pioneers of Islamic Revival*, Zed Books, 1994, pp. 251–272.

Mannan, M. A. *Islamic Economics: Theory and Practice*, Sh. Muammad Ashraf, 1970.

Mannan, M. A. "Indexation in an Islamic Economy", Journal of Development Studies, 1981, pp. 41–51.

Mansfield, Peter, *The Arabs*, Penguin Books, 1982.

Maunier, R., "Les Idees Economiques d'un Philosophe Arabe au XIV Siecle, Ibn Khaldūn", *Revue d'Histoire Economique et Sociale*, Vol. 6, 1913, p. 409ff.

Metwally, M. M., "Fiscal Policy in an Islamic Economy", in Ahmed, Ziauddin, Munawar Iqbal and M. Fahim Khan (eds.), *Fiscal Policy and Resource Allocation in Islam*, Institute of Policy Studies, and International Centre for Research in Islamic Economics, 1983.

Muhammad, Mi'rāj, "Shah Wali-Allah's Concept of the Sharī'ah, in Khurshid Ahmad, and Zafar Ishaq Ansari, (eds.), *Islamic Perspectives: Studies in Hounour of Sayyid Abul A'ala al-Maudoūī*, Islamic Foundation in association with Saudi Publishing House, 1979.

Muhammad, Faiz, "Relationship between Obligatory Official Zakāh Collection and Voluntary Zakāh Collection by Charitable Organisations", in Ahmed A. F. El-Ashker and Muhammad Sirajul Haq, (eds.), *Institutional Framework of Zakāh: Diemnsions and Implications*, Islamic Research and Training Institute (IRTI), Islamic Development Bank (IDB), 1995.

Muĥammad, Qutb Ibrāhīm, *Fiscal Policy of Uthman ibn Affan, al-siyasah al-maliyyah le Utman ibn Affan*, Egyptian Book Public Organisation, 1986 (in Arabic)
Mundell, Robert, "A Theory of Optimum Curency Areas", *American Economic Review*, Vol. 51, No. 3, 1961, pp. 509–517.
McKee, A. F., "Social Economics and Values", *International Journal of Social Economics*, Vol. 9, No. 6/7, 1982, pp. 5–19.
McKinnon, Ronald, "Optimum Currency Areas", *American Economic Review*, Vol. 53, No. 3, 1963, pp. 717–724.
Naqvi, S., *Ethics and Economics: an Islamic Thesis*, Islamic Foundation, 1981.
Nasr, Seyyed Hossein, and Oliver Leaman, *History of Islamic Philosophy*, Routledge, 1996, 2001.
Nasser Social Bank of Egypt, *Annual Reports*, and Law No. 66/1971 of the establishment of the bank (in Arabic).
Nicholson, R. A., *Literary History of the Arabs*, Curzon Press, 1993 (first published in 1930).
Nitsch, T. O., "Economic Man, Socio-Economic Man, and Homo-Economicus-Humanus", *International Journal of Social Economics*, Vol. 9, No. 6/7, 1982, 20–49pp.
Qattan, M. Khalil, "The Concept and Approach of Islamic Economics", in International Centre for Research on Islamic Economics, *Islamic Economics: Selected Researches from the First International Conference on Islamic Economics*, King Abdel-Azīz University, 1980 (in Arabic).
Qutb, Said, *Social Justice in Islam, al-adālah al-ijtima'iyyah fi al-Islam*, Dar Al-Shrouk, 6th ed., 1979, (in Arabic)
Rahim, Abdel, *Annukatu wal uyuun: Tafsir al-Māwardī*, Dar of Acedmic Books Publication, 1993 (in Arabic).
Rahman, Afzalur, *Economic Doctorines of Islam: Banking and Insurance*, The Muslim Schools Trust, London, 1979.
Rahnema, Ali (ed.), *Pioneers of Islamic Revival*, Zed Books, 1994.
Raymond, Andre, "The Economic Crisis of Egypt in the Eighteenth Century", in Udovitch, A. L. (ed.), *The Islamic Middle East, 700–1900: Studies in Economic and Social History*, The Darwin Press, 1981.
Rodinson, Maxine, *Mohammad* (Trans. Anne Carter), Penguin, 1974.
——, *Islam and Capitalism*, (trans. B. Pearce), Penguin, 1980.
Roll, Eric, *A History of Economic Thought*, Faber and Faber Ltd., 1973.
Salama, Abdin Ahmad, "Empirical Economic Effects of Obligatory and Non-Obligatory Payment of Zakāh to the State", in Ahmed A. F. El-Ashker and Muĥammad Sirajul Haq, (eds.), *Institutional Framework of Zakāh: Dimension and Implications*, Islamic Research and Training Institute, Islamic Development Bank, 1995.
Sadeq, Abull Ĥassan M., and Aidit Ghazāli, (eds.), *Readings in Islamic Economic Thought*, Longman Malaysia, 1992.
Sakr, Mohammad, *First International Conference on Islamic Economics: held in Makkah under the auspices of King Abdul-Azīz University, Jeddah, February 21–26, 1976*, International Centre for Research in Islamic Economics, King Abdul-Azīz University, Jeddah, 1979 (in Arabic).
—— "Islamic Economics: Concepts and Principles", in International Centre for Research on Islamic Economics, *Islamic Economics: Selected Researches from the First International Conference on Islamic Economics"*, King Abdel-Azīz University, 1980 (in Arabic).
Sagiv, David, *Fundamentalism and Intellectuals in Egypt, 1973–1993*, Frank Cass, 1995.
Sardar, Ziauddin, *The Future of Muslim Civilisation*, Croom Helm, 1979.
——, *Islamic Futures: the Shape of Ideas to come*, Selangor: Pelanduk Publications, 1985.
Schacht, J. and Bosworth, C. E., (eds.) *The Legacy of Islam*, Oxford University Press, 2nd ed., 1979.

Shahab, H. V. (ed), *Interest Free Banking: Introduction and Operation in Pakistan*, Asian Secretarial International, Association of Islamic Banks, Karachi, 1982.
Shahid, I., "Pre-Islamic Arabia", in *Cambridge History of Islam*, vol. 1, Cambridge University Press, 1970.
Shakir, Ahmad Muĥammad (Abū al-Ashbal), (ed.), *Kitāb al-Karaj by Yahya ibn-Adam al-Qurashi*, al-Ma'arif Publishing and Distribution House, 1979, (in Arabic).
Sharwani, H. K., *Studies in Muslim Political Administration*, Lahore, 2nd ed., 1945.
——, "Ibn-Taimiyah's Economic Thought", *Islamic Literature*, Lahore, vol. 8, no. 1, January 1956.
Siddiqi, Muĥammad, N., "Muslim Economic Thinking: a Survey of Contemporary Literature", in Khurshid Ahmad (ed.), *Studies in Islamic Economics*, Islamic Foundation, 1980.
——, "Islamic Economic Thought: Foundation, Evolution and needed Direction", in Abdul Hasan M. Sadeq and Aidit Ghazāli, (eds.), *Readings in Islamic Economic Thought*, Longman Malaysia, 1992.
——, *Banking Without Interest*, Islamic Publication Limited, Lahore, 1973.
Sivan, Emmanuel, *Radical Islam: Medieval Theology and Modern Politics*, enlarged edition, Yale University Press, 1990.
Smith, Adam, *An Inquiry into the Nature and Causes of the Wealth of Nations*, Greenland and Norris, London 1805, (original 1776).
Smith, Margaret, *An Early Mystic of Baghdad: A Study of the Life and Teaching of Ĥarith B. Asad al-Muĥasbī A.C. 781–857*, London: Sheldon Press, 1977.
Spingler, I., "Economic Thought of Islam: Ibn-Khaldūn", *Comparative Studies in Society and History*, the Hague, vol. 1, 1964.
Suha Taji-Farouki and Basheer M. Nafi, (eds.) *Islamic Thought in the Twentieth Century*, I. B. Tauris, London, 2004
Tawney, R. H., *Religion and the Rise of Capitalism: a Historical study*, Penguin, 1980
Tower, Edward, "*The Theory of Optimal Currency Areas and Exchange Rate Flexibility*, Princeton Special Papers in International Economics, Princeton University, 1976, pp. 1–20.
Tuma, Elias H., "Early Arab Economic Policies, 1st/7th–4th/10th Centuries", *Islamic Studies*, vol. 4, no. 1, March 1965, pp. 1–23.
Udovitch, A. L., *Partnership and Profit in Medieval Islam*, Princeton University Press, 1970.
—— (ed.), *The Islamic Middle East, 700–1900: Studies in Economic and Social History*, The Darwin Press, 1981.
Watson, Andrew M., "A Medieval green revolution: new farming and corps techniques in the early Islamic world", in A. L. Udovitch (ed.), *The Islamic Middle East, 700–1900: Studies in Economic and Social History*, The Darwin Press, 1981.
Weiss, Dieter, "Ibn Khaldūn on Economic Transformation", *International Journal of Middle Eastern Studies*, vol. 27, 1995, pp. 29–37.
Wilson, Rodney, "Economic Changes and Reinterpretation of Islamic Social Values", *British Society for Middle Eastern Studies Bulletin*, vol. 9, no. 2, 1982.
——, *Banking and Finance in the Arab Middle East*, Macmillan, 1983.
—— (ed.), *Islamic Financial Market*, Croom Helm, 1990.
——, *Economics, Ethics, and Religion: Jewish, Christian and Muslim Economic Thought*, Macmillan, 1997.
——, "The Contribution of Muĥammad Bāqir al-Sadr to Contemporary Islamic Economic Thought", *Journal of Islamic Studies*, vol. 9, no. 1, 1998, pp. 48–59.
—— "Exchange Rate Issues for Muslim Countries", *International Seminar on Macro Economics in Islamic Perspective*, International Islamic University Malaysia, September 2004, p. 17.
——, "the Development of Islamic Economics: Theory and Practice", in Suha Taji-Farouki and Basheer M. Nafi, (eds.) *Islamic Thought in the Twentieth Century*, I. B. Tauris, London, 2004, pp. 195–222.

World Development Indicators, World Bank, Washington, 2004.
World Bank, *Country Statistical Profiles*, 2002.
Yahya ibn-Adam al-Qurashi, *Kitāb al-Kharāj*, Shakir, Ahmad Muĥammad (ed.), Dar al-Ma'arif Publishing and Distribution, 1979 edition (in Arabic).
Yusri, Abdel-Rahman, *Development of Economic Thought*, Dar of Egyptian Universities, 2nd ed., 1987, (in Arabic).
Yusri, Abdel-Rahman, "Economic Relations Among Muslim Countries and their Effect on Economic Development", in International Cente for Research on Islamic Economics, *Studies in Islamic Economics: Selected Researches from The Second Internaitonal Conference on Islamic Economics*, King Abdel-Azīz University, 1985, pp. 265–314, (in Arabic).
Zaim, Sabahuddin, "Contemporary Turkish Literature on Islamic Economics", in Khurshid Ahmad (ed.), *Studies in Islamic Economics*, the Islamic Foundation, 1980.
Zaki, Ĥassan Abbās, "Economic Cooperation Among Muslim Countries", in International Centre for Research on Islamic Economics, *Islamic Economics: Selected Researches from the First International Conference on Islamic Economics*, King Abdel-Azīz University, 1980, pp. 535–548, (in Arabic).
Zarqa, Mohammad Anas, "An Islamic Framework of Social Welfare Function and Consumer Behaviour", in International Centre for Research on Islamic Economics, *Islamic Economics: Selected Researches from the First International Conference on Islamic Economics*, King Abdel-Azīz University, 1980 (in Arabic), also translated to English in Khurshid Ahmad (ed.), *Studies in Islamic Economics*, International Centre for Research in Islamic Economics, and Islamic Foundation, 1980.
Zarqa, Mustapha Ahmed, "Insurance in Economics in General and the Stand of Sharī'ah on it" *Nizamu al-Ta'amin wa mawqi'oho fi al-maidan al-iqtisadi bi waghin a'am wa mauqifu al-Sahri'ah minho*, in International Centre for Research on Islamic Economics, *Islamic Economics: Selected Researches from the First International Conference on Islamic Economics*, King Abdel-Azīz University, 1980 (in Arabic).

Websites

International Islamic Univeristy Malaysia, http://www.iiu.edu.my/about_iium.shtml January 2006
International Islamic University Islamabad, http://www.iiu.edu.pk/ January 2006
Islamic Development Bank (IDB): http://www.isdb.org/, July 2004
Islamic Research and Training Institute (IRTI): http://www.irti.org/, July 2004
Islamic Foundation England: http://www.islamic-foundation.org.uk/, January 2006
Organization of the Islamic Conference (OIC): www.oic-oic.org/, July 2004
Perspective on World History and Current Events (PWHCE), *Ĥassan al-Banna: Founder of the Muslim Brotherhood, Ikhjwan al-Muslimun* http://www.pwhce.org/maududi.html January 2006
Perspective on World History and Current Events (PWHCE), *Maulana maududi: Radical Islam's Missing Link*, http://www.pwhce.org/maududi.html January 2006
World Bank, www.worldbank.org
Zahoor, A., "Abū al-Hasan al Māwardī": http://www.users.erols.com./Zenithco.index, 1997

INDEX

Bold pagenumbers refer to the glossary.

THEMES IN ISLAMIC STUDIES

ISSN 1389-823X

1. Knysh, A. *Islamic Mysticism.* A Short History. 2000. ISBN 90 04 10717 7
2. Stillman, Y.K. and Stillman, N.A. (ed.) *Arab Dress, A Short History.* From the Dawn of Islam to Modern Times. 2003. ISBN 90 04 11373 8
3. El-Ashker, A. and Wilson, R. *Islamic Economics.* A Short History. 2006. ISBN-10: 90 04 15134 6, ISBN-13: 978 90 04 15134 5